THE INDIVIDUAL INVESTOR'S GUIDE TO
LOW-LOAD INSURANCE PRODUCTS

D0813348

THE INDIVIDUAL INVESTOR'S GUIDE TO
LOW-LOAD INSURANCE PRODUCTS

HOW, WHAT, WHERE TO BUY
INSURANCE WHOLESALE

GLENN S. DAILY

International Publishing Corporation
Chicago

© by International Publishing Corporation. All rights reserved. This publication may not be reproduced in whole or in part by any means without prior written consent. Requests for permissions should be sent to: Permissions, International Publishing Corporation, 625 North Michigan, Suite 1920, Chicago, IL 60611.

ISBN Number: 0-942641-20-5

Printed in the United States of America
10 9 8 7 6 5 4 3 2 1

This publication is designed to provide accurate and authoritative information in regard to the subject matter covered. However, it is sold with the understanding that the publisher is not engaged in rendering legal or professional investment services. If legal advice or other expert assistance is required, a competent professional should be retained.

368
D133i

TABLE OF CONTENTS

PREFACE

"Life insurance is sold, not bought" is one of the insurance industry's favorite sayings. Why do we need agents? Because life insurance is sold, not bought. Why does it often cost all of the first-year's premium to get a policy from the manufacturer to the consumer? Because life insurance is sold, not bought.

The premise of this book is that some people are capable of *buying* insurance products and should not have to pay the high commissions and other sales expenses that wait-to-be-sold people do. They deserve a better selection of products—and enough information to be able to make an informed purchase.

A few insurance companies have decided to provide the products. We have decided to provide the information.

HOW TO USE THIS BOOK

This book can be used in three ways:

1. If you already know what you're looking for, you can turn to the product and company profiles (Chapters 12 and 13), contact the distributors, and get any additional information that you need. Chapter 11 contains a brief explanation of the profiles.

2. If you want a little guidance, but not too much, you can scan Chapters 1-10, paying particular attention to the sections labeled "The Bottom Line" and "Shopping Suggestions." At the end of Chapter 1, you'll find "Suggestions for People in a Hurry."

3. If you want a lot of guidance on how to buy insurance products intelligently, you can read Chapters 1-10.

ORGANIZATION

The book is organized around decisions a buyer must make to find, apply for, and make proper use of insurance products. These decisions are summarized at the beginning of Chapter 2 (Life Insurance), Chapter 8 (Annuities), and Chapter 9 (Disability Income Insurance).

Chapter 1 contains a general discussion of low-load products and the difficulties of shopping for insurance. Chapters 2-7 explain what you need to know to buy and use life insurance products. Chapter 8 focuses on deferred and immediate annuities. Chapter 9 deals with disability income insurance. Chapter 10 discusses the important considerations in choosing an insurance company. Scattered throughout Chapters 1-10, you will find various sidebars with additional information related to the main text.

Chapter 11 contains a brief explanation of each item in the product and company profiles, which can be found in Chapters 12 and 13.

At the back of the book, you'll find eleven appendices and a glossary of terms. Appendix A contains an assortment of benchmarks for judging the competitiveness of various types of insurance products. Appendix B lists low-load products that can be used within qualified retirement plans. Appendix C lists low-load products expected to be available in the near future. Appendix D lists commercially-available surveys that may be helpful in finding a competitive product. Appendix E lists several organizations that provide fee-for-service insurance advice and/or referrals. Appendix F provides rating methods as well as the addresses of the major rating agencies for insurance companies. Appendix G contains the phone numbers of state insurance departments, for requesting information or filing a complaint. Appendix H contains the mortality rates from several standard tables that are often used as the basis for contractual guarantees. Appendix I reproduces the questions in two supplements to insurance company annual statements; these supplements deal with illustration practices and procedures for determining policy values and are therefore of interest to policyholders and prospective buyers. Appendix J is a list of books and articles for readers who want additional information about insurance products and the methods of evaluating them. Appendix K explains how to read a policy illustration.

SEXISM

In writing this book, we had to confront the fact that English has no gender-neutral, third person singular pronoun. We considered various solutions, including "he or she"; alternating "he" and "she" (either systematically or with a random number generator); or using one of the many neologisms invented during the last 140 years (e.g., ne, hiser, ir, co, tey, chim, s/he). In the end, we decided to abide by an 1850 act of the English Parliament, which ordered "that in all acts words importing the masculine gender shall be deemed and taken to include females..." No slight to women is intended.

DISCLAIMER

As a group, low-load products offer some of the best values in the insurance marketplace. However, not every low-load product is a good buy. Just as some load mutual funds outperform some no-load funds, some agent-sold products will provide better value for your money than some low-load products. If all other things are equal, low-load wins. But all other things are rarely equal, so you still have to do your homework. This is especially true if you have a significant health problem or if you need a lot of advice. Underwriting practices vary from one company to another, so a knowledgeable agent can be a valuable resource. (Insurance buyers in poor health can begin by reading "Risky History, High Premium" in the April 16, 1990 issue of *U.S. News & World Report*.) Also, you cannot expect to get free estate or business planning services from a low-load company. If you have a complex insurance problem, you can either buy a commission-paying product from an agent or buy a low-load product and pay a planning fee to a fee-for-service advisor. The fees may or may not be greater than the agent's hidden compensation, depending on the situation. More on this later.

ACKNOWLEDGMENTS

I owe a lot to the many actuaries, professors, financial planners, agents, clients, and journalists whose insights, experiences, and questions have shaped this book. Appendix J does double duty as both a bibliography and an acknowledgment. Special thanks go to James H. Hunt (National Insurance Consumer Organization), John M. O'Sullivan (Fidelity Investments), Timothy C. Pfeifer (Tillinghast/Towers Perrin), and Richard W. Vautravers (Ameritas Marketing Corp.) for their constructive comments on the company and product profiles and on various portions of the manuscript.

I have been greatly aided by the publications of the Society of Actuaries, whose motto is worth noting: "The work of science is to substitute facts for appearances and demonstrations for impressions." Actuaries are a breath of fresh air in a sales-driven environment overpopulated by appearances and impressions.

My list of acknowledgments must include the library of the College of Insurance in New York City. Although their photocopiers leave something to be desired, their collection of research materials is superb, and the staff has always been helpful.

Finally, very special thanks has been earned by my editor, Barbara Craig, for her constant encouragement, sound advice, and equanimity in the face of missed deadlines.

AN INVITATION

We welcome your comments, suggestions, and criticisms to help us improve future editions of this book. Correspondence should be sent to:

Glenn S. Daily
c/o International Publishing Corporation
625 N. Michigan Ave., Suite 1920
Chicago, IL 60611

1

INTRODUCTION

LOW-LOAD PRODUCTS: AN OVERVIEW

An insurance product is considered *low-load* if distribution costs are significantly below average because the product is sold directly to the public with limited advertising or through fee-for-service financial advisors. This definition is intended to exclude expensive mail-order policies whose vendors rely on mass advertising to reach their audience. It is also intended to exclude so-called no-load policies, which pay the usual commission to agents but have no front-end sales charge. *Low-load* simply means "low-distribution cost"; it says nothing about whether the policy has a front-end load, a back-end load, or no load at all. In fact, a policy could have a large front-end load and still be a competitive low-load product because of a higher interest rate or lower insurance charges. In this sense, low-load is a confusing term, but it has gained general acceptance within the insurance industry and is not as awkward as low-distribution cost.

Selling costs lie along a continuum from very high to very low, so no definition can eliminate the need for judgment when deciding which products should be called low-load and which should not. Although these gray areas can exist with *any* definition, the essential feature of low-load products is that they are designed to be distributed directly and efficiently and to reward the consumer for taking the initiative in gathering information and making a purchase decision.

Advantages of Low-Load Products

The insurance industry's traditional distribution system—commissioned agents and brokers—is very effective for a population that has to be badgered into buying insurance. It is clearly inappropriate, however, for the growing number of people who want to take charge of their own financial affairs—people who want to *buy* and not be *sold*. For these people, low-load products have several obvious advantages, discussed below.

Greater benefits. Some agents are able to say with a straight face that *you* don't pay the commission, the company does. The truth of course is that insurance companies price their products to recover expenses incurred in finding buyers for them. If they don't have to pay the commissions and other expenses necessary to attract a sales force, that money is available to increase policyholder benefits.

In a sense, when you buy an insurance product you are taking out a loan. The insurance company pays the commissions and other selling costs on your behalf, and it recovers them over time from various charges within the policy. With an agent-sold policy, you might be "borrowing" 100 percent of the first-year premium for selling costs, versus 25 percent for a low-load product. If the premium is $1,000, the difference in selling costs is $750, and that $750 will be reflected in future benefits or premiums.

Less risk. A company that issues low-load products can produce competitive benefits without resorting to controversial investment strategies, aggressive underwriting, overleveraging of capital, or fraudulent policy illustrations.

Greater flexibility. Low-load products typically have low or no surrender charges, so you can bail out if the product doesn't live up to your expectations. In contrast, commissionable products often have heavy surrender charges during the early years; once you buy them, you're locked in. Flexibility is especially important today, because of the increasing number of mergers, acquisitions, and insolvencies.

Less due diligence. In a broad sense, *due diligence* is the process of satisfying yourself that a product will live up to your expectations. Because the consequences of making a mistake are generally less serious with low-load products, you do not have to spend as much time examining them.

Separation of product and advice. When you buy an agent-sold product, you are an inseparable package of product and advice. If you want to tap the agent's implementation skills, you have to go along with that agent's product recommendations. In contrast, low-load products let you shop for product and advice independently.

Fee-for-service advice will often cost less than commission-based services, for three reasons. First, in some cases the fees will be tax-deductible. Second, you pay only for what you need, now and in the future. That's important, because if you pay attention the first time around you'll probably need less advice on subsequent purchases. In contrast, commissionable products make you pay over and over—regardless of whether you've learned anything. The third reason is the most subtle. The insurance company pays the selling expenses on your behalf and expects to recover them over time and make a profit, in accord with a targeted rate of return. Because the insurer's profit goal is probably higher than what you are earning on your own investments, you are better off paying the selling expenses out of your own pocket—in the same way that you should prepay a 12 percent mortgage if your assets are earning only 8 percent.

Moreover, although agents justify their commissions by pointing to the "lifetime of service" that you are entitled to, it's not always clear that you get what you pay for. One agent admitted as much in a recent article in a trade publication: "I have found most agents unwilling to waste their valuable time calling on old policyholders because they might ask uncomfortable questions about what was sold." Despite their advantages, however, low-load products will probably never capture a major share of the market in the United States, for reasons that have to do both with demand and supply.

Limitations on Demand

Several factors explain why low-load products are in limited demand:

- Most insurance buyers either do not know that low-load products exist or may not be aware of the importance of distribution costs in determining performance.

- Selling expenses are generally not disclosed, so consumers do not know what they are charged for the agent's services.

- Many people are not self-motivated and thus will not take the time to do the research necessary to make a prudent purchase decision. Others have little confidence in their own ability to make sound financial decisions and therefore look to someone else—even a salesperson—to help them.

- Life insurance buyers, in using policy illustrations to compare products, often make the mistake of focusing on hypothetical values in the distant future, rather than on more certain values in the next few years. This means that companies with commissionable products can easily produce illustrations that allow them to compete favorably with low-load products—on paper.

- Insurance buyers who need professional advice may find it easier to locate a commission-based agent or financial planner than a fee-for-service advisor. Also, many people resist paying fees for financial advice; they would rather pay a $2,000 undisclosed commission than a $1,000 disclosed fee. (This fact is not lost on fee-only planners. After a few experiences of charging $5,000 for a comprehensive plan and then seeing the client's agent pocket $8,000 in commissions for implementing one recommendation, even the most idealistic fee-only planners must wonder if they're in the right business.)

- High advisory fees can offset the cost advantage of low-load products. Insurance buyers who will need advice on a continuing basis may be better off with a commissionable product—but only after verifying that (1) the agent will in fact live up to the promise of a "lifetime of service" and

(2) service means more than just coming around next year to try to sell you something else.

- The cost differences between low-load and commissionable products will be reduced—but not eliminated—if the rebating of commissions is legalized or if more companies give agents the ability to reduce their compensation in order to close a difficult sale. Large corporations have been able to buy reduced-commission policies for years, and some agents may decide that it's now in their best interest to give knowledgeable consumers a similar deal.

- Agents' efforts to protect their commissions may instill doubts among potential buyers of low-load products. What is the consumer to think when a friendly agent calls these products junk, the worst kind of junk, or garbage? Or when the agent casually mentions negative rumors about the companies that issue these products?

Limitations on Supply

Low-load products are in limited supply for reasons that include the following:

- Many companies are afraid of antagonizing their sales force by experimenting with alternative channels of distribution. A company that depends on agents to promote its products runs the risk of being left with no distribution system if the experiment fails.

- In evaluating the potential market for low-load products, companies may be discouraged by the relatively small number of fee-for-service financial planners and insurance consultants. This is a chicken-and-egg problem, as more advisors might be willing to shift from commissions to fees if they had a larger selection of low-load products to choose from.

- Politically powerful agents may try to pressure state insurance departments into denying approval of low-load products, using creative arguments about unfair competition, antidiscrimination, and "disturbance to the marketplace." (Don't laugh; it already happened once in Florida.)

For the reasons outlined here, low-load products may remain a mere sliver on pie charts of total market share. However, those insurance buyers who venture beyond the industry's traditional distribution channels will be well rewarded for their enterprise.

SHOPPING FOR INSURANCE: AN OVERVIEW

Insurance products are worth looking at for several reasons:

- No other financial products can offer guaranteed protection against the economic risks of death, sickness, accidents, and extended life. Societies cannot function without some way of sharing risks, and that's what insurance does.

- Insurance products generally enjoy favorable tax treatment, giving them a competitive advantage over other types of investments.

- Insurance companies have a long history of financial stability. This tradition may be tested in the years to come, but most companies will continue to offer investors a safe haven from the volatility of the financial markets.

Looking for the Hazards

Insurance is good for you, but it's important to understand what you're up against when you enter the marketplace in search of an appropriate product. Some of the hazards you'll face are discussed in the following sections (in no particular order).

Misleading information—lots of it. Information is misleading when it causes you to buy something you wouldn't, (or *not* buy something you otherwise would) if you had all the facts. When you combine aggressive salespeople, aggressive companies, and underfunded regulatory agencies, you have a marketplace where anything goes. Companies can make fifty-year projections of future cash values and death benefits based on assumptions they know are false. Agents can claim that a universal life policy provides a 22.67 percent average yield, or that an immediate annuity offers a 14.89 percent risk-free rate of return, or that life insurance lets you pay your estate taxes for 2.5 cents on the dollar. Anything goes.

There's a curious double standard here. In designing their products, insurance companies make use of mathematical techniques that are among the most sophisticated used in any industry—and they arm their agents with the shoddiest pieces of analysis and turn them loose on consumers.

Conflicting advice. Those who make it their business to advise consumers do not agree on the strengths and weaknesses of different types of products, on the best way to compare products, or even on basic analytical techniques. For example, you may run across three different ways to calculate the rate of return on your investment in a whole life policy. You will also have to navigate between industry apologists, whose "abuse-vision" contains many blind spots, and industry bashers, who see an abuse lurking behind every activity and product feature.

Policy illustrations. In theory, policy illustrations (or *ledger statements*) are useful tools for comparing products with different cost structures. In practice, however, illustrations are weapons that companies and agents fling about to destroy the competition and capture your business. The sequence of events goes something like this:

1. The agent gives you some pieces of paper with lots of numbers on them.

2. The agent points out that the numbers on these pieces of paper are better than the numbers another agent has given you.

3. Impressed by the "better" numbers, you buy the product.

4. Several years pass. When the numbers don't come true, you complain to the company, which sends you a short letter directing your attention to the footnote at the end of the illustration that says "the figures shown on this illustration are neither estimates nor guarantees."

If the numbers aren't estimates or guarantees, what are they? That's for you to figure out. Even before you can begin that task, however, there's another problem to consider: the lack of a standardized format. Each company prepares its illustrations as it sees fit and leaves the deciphering to you. Table 1.1 is an example of a term insurance illustration from a well-known New York company.

Table 1.1. Term Insurance Illustration
Male nonsmoker, age 32, $100,000

| | Year-by-Year Figures | | |
Year	Annual Premium	End-of-Year Dividend	Net Outlay
1	$134	$—	$134
2	145	—	145
3	145	—	145
4	159	88	71
5	247	101	146

Look at the column labeled "Net Outlay." At the beginning of year 4, you'll have to write a check for $71, right? Wrong. The $88 dividend is received at the end of year 4, so the fourth-year premium is really $159. The $88 reduces the fifth-year premium, which stays level at $159 ($247 - $88). What, then, does net outlay mean? Whatever a company wants it to mean. In this case, it means the difference between the gross premium and the dividend that is received a year later. Remember, anything goes.

Unique products (or companies that just want to be different). To distinguish themselves from the competition, some companies come up with unique product designs and features that add little or no value but merely serve to make comparisons more difficult. The marketing strategy of these companies is based on two simple rules:

1. Every product is unique.

2. No product is so unique that it cannot be compared with other products if the comparison would be favorable. But

if the comparison would be unfavorable, then the product is truly unique.

Inadequate performance data. Publicly available databases typically focus on each insurer's most popular products; as newer products emerge, older ones are dropped from the database. Also, the performance of life insurance products can vary by issue age, face amount, and premium pattern; but obviously it's impractical to keep track of every possibility. Data-gathering organizations typically select a few representative cases and then publish their surveys with a warning that the information should not be used to draw any general conclusions.

The lack of solid data makes it hard to compare the performance history of different companies in a relevant way. It also means that you'll probably never know if you made the right choice, because there is no practical way of tracking how you would have fared if you had chosen differently.

Overemphasis on the distant future. Many life insurance buyers follow the agent's finger as it moves down the policy illustration to the riches emerging at year 20 and beyond. The numbers will be impressive—and so are the odds against keeping a policy in force that long. Using typical lapse rates for cash value policies, Table 1.2 shows the expected number of policies in force per hundred issued, displayed side by side with the average annual rate of return for one competitive commissionable product over each holding period. (The *average annual rate of return* is the rate you would have to earn to match the policy's cash value if you bought term insurance and invested the difference.)

Agents' sales pitches often stress tax-deferred savings, low-cost protection, and accumulated wealth, but it's clear from Table 1.2 that a more honest sales pitch might sound like this:

> Mr. Prospect, how would you like an investment that gives you a 15 percent chance of losing all of your money, a 30 percent chance of losing part of it, a 15 percent chance of making less than you could in the money market, and a 40 percent chance of doing about the same or somewhat better than if you bought short- or intermediate-term bond funds? That's the magic of life insurance!

Table 1.2. For Many People, An Agent-Sold Policy Is a Bad Investment

End of Year	Cash Value	Average Annual Return	Policies in Force (out of 100)
1	$0	(100.0)%	85
2	385	(66.7)	75
3	1,454	(26.3)	67
4	2,606	(10.9)	61
5	3,847	(3.7)	56
10	12,861	7.5	42
15	26,486	9.0	33
20	47,310	9.4	25

Note: Based on an April 1989 policy illustration for a male non-smoker, age 35, $100,000 level death benefit, $1,000 annual premium, 8.75 percent interest; ignores income tax due upon surrender. During this period, taxable bond funds were yielding: 8.5-9.5 percent.

Not surprisingly, insurance companies often downplay the high lapse rates on life insurance products. In its marketing materials, one Iowa company tells prospective buyers: "You are about to purchase an insurance contract that you will probably own for a long time." (Oh, really?)

A Massachusetts company recently sent a newsletter to policyholders that contained a brief discussion of persistency, with this sentence in bold type: "An analysis of all death claims paid during 1988 shows that the average policy had been in force for 34 years." Sounds impressive, until you realize that death claims can be paid only on policies that don't lapse. Misleading statistics aside, this company, by industry standards, really does have excellent persistency. It is proud that "only" 6 percent of its policies are dropped each year—or almost half over a ten-year period.

And what about the New York insurer that calls itself "The Company You Keep"? Each year about 10 percent of its policyholders don't think so.

Insurer control over performance. Every issuer of a financial product has some control over performance. For example, the yield of a money market fund can be increased by waiving the management fee. Yields on certificates of deposit are set by the issuing bank, so any bank can have the highest rate if it's willing to lose money to achieve it. Similarly, insurance companies can control the performance of their products by changing nonguaranteed premiums, dividends, interest rates, and insurance and expense charges. As a rule, you will not know what the pricing strategy is, and you should not assume that a company will always be better off by keeping its products competitive.

Consider single premium deferred annuities. In setting the interest rate, a sophisticated company might construct a cash flow model that links the expected lapse rate to the difference between its own credited rate and the interest rate on competing contracts. For example, the formula for expected lapses might be:

$$\text{Lapse rate} = 15\% - 3(\text{surrender charge}) + 2C(\text{competitors' rate - credited rate})^2$$

where C is 1 if the credited rate is less than the competitors' rate and -1 if it is greater. This would generate the termination rates shown in Table 1.3 for contracts with a 3 percent surrender charge and a competitors' rate of 9 percent.

Table 1.3. Interest-Sensitive Termination Rates for a Hypothetical SPDA Contract

Credited Rate	Competitors' Rate	Difference	Lapse Rate
10.0%	9.0%	1.0%	4.0%
9.5	9.0	0.5	5.5
9.0	9.0	0.0	6.0
8.5	9.0	(0.5)	6.5
8.0	9.0	(1.0)	8.0
7.5	9.0	(1.5)	10.5
7.0	9.0	(2.0)	14.0

Using this model, the company might find that its expected profits would be greatest if it pays 1 percent less than its competitors, because it believes that most of its policyholders will not jump ship. But in the single premium deferred annuity (SPDA) market it doesn't take much to move a contract from the top quartile to the bottom quartile—the corresponding difference in credited rates is generally less than 1 percent.

In comparing insurance products, you can make some guesses about future performance by using common sense and a little knowledge of the pricing process. But insurance advisors have nothing in their bag of tricks that can make a black box transparent. If a company really wants to fool you, it will succeed because it holds all the cards—or, rather, all the profit tests, the asset/liability matching tests, the pricing assumptions, and the information about its own investment, mortality, and expense experience.

This poses a real problem for financial planners and other advisors. Out of necessity, everyone goes along with the insurance industry's game. When asked by clients to evaluate products that cannot be evaluated on the basis of publicly available information, advisors try to make do with what *is* available; namely, compilations of policy illustrations, limited performance histories, and information about the company's overall operations. In contrast, an independently wealthy advisor would have the luxury of refusing the assignment altogether, on the grounds that you can't do an analysis when you have nothing to analyze.

Uncertain investor protections. Most insurance products are not securities, so investors are not protected by the antifraud provisions of the securities laws. In the past, courts have generally ruled that insurers have broad discretion to determine dividends and other nonguaranteed policy values, so it is unclear whether policyholders have any legal recourse when product performance does not live up to expectations. Given the widespread use of deceptive marketing practices, this is an issue that investors and their attorneys will surely be exploring in the years to come.

Corporate reorganizations. Sometimes a company gets tired of being in the insurance business, or it may decide to sell a block of policies to raise capital for a new project. An agent will stress the "peace of mind" that comes from knowing that your insurance company is backed by a huge financial organization, but then a few months later you'll read in the newspaper that the company is up for sale, and no one knows who the new owner will be. The huge financial organization that tells you "you're better off under the umbrella" angered a Connecticut investor not long ago when it sold the subsidiary he had purchased an annuity from. So much for umbrellas.

Insurance companies can also get rid of you through assumption reinsurance, an arrangement in which the issuing company transfers its obligations to another insurance company, which may or may not be financially sound. A recent issue of *The Insurance Forum*, a monthly newsletter published by industry critic and insurance professor Joseph M. Belth, described the unhappy experiences of three insurance buyers who got a quick education in how reinsurance works. In the past, insurers have not bothered to ask their policyholders if they minded being turned over to another company, but this may change as more litigation moves through the courts.

Consumer foibles. Insurance buyers share the blame for making the insurance marketplace a dangerous place to do business. Many people prefer not to think about the various catastrophes that might befall them, so they don't make an effort to become knowledgeable purchasers of insurance products. They unwittingly encourage misleading sales pitches because nothing else will get their attention.

Some consumers also enter the marketplace with unrealistic expectations. They want the "best" product, even though they're not sure what they mean by "best." They want answers that are both simple and right, in a world where these two qualities are rarely found together. They want sound advice, but they don't want to pay for it.

THE BOTTOM LINE

The insurance industry wants its products to be viewed as attractive investment vehicles, but the hazards discussed above show that many companies have not yet learned how to deal with prudent investors—that is, people who refuse to buy a pig in a poke. Of course, it's equally true that prudent investors haven't figured out how to deal with insurance companies. It might be helpful to keep a few things in mind:

1. Insurance products enjoy tax advantages that can give them a competitive edge over other types of investments.

2. You cannot reasonably hope to outsmart insurance companies, because *they* decide what you're going to get. Oh, you may win an occasional victory during periods of fierce competition, but over the long run you'll get what they decide to give you.

3. Insurers control performance, but *you* control their revenues. A company cannot get at your money unless you sign the check.

4. It takes no talent to design a financial product that cannot be evaluated by an informed buyer. Anyone can do it if they're allowed to hide behind the convenient phrase, "that's proprietary information." The real challenge is to design a product with competitive advantages that can stand up to scrutiny.

All of this suggests that the appropriate response to the hazards is not to avoid the products altogether but rather to look for companies willing to compete on disclosure as well as price. You might even consider a kind of partnership in which you acknowledge the company's right to an adequate profit and endeavor to behave responsibly as a consumer, and the company acknowledges your right to understand what you're buying and endeavors to provide a reasonably priced product with as few surprises as possible. In short, quiet commerce instead of a noisy bazaar.

The Purchase Decision

The purchase decision actually involves a whole series of choices —as anyone who has filled out an application knows—and once the purchase has been made, there are still more options to consider. Here's the list:

Before the purchase:

- Suitability
- Time to be spent
- Definition of success
- Advisor
- How much coverage
- Type of policy
- Company and product
- Premium
- Owner/beneficiary/premium payer/annuitant
- Other policy options
- Personal information

After the purchase:

- Keep in force/surrender/exchange?
- Add/withdraw/borrow money?
- Other changes

We'll look at these choices more closely later, but for now, let's look at suitability, time to spend, defining success, choosing an advisor, and listing personal data.

Suitability. There's no reason to look at a product if it doesn't do what you want it to. Of course, the people who sell insurance products can make it sound like every product is suitable for almost everything. Some of these uses are reasonable; others are quite contorted.

Table 1.4 offers some guidance on the appropriate uses of life insurance and annuities. Unless otherwise noted, the comments for life insurance presuppose that you need insurance protection. If you don't need insurance, you will generally be better off investing your money elsewhere.

Time to be spent. Shopping for insurance can really eat up your time if you let it, and let's face it, you probably have better things to do than listen to sales pitches for insurance products. That's why it's a good idea to set some limits at the beginning, even if they turn out to be unrealistic. Figure 1.1 lists the steps in the shopping process, and should help you prepare a preliminary time-budget to move the purchase decision along at an appropriate pace.

Table 1.4. Uses for Life Insurance and Annuities

Financial Planning Goal	Cash Value Life Insurance	Annuities
Emergency fund	Good place for a portion of emergency fund if policy has high early cash value (e.g., low-load policy), since money grows tax-deferred and can be accessed for short periods through withdrawals or policy loans.	Not appropriate; loans or withdrawals are taxable.
Protection against losses due to early death	Can be viable alternative to term insurance if a competitive product is bought and kept in force.	Not appropriate.
Retirement planning	Can be viable alternative to buying term and investing on your own if a competitive product is bought and kept in force. Cash value is available through withdrawals, loans or annuitization.	Deferred annuities can be appropriate if the money is not needed for other goals. Immediate annuities can provide a good foundation of retirement income to build on.
Education funding	Can be a viable alternative to buying term and investing on your own. Cash value withdrawals may be preferable to loans.	Probably not appropriate, since holding period may be too short and tax treatment is unfavorable.
Capital accumulation for yourself	Can be viable alternative to term and investing on your own if a competitive product is bought and kept in force.	Deferred annuities can be appropriate if the money is not needed for other goals.
Capital accumulation for your heirs	Can be viable alternative to investing the premiums on your own, even if you don't need insurance in the usual sense.	Generally not as effective as life insurance, but may be a viable alternative to investing elsewhere, in some cases.
Business needs	Can be appropriate for key person and buy-out situations; also some limited uses with pension plans.	

Figure 1.1. How Much Time are You Willing to Spend?

	Time (hours)	
	Planned	Actual
Reading relevant sections of this book	_____	_____
Reading other books or articles	_____	_____
Choosing an advisor	_____	_____
Consulting with advisor	_____	_____
Getting product information from companies	_____	_____
Reviewing product information and getting additional information	_____	_____
Making a decision	_____	_____
Implementing decision	_____	_____
Total	_____	_____

The biggest time-waster is simply the large number of companies and products out there, constantly elbowing one another for market share. One investment analyst believes that two-thirds of all mutual funds serve no useful purpose; they exist only to provide a livelihood for the nation's money managers, each of whom wants to stay in business even if he has no special talent. The same thing is true of insurance products. Most of them just clutter up the marketplace, and consumers would be no worse off if they disappeared. In this regard, one advantage of low-load products is that they let you narrow down the choices faster.

Defining success. This choice is often overlooked, but it's one of the most important. At what point will you be satisfied that you have found the right product? Here are some possibilities:

The best. Some insurance buyers assume that there really is such a thing as a "best" whole life policy, a "best" term policy, or a "best" annuity. Well, there isn't. Consider for a moment what it would take to find the "best" universal life policy. Are you going to look at every product in the marketplace—and maybe even those under development? Are you going to accept policy illustrations at face value, or will you make adjustments for their reliability? What does "best" mean, anyway? Highest cash value? When—in five years, ten years, twenty years? Lowest premium? Under what assumptions about interest rates, policy charges, and future death benefits? The best way to find the right product is to forget about finding the "best" one.

Top decile, top quartile, etc. This definition of success still suffers from some of the problems that sink "the best," but at least it acknowledges that we live in an uncertain world. Also, it is not an impossible goal. By any reasonable measure, most low-load products should be in the top quartile of their respective groups of products. Top decile, on the other hand, is much more of a challenge.

Good value for your money. This definition is vague, but that may be one of its merits. Sometimes it's enough to know that you're not being ripped off. Given the difficulties of comparing insurance products and predicting future performance, this definition may be all that you can reasonably hope for.

Doing better than you would with a taxable investment. Because insurance products generally enjoy favorable tax treatment, you might define your goal in terms of achieving a higher after-tax return than you could if you invested in something else. The focus here is on finding an insurance product that is simply good enough to outperform the taxable alternatives.

Choosing an advisor. Who will counsel you on insurance matters? Before you can answer this question, it's important to understand that insurance expertise is fragmented. Agents, actuaries, accountants, attorneys, and financial planners all have something to contribute, and no single group of professionals possesses an all-encompassing perspective. The following sections explore your choices.

Do it yourself. This may be appropriate if your financial life is relatively simple or if you are willing to do some research.

You may also decide to do your own insurance product selection and hire an attorney or other professional to take care of some of the details of implementation. Sometimes you'll wind up doing it yourself by necessity, rather than by choice, because the agent you turn to is poorly trained in finance or has only a superficial understanding of the available products. Such an agent will send you a couple of policy illustrations and concentrate on overcoming your objections instead of helping you make an informed decision.

Commission-based agents and brokers. Agents vary greatly in their expertise and in the seriousness with which they take their advisory role. When you buy a fully-loaded product, you are paying for a relationship; that relationship is likely to be better if you choose *one* agent as your advisor and refrain from playing several agents against one another. It is certainly reasonable to interview a few candidates, however, just as you might do if you needed a financial planner, attorney, or other professional. Some appropriate questions to ask:

- Which companies do you represent, how long have you represented them, and why did you choose them?

- What percentage of your business goes to the top company?

- How do you make judgments about future product performance and the reliability of policy illustrations?

- Who are your contacts at each company's home office, and what questions have you asked them recently?

- Upon whom do you rely for advice when technical questions arise about implementation strategies?

- How do you resolve conflicts of interest between buyer and seller in the sales process?

- What services do you provide after the sale, and what happens if you decide to stop representing the companies whose products you are currently recommending?

There's a good legal reason to ask these questions and to write down the answers: If something goes wrong later on, you'll have a better chance of winning a lawsuit for malpractice if you can demonstrate that the agent presented himself as a knowledgeable professional, instead of just a salesman pushing a product.

Fee-and-commission financial planners. Although most financial planners earn most of their income from commissions, and in that respect resemble agents, planners are trained to look at insurance problems in the context of a client's *total* financial life. The trade-off is that a generalist may not be as familiar with products and procedures as the full-time specialist.

In addition to asking the same questions you would ask an agent, inquire about the planner's professional background and qualifications for offering insurance advice. As a generalist, can the planner offer the same level of expertise that a full-time agent can?

Fee-for-service consultants and financial planners. Several hundred fee-only insurance consulting and financial planning firms throughout the United States offer insurance advice either on a stand-alone basis or as part of a comprehensive plan. Some commission-based agents also consult for fees. Many questions you would ask an agent and a fee-and-commission financial planner would also be appropriate for a fee-for-service advisor. You should come away from the interview with an understanding of how the advisor arrives at recommendations.

Accountants and lawyers. Accountants and lawyers can provide a second opinion on agents' proposals, as well as tax and legal advice when appropriate. Like other fee-for-service advisors, accountants and lawyers occasionally experience conflicts of interest as a result of cross-referral arrangements with insurance agents. Also in some states, practicing accountants are allowed to accept commissions from the sale of insurance products.

Consulting actuaries. Consulting actuaries are well qualified to offer advice on insurance products because they understand how the pricing process works. However, they generally work with insurance companies and corporate insurance buyers, rather than with individuals. In addition, they are often reluctant to recommend specific products.

Insiders. Insiders include company employees, consulting actuaries, auditors, and, in some cases, agents. Unlike the issuers of stocks, bonds, and limited partnerships, insurance companies have only a vague obligation to disclose material information about their products, so insiders can be an especially interesting source of advice. For example, one agent tells of selling a life insurance policy to an actuary who worked for a large insurer. Why didn't the actuary get his coverage—with an employee discount, no less—from his own employer? "I've seen the numbers," he reportedly replied.

Listing personal information. Should you lie on an application? Aside from the questionable ethics, there are other good reasons to refrain from misrepresentation on an insurance application.

Contestability period. Insurance companies have a period of time—typically two years—in which to verify the information you provide. If you die under suspicious circumstances during this period, the company may withhold payment of the death claim, and the whole matter could wind up in court. Note in particular that companies are becoming more aggressive in dealing with applicants who lie about their smoking habits. Misrepresentations on applications for health and disability income insurance can lead to similar claim problems.

Personal history interview. Some companies follow up the written application with a phone interview. One of the problems with lying is that it can be difficult to keep your story straight.

Vulnerability to blackmail. Lying sometimes requires collusion with an agent or a doctor, which can leave you exposed to a "unilateral renegotiation" of the original agreement.

If you have a significant health problem, a good alternative to lying is to work with an agent who specializes in substandard risks.

SUGGESTIONS FOR PEOPLE IN A HURRY

It is not advisable to buy insurance products hastily, but if you must here are some general suggestions:

1. Before investing in tax-deferred insurance products, take advantage of opportunities to make tax-deductible contributions to retirement plans, such as IRAs and 401(k) plans. (In some limited cases, it may be appropriate to use a tax-deferred insurance product within a qualified retirement plan.)

2. Be prepared to make a long-term commitment to the product that you are buying. "Long-term" means five to fifteen years, depending on the product. In this sense, insurance products are like limited partnerships that you buy and hold for a long time.

3. Forget about finding the "best" product. Be satisfied with getting good value for your money. If you can find a product with performance in the top quartile of similar products, you've done well.

4. Stay away from products that appear to be much better than all the rest. That's a good sign that there's something fishy, since competitive advantage in the life insurance industry is a matter of inches, not miles.

5. Don't buy a product just because it's hot or new. Hot products come and go. New products are generally priced with higher profit margins; if you wait awhile, competition produces better choices.

6. Look for products that perform their main function well, and don't get distracted by the gimmicks that companies add to make their products stand out from the crowd.

7. If you're making a big purchase, consider diversifying your insurance portfolio by buying two or more different products.

8. Start your search with low-load products. Obtain information from several companies and then weed out the products that seem to be less competitive. You can use

the benchmarks in Appendix A to get some idea of a product's competitive position in the marketplace.

9. If you want to expand your search to include commissionable products, use the more competitive low-load products as points of reference to help you find a competitive agent-sold product. When making comparisons, be sure to take into account any additional fees that you have to pay to get the low-load product.

10. Finally, don't be surprised if you find it difficult to obtain the information that you need to make an intelligent choice. Insurance salespeople often get annoyed when you try to be as careful in deciding whether or not to buy a product as the company was in deciding whether or not to offer it for sale. This is just one of the little hypocrisies that permeate the financial services—or as we prefer to call it, the financial *dis*services—industry.

2

LIFE INSURANCE:
AN OVERVIEW

Consider buying life insurance if you want to protect other people from the financial losses that would be caused by your death and/or you want to stabilize the value of the estate you will leave to your heirs. A life insurance policy is a contract that obligates the insurer to fulfill certain promises to you (the insured) in exchange for one or more payments, or *premiums*. All life insurance policies have a *death benefit*—the amount the insurer promises to pay upon your death. Some policies have a cash value—the amount the insurer promises to pay if you terminate the contract before you die.

The decisions you must make to complete a life insurance purchase are listed in Figure 2.1. These choices will be explored in detail in this and later chapters.

TYPES OF PRODUCTS

Table 2.1 shows the types of life insurance products you are most likely to run across.

Term

Term insurance is pure protection and has no cash surrender value. The amount you pay is closely related to the actual risk of death each year, with an appropriate loading for the company's expenses and profit. Common forms are explained in the following sections.

Figure 2.1. Life Insurance: A Checklist

I. BEFORE THE PURCHASE

1. What is your definition of a successful search?
   ____ the *best* product (sorry, this book can't help you)
   ____ top decile in expected performance
   ____ top quartile in expected performance
   ____ good value for your money
   ____ better than a taxable investment

2. Who will advise you?
   ____ do it yourself
   ____ commission-based agent or broker
   ____ fee-and-commission financial planner
   ____ fee-for-service consultant or financial planner
   ____ accountant
   ____ attorney
   ____ consulting actuary

3. How much coverage do you need?
   ____ amount needed to protect dependents
   ____ amount desired as an investment for heirs
   ____ amount desired for emotional reasons
   ____ amount that can be afforded

4. What type of policy will you buy?
   ____ term
   ____ cash value
       ____ traditional whole life
       ____ adjustable life
       ____ current assumption whole life
       ____ universal life
       ____ single premium whole life
       ____ variable life
       ____ variable universal life
       ____ second-to-die

5. How will you choose among several companies?
   ____ ratings
   ____ analysis of financial statements
   ____ management quality
   ____ valuation actuary's report
   ____ other judgments

6. How will you choose among several products?
   ____ product features (flexibility, load structure, riders)
   ____ comparison of similar illustrations
   ____ comparison with term insurance
   ____ company reputation and track record
   ____ profit testing

7. If you have a choice, what premium will you pay?
___ maximum allowed by current tax law
___ to qualify as life insurance
___ to avoid being a modified endowment contract
___ amount needed to make future cost basis equal future cash value
___ amount justified by rate of return on additional dollars
___ amount justified by desired asset allocation
___ affordable amount
___ amount needed to keep policy in force
___ minimum/maximum set by company

8. Who will own the policy?
___ insured
___ spouse
___ other relative or associate
___ business
___ retirement plan
___ trust
___ tax-exempt organization

9. Who will the beneficiary(ies) be?
___ estate
___ spouse
___ other relative or associate
___ business
___ retirement plan
___ trust
___ tax-exempt organization

10. Who will pay the premiums?
___ insured
___ spouse
___ other relative or associate
___ business
___ retirement plan
___ trust
___ tax-exempt organization

11. What other decisions might be required?
___ dividend option (if applicable)
___ option A or option B (universal life)
___ investment allocation (variable life)
___ settlement option
___ riders
___ premium payment mode (if applicable)

_____

II. AFTER THE PURCHASE

1. ___ Will you keep the policy in force/ surrender it/exchange it?

2. ___ Will you add money/ withdraw money/ borrow?

3. ___ Will there be other policy changes?

Annual renewable term. Premiums typically increase each year, and the policy can be renewed to some maximum age.

N-year renewable term. Premiums remain level for a specified period, typically five or ten years, at which time you can renew the contract at a higher premium level for another multiyear period.

Table 2.1. Types of Life Insurance Products

Term	Cash Value	
	General Account	Separate Account
• Annual renewable term	• Whole life	• Variable life
• N-year renewable term	—Traditional	• Variable
• Graded premium	—Current assumption	universal life
whole life	—Single premium	• Second-to-die
• Decreasing term	• Adjustable life	
	• Universal life	
	• Second-to-die	

Graded premium whole life. This is technically a whole life policy, but it looks like annual renewable term for the first fifteen to twenty years, until the premium becomes level and cash values appear.

Decreasing term. Decreasing term is usually used to pay off an outstanding debt, such as a mortgage.

Cash Value

In contrast to term insurance, cash value life insurance combines protection with savings. The amount you pay exceeds the actual death claims and expense loadings during the early years. This excess accumulates at interest and can be drawn upon in later years to reduce the premium that would otherwise be necessary or to provide funds for some other purpose, such as retirement.

With some products, the excess funds are invested in the company's *general account*, which may include bonds, mortgages, preferred and common stock, real estate, and other investments.

The insurance company makes the investment decisions; it also bears the risk of loss from defaults, changing interest rates, and market fluctuations.

With *separate account* products, the policyholder chooses from among several investment options that are similar to mutual funds. These options usually include stocks, bonds, and money market instruments. In exchange for greater investment control, the policyholder bears the same economic risks as if investing independently.

All cash value products work essentially the same way. As shown in Figure 2.2, there is a death benefit, an internal fund, and a *net amount at risk*—the amount that represents the insurance company's actual risk exposure. In Figure 2.2, the death benefit is level, so the net amount at risk gradually decreases. If the policy has an increasing death benefit, the net amount at risk could remain constant or even increase.

Figure 2.2. Death Benefit = Fund + Net Amount at Risk

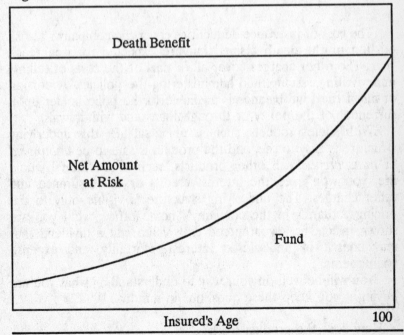

Premiums are deposited into the internal fund, insurance and other charges are deducted, and investment income is credited. This process, similar to what goes on with an interest-bearing checking account, is illustrated in Table 2.2.

Table 2.2. How Cash Value Products Work

Year	Beginning Fund Balance	Premium	Cost of Ins.	Other Charges	Invest. Income	Ending Fund Balance
1	$0	$1,000	$(100)	$(500)	$32	$432
2	432	1,000	(102)	(50)	102	1,382
3	1,382	1,000	(104)	(50)	178	2,406
4	2,406	1,000	(107)	(50)	260	3,509
.						
.						

The cost-of-insurance deductions cover the company's at-risk portion of the death claims that are expected to occur each year. The other charges cover all or part of the costs of selling, underwriting, issuing, and administering the policies. A portion or all of the fund balance is available to the policyholder upon surrender of the policy or through loans and withdrawals.

With some products, such as universal life, this underlying structure is easy to see, and the product is said to be *unbundled* or *transparent*. With other products, such as traditional whole life, you won't see the interest credits or the insurance and other charges. The underlying structure is visible only to the pricing actuaries in the company's home office; what you are shown instead is a guaranteed cash value and a dividend that may consist of undisclosed interest, mortality, and expense components.

You will be well on your way to understanding what you are buying if you keep these questions in mind:

• How does the product work?
  —How is interest credited?

—How is the cost of insurance deducted?
—How are other charges deducted?
—How does the company recover its expenses and make a profit?

- How flexible is the product?
  —How can you change the premium?
  —How can you change the death benefit?
  —How can you change the cash value?

- What competitive advantages and disadvantages does it have?
  —In theory?
  —In reality?

Table 2.3 summarizes key features of several types of cash value policies, which we will examine in more detail later. The terminology can be confusing because some types of policies have more than one name, and some names refer to more than one type of policy. This lack of standardization makes it all the more important to look at the product's features and not just the name. Some of the features in Table 2.3 may not be available on all contracts, or the feature may be an extracontractual provision available only upon request.

TAX CONSIDERATIONS

The tax treatment of life insurance products in general, and cash value products in particular, is complex. You can probably find answers to many of your questions in *Tax Facts 1*, published and revised annually by The National Underwriter Company (see Appendix J, "Other Sources of Information"). Table 2.4 provides a brief overview that necessarily glosses over many of the finer points. The complexity has increased in recent years as a result of numerous tax reforms. Because legislators often are unable to anticipate all of the questions their handiwork raises, you may run into tax provisions that simply are not clear.

Table 2.3. Important Features of Cash Value Life Insurance Products

	Other Names	How Interest is Credited	How COI is Deducted	How Other Charges are Deducted
Traditional whole life	Straight life, ordinary life, n-pay life, life paid up to 65	Implicitly, through determination of dividends and guaranteed cash values. Interest credits and mortality and other deductions are not separately identified, although some of the pricing factors may be disclosed.		
Adjustable life		(Same as *traditional whole life*)		
Current assumption whole life	Interest-sensitive whole life, excess-interest whole life, fixed-premium universal life	Explicit credits, based on current interest rate	Explicit charges, based on current COI rates	Front-end load, periodic loads, surrender charge
Single premium whole life	Single premium life	(Same as *current assumption*)	Usually implicit in current interest rate	Surrender charge, periodic loads
Universal life	Flexible-premium universal life, adjustible life, flexible-premium ajustible life	(Same as *current assumption*)		
Variable life	Fixed-premium variable life	Net investment return on funds	(Same as *current assumption*)	
Variable universal life	Universal variable life, flexible-premium variable life	(Same as *variable life*)		

Table 2.3. *Continued*

How Company Recovers its Expenses and Makes a Profit	Premium Adjustments	Death Benefit Adjustments	Cash Value Adjustments
Premiums in excess of what is needed to pay death claims, expenses, cash values, and dividends	Fixed premium; outlay adjusted through dividend option, riders	Limited, through paid-up additions and partial surrenders	
(Same as *traditional whole life*)	Wide range of amounts	Through change of plan after issue	
Interest and mortality spreads; policy loads	Can periodically choose among several amounts		Limited, through partial surrender
Interest spread; policy loads	Single premium is chosen at issue	Generally none	Partial withdrawals or surrenders may be possible
(Same as *current assumption*)	Wide range of amounts and timing	Can be increased or decreased	Through additional deposits or withdrawals
Mortality spread; mortality and expense risk charge; policy loads; investment advisory fee	Generally fixed. Some adjustments may be possible	Limited adjustments may be possible	
(Same as *variable life*)		(Same as *universal life*)	

Table 2.4. Tax Treatment of Life Insurance

General Rule	Exceptions
• No income tax on death proceeds.	• Situations involving corporate alternative minimum tax or transfers for value.
• Death benefits are included in the insured's estate.	• Not included if insured has never possessed policy ownership rights
• Premiums are not tax-deductible.	• Charitable contributions.
• Investment gains within the policy are tax-deferred.	• Situations involving corporate alternative minimum tax.
• Cost basis is the sum of premiums plus any prior taxable distributions, unreduced by insurance charges within the policy.	• Transfers for value, rollouts from split-dollar and pension plans.
• Premiums paid for riders do not increase the cost basis.	• There may be exceptions; clarification is needed.
• Any taxable gains are treated as ordinary income, not capital gains.	
• Losses from the surrender of a life insurance policy are not deductible.	• Losses due to insurer insolvency; possibly other exceptions i business/investment situations.
• Dividends are not taxable unless sum of dividends received exceeds the sum of premiums paid.	• For modified endowment contracts, some dividends may be taxable.
• Policy can be exchanged tax-free for another policy or an annuity.	• Limitations exist on what qualifies as a tax-free exchange.
• Withdrawals may or may not be taxable—depends on the type of contract and policy year.	• More favorable for contracts is sued before 1/1/85; least favorable for modified endowment contracts.
• Loans are not taxable distributions.	• Modified endowment contracts.
• Policy loan interest is not tax-deductible. (10 percent deduction in 1990.)	• Probably deductible if loan is used for investment/business purposes.
• No penalty tax on income distributions.	• Modified endowment contracts—10 percent penalty.

PRICING CONSIDERATIONS

You can avoid some of the pitfalls of buying insurance products if you try to understand them from the company's point of view. Let's look at the important issues a product manufacturer must address.

Initial Surplus Strain

One feature of almost all insurance products is that they require a company to invest some of its capital—or *surplus*—at the beginning, with the expectation of receiving a stream of profits over time. This investment is necessary because the company incurs sizable expenses in obtaining the business, and it also has to establish a liability on its balance sheet to reflect its obligations to policyholders. The sum of these two items—capital investment and liability—is generally greater than the premium the company receives in the first year. In fact, for agent-sold policies the distribution costs alone will sometimes exceed the first-year premium. If the product is adequately priced, the company will recover its investment and earn a targeted rate of return. The initial acquisition costs and subsequent expenses can be recovered in a variety of ways, depending on the type of product. A company can recover them immediately through a front-end load, or over time through the spread between earned and credited interest rates and the difference between cost of insurance deductions and actual death claims.

Front-end loads are distasteful to consumers, but you should generally welcome them for two reasons. First, by matching more closely the timing of its expenses and its revenues, a company can reduce its own risks and therefore lower its targeted rate of return. Second, the company is in effect lending you money to pay the policy acquisition costs and charging you for the use of that money. The company's targeted rate of return is probably greater than what you are earning on your own investments, so you will be better off by repaying the "loan" as quickly as possible. Many insurance buyers mistakenly believe they are getting a better deal with a so-called no-load—that is, no front-end load—product that "puts all of their money to work for them," but the acquisition costs are simply being recovered more furtively. The world is full of people who want to believe in free lunches, so for marketing reasons insurance companies usually avoid large front-end loads.

Early Lapses

High acquisition costs create another problem for pricing actuaries: how to maintain equity between policyholders who keep their contracts in force and those who don't. What would you think, for instance, of someone who shows up at a party with a bottle of wine, drinks all of it himself, and then leaves the party half an hour later with someone else's bottle? Consistency calls for the same opinion of those who buy life insurance policies only to drop them within a few years. If the company collects a $1,000 first-year premium and spends $1,200 on agent commissions and other expenses, how much does the policyholder deserve to get back if the policy is dropped after a year? The reasonable answer is that he deserves to get a bill for another $200. That's not possible, however, because cash values cannot be less than $0. So the end result is that the pool of assets available for the remaining policyholders is reduced, and this will be reflected in policy values. Unseen costs can be significant. If a company knew in advance that lapses on its universal life product would be very low, it might be able to increase the credited interest rate by 0.5 percent. Term insurance prices are probably 10-20 percent higher than they need to be, because many people drop their policies within a few years of issue—after finding another product that is 5-10 percent cheaper.

Actuaries can sometimes make a cash value product "lapse-proof" through reduced acquisition costs and high surrender charges. In most cases, however, even though an early dropout might get back little or nothing, that individual would still leave with more than he deserved.

Book Value-based Cash Values

With separate account products, such as variable life, the cash value moves in tandem with the market value of the underlying assets. With general account products—traditional whole life, universal life, and others—the cash value reflects the yield on the supporting assets (primarily bonds and mortgages) and is not adjusted for changes in market value. This introduces an additional element of risk for the insurer.

For example, suppose you put $10,000 in a single premium whole life policy, with an 8.5 percent declared interest rate that is guaranteed for one year. To support the policy, the insurer buys a ten-year corporate bond with a 10 percent yield. A year later, interest rates rise to 12 percent. The policyholder now has the right to drop the policy and receive a guaranteed cash value of $10,090, assuming a 7 percent surrender charge. But the corporate bond has lost 11.5 percent of its value and is now worth only $8,850. Add in the year's coupon interest and the company still has only $9,850—$240 short, not counting sales commissions paid out and other expenses that will never be recovered.

The practice of providing guaranteed cash values arose in the late nineteenth century as a way of protecting people who, for various reason, did not keep their policies in force. It is a mandatory feature of all general account cash value products issued today, but it is also a subject of discussion among actuaries and regulators.

During periods of volatile interest rates, are guaranteed loan and surrender values a luxury that the insurance industry can no longer afford? Do generous guarantees actually *prevent* companies from developing products that might be more beneficial to consumers in the long run? A few states have already authorized *modified guaranteed* (or *market value adjusted*) products that would provide a guaranteed cash value at the end of some period—ten years, for example—but would adjust interim cash values up or down to reflect current market conditions at the time of surrender. This area of product development is likely to receive more attention in the future.

Asset/Liability Management

Product guarantees create a need to monitor the relationship between assets and liabilities to reduce potential losses, increase potential gains, or, at the extreme, avoid insolvency. In the previous example, the company chose to mismatch its assets and liabilities by investing in a ten-year bond to support a product with an uncertain lifetime. It could have reduced its interest-rate risk by investing in a lower yielding short-term bond, but that might have made the product unprofitable. It could have lowered the credited interest rate, but that might have made the product uncompetitive. Insurance companies are constantly struggling to balance the profitability and competitiveness of their products, and their sophistication has grown dramatically in recent years. Some companies make use of option-pricing models, immunization techniques, and exotic investments with customized yield and sensitivity characteristics. Regardless of what approach is used, most insurance executives agree that skillful asset/liability management plays a key role in product success. In fact, asset/liability analysis is now becoming inter-twined with the pricing process itself.

Load Versus Low-Load

Distribution costs are an important factor in determining the performance of life insurance products. Selling expenses for a typical agent-sold cash value policy can range from 80 percent to 120 percent of the first-year premium, versus 30 percent or less for a low-load product. Lower expenses mean a higher cash value (given the same premium and death benefit), a higher death benefit (given the same premium and projected cash value), or a lower premium for the same coverage. Some companies view agents as their primary customers—while on the other side of their mouths they talk about their "consumer-oriented" products. It costs money to attract and maintain a sales force to sell life insurance the old-fashioned way; that is, door to door, one-on-one, or one sale per week. Commissions are only part of the cost. Table 2.5 compares the types of sales expenses associated with agent-oriented and consumer-oriented distribution systems.

When insurance products are sold directly to consumers, or through fee-for-service advisors, most of the usual selling expenses can be eliminated. Of course, home office marketing expenses are still required for the preparation of sales materials, advertising, and other functions. Proposal software and other

Table 2.5. Types of Distribution Costs: Agent-Sold Versus Low-Load

Agent-Sold	Low-Load
Base commission	—
Production bonus	—
Expense allowance	—
Override	—
Recruiting and training	Recruiting and training
Training	—
Proposal software	Proposal software
Proposal hardware	—
Office equipment	—
Sales convention (i.e., vacation)	—
Other sales incentives	—
Benefit plans	—
Profit sharing	—
Home office marketing	Home office marketing

expenses may be necessary when the company uses outside distributors. Compare that with what it takes to train and motivate a sales force to undertake the difficult task of finding prospects and then convincing them to make a purchase. There will likely be several layers of sales personnel, each with various forms of incentives to encourage production.

Profit sharing deserves special mention because of its growing popularity and potential for conflicts of interest. One way to share profits is through agent-owned reinsurance companies, which reinsure the policies that the agent-shareholders sell. If persistency and death claims are favorable, the agents will make money from their reinsurance activity; this gives them an incentive to place "quality" business with the issuing company. Of course, there are several ways of looking at this. You might wonder, for example, why the agent should be rewarded for *your* commitment and *your* good health—after all, *you're* paying the premiums. You might also wonder if, to make more money for themselves, agents will pressure the company to pay you less in the future. On the other hand, it's the agent who found you, persuaded you to buy the policy, and now keeps you from dropping it (and maybe even pays for your health club membership). Doesn't that agent deserve to be rewarded? Also, favorable persistency and mortality should produce a bigger pie, with bigger slices for everyone.

Because these profit-sharing arrangements typically take place without consumer oversight, it's a safe bet that the division of the pie—bigger or not—among the company, agents, and policyholders will be different from what it would be if the policyholders were as well organized and well informed as the agents. Fortunately, consumers who are willing to take the initiative in making a life insurance purchase can bypass the conflicts of interest by bypassing the agent-oriented distribution system. You might begin by trying to assess your own insurance needs.

Terminology

As with mutual funds, insurance product categories can be fuzzy. Here are some reasonable definitions.

Commissionable: Agent-sold products with the usual level of commissions and other distribution costs. These might also be called *load* or *full-load products*.

Adjustable-commission: Commissionable products that allow an agent to adjust the compensation. Some products permit limited reductions through the use of low- or no-commission term riders and additional deposits. A few products allow the agent to forgo almost all of the commission, with a corresponding increase in policy values. Overall distribution costs will therefore be less than with a full-load product. However, they may still be greater than with a low-load product, because (1) there may be other agent-related expenses, such as production bonuses and fringe benefits, that are not refundable; and (2) the product is priced to recover all distribution costs, at a required rate of return that will usually exceed the buyer's rate of return on the amounts refunded. As a simple example, suppose the company incurs $1,000 in distribution costs and prices the product to recover the costs evenly over ten years at a 12 percent implicit rate of return; i.e., the policyholder is charged $158 a year. If the company allows the agent to refund $800 within the policy, and the credited interest rate is 8 percent, the buyer is still worse off than if the $800 had not been priced into the product to begin with.

Mail order: Also called *direct response*. Products that are marketed through radio, television, newspapers, magazines, or direct mail. Distribution costs are generally at least as high as with agent-sold products, because of the expenses incurred in advertising. Underwriting is limited, and persistency is often poor.

Low-load: Products that are designed and sold without the usual agent-related or mail-order distribution costs. Marketing expenses are limited because the product is sold through fee-for-service advisors or to a targeted audience of informed buyers.

No load: This simply means that the product has no front-end or ongoing loads and says nothing about the level of distribution costs. No load products with high distribution costs will have high surrender charges, high insurance charges, and/or a low interest rate.

3

LIFE INSURANCE: HOW MUCH TO BUY

How much life insurance should you buy? Table 3.1 lists the many ways you can answer this question.

LIFE INSURANCE AS PROTECTION FOR YOUR HEIRS

Most people buy life insurance to protect their dependents from the economic consequences of an untimely death. There are two ways of thinking about how much protection is needed.

Table 3.1. Methods of Deciding How Much Life Insurance to Buy

Life Insurance as Protection for Your Heirs	Life Insurance as an Investment for Your Heirs	Life Insurance as a Source of Good Feelings	Life Insurance as an Expense
• Human life value	• Discounted dollars	• Love	• Optimization
• Capital needs	• Rate of return upon death	• Relief from guilt	• Other methods
—rough guess	• Expected value	• Relief from fear	
—multiple of income	• Expected utility	• Immortality	
—cash flow modeling		• Heroism	
		• Power	

Human Life Value

From this point of view, life insurance is needed to replace the decedent's economic value to others, a value that has been destroyed by death. Few practitioners use this method to determine insurance needs, although it is frequently used in court cases to estimate losses arising from wrongful death.

Capital Needs

From this point of view, life insurance is needed to fill the gap between the resources that would be available upon your death and the resources that would actually be required to carry out your wishes. You can use one of several methods to determine this capital need.

Rough guess. In addition to saving time, this approach recognizes that life is not a series of optimization problems, and that people can successfully adapt to a fairly wide range of situations. This means that you have fulfilled your responsibilities if you leave an amount that is in the ballpark—and then let the normal processes of adjustment take it from there. The danger, of course, is that you may be a poor guesser. For example, $500,000 sounds like a fortune, but it won't be enough to send your two kids to a top-notch college and provide your spouse with an inflation-adjusted income of $30,000 for forty years.

Multiple of income. This is a form of rough guessing. Multiply your pretax annual income by some number—five is often suggested—and that's how much insurance you need. Although in some cases this may give you a reasonable estimate, the method is so simple it is likely to be off the mark more often than not.

Cash flow modeling. This is the method most financial planners and insurance agents are trained to use. The idea is to calculate how much capital would be needed to accomplish each of your objectives, and then subtract from that the value of the available resources, including Social Security payments and spousal earned income. The answer you get will depend on a long list of assumptions, as well as the model itself. Reasonable people can disagree about the proper level of detail.

There's a consensus, though, that you need to estimate future as well as present insurance needs, because that will help you decide what type of policy to buy. For example, term insurance or a flexible cash value policy might be appropriate if your growing assets will reduce the need for insurance protection in the near future.

In most cases, cash flow models will give you a wide range of answers, depending on the assumptions you make. You can find detailed examples in personal finance books; meanwhile, Table 3.2 illustrates a "quick and dirty approach" that will at least get you started. The trick to keeping things simple is to choose your assumptions carefully.

Assumption 1: If the after-tax rate of return equals the rate of inflation, the present value of an inflation-adjusted series of expenses is equal to the annual expense times the number of years of expenses. For example, $60,000 is just enough to pay for four years of college with an annual cost of $15,000 in today's dollars. Here's a demonstration, assuming that expenses start two years from now (and inflation and investment return are both 7%):

Year	Beginning Balance	Expense	Interest (at 7%)	Ending Balance
1	$60,000	$0	$4,200	$64,200
2	64,200	0	4,494	68,694
3	68,694	(17,174)	3,606	55,126
4	55,126	(18,376)	2,573	39,323
5	39,323	(19,662)	1,376	21,037
6	21,037	(21,037)	0	0

Assumption 2: At 7 percent interest, money doubles in about ten years.

Taken together, these assumptions allow you to easily compute the present value of expenses and Social Security benefits now and in the future. To compute the capital that would be needed ten years from now to pay any remaining expenses, simply double the current annual expense (to adjust for ten years of inflation at 7 percent) and multiply by the remaining number of years. You can perform a similar calculation for different inflation rates if you use these factors, rather than 2: 4%, 1.5; 5%, 1.6; 6%, 1.8; 8%, 2.2; 9%, 2.4; 10%, 2.6.

Table 3.2. A "Quick and Dirty" Capital Needs Analysis

Assumptions:

1. The after-tax rate of return on your invested assets and the rate of inflation are both 7 percent (this makes the calculations easier).

2. Your after-death objectives are:

a. Provide your spouse with an annual after-tax income of $36,000 until your daughter is 18 (she's 7 now), and $24,000 for forty years beyond that. Amounts will increase each year with inflation.

b. Provide for four years of college, with a current cost of $15,000 per year. College expenses will increase each year with inflation.

c. Pay off the mortgage. Current outstanding balance is $100,000.

d. Provide $25,000 for miscellaneous needs, to be adjusted for inflation.

e. Provide $30,000 for final and probate expenses, to be adjusted for inflation.

f. Provide your daughter with a minimum inheritance of $100,000.

3. Your annual savings will be $10,000.

4. Monthly Social Security payments would be $1,700 until your daughter is 16, and $850 until she is 18. Your spouse would elect to receive a $1,130 monthly benefit at age 65, for 21 years (until death). All payments are adjusted each year for inflation, and income taxes are ignored.

Capital needed to accomplish goals:

	Now	10 Years From Now
Living expenses for survivors		
—until daughter is 18	$396,000[a]	$72,000[c]
—after daughter is 18	960,000[b]	1,920,000[d]
College expenses	60,000[e]	120,000[f]
Mortgage payoff	100,000	75,000[g]
Fund for miscellaneous needs	25,000	50,000[h]
Final and probate expenses	30,000	60,000[i]
Daughter's inheritance	100,000	100,000
Total Capital Needed	**$1,671,000**	**$2,397,000**

Capital available to accomplish goals:	Now	10 Years From Now
Investments		
—already accumulated	$200,000	$400,000[j]
—future additions		138,000[k]
Social Security		
—until daughter is 16	183,600[l]	-0-
—until daughter is 18	20,400[m]	20,400[o]
—after spouse is 65	284,760[n]	569,520[p]
Total Capital Available	**$688,760**	**$1,127,920**
Shortfall/(Excess)	**$982,240**	**$1,269,080**
Adjustment for more conservative (+30%) or more aggressive (-20%) investment strategy	0	0
Other adjustments	0	0
LIFE INSURANCE NEEDED	**$982,240**	**$1,269,080**

What if...
—inflation is 5 percent and you reduce the insurance need by 10 percent to reflect a more aggressive investment strategy? $931,190

—inflation is 10 percent and you increase the insurance need by 10 percent to reflect a more conservative investment strategy? $1,779,470

[a] $36,000 annual income x 1 year
[b] $24,000 annual income x 40 years
[c] $36,000 annual income in today's dollars x 2 x 1 year
[d] $24,000 annual income in today's dollars x 2 x 40 years
[e] $15,000 annual cost x 4 years
[f] $15,000 annual cost in today's dollars x 2 x 4 years
[g] Assumes $25,000 of principal has been repaid
[h] $25,000 x 2
[i] $30,000 x 2
[j] $200,000 x 2
[k] $10,000 annual savings accumulated at 7 percent
[l] $1,700 monthly payment x 12 months x 9 years
[m] $850 monthly payment x 12 months x 2 years
[n] $1,130 monthly payment x 12 months x 21 years
[o] $850 monthly payment in today's dollars x 2 x 12 months x 1 year
[p] $1,130 monthly payment in today's dollars x 2 x 12 months x 21 years

There is no simple relationship between future insurance needs and inflation. With each passing year, the number of years of survivor expenses is reduced by one, but the annual expense increases with inflation. In the beginning, the impact of inflation will probably overshadow the impact of each one-year reduction in the support period, and more capital will be needed to accomplish your objectives. At some point, however, the relative impact of these factors will reverse, and less capital will be required.

The assumption that your survivors can earn an after-tax rate of return equal to inflation implies a diversified portfolio that is about 50 percent in stocks, real estate, and other equity investments, and about 50 percent in bonds and cash. If this seems too aggressive (or too conservative), you can adjust the amount of life insurance needed. Again, there is no "simple and right" way of doing this; however, a reasonable range is +30 percent to -20 percent. You may also want to increase the estimated need if you believe that Social Security benefits will be reduced in the future, or if a significant portion of your assets is in qualified retirement plans and will be taxed upon withdrawal. Of course, many other refinements are possible.

The two what-ifs at the bottom of Table 3.2 show how difficult it is to forecast future insurance needs with any degree of confidence. Clearly the results are very sensitive to the assumptions you use, which suggests that you should keep your insurance program flexible so that you can react to changing circumstances as they arise.

LIFE INSURANCE AS AN INVESTMENT FOR YOUR HEIRS

Maybe you don't need insurance to fill the gap between actual and required resources. But what about as an investment? Will life insurance let you leave more money to your heirs than you otherwise could? There are four ways to answer that question.

Discounted Dollars

This is a primitive method often used by agents to convince consumers to buy life insurance to pay their estate taxes. The sales pitch goes something like this:

Mr. Prospect, if you were to die tomorrow, your estate would owe Uncle Sam $1 million. Now there are only four ways that I know of to pay this bill. You can pay it when it comes due, with the assets of the estate; that's 100 cents on the dollar. You can borrow the money; that's 100 cents on the dollar plus accrued interest. You can set aside some money in advance. Let's say you die ten years from now. If you could earn 7 percent after tax, you'd need to set aside about $510,000 right now; that's 51 cents on the dollar. But here's the good news: I can get an insurance company to assume the burden for a single premium of about $150,000. That's an 85 percent discount! That's the magic of life insurance! (Prospect then begs Agent to sell him an insurance policy that will let him pay his estate taxes with "discounted dollars.")

Although this simple argument may sound appealing, the results depend on the assumptions made. For example, if you assume an 8 percent after-tax return and death in twenty-five years, you'd only need to set aside $146,000, rather than $510,000. The comparison can easily be fudged because it focuses on only one of many possible outcomes. If you do the calculations for a range of outcomes, you'll get lots of numbers but no conclusions.

Rate of Return Upon Death

This is another primitive method that agents seem to like. The rate of return upon death is the interest rate you would have to earn on invested premiums in order to match the policy's death benefit at the end of the measurement period. It looks like this:

Year	Premium	Face Amount	Rate of Return Upon Death	Before-tax Equivalent (30% tax)
1	$1,000	$100,000	9,900.0%	14,142.9%
2	1,000	100,000	851.2	1,216.0
3	1,000	100,000	326.4	466.3
4	1,000	100,000	184.9	264.1
5	1,000	100,000	124.0	177.1
20	1,000	100,000	13.7	19.6
40	1,000	100,000	4.0	5.8

This method is particularly effective when used with a typical policy illustration that stops at year 20, because the rate of return upon death goes down over time. The column labeled "Before-tax equivalent" may or may not be shown, depending on how desperate the agent is to make the sale.

Expected Value

If the odds of winning a $100 lottery prize are 1 out of 200 and it costs $1 to enter, the expected value of the bet is -$0.50 ($100 x 1/200 - $1); that is, you'll lose $0.50 on average for each $1 bet. On the other hand, if you can find someone to sell you a lot of tickets for $0.40, you can expect to make $0.10 per ticket.

The president of a large university recently made headlines by suggesting that his institution could increase its endowment by taking out life insurance policies on its students. "Ghoulish and morbid," one alumnus said. Perhaps, but is it smart? Can people make money, on average, by buying cash value life insurance—in other words, does it have a positive expected value? To find out, let's begin by looking at some commercially-available universal life policies. The left-hand side of Figure 3.1 shows the range of single premiums a 55-year-old man could pay in order to keep a $250,000 policy in force until age 95. These amounts are based on a compilation of 98 illustrations prepared in June 1989 by Tillinghast/Towers Perrin, a large actuarial consulting firm.

Now consider this alternative: One sunny afternoon fifty thousand healthy 55-year-olds get together in a football stadium and form an association that will issue a $250,000 life insurance policy to each member. The association gets free actuarial advice, and its other administrative costs are negligible. Unlike an insurance company, however, the association receives no special tax treatment, so the interest income on the premiums collected will be taxed each year. What single premium would the association have to charge each member in order to provide the same $250,000 benefit as the universal life policy?

The right-hand side of Figure 3.1 shows some of the possibilities, based on various assumptions about gross investment yield, mortality experience, and tax rate. (These estimated

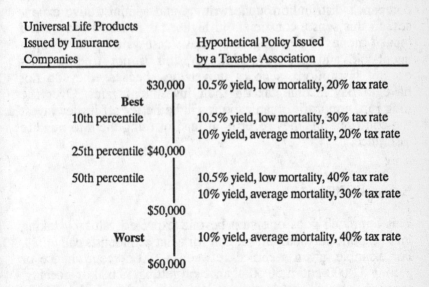

Figure 3.1. Single Premium for a $250,000 Policy Issued to a 55-Year-Old Male Nonsmoker

Universal Life Products Issued by Insurance Companies	Hypothetical Policy Issued by a Taxable Association
$30,000	10.5% yield, low mortality, 20% tax rate
Best	
10th percentile	10.5% yield, low mortality, 30% tax rate
	10% yield, average mortality, 20% tax rate
25th percentile $40,000	
50th percentile	10.5% yield, low mortality, 40% tax rate
	10% yield, average mortality, 30% tax rate
$50,000	
Worst	10% yield, average mortality, 40% tax rate
$60,000	

premiums also take into account the income tax on the universal life proceeds at maturity, which reduces the benefits provided by the insurance company.) The assumed investment yields and mortality rates are probably close to what the surveyed companies used in their own pricing. For example, the commission-paying companies with the best illustrations might have implicitly assumed they could earn 10.5 percent on their assets and that mortality rates would gradually improve over time. Figure 3.1 shows that for higher tax rates, such as 40 percent, many of these commissionable products would cost less than the association's policy. Of course, this conclusion is likely to be even more valid for low-load products. With a 30 percent tax rate, a 10 percent gross investment yield, and average mortality, the association might have to charge about $48,000. Using similar investment yield and mortality assumptions, one company's low-load product would cost about $37,000.

In short, insurance companies may be able to provide benefits that individual investors acting on their own could not duplicate at the same price. This is possible because the tax advantages of cash value life insurance can more than offset the company's distribution, underwriting, and administrative expenses. In this sense, consumers in higher tax brackets can indeed "make money" by buying competitive cash value policies—both agent-sold and low-load. However, this is not true for tax-exempt institutions, such as universities, because they do not have to pay income tax on their investment gains. Over the long run, nonprofit organizations will be better off if they invest the contributions they receive, instead of using them to buy life insurance.

Expected Utility

This approach goes one step beyond expected value by taking into account personal satisfaction—or what economists call *utility*. For example, given a choice between a 100 percent chance of getting $1,000 and a 50/50 chance of getting $3,000 or nothing, many people will choose the sure thing, even though the gamble has a higher expected value. This decision is not irrational; it simply reflects an aversion to risk. When you buy life insurance as an investment for your heirs, you are exchanging an uncertain pattern of wealth for a certain one, as shown in Figure 3.2. By investing the premiums on your own, you might be able to leave your heirs more money if you live a long time, but you will almost certainly leave less if you die early. Life insurance stabilizes the value of your estate.

For most people, then, if life insurance has a favorable expected value (as shown by case 1 in the diagram), it will automatically have a favorable expected utility, because it reduces risk. Furthermore, if the expected value is only mildly unfavorable (as in case 2), the expected utility might still be favorable. In short, introducing the concept of utility strengthens the case for buying life insurance as an investment for your heirs.

Figure 3.2. Life Insurance Stabilizes the Value of Your Estate

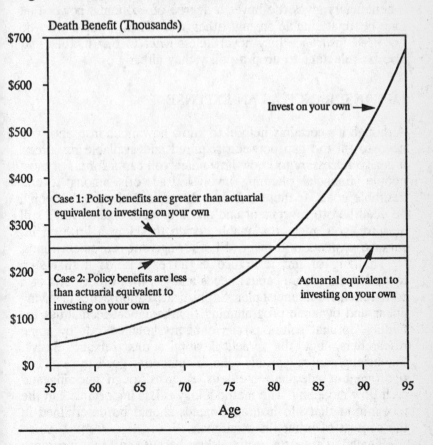

Death Benefit (Thousands)

Invest on your own →

Case 1: Policy benefits are greater than actuarial equivalent to investing on your own

Case 2: Policy benefits are less than actuarial equivalent to investing on your own

Actuarial equivalent to investing on your own

LIFE INSURANCE AS A SOURCE OF GOOD FEELINGS

Life insurance is often sold by appealing to love, guilt, and fear (e.g., "What would happen to your loved ones if you were to die tomorrow?"). In a 1987 article in the *Journal of the American Society of CLU & ChFC*, Professors Mark S. Dorfman and Charles P. Flynn suggested that other motivations—immortality-striving, heroism, and power—may deserve even more attention.

Life insurance enables people to leave something behind, thereby satisfying a need to be remembered after death. It also provides a victory over the economic consequences of death and thereby turns the buyer into a hero. Finally, the right to name a beneficiary gives the buyer a degree of economic power that may be unattainable in any other way. Thus, people who do not *need* insurance may nevertheless *want* to buy it; they may also be reluctant to drop a policy they already own.

LIFE INSURANCE AS AN EXPENSE

Although it's certainly helpful to know how much insurance you need to fill the gap between required and available resources, it is also necessary to know how much you can afford. For most people, financial planning involves trade-offs among several desirable goals. If there is only a 20 percent chance that you'll be dead before retirement and an 80 percent chance you'll still be alive, you might reasonably decide to skimp a little on insurance protection in favor of bolstering your retirement funds.

Thinking of life insurance as an expense is a first step toward integrating a capital needs analysis with other parts of a comprehensive financial plan. Sophisticated approaches involving linear and dynamic programming (mathematical techniques for finding optimal solutions) have been sketched out by some researchers, but the practical applications remain elusive. Financial planners typically balance competing goals through less rigorous—but adequate—methods, such as rough guessing and cash flow modeling. The methodology is less important than the recognition that life insurance needs should be determined in the context of other financial goals.

Finally, it's worth noting that because of the insurance expenses that must be incurred, it will rarely make sense to buy life insurance as an investment *for yourself.* Instead, consider annuities, certificates of deposit, or similar types of investments.

THE BOTTOM LINE

To sum up, you can decide how much life insurance to buy in various ways. It may be worthwhile to prepare an estimate using more than one of these approaches:

	Amount
Life insurance as protection for your heirs	
Capital needs: rough guess	_____
multiple of income	_____
cash flow modeling	_____
Life insurance as an investment for your heirs	_____
Life insurance as a source of good feelings	_____
Life insurance as an expense	_____

Life Insurance as a Substitute For A Spouse's Pension Benefits

Life insurance can sometimes be used as a substitute for a survivor's pension benefits. Instead of electing a joint and survivor annuity option at retirement, you choose a single life option and use the higher monthly payments to fund a life insurance policy for your spouse. Unfortunately, there is no simple way of determining if this is a viable alternative, since the answer depends on your current ages, your ages at death, your tax rate, the difference in pension benefits, and the required premium for the insurance policy. Other considerations may also apply, such as future cost-of-living adjustments and state income tax. The best advice is to avoid leaping until you have carefully examined the choices. As a starting point, here's a rough analysis:

You're 65 and your spouse is 63. Your two pension options are (1) $2,100 per month while you are both alive and $1,400 per month to the survivor or (2) $2,300 while you are alive and nothing after your death. If you elect the single life option, you'll receive an additional $2,400 a year before tax (or $1,680 after tax, assuming a 30 percent tax rate), which you can use to buy a $100,000 universal life policy. Upon your death at age 82, your spouse uses the policy proceeds to buy a single life annuity with a monthly benefit of $1,300 before tax or about $880 after tax. In contrast, with the joint and survivor pension option, your spouse would receive $1,400 before tax or $980 after tax. In this example the life insurance alternative doesn't work, but there will be instances where it does.

4

LIFE INSURANCE:
TYPES OF POLICIES

OVERVIEW

Once you have some idea of why you are buying life insurance and how much you want, you can begin to think about what type of policy is most appropriate. Important considerations include affordability, performance, flexibility, ease of understanding, and disclosure. To a certain extent, a product's beauty and blemishes are in the eye of the beholder. You can find a range of opinions among agents, actuaries, and consumers about each policy type.

It's important to remember that all cash value products are essentially the same. Somewhere, somehow, the company is recovering the distribution, underwriting, issuing, and administrative costs that it incurs. And somewhere, somehow, the company is crediting you with investment earnings and charging you for death claims.

Choosing between term and cash value life insurance is the first task many buyers will face. In general, short-term needs require term insurance, and long-term needs—those lasting beyond age 60 or so—require cash value insurance. Insurance needs that can be met with either type of policy. It basically comes down to an investment decision: Do you want to put your money in a life insurance policy or in some other asset? This is a personal decision, but it should be made with some understanding of the advantages and disadvantages of cash value products.

The disadvantage is that cash value policies generally have higher distribution, issuing, and administrative costs than is typically the case for term insurance. This means that the savings portion of the policy gets hit with various charges that lower the effective yield. On the other hand, cash value life insurance enjoys several tax advantages, some of which are just different ways of saying the same thing:

- Investment earnings within the policy grow tax-deferred and escape income tax entirely upon death.

- The cost basis is the sum of premiums paid, without any reduction for the cost of insurance or other charges. This shields a portion of the investment earnings from tax.

  Example: Suppose you put $2,000 into a universal life policy, and the company deducts $80 for insurance protection and credits $154 interest. If you surrender the policy and receive $2,074, the taxable gain would only be $74, not $154.

- The insurance and other charges within the policy can be paid with pretax dollars by drawing upon the investment earnings.

  Example: Suppose you have $5,000 in a universal life policy that is credited with $400 interest. If you don't want to pay any more premiums, the entire $5,400 account balance can be used to pay for the insurance costs. On the other hand, if you buy term insurance and invest separately, you will have to pay tax on the interest and pay the term premiums with after-tax dollars.

- In some cases, future insurance costs can be prefunded at a discount rate that is equal to the gross interest rate.

  Example: If you own a universal life policy with a 9 percent declared interest rate and you estimate that next year's insurance charges will be $500, you can prefund those charges by depositing $459 today (500/1.09). On the other hand, if you want to prefund $500 of term premiums you will need more than $459, unless your after-tax rate of return is at least 9 percent.

The question, then, is whether the tax advantages of cash value life insurance are sufficient to offset the higher expenses. Not surprisingly, the answer depends on the particular products you compare. However, competitive cash value products—both commissionable and low-load—will offer a reasonable rate of return if you keep them in force for a while. The threshold is generally shorter for low-load products because of their lower acquisition costs.

The comparison in Table 4.1 is equivalent to testing the strength of a household glue in a helicopter-lifts-truck commercial. It pits a low-load universal life policy against very cheap

---

Table 4.1. Cash Value Life Insurance Versus Term: An Extreme Case

- Male nonsmoker, age 30
- $1,000 annual premium
- $300,000 level death benefit
- 30% marginal tax rate

Cash value policy: Low-load universal life, 8.5% interest
Term policy: 10-year level-premium term, with re-entry

Policy Year	Before-Tax Cash Value	Average Annual Rate of Return	Benchmark
1	$791	8.7%	6.7%
2	1,518	2.8	6.7
3	2,247	1.4	6.7
4	3,000	1.2	6.7
5	3,800	1.4	6.7
10	9,627	5.0	6.7
15	19,216	6.7	6.7
20	32,948	6.9	6.7

---

ten-year renewable term. The illustrated values for the low-load policy assume that the company earns about 10 percent on its assets and credits 8.5 percent. The column labeled "Average annual rate of return" shows what you would have to earn on separate investments, after tax, in order to match the universal life policy's after-tax cash surrender value at the end of each holding period. The column labeled "Benchmark" shows what your after-tax rate of return would be if you made the same investments as the insurance company, assuming a 10 percent gross yield, 0.5 percent annual investment expenses (investment advisory fee, bid/ask spread, etc.), and a 30 percent tax rate.

Clearly, it would be inadvisable to buy this policy if you didn't plan to hold it for at least fifteen years, since you could do far better investing on your own. However, the policy does offer a competitive rate of return over the long run. Moreover, this comparison represents a worst-case scenario for several reasons:

- It uses a very cheap term policy and assumes that after ten years you will qualify for re-entry at low rates.

- It uses a young age group, for which cash value life insurance is least likely to offer attractive rates of return.

- The benchmark is optimistic. It assumes that you can get the same gross yield as an insurance company, even though the company may have opportunities—such as private placements—not available to you. Also, most people probably incur expenses above 0.5 percent a year, and the 30 percent marginal tax rate is too low for many people today—and it may be too low for everyone tomorrow.

- The results ignore differences in risk. Unlike many other investments, universal life cash values are free from interest-rate, market, and default risks. In contrast, if you invest in an intermediate- or long-term bond fund, you will suffer a capital loss when interest rates go up.

This face-off was intended to be unfair in order to make a point. In general, competitive cash value policies—both agent-sold and low-load—will provide a good to excellent rate of return in relation to risk if you treat them as long-term commitments. In addition, a low-load policy with low surrender charges is an ideal place to keep a portion of your emergency fund, since the money will grow tax-deferred and can be accessed through withdrawals or short-term policy loans.

Now let's look at each type of life insurance product in more detail.

CASH VALUE LIFE INSURANCE

Traditional Whole Life

Traditional whole life is the oldest form of cash value life insurance, and it still accounts for a significant share of all sales to individuals. There are three versions in the marketplace today: nonparticipating, adjustable premium, and participating.

Nonparticipating whole life. This form of whole life used to be quite common, but companies have moved on to other things and generally make it available only as an accommodation to agents and consumers. Premiums, death benefits, and cash values are all predetermined, fixed, and guaranteed: What you see is what you get. The product is most appropriate for people who hold an apocalyptic view of the world and expect investment returns or mortality to deteriorate significantly.

Adjustable premium whole life. Adjustable premium whole life offers guaranteed cash values, guaranteed death benefits, and two premium schedules: a maximum premium and a lower current premium that may be guaranteed not to change for several years. Premiums are adjusted periodically based on the company's investment, mortality, and expense experience.

Participating whole life. This is the most common version. Premiums are fixed and guaranteed; the policy will stay in force until maturity as long as the premium is paid each year. Premiums are based on conservative assumptions about interest and mortality rates and may be payable for life (straight life) or for a limited number of years (life to age 65, 10-pay life, 20-pay life).

Each year the company pays a dividend that reflects the difference between actual and assumed experience. Typically the dividend can be used in one or more of five ways:

- It can be received in cash.

- It can be applied to reduce the premium.

- It can accumulate at interest; the company holds the dividends for you and pays taxable interest, just like a money market account.

- It can buy paid-up additions; these are small, low-load, single premium whole life policies that have guaranteed cash values and death benefits and pay dividends themselves.

- It can buy one-year term insurance; this is often used together with policy loans to keep the death benefit from being reduced.

Dividend options add some flexibility to an otherwise-inflexible product. For example, you can set up a *vanishing premium* plan by purchasing paid-up additions for several years and then surrendering them to pay future premiums. Dividend

---

How One Agent Explains It

Many people do not like technical explanations of the things they buy. Here's how one very successful agent explains cash value life insurance to his prospects:

Starting an insurance program is like planting a tree. First, you plant the seed, then the seed germinates, a young tree sprouts and more and more leaves come, then the first fruit appears. Later, more and more fruit is borne by the tree. In the same way, a life insurance policy grows. There's very little cash value in the early years of its life, but the cash values grow. Later on when money is needed, it's there in abundance. Just as a tree provides shade, the policy provides cash for emergencies. Later on, you can eat fruit off the tree. With an insurance policy, in later life you can take retirement income from the policy.

To complete the analogy, a low-load policy will likely grow faster and bear more fruit than a commissionable policy. And it needs less fertilizer to make it look attractive.

---

options also make it possible to combine whole life with term insurance in numerous ways, to reduce the initial outlay without sacrificing the long-term protection that whole life provides.

Flexibility and performance can be further enhanced with paid-up additions riders that let you deposit a lump-sum payment to finance future premiums or to accelerate the growth in the death benefit.

An inside view. On the surface, all of this seems simple enough, but in fact, no life insurance product tells you less about itself than traditional whole life does. From the outside you see premiums, death benefits, guaranteed cash values, and dividends, while the *real* activity takes place out of view. Table 4.2 shows you what traditional whole life looks like from the inside; items you can see from the outside are in boldface type. As with any cash value product, there are investment earnings and insurance and expense deductions, except that it all happens in a roundabout way. Here's a step-by-step explanation, moving left to right, column by column, across the table.

When any life insurance policy is issued, the company assumes certain obligations, in accordance with the contractual guarantees. A liability, the *reserve*, is set up to reflect the amount the company needs to have on hand to meet its promises in the future. The balance at the beginning of each policy year is called the *initial reserve*.

The insured pays a *gross premium* of $1,910, which is fixed for life.

In the first year, the company subtracts $1,594 as an initial expense allowance (which may be higher or lower than its actual acquisition costs). The remaining $316—called the *valuation net annual premium*, or sometimes just the *net premium*—is added to the initial reserve. (Note that *net premium* can also mean the difference between the gross premium and the dividend; the terminology can be confusing if you're talking with an agent and an actuary at the same time.) In subsequent years, the company subtracts $244 as a renewal expense allowance and deposits the $1,666 net premium.

The balance in the reserve is credited with interest—called *tabular interest*—at the valuation interest rate; in this case, 5 percent. This is a deliberately conservative rate, used to value the company's obligations to policyholders so that reserves are

Table 4.2. What Traditional Whole Life Looks Like from the Inside

- Male nonsmoker, age 45
- $100,000 face amount
- $1,910 level premium

- Valuation interest rate: 5%
- Dividend interest rate: 10%

Year	Initial Reserve	Valuation Net Annual Premium Gross Premium	Loading	Tabular Interest	Tabular Cost	Terminal Reserve
1	$0	$1,910	$(1,594)	$16	$(332)	$0
2	0	1,910	(244)	83	(352)	1,395
3	1,395	1,910	(244)	153	(378)	2,836
4	2,836	1,910	(244)	225	(402)	4,325
5	4,325	1,910	(244)	300	(428)	5,863
10	12,490	1,910	(244)	708	(609)	14,255
15	21,707	1,910	(244)	1,169	(876)	23,666
20	31,799	1,910	(244)	1,673	(1,258)	33,880

sufficient. (The aggregate amount of tabular interest credited by the company on all of its policies is shown in the annual statement filed with state insurance departments.)

A cost of insurance—called *tabular cost*—is deducted, based on the net amount at risk and a conservative mortality table; in this case, the 1980 Commissioners Standard Ordinary Table for male nonsmokers. This is a deliberately high insurance charge used to ensure sufficient reserves. (The aggregate tabular cost charged by the company on all of its life policies is shown in its annual statement.)

The balance at the end of the year is called the *terminal reserve*.

In effect, a *surrender charge* is deducted to get the *guaranteed cash value*. This surrender charge arises from differences between the Standard Valuation Law, which governs the computation of reserves, and the Standard Nonforfeiture Law, which governs the computation of minimum guaranteed cash

Table 4.2. Continued

- Valuation mortality rates: 1980 CSO Male Nonsmoker Table
- Dividend mortality rates: 80% of 1975-80 Select & Ultimate Table
- Reserve basis: 1980 CSO 5% CRVM

Surrender Charge	Guaranteed Cash Value	Dividend			Total Dividend
		Interest	Mortality	Expense	
$0	$0	$16	$238	$(158)	$96
(1,290)	105	83	218	(187)	114
(1,029)	1,807	153	197	(217)	133
(709)	3,623	225	190	(250)	165
(445)	5,418	300	192	(284)	208
0	14,255	708	259	53	1,020
0	23,666	1,169	264	129	1,562
0	33,880	1,673	321	129	2,123

values. The Standard Nonforfeiture Law allows companies to recover all or most of their acquisition costs, while requiring a minimum level of cash values to prevent abuses. In practice, the guaranteed cash values may be greater than the required minimums, and they will always be less than or equal to the terminal reserve. In this example, the surrender charge gradually disappears within ten years.

At the end of each year, the company pays a dividend, based on its actual investment, mortality, and expense experience. In this example, the company uses a three-factor formula with interest, mortality, and expense components, to determine the dividend each year.

The *interest component* represents the excess interest earned on the initial reserve plus the net premium, over and above the 5 percent tabular interest. The *dividend interest rate* is 10 percent, so the excess is 5 percent. For the third year, the calculation would be $(1,395 + 1,910 - 244)(.05) = \$153$. In this example, the dividend interest rate is determined on a *portfolio-*

average basis; that is, everyone gets the same rate regardless of when they paid their premiums. In contrast, under an *investment-year* approach several interest rates would be used to reflect the timing of premium payments.

The *mortality component* represents the difference between assumed and actual death claims. It is equal to the net amount at risk multiplied by the difference between the valuation mortality rate and the actual mortality rate. In the third year, the conservative mortality rate used to compute reserves is 3.88 deaths per 1,000, whereas the actual rate is only 1.85 per 1,000. The difference of 2.03 is multiplied by the net amount at risk ($100,000 minus the $2,836 terminal reserve, expressed in thousands of dollars), to get $197.

The *expense component* represents the difference between the expense loading in the gross premium and the actual expenses. In this example, the actual expenses exceed the loading during the early years, so the expense component is a negative value, -$217.

The end result of all of this activity is that:

- You receive a current rate of interest. Interest is credited in two pieces: reserve interest (5 percent) and the interest component of the dividend (5 percent).

- You are charged a current cost of insurance. An excessive charge is made in the reserve and then a portion is refunded through the mortality component of the dividend. The net charge reflects the company's actual experience.

- You are charged for the company's current expenses. Expenses are recovered from the premiums you pay and the dividends you receive. If you drop the policy, you may also receive less than the terminal reserve; in effect, there is a surrender charge.

In designing a traditional whole life product, the company sets the gross premium, the valuation net premium, the guaranteed cash values, and the dividends—but it has to operate within regulatory and marketplace constraints.

The gross premium will generally be greater than the valuation net premium, in order to achieve adequate profit levels and avoid having to set aside additional reserves. A higher gross premium will allow dividends to be higher, since more money is being collected for investment. On the other hand, a low gross premium may be more appealing to some buyers, even if it means lower dividends. Marketing considerations will play an important part in the final decision. The valuation net premium is determined indirectly through the selection of a *reserve basis*; that is, the method and assumptions the company uses to determine the reserve. In the example in Table 4.2, the company uses the *Commissioners' Reserve Valuation Method (CRVM)*, which produces a large front-end load in the first year and a smaller load in all renewal years. Many companies use this method because it produces lower required reserves and therefore reduces surplus strain. Some companies use the *net level premium method*, a more conservative valuation method that spreads the expense loading evenly over all of the gross premiums and produces a higher level of reserves. In Table 4.2, this method would produce a constant load of about $330 each year.

The reserve basis also contains assumptions about future interest and mortality rates. For example, "1980 CSO 5%" means that the company is using a 5 percent valuation interest rate and the 1980 Commissioners Standard Ordinary Mortality Table (CSO Table). State law determines the highest interest rate and the lowest mortality rates that can be used. Guaranteed cash values must be greater than the minimums required by the Standard Nonforfeiture Law and less than or equal to the terminal reserve. Within this range, marketing considerations will determine what level of values the company actually decides to offer.

Dividends allow the company to adjust the competitiveness and profitability of the product. The process of dividend determination is governed by actuarial standards of practice and, in some cases, state law. The company begins by deciding how much money it wants to pay out in total—the *divisible surplus*. The allocation of divisible surplus among policyholders is governed by the *contribution principle*, which states that divisible surplus should be distributed in the same proportion as each policy has contributed to it.

Numerous ways of implementing the contribution principle exist to achieve a defensible dividend scale. The most common approach is the *contribution method* (also called the *source of earnings method*), which views a dividend as the sum of contributions from interest, mortality, and expense experience. This leads to a three-factor dividend formula, as in Table 4.2. Other formulas are possible; some years ago, an actuary proposed a nine-factor formula.

Insurance companies often regard the dividend formula as proprietary and will not disclose it to policyholders. In recent years, perhaps in response to the popularity of universal life, some companies have chosen to disclose the dividend interest rate—sometimes in flashy advertisements in trade publications. However, as Table 4.2 shows, the dividend interest rate by itself tells you nothing, because you don't know what the hidden charges are. A 10 percent rate applied to a small reserve balance could be worse than a 9 percent rate applied to a larger balance.

It is just as misleading to compare the dividend interest rate with the gross interest rate on universal life products. With universal life, more of the expenses tend to be recovered through the interest rate spread—as opposed to the hidden premium loads on traditional whole life—so you would expect the gross interest rate on universal life to be less than the dividend interest rate on traditional whole life, given the same portfolio yield. Of course, companies are quite happy to announce an 11 percent dividend interest rate and let you draw your own favorable—and possibly erroneous—conclusions.

Ultimately, policyholders have to trust the company's actuaries to determine dividends in an equitable manner, but sometimes their trust is misplaced. Here's an excerpt from a 1987 examiner's report on a New York company, covering the three-year period ending in 1985:

> The dividend interest rate for ordinary life insurance dividends was obtained by deriving a weighted blend of the array of dividend interest rates in the previous dividend resolution. No new study of actual investment experience was done. The most recent such study involves experience through the year 1981.

In the current resolution, the maximum dividend interest rate is a rather low 6 percent. By comparison, the Company's Exhibit Two net return was 10.02 percent and in December 1985 the Company was crediting 10.50 percent on Universal Life products. This suggests the need for an upward revision in the dividend interest rate. . .

The most recent study supporting dividend mortality rates covered the one-year period ending July 1, 1981. It is suggested that the Company conduct a new mortality study encompassing several years' experience to determine whether the current dividend mortality basis remains appropriate.

Documentation supporting the expense element of the loading refund factor was somewhat sketchy. The Company stated that an "asset share approach" had been used, but did not provide an asset share study nor a derivation of expense factors from such a study. Much judgment appears to have been used. . .

The examiner was being polite. A less restrained observer might have accused the company of cheating its old policyholders by using out-of-date interest, mortality, and expense factors in its dividend calculations. This case is certainly not typical of insurance companies that issue dividend-paying products, but it highlights the folly of assuming that your dividend is exactly what it should be.

Advantages and disadvantages. Despite its opacity and limited flexibility, traditional whole life does have some advantages. The semi-compulsory nature of fixed premiums may be of benefit to people who are not disciplined savers. Fixed premiums also reduce administrative costs and the company's uncertainty about its cash flows. In theory, this should lead to higher investment yields, lower expense loads, and a lower profit objective. In practice, however, there is little evidence that fixed premiums actually produce significant improvements in benefits for policyholders.

Some critics have "exposed" traditional whole life as an ill-conceived scheme in which companies overcharge their policyholders and then refund a portion of the overcharge through dividends. The only thing exposed in these attacks is the critics' own ignorance about insurance products. A high fixed premium allows the company to guarantee that the policy will stay in force until maturity regardless of interest rates, mortality, or expenses. Without the cushion provided by the high premium, a company has two choices. It can issue an adjustable-premium product with a lower current premium and a higher guaranteed premium, *or* it can issue a nonparticipating product with a low premium guaranteed for life and hope nothing happens to drive the company into bankruptcy. Few informed consumers would welcome the second choice.

In general, a high fixed premium *does* mean higher expenses, because commissions and related sales costs, as well as state premium taxes, will be based on the entire premium. Even so, the overall impact on long-term performance is not obvious. Let's say the company collects an additional $100 a year. In Year 1, it loses the entire $100, due to commissions and other variable expenses. In subsequent years, it loses 7 percent—5 percent for commissions and 2 percent for state premium tax. This looks like a terrible deal for a policyholder who could invest the $100 a year elsewhere at 7 percent after tax and have $4,387 after twenty years. But the insurance company has Uncle Sam on its side; if the company can pay 10.3 percent tax-deferred interest on whatever remains of the $100 each year, a policyholder in the 30 percent tax bracket would have an extra $4,393 upon surrender. Needless to say, the comparison would be much more favorable if the company refused to pay full commissions on the entire premium. Remember, too, that most people do not keep their policies in force for twenty years, so they will be worse off by having given the company the additional $100 a year.

The continued popularity of traditional whole life is best explained by looking at the supply side. Agents like it because of the higher commissionable premium and the mystique of guarantees; from the company's point of view, inscrutability can be a real plus. Here's how Paul T. Bourdeau, former president and CEO, Beneficial Standard Life, put it some years ago, as he discussed the problems of making money on universal life policies:

The current interest rate [on universal life] is featured in sales presentations—it is there for everybody to see, challenge and compare. This visibility and the resulting comparisons lead to a highly competitive environment with resulting downward pressure on the earnings of life insurance companies. The traditional participating policy dividend is, by comparison, a piece of cake. The mysterious calculation of dividends creates a relatively desensitized competitive environment resulting in less pressure on earnings.

In other words, when you can't figure out what's going on, the company can get away with paying you less.

Shopping for traditional whole life. Here are some suggestions for finding a reasonably priced policy:

- Try to avoid comparing two traditional whole life products. If you must, obtain illustrations that assume the same gross premium, with dividends received as paid-up additions, and then compare the death benefits and cash values for each year to maturity. If you get inconclusive results, try to mentally adjust the cash value of one policy for the assumed value of any difference in death benefits; for example, by using term insurance prices or standard mortality rates.
- Ask about the company's dividend illustration practices. Do illustrated values make use of pricing factors that are different from current factors? Do illustrated values make use of pricing factors that may not be sustainable over the long run?
- If you are buying an agent-sold product, make sure that the proposal is what is best for *you*, not the agent. Ask about noncommissionable paid-up additions and term riders that might improve performance.
- Do not buy high-profit riders, such as waiver of premium and accidental death benefit, unless you really have a need for them.
- Consider using dividends to buy paid-up additions, since they will often be a good value. To verify this, look at the annual percentage increase in the cash value of the paid-up additions, ignoring the death benefit; then compare this with the interest rate on fixed deferred annuities.

- If you want to better understand what you're buying, ask the company to show you the internal interest credits and mortality and expense deductions, including the components of the dividend.
- Save all illustrations and other documents, so that you have a basis for monitoring future performance.

Adjustable Life

Adjustable life was developed in the 1970s as a more flexible version of traditional whole life. It allows you to move between different plans of insurance, such as "whole life paid up at age 65" and "term to age 67," as your needs change. The policy might start off as term insurance, but you can use dividends and additional premium payments to change it into whole life. As with traditional whole life, you do not see the separate interest credits or insurance and expense charges.

Universal Life

Universal life was conceived some decades ago, but its commercial birth occurred in the late 1970s. It is both flexible and transparent. Premiums are deposited into an accumulation account that earns a declared rate of interest, and monthly charges are deducted for the cost of insurance. Many policies also have front-end loads, percent-of-premium loads, monthly administrative fees, or declining surrender charges. All credits and deductions are shown on an annual report to the policyholder.

Policyholders can choose between two death benefit options. Option A is a level death benefit where the net amount at risk gradually decreases as the accumulation account builds. Option B is an increasing death benefit that equals the initial face amount plus the accumulation account balance; the net amount at risk remains constant.

Premiums can be increased, decreased, or stopped altogether. However, the policy will lapse if the accumulation account balance cannot cover the cost of insurance and other charges.

The death benefit can be increased (subject to evidence of insurability) or decreased (subject to a required minimum). The death benefit option can also be changed.

The cash value can be increased by depositing additional amounts or decreased by making withdrawals.

So much flexibility can be a curse as well as a blessing; it also can be more theoretical than real. Universal life is easy to abuse because it lets you pay a low premium in anticipation of favorable interest and mortality experience. If interest rates go down or the insurance charges go up, you may have to deposit more money into the policy. You may also find that the flexibility goes unused, because of complex tax code provisions of your own inertia. If you put too much money into the policy, it will become a modified endowment contract and lose some of its tax advantages (see Chapter 6, "Premiums"). This can also happen if you reduce the coverage during the first seven years. If you increase the coverage at *any* time, you might inadvertently limit the premiums you can pay during the *next* seven years. The option to make withdrawals is also nice in theory, but you may not like the tax consequences.

Two myths about universal life have been surprisingly durable, perhaps because agents who sell traditional whole life find it convenient to keep them alive.

Myth 1: Universal life has fewer guarantees than traditional whole life. Nonsense. Without exception, universal life policies have a guaranteed interest rate (typically 4-6 percent), a guaranteed cost of insurance (generally based on some version of the 1980 CSO Table), and guaranteed expenses. The difference between the two types of products is that universal life allows you to reduce the premium today, whereas traditional whole life makes you wait until the favorable experience actually occurs and can be passed along in dividends.

You don't have to buy traditional whole life to get traditional whole life, however. You can get the same level of guarantees with universal life. Just follow these steps:

1. Ask the company for the *guideline annual premium* (the maximum annual premium that is permitted under current tax law).

2. Obtain a policy illustration showing the guaranteed account values for each year to maturity, assuming payment of the guideline annual premium each year.

3. In the first year, pay the guideline annual premium.

4. At the end of the year, look at the difference between the actual and the guaranteed account values. That difference is your "dividend," which you can use to reduce the premium in the following year or leave on deposit within the policy.

Of course, unlike a real traditional whole life policy, this simulated whole life policy lets you revert to universal life at any time.

Myth 2: Universal life is backed by short-term (and therefore lower yielding) investments, whereas traditional whole life is backed by long-term (and therefore higher yielding) investments. Near-nonsense. For both types of products, the actual investment strategy will depend on the company's willingness to accept risk. Cash flows for universal life are less predictable than they are for traditional whole life, so this argues in favor of a shorter term portfolio of bonds and mortgages. However, traditional whole life policies allow policyholders to surrender at book value, so companies cannot load up on thirty-year bonds if they want to stay in business during the next period of rising interest rates. On average, universal life portfolios probably have a shorter duration than those for traditional whole life, but the yield differences are much less important than many other factors that affect performance.

A closer look. The insurance company recovers its expenses and makes a profit from (1) the difference between what it earns on its investments and what it credits, (2) the difference between the insurance charges and actual death claims, and (3) other policy loads. Insurance charges and policy loads vary greatly among products. Interest rates tend to be more uniform; the interest rate is the most visible feature of universal life, so companies try to keep it attractive.

Interest can be credited in several ways. Under a pure *portfolio average* approach, the same rate is paid on all policies, regardless of the timing of premium payments. Under a pure *investment generation* approach, premium payments are grouped by year (or month or some other period) and a credited rate is declared for each "generation," based on investment results.

In practice, many companies use an interest crediting approach that lies somewhere between the two extremes. There may be one interest rate for *new money* and another for all previous deposits; at the end of each year, new money becomes old money and earns the pooled rate. Or a company that uses the portfolio average approach might decide to close off the block of business as interest rates rise and start a new portfolio for newly issued policies, in order to remain competitive with new-money rates. For new policyholders, a portfolio average approach is better during periods of falling interest rates, since the credited rate is buoyed by the earlier, higher yielding investments. A new-money approach is better during periods of rising interest rates, since the credited rate is not held back by the earlier, lower yielding investments. Over the long run, however, the choice of method is less important than the consistency with which it is applied. When a company manipulates the interest crediting method to attract new business, that should be a red flag for both new and existing policyholders.

Cost of insurance rates can also be structured in several ways, similar to term insurance. With *aggregate* (or *attained-age*) rates, everyone of the same age and underwriting class pays the same rate, regardless of when the policy was issued. With *select and ultimate* rates, new policyholders pay a lower rate than existing policyholders of the same age, since they have just been underwritten and should therefore have fewer death claims. This advantage eventually wears off, and everyone then pays the same ultimate rate, similar to an aggregate rate structure. Some companies use a *reverse select* schedule, in which insurance charges are increased during the early years to recover policy acquisition costs.

Banded and *tiered* rates add another dimension to the rate structure. With banding, the face amount or net amount at risk will determine which set of charges will be used; generally, the cost of insurance rates are lower for larger policies, since the charges cover some fixed expenses as well as pure mortality risk. Under a *tiered* rate structure, one set of rates is applied to each portion of the net amount at risk; for example, the first $50,000 of coverage might cost $1.00 per $1,000, the next $50,000 might cost $0.94, and all amounts above that might cost $0.86.

In addition to the insurance charges, other policy loads may reimburse the company for acquisition costs, ongoing administrative costs, and state premium taxes. This aspect of product design is often driven by marketing considerations; the company may decide that the product will be easier to sell if the expenses are hidden in the interest-rate and mortality margins, instead of being trumpeted in a large front-end load and smaller ongoing loads. At the extreme, a company's actuaries can create a so-called no-load product with a declining surrender charge and no other explicit loads. Then the marketing department can put together a nice brochure emphasizing that "100% of your money goes to work for you immediately," which is, of course, deceptive advertising, because the interest rate or mortality charges have been adjusted to make up for the reduced loads. (Which is better: working quickly for five hours starting one hour from now, or working slowly for six hours, starting immediately?)

Recent developments. In the early 1980s, universal life sales were swept along by high interest rates, and many companies rushed to develop "interest sensitive" products. Consumers have since learned that interest rates can go down as well as up, and companies have learned that it's hard to design a universal life product that is both competitive and profitable. To restore excitement and profitability to the product, some companies have introduced two innovations: *persistency bonuses* and *living benefits*.

Persistency bonuses. Also called *policy enhancements*, persistency bonuses are intended to give policyholders an incentive to keep their contracts in force. These incentives include:

- declaring a retroactively higher interest rate after some period, usually at least ten years (cash values are recalculated as if the higher rate had been in effect the whole time)

- declaring an interest-rate bonus after some period or after cash values exceed a certain amount (for example, paying an extra 0.50 percent if cash values exceed $10,000)

- declaring a premium bonus after some period (for example, adding 45 percent of the scheduled premium to the cash value each year, starting ten years from issue)

- refunding a portion or all of the insurance charges after some period (for example, every ten years)

The key feature of all of these enhancements is that they are scheduled to take place in the future—usually a long time in the future—but they can greatly improve the illustrated long-term performance of the product and therefore make it look more competitive on paper.

Concerned actuaries and other observers have pointed out several risks that the buyers of enhanced products should be aware of. If the bonus is not guaranteed, there is no assurance that it will be paid when the time comes. If the company's management changes after the policy is issued, the new management may not feel obligated to continue the practices of its predecessors. Or, the company may not set aside enough money to pay the bonuses. On the other hand, if money *is* set aside the company may become a tempting target for corporate raiders. Even if the bonus is guaranteed, the company usually retains the right to change other factors, such as the monthly insurance charges or the interest rate, thereby offsetting the bonus. Also, a guaranteed bonus can become meaningless if the company no longer sells the product being used as a reference point.

Note, too, that a guaranteed bonus is only as good as the company that makes the guarantee. If the company is driven into bankruptcy because of its outlandish promises, you may never see the bonus.

If nothing else, persistency bonuses have added a new level of complexity to policy comparisons. Some bonuses are legitimate ways of rewarding policyholders who make regular premium payments or who simply keep their contracts in force. Lower lapse rates and more money under management can generate enough additional profits to finance the bonus.

In contrast, some bonuses are merely lures, with little chance of actually materializing. The company uses them to attract sales but is not really committed to paying them. In most industries, this would be called fraud; journalists would expose it, and the victims would sue. In the life insurance industry, however, it's simply called a "current illustration practice." There's always a footnote at the end of the ledger statement that says something like "Illustrated values are not guaranteed"—and *that's* what the company will point to if you try to take them to court.

Finally, some bonuses are *tontines*, an arrangement in which surviving policyholders benefit at the expense of those who die or lapse. Dropouts receive less than they normally would, and these funds are used to finance the bonuses for those who remain. Tontines were popular for a while in the late 19th century, but they led to many abuses and lawsuits and were eventually prohibited. Time will tell if this latest incarnation of the tontine has a different karma.

In sum, when a universal life policy has a persistency bonus, you may be looking at an equitably priced product, an instance of fraud, or a tontine. Only the company's pricing actuaries and executives know for sure.

Living benefits. Also called *accelerated death benefits*, living benefits are usually offered as a rider to a flexible or fixed-premium universal life policy (and sometimes to whole life). They are designed to make life insurance more appealing by providing a benefit while the insured is still alive. The benefit is triggered by one or more covered conditions, such as a heart attack or an extended stay in a nursing home, and can be paid in a lump sum or in a series of monthly payments. Living benefits are of two designs: *lien* and *partial surrender*. Under the lien approach, the benefit payments are treated as a non-interest bearing loan against the death benefit and cash value, on a dollar-for-dollar basis. Under the partial surrender approach, there is a proportionate reduction in the death benefit, cash value, and, for fixed-premium contracts, the premium.

The attraction of living benefits is that you don't have to die to receive money from the insurance company. Also, many people are concerned about the expenses of long-term care, so they are likely to be receptive to anything that addresses this problem. Beyond the hype, however, it appears that living benefits offer only two advantages over the alternative of buying separate life and health insurance policies. First, there should be some savings on underwriting costs; that might be worth about

$150, if you can satisfy all of your insurance needs with one policy instead of two. Second, with some flexible-premium policies you can prefund the future insurance charges at a discount rate that is equal to the policy's gross interest rate. If the long-term care benefit costs $300 a year for twenty years, the present value at 6 percent would be $3,647, versus only $2,985 at 9 percent.

Now consider the disadvantages. The living benefits reduce the death benefit, so your beneficiaries will receive less money than if you purchased adequate coverage for each need separately. That's all right if you're just buying life insurance as an investment for your heirs, but not if you're trying to protect them from the consequences of your death. The triggering conditions may be open to misunderstanding or dispute. There may be exclusions or other limitations that the insured is not aware of until a claim is filed.

The benefits may not be reasonably priced. Some companies are using accelerated death benefit riders to increase the profitability of the base policy. As more companies offer these benefits, the price should come down.

Living benefit provisions are not standardized, so it's hard to compare policies. (Of course, that's a good feature from the company's point of view.) Also, some companies use misleading methods of expressing the cost of the accelerated death benefit.

Several tax-related issues still need to be addressed. Do the monthly charges for the living benefits reduce the cost basis? What is the tax treatment of the benefits received? If the accelerated payments are taxable, that could greatly reduce their attractiveness.

Living benefit policies may be appropriate for some people, but most insurance buyers should buy separate coverages for now and let others be the guinea pigs. In fact, at least one company has taken a different approach that deflects some of the criticisms of living benefit riders. In cases of terminal illness or permanent nursing home care, it pays a discounted death benefit to the insured, without any additional charges.

Shopping for universal life. Here are some suggestions for finding a reasonably priced policy:

- Obtain illustrations assuming the same premiums and death benefits, and then compare the cash surrender values for each year to maturity.

Two Ways to Provide Living Benefits

To keep things simple, imagine a $100,000 one-year term policy that is sold to a group of 75-year-olds. Assume that the group's mortality rate is 50 per 1,000; all deaths take place at the end of the year; and 40 percent of the deaths (i.e, 20 per 1,000) result from a terminal illness.

If the insurance company can earn 8.16 percent per year (4 percent semiannually) on its assets, has no expenses, and wants to just break even, it would have to charge $4,623 for a $100,000 term policy with no living benefit (100,000 x 0.05/1.0816).

Now suppose the company wants to add a terminal illness benefit to its policy. There are two ways it can do this.

The first approach is to pay the full $100,000 death benefit when a policyholder is diagnosed as having less than six months to live. To offset the lost interest income, it charges every policyholder an additional $74 premium at the beginning of the year.

The second approach is to pay each terminally-ill policyholder a reduced death benefit of $96,154, using a discount rate of 4 percent. Since the lost interest is being accounted for in the discounting process, no additional premium is needed.

The main difference between the two approaches is who pays. In the first case, 1,000 people pay for a benefit that will actually be used by only twenty of them. In the second case, the cost of the benefit is borne by those who receive it.

- Ask about the company's illustration practices. Do illustrated values make use of any pricing factors that are different from current factors? Do illustrated values make use of any pricing factors that may not be sustainable over the long run? Be especially wary of persistency bonuses.
- If you are buying an agent-sold product, make sure that the proposal is what is best for you, not best for the agent. Ask about noncommissionable term riders and dump-ins and similar products from the same company that pay lower commissions.

- Save all illustrations and other documents and get a schedule of the *current* cost of insurance rates at the time of issue.

Current Assumption Whole Life

Also called *interest sensitive whole life* or *fixed premium universal life*, current assumption whole life resembles flexible premium universal life because there are separately identifiable interest credits and mortality and expense charges. The difference is that premiums are fixed for a certain period of time, such as five years, based on anticipated interest, mortality, and expenses. At the end of each period, the premium is recalculated, taking into account the actual fund value and new experience assumptions. The new level premium can be lower or higher, subject to a guaranteed maximum.

If the recalculated premium is lower, the policyholder may have the option to pay the lower premium and continue the coverage as before, pay the old premium and let the fund value increase, or pay the old premium and increase the death benefit.

If the recalculated premium is higher, the policyholder may have the option to pay the higher premium and continue the coverage as before, pay the old premium and reduce the death benefit accordingly, or pay the old premium and draw on the accumulated fund value to make up the difference.

As with traditional whole life, the fixed-premium structure offers some advantages to the insurer and may be appropriate for the buyer as well.

Single Premium Whole Life

Single premium whole life has been around in one form or another for a long time, but it became popular in recent years as a tax shelter. The Technical and Miscellaneous Revenue Act of 1988 eliminated some of its highly touted features, but it still remains a viable product for some purposes.

The most common version is like a certificate of deposit with some life insurance tacked on. At age 55, you might pay $20,000 for a policy with a $40,000 death benefit. The single premium earns interest at a declared rate—for example, 8 percent. There is usually no front-end load, no maintenance fee, and no insurance charges, although the company generally reserves the right to impose them in the future. Instead, acquisition costs, death claims, and ongoing expenses are recovered from the spread between what the company earns on its investments and what it pays you. If you drop the policy within a few years of purchase, the account balance will be reduced by a declining surrender charge. As the account balance grows, the death benefit also increases, in order to qualify the contract as life insurance under the provisions of the Internal Revenue Code (see Chapter 6, "Premiums.").

The most interesting—and misunderstood—feature of single premium whole life is the policy loan provision, which gives you a way to access your money for retirement or other purposes without surrendering the policy. Many policies provide *zero net cost* loans for accumulated interest and 1-2 percent *net cost* loans for principal. For example, assume that the current interest rate is 8 percent. If you borrow accumulated interest, the policy loan interest rate is 6 percent, and the interest rate on the offsetting portion of your account value that is held as collateral drops to 6 percent; therefore, zero net cost. If you borrow against principal, the policy loan interest rate is 6 percent, and the interest rate on that portion of your account value drops to 4 percent; therefore, 2 percent net cost.

The confusion surrounding the true cost of borrowing is explored in detail in Chapter 7 (see "Policy Loans and the Cost of Borrowing"). Suffice it to say that the cost is not 0 percent or 2 percent.

Since the insurance company recovers all of its expenses through the interest rate spread, you might wonder what happens when policyholders borrow the accumulated interest, leaving no spread. The answer is that companies price the product with some expectations about the level of loan usage. If loans exceed that level, the company may have to reduce the credited interest rate on everyone's money or make explicit charges for the insurance protection.

The 1988 tax law eliminated the favorable treatment of policy loans against single premium contracts, so companies are now developing new product designs that may permit tax-free loans. Even without tax-free loans, single premium whole life may be appropriate for people who have "excess" money that they will not need in retirement and are looking for someplace to put it.

Variable Life

Unlike general account products, *variable life* lets you choose among several types of investments. These may include stocks, bonds, money market instruments, gold, and real estate. Some products also offer a guaranteed-interest option that is similar to the declared interest rate on universal life.

As with universal life, premiums are deposited in an accumulation account after subtracting any front-end or ongoing loads, and charges are made for the cost of insurance and recordkeeping. Investment returns are passed through to the policyholder after deducting *mortality and expense risk charge* ("m & e charge" to the cognoscenti) and the usual fund expenses for investment management and administration. The mortality and expense risk charge covers the risk of fluctuations in mortality and expense experience and is also a source of profit to the insurer. Based on Securities and Exchange Commission (SEC) guidelines, the m & e charge is generally limited to 0.60 percent for fixed premium products and 0.90 percent for flexible premium products.

The amount of flexibility depends on the product. Some products allow limited withdrawals or changes in the death benefit. Some single premium products allow additional premiums; this may be presented as a boon for the buyer, but it also allows the company to increase the risk charge. Restrictions on the allocation of the account value among the investment options vary from one product to another.

In a sense, variable life is even more transparent than most universal life products, because you can see the spread between the gross and net rates of return. The investment gains and insurance and other charges are detailed in an annual report to the policyholder.

One distinguishing feature of variable life is that the death benefit fluctuates with investment performance, although it typically cannot drop below the initial face amount. Companies use two methods to establish the linkage: *corridor percentage* factors and *net single premium* factors. Under the corridor percentage approach, the death benefit is periodically adjusted so that it is at least equal to a specified percentage of the cash value, as required by current tax law. The mandated corridor percentage is 250 percent until the insured reaches age 40 and then gradually declines to 100 percent by age 95.

> *Example*: Assume that the cash value is $50,000 at the beginning of the period and $60,000 at the end. The insured is 55 years old. The initial death benefit is $75,000, and the corridor percentage factor is 150 percent. At the end of the period, the death benefit will be 150 percent of $60,000, or $90,000. Each $1 increase (or decrease) in the cash value will cause the death benefit to go up (or down) by $1.50.

Under the net single premium approach, the death benefit is periodically adjusted so that it matches the insurance that could be purchased with a single premium equal to the cash value, assuming guaranteed mortality rates and a low rate of return, such as 4 percent. The net single premium factor is only used to calculate the change in the death benefit; the actual cost of insurance is based on current rates, and the actual rate of return is based on fund performance. In the same example, assume that the net single premium factor is 0.45929; that is, it takes $0.45929 to buy a $1 whole life policy. At the end of the period, the death benefit will be $60,000/0.45929, or $130,636. Each $1 increase (or decrease) in the cash value will cause the death benefit to go up (or down) by $2.18 (1/0.45929).

Neither method is inherently better or worse than the other, although the corridor percentage factor may be easier to understand.

Suitability. Variable life products are most appropriate for buyers looking for an investment for their heirs. You can pay one or more premiums, choose the funds with the best prospects for long-term growth, and let the favorable investment performance drive up the death benefit.

You can also take advantage of the ability to move from one fund to another without tax consequences. However, you should generally avoid the guaranteed-interest option because (1) there are likely to be restrictions on getting your money out; (2) the interest rate may not be as high as on universal life products (if you want a fixed interest rate, why buy variable life?); and (3) the supporting assets are held in the company's general account, where there is less protection in the event of insolvency.

Variable life is less appropriate for investors trying to accumulate money for themselves. The overall expenses tend to be higher than for a combination of taxable no-load mutual funds and term insurance or universal life, and these higher expenses offset some or all of the gains from tax deferral. You can check this for yourself by doing a Linton yield analysis (discussed in Chapter 5), using the same assumed gross rate of return on the taxable funds and the funds within the variable life policy.

Shopping for variable life. Here are some suggestions for finding a reasonably priced product:

- Look for products that have a range of investment options, so that you can respond to future economic changes.
- In evaluating the internal funds, use the same criteria that you use for taxable mutual funds (e.g., historical performance, expected future performance, continuity of management).
- Compare the current cost of insurance rates with those for universal life or term insurance.
- Make a list of all other contract charges.
- To compare the impact of all charges, obtain illustrations assuming the same premiums, and then compare the death benefits and cash values for each year to maturity. If you get inconclusive results, try to mentally adjust the cash value of one policy for the assumed value of any difference in death benefits; for example, by using term insurance prices or standard mortality rates.
- Ask about the company's illustration practices. Do illustrated values make use of any pricing factors that are different from current factors? Do illustrated values make

use of any pricing factors that may not be sustainable over the long run?

- Use a "buy term and invest the difference" approach to satisfy yourself that a variable life policy is better than the alternative of buying term insurance and investing in taxable no-load mutual funds.
- To convince yourself that a variable policy is better than universal life, check what gross rate of return you would have to earn on the variable accounts to match the cash values of universal life, assuming similar premiums and death benefits.

Variable Universal Life

As the name suggests, *variable universal life* combines features of both universal and variable life. Premiums, death benefits, and cash values are flexible, as with universal life. As with variable life, the account value can be allocated among different types of investments. Some contracts also provide a limited death benefit guarantee if you pay a minimum premium each year.

The strengths and weaknesses of variable life carry over to variable universal life. In comparison with universal life, you have greater control over how your money is invested, and you can make adjustments to the allocation without getting a tax bill. However, the insurance company incurs greater costs for policy administration and regulatory compliance, and these costs are passed along to policyholders in the various loads.

Before buying a variable universal policy, you should compare it with the alternative of buying term insurance and investing in no-load mutual funds. You can also check to see what gross rate of return you would have to earn on the funds within the variable policy to match the performance of a comparable universal life policy.

Survivorship Policies

Survivorship (also called *second-to-die* or *last survivor*) policies pay off at the second of two deaths. They have become popular in recent years as a result of the unlimited marital deduction, which allows couples to postpone paying estate taxes until the second spouse dies. They can also be useful in business and charitable giving, situations where the death proceeds are not needed at the first death.

Survivorship policies are the most difficult insurance products to evaluate, because of the many possible combinations of deaths. Comparisons prepared by agents often focus on the lower premiums of these policies in relation to single-life policies. For example, a prospective buyer might be shown something like this:

Alternative 1: Buy two $500,000 single-life policies

Male, age 50	$9,000 annual premium for 10 years
Female, age 50	7,000 annual premium for 10 years
Total	$16,000 annual premium for 10 years

Alternative 2: Buy a $1,000,000 survivorship policy

Male and female, both age 50	$8,000 annual premium for 10 years

It looks like the $1,000,000 survivorship policy costs half as much as the alternative of buying a $500,000 policy on each life, but the comparison is misleading because the events being insured against are not the same. It's like comparing the premiums for homeowners and automobile insurance.

To see this more clearly, let's suppose that there are three possible dates of death for each person in the example above: immediately, at age 70, or at age 90. The survivorship policy pays $1,000,000 upon the second death, regardless of when the two deaths occur. In contrast, the two single-life policies will provide $500,000 at the first death, which can then be invested until the second death. Assuming a 7 percent after-tax rate of return, the matrix in Table 4.3 shows what the total proceeds would be for each combination of deaths.

Table 4.3. Total Death Proceeds Upon Second Death

| | Female Dies | | |
Male Dies	Now	at Age 70	at Age 90
Now	$1,000,000	$2,500,000	$8,500,000
at Age 70	2,500,000	1,000,000	2,500,000
at Age 90	8,500,000	2,500,000	1,000,000

A *pair* of single-life policies provides a very different benefit than *one* survivorship policy, so it's not appropriate to compare the premiums. What you can do, however, is compare the efficiency of the two alternatives. A second-to-die policy is the most efficient way of providing a fixed sum of money at the second death, in the same way that an annuity is the most efficient way of providing a fixed sum of money for life. The example above shows that it is wasteful to buy two single life policies if your goal is to have exactly $1 million at the second death. Most of the time you'll have more than you want, but you can't reduce the combined coverage below $1 million without running the risk of having less than you want if both deaths occur close together.

The problem of comparing survivorship and single life policies is just the beginning. Survivorship policies come in various forms: traditional whole life, current assumption whole life, universal life, and variable life. For each form, there are two basic designs—what actuaries call method I and method II. With method I, there is an increase in the cash value at the first death, and the insurance charges also increase to reflect the fact that there is only one survivor and therefore a greater probability that the company will have to pay the death benefit in any given year. Premiums may or may not be required after the first death.

In contrast, method II policies have no jump in cash value or insurance charges at the first death; the policy values increase at the same pace as before, and premiums continue unchanged. Many actuaries believe that method II is theoretically more correct than method I, but for marketing and regulatory reasons method I is still widely used.

In general, the cash value under method II will be somewhat greater than with method I until the first death, and less after that. Since you don't know when the first death will occur, this makes it hard to compare cash values, even if you are able to make the premiums and death benefits the same. Comparisons are also made difficult by the use of paid-up additions and term insurance riders that are designed to improve product performance or reduce the outlay, thereby making the product more palatable to price-sensitive prospects.

Instead of pure survivorship policies, some companies offer a "beneficiary insurance purchase rider" to a single-life policy that allows the beneficiary to use a portion or all of the death proceeds to purchase a policy on a second life. The advantage of this approach is that it can be adapted to changing tax laws and family situations. For example, it might be appropriate in some cases to pay some estate taxes at the first death, or a portion of the death proceeds might be needed for some other purpose. The combination of single-life policies and riders will create different patterns of premiums, death benefits, and cash values, thus adding one more wrinkle to the comparison dilemma.

Shopping for survivorship policies. Insurance advisors are still trying to figure out how to evaluate second-to-die policies and their substitutes. One popular approach is to look at the rate of return on death, for a fixed period or at life expectancy. For example, if you pay a single premium of $60,000 for a $1 million policy and your joint life expectancy is thirty-two years, the agent might say that the "internal rate of return" (IRR) is 9.2 percent. And he might go on to compare this with thirty-year zero-coupon bonds or some other investment alternative.

The rate of return on death has several drawbacks as a performance measure for second-to-die policies:

- It's easy to manipulate. Once insurance companies see that policies are being compared on this basis, they can simply design their products with that measure in mind.
- To be of any use, the rate of return would have to be supplied for every year until maturity, along with the corresponding probability of occurrence.
- The rate of return at life expectancy can be misleading for two reasons. First, it depends on the mortality table that

you use. In the example above, if you use a table that implies a life expectancy of thirty-five rather than thirty-two years, the rate of return would drop to 8.4 percent. Second, for whole life insurance in general, the IRR on death at life expectancy will often be lower than the credited interest rate. For example, one of the hypothetical policies in Figure 3.1 would have an IRR of only 6.1 percent, even though the premium was based on 7 percent after-tax interest. This is just a mathematical curiosity, and it does not mean that whole life insurance is a bad deal. (But it *does* make you wonder how agents' numbers can always look so good—where are they getting their estimates of life expectancy?)

- In general, internal rate of return can be a dangerous measure of performance if the investment projects have different patterns of cash flows; in this case, premium payments.

Until a more thoughtful consensus emerges about how to compare survivorship policies, it appears that the best approach is to request illustrations to maturity for several combinations of deaths and then scrutinize the premiums, death benefits, and cash values side by side. For most buyers of second-to-die policies, the cash values will be of less importance than the premiums and death benefits.

As always, you need to be concerned about the reliability of the policy illustrations. In particular, be aware that some vanishing premium plans are very sensitive to changes in mortality and interest assumptions. Make sure you understand what will happen at the first death, and find out if you can split the contract into two single-life contracts if your circumstances change.

TERM LIFE INSURANCE

At first glance, buying term insurance seems easy. Just shop around for a cheap policy issued by a financially sound company, and you're done. That's a sensible strategy, but you have to do a little homework to implement it.

The most common forms of term insurance are *annual renewable term* and *n-year level term* (where *n* can be 3, 5, 7, 10, or some other number).

Annual Renewable Term

Annual renewable term, also called *yearly renewable term*, is generally lower in cost during the early years, but premiums increase each year. There are two different rate structures: *aggregate* (or *attained age*) and *select and ultimate*. With aggregate pricing, the premium is the same for all insureds of the same age, regardless of when the policy was issued. With select and ultimate pricing, the premium depends on the issue age and the policy year. These two rate structures are shown in Table 4.4. Note that aggregate rates can be displayed in a single column, whereas select and ultimate rates require a matrix. In this example, there is a twenty-year *select* period, followed by *ultimate* rates that are based on attained age.

The advantage of select and ultimate pricing is that the premiums can be lower in the early years because people who have just passed a medical exam are less likely to die. Aggregate rates lump everyone together, so longtime policyholders are being subsidized by new policyholders.

The disadvantage of select and ultimate pricing is that it produces greater premium increases from year to year and therefore encourages healthy policyholders to shop for a new policy after a few years. Higher lapse rates and deteriorating mortality experience can make the product more expensive for those who remain.

N-Year Level Term

Generally, n-year level term is more expensive than annual renewable term during the early policy years, because premiums remain level—and are often guaranteed—for a longer period, such as three, five, seven, ten, or fifteen years. The level rate structure encourages persistency and tends to produce a lower overall cost if the policy is held for some years. At the end of

Table 4.4. Annual Renewable Term: Aggregate Versus Select & Ultimate

Company A: Aggregate

Male nonsmoker rates, add $30 policy fee

Attained Age	Rate per $1,000
35	0.92
36	0.95
37	0.97
38	1.01
⋮	⋮
54	4.13
55	4.37
56	4.70
57	5.04

Company B: Select and ultimate

Male nonsmoker rates, add $75 policy fee

Issue Age	Policy Year						21 & Later	Attained Age
	1	2	3	4 ...	19	20		
35	0.59	0.73	0.89	1.09	6.53	7.25	7.32	55
36	0.61	0.77	0.97	1.18	7.22	7.98	8.07	56
37	0.64	0.83	1.03	1.28	7.95	8.78	8.90	57
38	0.68	0.88	1.12	1.38	8.75	9.64	9.79	58
⋮								
54	1.71	2.67	3.69	5.02	—	—	—	—
55	1.89	2.85	3.95	5.65	—	—	—	—
56	2.09	3.20	4.69	6.04	—	—	—	—
57	2.33	3.67	5.09	6.51	—	—	—	—

the n-year period, premiums will increase each year as with annual renewable term, or you can reapply for another period of level premiums.

Other Features

Other product features to be aware of are discussed below.

Renewability. Most products are guaranteed renewable to at least age 70, and some can be renewed up to age 100.

Guarantee period. Many products have only a one-year guarantee, but some companies guarantee their current rates for ten years or more.

Convertibility. Most term policies are convertible to one or more of the issuing company's cash value products without evidence of insurability. To encourage conversions, companies often credit a portion of the term premium against the first-year whole life premium.

Revertibility (or re-entry). This lets you qualify for lower premiums in future years as if you were a new applicant, by submitting evidence of insurability—sometimes at your own expense. Since healthy people can always shop around for better coverage, this provision is of value only if the company makes some underwriting concessions. Otherwise, it's just a marketing gimmick designed to focus your attention on a set of low rates that you may never enjoy.

Banding. Many companies charge a lower rate per $1,000 for greater amounts of coverage. The breakpoints vary by company.

Discount for prepayment. Some companies offer a discount if you pay one or more annual premiums up front. You should always ask about this, though sometimes the discount may not be worth taking. For example, at least two companies offer a 20 percent discount on the fifth-year premium if you prepay it—that's equivalent to a 5.7 percent annual rate of return.

Fractional premiums. Most companies allow you to pay premiums semi-annually, quarterly, or monthly. Unless you're strapped for cash, however, you should pay annually, since the implicit interest charge will often exceed your own cost of capital (see Chapter 6, "Premium payment mode").

Face amount reductions. Some companies allow you to reduce the face amount in later years without getting a new policy.

Comparing Term Policies: A Case Study

To illustrate the difficulties of choosing a term policy, Table 4.5 compares two $500,000 policies issued to a 35-year-old male nonsmoker. Policy A is revertible, nonconvertible ten-year level term, with three sets of rates: current rates, assuming re-entry at the end of ten years; current rates, assuming no re-entry; and guaranteed rates. Premiums are guaranteed for 10 years.

Table 4.5. Cost of a $500,000 Policy Issued to a 35-Year-Old Male Nonsmoker

| | Policy A | | | Policy B | |
Age	Current, with Reversion	Current, without Reversion	Guaranteed	Current	Guaranteed
35	$565	$565	$565	$490	$490
40	565	565	565	595	1,860
45	1,250	1,520	2,415	890	2,825
50	1,250	2,400	4,070	1,610	4,400
54	1,250	3,435	5,945	2,095	6,285

Policy B is convertible annual renewable term, with no re-entry provision and two sets of rates: current rates, guaranteed for one year; and guaranteed rates.

The premiums are compared for selected years. Figure 4.1 shows the present value of premiums for each holding period up to twenty years, assuming a discount rate of 5 percent. From this graph, you can see that:

- On a current basis, policy A is slightly more expensive than policy B for twelve of the twenty periods (through ages 35-42 and 46-49) if you assume re-entry. For the entire twenty-year period, policy A is about 10 percent cheaper ($10,800 versus $12,000). However, this difference would be almost eliminated if you switched from policy B to policy A in Year 11.

- Without re-entry, policy A is more expensive for all holding periods except two (ages 43-44). It is about 30 percent more expensive over the twenty-year period.

- On a guaranteed basis, policy A is significantly cheaper than policy B for all periods except the first year.

Figure 4.1. Present Value of Premiums

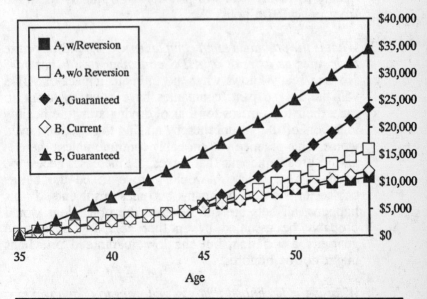

To make a decision, you would need to answer these questions:

1. *How long do you plan to keep the policy in force?* The answer depends on your own needs, which can easily change. In addition, newer types of policies may come along that offer attractive features, although it is unlikely that term prices will decline for younger buyers in the near future.

2. *What is the probability that you will be able to take advantage of policy A's reversion provision in year 11?* This question will be hard to answer, because the insurance industry does not yet have enough data on actual experience to determine the odds that a healthy person will become uninsurable in the future. Also, some companies may try to wiggle out of the reversion provision by changing the underwriting standards. Remember, too, that revertibility should be viewed as a marketing ploy unless the company offers some underwriting concessions. Otherwise, revertibility doesn't matter because, if you qualify to revert, you will probably also qualify to switch from policy B to policy A.

3. *What is the probability that companies will significantly raise their rates as a result of AIDS and other health hazards?* No one really knows what the ultimate impact of AIDS will be. In the past, companies have been reluctant to raise their term prices for fear of driving away the healthy members of the group, thereby making the situation even worse. This practice will probably continue unless there is a widespread epidemic that makes rate increases necessary. In that case, policy A would prove to be the better choice—unless the company becomes insolvent. If this happens, all bets are off, because the obligations would probably be assumed by another company or a state guaranty association, but the low guaranteed premiums might not be honored.

4. *What is the likelihood that you will want to take advantage of policy B's conversion provision?* This will depend on your own insurance needs and the competitiveness of Company B's cash value products.

5. *Do you prefer premiums that remain level for ten years, with the possibility of a large increase later on, or premiums that gradually increase over time?* Clearly, this is not an easy choice. You might reasonably decide to buy either policy, depending on your own guesses about what the future holds.

Shopping suggestions. Here are some suggestions for finding a reasonably priced product:

- Before selecting a term product, give some thought to how long you will need the coverage, and remember that some people find it emotionally difficult to drop coverage once it is in place.
- Use this book, an agent, and/or a computerized shopping service to come up with a short list of low-cost products issued by reputable companies. Note that the computer-based services usually include a limited number of products in their databases, and their selection criteria may not be appropriate for your situation.

    Most services are actually insurance agencies that collect a commission for the sale. However, Insurance Information, Inc. (800/472-5800) is a fee-based organization. Commission-based services include InsuranceQuote (800/972-1104), LifeQuote (900/246-5433), SelectQuote (800/343-1985), and TermQuote (800/444-8376).

    You might also consider looking for an agent that subscribes to Quotesmith (800-556-9393), an online term insurance proposal service that allows the user to choose among several selection criteria.
- Compare the cost of different policies by computing the present value of premiums for several holding periods. If you're comparing revertible policies, assume that you will not qualify for lower rates in the future. Do not pay much attention to the first year cost, unless you only plan to hold the policy for one year.
- Look for policies that are renewable and convertible, because these features will let you keep the policy in force if your health deteriorates.
- To avoid future price increases, buy a level-premium product with a guarantee period of at least five to ten years.
- If you need a lot of insurance, consider using more than one company. This will usually result in a higher cost because of duplicate policy fees (typically $25 to $50) and possibly a less favorable price per $1,000, but it will give you more flexibility.

- If you're tempted to shop for a "cheaper" policy every year, keep these disadvantages in mind:

—The contestability period will start over again.

—If your health deteriorates, your bargain hunting will stop, and your last "bargain" may turn out to be expensive over the long run.

—Primary insurers and their reinsurers generally lose money on policies that are dropped soon after issue, so frequent switchers may find that their business is not wanted.

5

LIFE INSURANCE: COMPARING PRODUCTS

After you have decided what type of policy you are most interested in, you will still have to choose among hundreds of products in the marketplace. Simply stated, your goal is to find a competitive product issued by a financially-sound company. The types of information that are useful in assessing a company's financial strength are discussed in Chapter 10. We'll focus here on various methods you can use to determine a product's competitiveness.

PREMIUMS

Novice insurance buyers often equate premium with cost. "How much will it cost me?" they ask, and then they go with the product that has the lowest illustrated premiums. There are at least three reasons why this is not a smart move.

First, it ignores cash values. A policy with a $1,500 annual premium and a 10-year cash value of $20,000 might be better than one with a $1,000 premium and a 10-year cash value of $12,000. Even if you have no intention of surrendering the policy, you still can't ignore the possibility that you will live until the maturity date, at which time you will receive the cash value.

Second, the death benefits of the two policies may not be the same at all ages—and particularly at the later ages, when high cash values may cause the death benefit to rise. Third, illustrated premiums can be manipulated by changing interest rate or dividend assumptions.

As an example, Table 5.1 shows the range of premiums that you could be shown for one low-load universal life policy, depending on how the illustration is prepared. If you use an interest rate below the current rate in order to be conservative, you will drive the premium up. On the other hand, you can reduce the projected premium by using a higher interest rate or by assuming that the cash value will be depleted in the later years to pay for the insurance costs, leaving nothing at age 95.

There is only one situation in which it might make sense to use premiums as a proxy for cost; namely, when you are comparing policies with identical death benefits and identical cash values at maturity and with similarly reliable illustrations.

Table 5.1. Same Policy, Different Premiums
$500,000 policy issued to a male nonsmoker, age 50;
policy matures at age 95; 8.5% current interest

Assumed Interest	Targeted Cash Value	Annual Premium to Age 65
7.5%	$500,000 at age 95	$7,106
8.5	$500,000 at age 95	6,232
8.5	$0 at age 95	6,067
8.5	Policy lapses at age 90	5,864
9.0	$500,000 at age 95	5,858

TRADITIONAL NET COST

This method is appropriate if you keep all of your money in a non-interest-bearing checking account or under a mattress. You can also use it to help children learn addition and subtraction.

The procedure is simple: Select a measurement period (e.g., twenty years), compute the sum of all premiums paid, and then subtract the ending cash value and the sum of all dividends and withdrawals received. The lower the net cost, the better the policy. The problem, of course, is that this method fails to take account of the time value of money; that is, it gives equal weight to benefits that are received next year and twenty years from now.

A few unsophisticated agents still feel that the time value of money is a ball and chain, which they are unfairly forced to drag around to sales presentations. If you run across some-one like this, don't forget to ask him for an interest-free loan.

INTEREST-ADJUSTED COST INDEXES

Among insurance professionals, interest-adjusted cost indexes are something of a joke. They were invented in the 1970s in response to pressure from consumer groups and Congress for better disclosure of policy costs. A majority of states now require that cost indexes be provided to prospective buyers, but there is little evidence that consumers or insurance agents make much use of them, or even understand them.

The Surrender Cost Index is intended to be used when you are concerned about future cash values and want to take them into account in comparing policies. The Net Payment Cost Index is intended to be used when you are only concerned about the premium payments. In both cases, a lower cost index supposedly means a cheaper policy.

Table 5.2 shows how the two indexes would be calculated for a term and a cash value policy. The Surrender Cost Index is computed in four steps. First, accumulate the net premiums at 5 percent interest over the desired period (in this example, three years).

Next, subtract the cash surrender value and any terminal dividend at the end of the period, and then divide by the future value of a $1 annuity due (again, assuming 5 percent interest). Finally, express the result on a per-thousand basis by dividing by the "equivalent level death benefit," which is computed by accumulating the death benefits for each year at 5 percent interest, and then dividing by the same annuity factor as before.

To compute the Net Payment Cost Index, follow the same steps, but do not subtract the cash surrender value and terminal dividend.

The two indexes can be interpreted as the average annual cost of the policy. The Net Payment Cost Index represents the amount that you would have to deposit at the beginning of each year into an account paying 5 percent interest after tax in order to keep the policy in force until your death at the end of the period. For example, an annual deposit of $157 would be just enough to keep the term policy in Table 5.2 in force for three years, assuming, of course, that you remain alive.

Similarly, the Surrender Cost Index represents the amount that you would have to deposit each year under the assumption that you will borrow money at 5 percent interest to pay the premiums, and will later use the cash surrender value to repay the loans plus all accrued interest. For example, a $65 deposit is just enough to keep the cash-value policy in Table 5.2 in force if you borrow an additional $935 each year to pay the $1,000 premium, and then use the $3,095 cash surrender value to repay the loan principal ($2,805) plus accrued interest ($290) at the end of three years, assuming, again, that you are still alive.

Although the cost indexes seem complicated, they are simply present values in disguise. To see this, multiply the Surrender Cost Index for the cash-value policy (65) by the future value of a $1 annuity due (3.31) and then divide by 1.05^3, or 1.16. The result is $185, the net present value of the premiums and cash surrender value, assuming a discount rate of 5 percent. Similarly, the Surrender Cost Index of the term policy can be unscrambled to show the present value of the premiums—$448.

Buyer's guides invariably warn against using the indexes to compare dissimilar policies, such as whole life and term, but no explanation is given. The indexes are computed in exactly the same way for both types of policies, so why can't you compare them? The reason, in a nutshell, is that you would be comparing the net present values of two insurance programs that are not comparable.

The death benefit of the cash value policy is $100,000, whereas the term policyowner's beneficiaries will receive $100,000 plus the difference in premiums that can be invested. The term policy is penalized in two other ways as well. First, the 5 percent discount rate is too low in relation to the assumed interest rate within the cash value policy (10 percent). Second, the Surrender Cost Index is based on before-tax cash values and ignores the income tax due upon surrender.

Table 5.2. Calculation of Interest-Adjusted Cost Indexes for Two $100,000 Life Insurance Policies

		Term	Cash-Value
Premium:	Year 1	$150	$1,000
	Year 2	153	1,000
	Year 3	170	1,000
Cash surrender value:	Year 3	0	3,095

Surrender Cost Index

	Term	Cash-Value
Premiums accumulated at 5%	521	3,310
less cash surrender value	0	(3,095)
	$521	$215
Future value of $1 annuity due	$3.31	$3.31
Equivalent level death benefit	$100,000	$100,000
3-Year Surrender Cost Index	1.57[a]	0.65[b]

[a] (521/3.31)/100   [b] (215/3.31)/100

Net Payment Cost Index

	Term	Cash-Value
Premiums accumulated at 5%	$521	$3,310
Future value of $1 annuity due	$3.31	$3.31
Equivalent level death benefit	$100,000	$100,000
3-Year Net Payment Cost Index	1.57[c]	10.00[d]

[c] (529/3.31)/100   [d] (3,310/3.31)/100

Note: The calculations in this table are equivalent to, but do not exactly follow, the steps outlined in the 1976 Life Insurance Solicitation Model Regulation.

Difficulties can also arise with "similar" cash-value policies that have different premiums or death benefits. For example, which of these two products is better?

	20-Year Surrender Cost Index
Policy A	1.42
Policy B	(2.11)

The obvious answer is Policy B—except that both products are really the same. Policy A is a $200,000 universal life policy paying 8.5 percent interest, with a $1,000 annual premium. Policy B is the same product, with a $2,000 annual premium.

In addition to misleading consumers, the cost indexes can have unintended consequences for public policy. In 1983, Montana became the first state to require unisex pricing for all individual life insurance policies. The law was opposed by the insurance industry and generally supported by women's rights organizations. Since mortality rates are lower for women than for men, and since this is reflected in the insurance charges within a policy, it has long been a mystery to some observers why women would lobby to pay more for their life insurance. Some advocates of non-gender insurance argue that the cost savings of sex-distinct policies are illusory, because the higher premiums that men pay result in higher cash values and higher dividends, making their policies a better value overall. Just look at the interest-adjusted surrender cost indexes, they say.

And that's the problem. When market interest rates are above 5 percent, policies with higher premiums will tend to have lower surrender cost indexes, simply because you are implicitly compounding the additional outlay at one rate—say, 9 percent—and discounting it back at 5 percent. If instead of paying the higher premium, you invested the difference in premiums in a side fund growing at some reasonable rate, you would find that the sex-distinct policy produces greater total wealth, as you would expect. There are legitimate arguments for unisex pricing, but a lower cost for women is not one of them.

Even though the interest-adjusted cost indexes are of limited value in buying life insurance intelligently, they do offer some insight into the regulatory process.

Cost disclosure regulations are the product of negotiations among insurance industry factions (principally, stock and mutual companies), regulators, and, to a lesser extent, academics and consumerists. The decision to provide some types of information but not others is influenced by considerations that have nothing to do with helping consumers make informed purchase decisions. For example, the Net Payment Cost Index exists in part because companies with low premiums and a mediocre Surrender Cost Index wanted a measure that would make them look good, too.

The insurance industry has often opposed the required disclosure of rates of return on cash value policies, even though the choice between whole life and term insurance is probably the most important choice that an insurance buyer faces. They are concerned that rates of return will confuse us—seeing a low rate of return, we might become "confused" and buy term insurance instead—or that Congress might use this information as an argument for eliminating the tax advantages of life insurance.

Recognizing the inadequacies of the current cost indexes, the National Association of Insurance Commissioners has proposed *yield index* for universal life policies. The index is similar to, but not exactly the same as, the Linton yield (discussed later). Much time has been spent arguing about how the calculation should be done and how it should be presented to consumers, if at all. Just as the interest-adjusted cost indexes are a mystification of present values, the yield index promises to mystify rates of return. At best, it will become just another number that salesmen can easily brush aside when it's convenient to do so.

There will undoubtedly be more government-sponsored attempts at cost disclosure in the future. For people who want to follow along as the government cooks, here's the recipe for an official cost index:

> Start with a measure of value that may or may not be flawed, but is at least understandable. Remove all of the meaning. Let simmer for a few years. Serve cold, or garnish with a buyer's guide.

Bon appetit.

How Should You Analyze an Investment?

In the corporate world, the process of evaluating investment projects is called *capital budgeting*. Individuals face similar capital budgeting decisions when they have to decide where to invest their money. Although there are many ways of describing the decision-making process, here's one four-step approach:

Step 1: Map out all of the cash flows. What amounts go into the investment, and when? What amounts come out of the investment, and when? Note that *cash flows* are not comprised only of cash; they include every cost or benefit attributable to the investment. A *cash flow diagram* can be a handy tool for organizing information about an investment. The diagram is simply a time line, with each cash flow placed at a corresponding point in time. Amounts invested are usually shown below the line, and amounts received are shown above. For example, a diagram for a $1,000 three-year promissory note, purchased for $900 with 10 percent interest paid annually, would look like this:

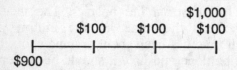

Step 2: Decide what criterion you will use to determine which of the alternatives is best. The criterion is whatever completes this sentence: "I am making this investment because..." Although it may not be stated explicitly, in most cases the objective will be to maximize future after-tax wealth; in other words, to have more money at the end of some measurement period. By making the goal explicit, you can avoid pursuing a false objective–such as minimizing this year's tax bill–when your real objective is to have more money. Insurance buyers need to be especially careful in defining the goal, because sales presentations will often tout tax deferral while conveniently overlooking high expenses that eat into your return.

Step 3: Using the cash flows that you mapped out earlier, compute some measure of performance that is appropriate for your situation. Financial analysis is a kind of storytelling, with numbers as the main characters. Good financial analysts tell stories that make sense; bad financial analysts forget that they are storytellers and just throw a bunch of numbers into a calculator. Each of the performance measures described in Table 5.A has a story that goes along with it. For example, the three-year promissory note mentioned earlier has a *net present value* at 8 percent in the amount of $152, computed as follows:

Present value of:	Year 1 interest	$93
	Year 2 interest	86
	Year 3 interest	79
	Maturity proceeds	794
	Total	$1,052
Initial investment		$900
Net present value @ 8%		$152

The story here is that a $900 investment in the promissory note will produce the same benefits (ignoring taxes) as a $1,052 investment earning 8 percent a year. In effect, the promissory note makes you $152 wealthier today, because you could invest $900 in the note, spend $152 on a shopping spree, and receive exactly the same amounts during the next three years as if you had invested $1,052 at 8 percent.

The promissory note also has an *internal rate of return* (IRR) of 14.33 percent. This tells you what interest rate you would have to earn on your $900 investment in order to produce all of the benefits of the promissory note. The IRR is computed by trial and error. You can verify that 14.33 percent is correct by setting up an imaginary interest-bearing checking account and paying out each benefit as it comes due:

Year	Beginning Balance	Interest @14.33%	Payment	Ending Balance
1	$900	$129	$(100)	$929
2	929	133	(100)	962
3	962	138	(1,100)	0

Table 5.A. Some Measures of Investment Merit

Measure	Description	Accept Proposal If...
Payback period	Compute the point at which the amounts received equal the amounts invested	Payback period is less than the minimum required period
Internal rate of return (IRR)	Compute the discount rate that equates the present value of the amounts received and invested	IRR is higher than the required rate of return
Modified IRR, adjusted IRR, financial management rate of return	Transform the pattern of cash flows by choosing one or more discounting or compounding rates, then compute a new IRR	IRR is higher than the required rate of return
Net present value (NPV)	Choose a discount rate, subtract the present value of amounts invested from the present value of amounts received	NPV is positive
Net future value	NPV in reverse: Choose a compounding rate, subtract future value of amounts invested from future value of amounts received	Net future value is positive
Profitability index	Divide NPV of amounts received by NPV of amounts invested	Index is greater than one
Expanded net present value (contingent claims analysis)	Compute traditional NPV and add the value future options (e.g., option to invest more)	Expanded NPV is positive

How to Rank Proposals	Insurance Industry Equivalents
Select the shortest payback period	Column labeled "Cumulative premiums less cash value" on some policy illustrations
Select the highest IRR	Linton yield, rate of return on death, rate of return on surrender, proposed "yield index"
Select the highest IRR	Some methods of determining rate of return on policyholder's investment
Select the highest NPV	Interest-adjusted cost index, traditional net cost, company retention (present expected value of premiums minus present expected value of benefits)
Select the highest net future value	Cash accumulation method
Select the highest index	Proposed "probable cost index" is closely related
Select the highest expanded NPV	

You will sometimes hear that the internal rate of return implies that each cash flow is reinvested at the same rate. Not so. The IRR is the same no matter what reinvestment assumption you make; it is determined by the cash flows that you identify and nothing more.

Each of the approaches in Table 5.A can be used to accept or reject a proposal or–if you're careful–to rank several proposals in order of attractiveness. Ranking projects can be difficult because of differences in scale or timing. For example, which is better–a $100 investment with an IRR of 20 percent or a $1,000 investment with an IRR of 12 percent? The answer depends on what you will do with the remaining $900 if you choose the $100 project.

Step 4: Take account of the riskiness of the project. This can be accomplished by adjusting the cash flows, the discounting or compounding rates, or the required rate of return. You can also use computerized simulation techniques to produce a probability distribution of possible outcomes, if you are able to specify how each of the cash flows is affected by some variable (such as interest rates).

The insurance industry lives in the same world as the rest of us, so it's not surprising that their products can be evaluated using the standard methods of finance. You can easily lose sight of this fact, however, because insurance people have their own names for everything, some of which are shown in the last column in Table 5.A.

For example, internal rate of return shows up in various guises, depending on which cash flows you choose to include in the calculation. If you take into account premiums, cash values, and the value of the insurance protection each year, you have the *Linton yield*. If you look only at premiums and death benefits, you have the *rate of return on death*. If you look only at premiums and cash values, you have the *rate of return on surrender*.

By keeping your feet firmly planted in the investment world, you can take a big step toward demystifying life insurance.

CASH ACCUMULATION METHOD

The cash accumulation method is based on a simple principle that appeals to common sense: If product A and product B are the same in all respects except one, and if product A is better in that one respect, then product A is better than product B. Few people would challenge this in the abstract; the criticisms begin when you present the results to the vendors of product B.

For cash value life insurance, the important features are: outlay (i.e., premiums paid); death benefits; cash values; and all other, including financial stability and agent service.

As we have seen, if you try to compare alternatives that have different outlays, different death benefits, and different cash values, you get a mess. One solution, therefore, is to deliberately construct alternatives that have identical outlays and identical death benefits, and then compare the cash values. You can bring in "all other" at the beginning—for example, by refusing to consider companies that do not have an A+ rating by A.M. Best—or at the end.

The cash accumulation method can be used to compare cash value products or to compare cash value and term insurance. This second application involves setting up a hypothetical side fund where you will invest the difference in premiums at some assumed rate of return. To see which is better—whole life or term—you then compare the whole life cash values with the side fund balance at each point in time. We'll look at the mechanics of this shortly when we discuss the Linton yield method.

To compare cash value products, follow these four steps:

1. Decide how much coverage you want.

2. Try to obtain policy illustrations with similar premiums and death benefits at all points in time.

3. Compare the year-by-year *current* or *assumed* cash values.

4. Try to determine if the policy illustrations are equally reliable; if not, try to make any necessary adjustments.

Clearly, there's a lot of "trying" here, but that's because there is no set of instructions that can guarantee success. The variety of product designs can make it hard to find alternatives with identical premiums and death benefits, so you may have to settle for something close, perhaps making some mental adjustments along the way.

Determining the reliability of policy illustrations may be impossible without insider information. The problem is that an illustration can be any of the following:

- a best-guess or most-likely projection

- a projection of future values based on current pricing factors that may or may not be sustainable over the long run

- a projection of future values based on assumed pricing factors that are different from current pricing factors and that may or may not be sustainable over the long run

- a projection of future values based on whatever assumptions are needed to beat a competitor's illustration

- a sales tool intended to show how the product works, and nothing more

There are many ways in which you can be fooled by policy illustrations as we'll see in the next sections.

Universal Life

Companies can declare a high current interest rate with the intention of lowering it in future years. When the high current rate is projected for fifty years in the illustration, the product looks great.

Companies can assume that cost of insurance rates will be reduced in the future due to improved mortality. Or, they can use artificially low current rates for older ages, knowing that this will not cost them much money for now because they have very few 80-year-old policyholders. The lower insurance charges allow the company to illustrate a lower required premium and make the product look great. To demonstrate the point, here are four companies' current rates (as of early 1989) for male nonsmokers at advanced ages:

Current Annual Cost of Insurance Rates per $1,000

| | Company | | | |
Age	A	B	C	D
76	$13.12	$20.39	$24.40	$41.06
80	20.66	27.80	33.68	72.91
85	45.58	35.20	54.32	132.34

Not surprisingly, company A is able to beat the competition when the focus is on the outlay required to keep the policy in force to age 95, based on current pricing factors. But why is company A charging so little? Why is company D charging so much? Is it reasonable to believe that all of these numbers are equally reliable—that is, equally likely to occur?

Companies can ignore some of the acquisition costs in pricing the product, with the understanding (theirs, not yours) that they will increase the profit margin at the first available opportunity. They can also assume that business volume will increase, thereby lowering unit costs.

Companies can add various *persistency bonuses* that, based on current illustrations, can make a product look better. Whether the bonuses will actually be paid, or simply offset in some way, is another matter.

Table 5.3 shows how the illustrated performance of an unremarkable universal life policy can be improved by tinkering with one or more pricing factors. Some persistency bonuses and interest rate projections can move a product from the median to the top decile. That's how easy it is to design a superior product—on paper.

Table 5.3. The Effect of Enhancements on Product Rank [a]

	20-Year Cash Value	Rank (out of 172)
Unenhanced [b]	$53,038	86
No monthly fee or premium load after year 10	54,798	59
2% annual improvement in mortality, reflected in COI rates every four years	56,582	43
0.5% higher interest, projected for 20 years	56,750	41
1.0% higher interest, projected for 20 years	60,728	18
0.25% retroactive interest rate bonus every five years	60,728	18
45% annual premium bonus after year 10	64,226	9
Interest rate bonus: 0.5%—years 2-5, 1.0%—years 6-10, 1.75% thereafter	64,246	9
Refund of insurance charges every 10 years	69,500	6
"Author's Special" [c]	75,000	1

[a] For a $100,000 policy with a $1,500 annual premium, issued to a 45-year-old male nonsmoker. Rankings are based on a survey of universal life products in the March 1989 issue of *Best's Review*, published by the A.M. Best Company.

[b] 9% current interest, 4.5% guaranteed interest, 4% premium load, $4 monthly fee, COI rates equal to 52% of 1980 CSO Table.

[c] This product was designed by the author and contains this contractual guarantee: "We promise that something wonderful will happen 20 years after you buy this policy, but we can't tell you what it is."

Whole Life

Illustrated dividends can be based on portfolio yields that are not sustainable if market interest rates remain unchanged. This can occur when a company invests in long-term bonds as interest rates are falling. The average portfolio yield—and therefore the dividend interest rate—will exceed market interest rates for a while, but the yield will gradually fall as the company is forced to invest new money at lower rates. Meanwhile, the policy illustration will project a high portfolio yield for the next half-century, so the product looks great.

Although an uncommon practice, some companies may be using dividend formulas that assume higher interest, lower mortality, or lower expenses at some point in the future, analogous to persistency bonuses. In other words, such companies play games with their illustrated dividends to remain competitive with companies that play games with universal life.

Variable Life

As with universal life, companies may set low current cost of insurance rates at later ages, thereby reducing the required premium or increasing the future illustrated death benefits and cash values.

In preparing illustrations based on an assumed gross rate of return, companies may assume that fund expense ratios drop from current levels as more money is invested. This will cause the net rate of return—and therefore projected benefits—to be overstated if the product line is not as successful as the company hopes.

Comparing Illustrations: A Case Study

In comparing policy illustrations, two questions quickly arise. First, should you focus on the cash values during the early years or the later years? You really need to look at both. The early cash values are more reliable because pricing factors are likely to change slowly over time as the insurer gains more information about actual performance. However, it would be foolish to buy a product that has high early cash values if you have good reason to believe that its long-term performance will be unimpressive. By examining the values at all durations, you may discover incongruities that will lead to questions that, hopefully, will lead to some answers—and a better purchase decision.

Second, should you focus *current* or on *guaranteed* values? The guaranteed values represent a worst case; they assume that interest rates immediately drop to very low levels and stay there, and that death rates immediately go up to high levels and stay there. Because neither of these events—much less both of them together—is likely to happen tomorrow, you will almost certainly receive more than the guaranteed values if you make the scheduled premium payments. The guarantees are worth looking at, just to make sure you're not missing an important feature; but you should place more emphasis on scenarios that are more likely to happen.

All of these considerations are brought together in Figure 5.1, which shows current, guaranteed, and maximum cash values for two products. Product B's *guaranteed* values are higher than product A's after 12 years, and product B's *current* values are based on aggressive assumptions and surpass product A's after 10 years. However, if interest and mortality remain constant, these illustrated current values may not materialize. Also, there is little room for further improvement if interest and mortality experience are favorable, because insurer B will need those margins to meet its profit objectives. In contrast, insurer A bases its current values on realistic pricing factors and would be able to pay those amounts if current conditions remain unchanged. If interest and mortality improve, the actual values could increase significantly.

To make a choice between these two products, it's clear that you need to go beyond a simple comparison of illustrated values and look more carefully at the chances that one product will in fact be able to outperform another.

Figure 5.1. An Illustration Shows You Just One Possibility Out of Many

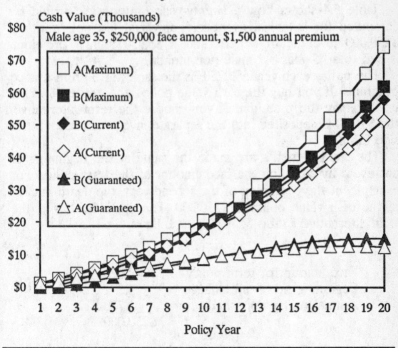

Cash Value (Thousands)

Male age 35, $250,000 face amount, $1,500 annual premium

- ☐ A(Maximum)
- ■ B(Maximum)
- ◆ B(Current)
- ◇ A(Current)
- ▲ B(Guaranteed)
- △ A(Guaranteed)

Policy Year

LINTON YIELD METHOD

The Linton yield can be useful for those consumers trying to decide between term and cash value life insurance. It is also applicable even when term insurance is not an option, if you interpret the results carefully.

This approach is named for M. Albert Linton, a distinguished actuary who wanted to silence the critics of whole life insurance by demonstrating that it offered a competitive rate of return. The first of his periodic rate-of-return studies was presented to a gathering of insurance agents in 1928. Ironically, the Linton yield method is now associated with "buy term and invest the difference" and is generally not popular with insurance companies or their salespeople. Linton's idea was to compare the whole life policy to a combination of term insurance and a separate investment account, and then compute the rate of return that would be necessary to generate the same wealth at the end of the measurement period.

Table 5.4 shows how a twenty-year Linton yield would be computed for a typical agent-sold universal life policy with a $250,000 level death benefit and a $3,750 annual premium, issued to a 45-year-old male nonsmoker.

The outlay each year—$3,750—is the same for both insurance programs. If you buy the cash value policy, the entire $3,750 is used to pay the premium. If you choose the term alternative, the $3,750 is deposited into the separate investment account, or side fund.

The death benefits are made the same at the beginning of each year by adjusting the face amount of the term policy. For example, at the beginning of the second year, the death benefit of the cash value policy is $250,000. The death benefit of the term alternative is also $250,000, as follows:

Face amount of term policy	$242,679
Beginning side fund balance	3,571
Annual outlay deposited	3,750
	$250,000

The premium for the decreasing term policy is paid from the side fund each year, and the balance remains invested. The question is: What after-tax rate of return would you have to earn on the side fund to have an amount that is exactly equal to the after-tax cash surrender value of the universal life policy at the end of twenty years? As Table 5.4 shows, the answer—found by trial and error—is 7.4 percent (actually, 7.3648 percent). If you surrender the cash value policy, you'll get $161,559 and owe $25,968 in taxes, assuming a 30 percent tax rate. That's $135,591 after tax, which is exactly what you would have if you "bought term insurance and invested the difference" each year at 7.4 percent after tax.

A similar calculation can be done for each policy year. Figure 5.2 shows the results for this agent-sold policy and a comparable

Table 5.4. Cash Value Life Insurance Versus Term-Plus Side Fund

- After-tax return on side fund: 7.4%   • Tax rate upon surrender: 30%

Age	Term Face Amount	Side Fund					Cash Value	
		Begin. Balance	Deposit	Term Premium	Interest	Ending Balance	Before Tax	After Tax
45	$246,250	$0	$3,750	$(424)	$245	$3,571	$0	$0
46	242,679	3,571	3,750	(471)	505	7,355	1,878	1,878
47	238,895	7,355	3,750	(523)	779	11,361	5,690	5,690
48	234,889	11,361	3,750	(583)	1,070	15,599	9,832	9,832
49	230,651	15,599	3,750	(646)	1,377	20,080	14,331	14,331
50	226,170	20,080	3,750	(715)	1,702	24,818	19,221	19,221
51	221,432	24,818	3,750	(753)	2,049	29,864	24,535	24,535
52	216,386	29,864	3,750	(792)	2,417	35,239	30,306	30,214
53	211,011	35,239	3,750	(827)	2,811	40,973	36,578	35,730
54	205,277	40,973	3,750	(848)	3,231	47,106	43,392	41,624
55	199,144	47,106	3,750	(870)	3,681	53,667	51,774	48,617
56	192,583	53,667	3,750	(936)	4,160	60,641	60,807	56,065
57	185,609	60,641	3,750	(1,000)	4,669	68,059	70,558	64,016
58	178,191	68,059	3,750	(1,067)	5,210	75,952	81,104	72,523
59	170,298	75,952	3,750	(1,138)	5,786	84,350	92,523	81,641
60	161,900	84,350	3,750	(1,216)	6,399	93,283	103,934	90,754
61	152,967	93,283	3,750	(1,271)	7,053	102,815	116,416	100,616
62	143,435	102,815	3,750	(1,317)	7,751	112,999	130,086	111,310
63	133,251	112,999	3,750	(1,348)	8,499	123,900	145,081	122,932
64	122,350	123,900	3,750	(1,359)	9,301	135,591	161,559	135,591

Side fund balance=After tax cash value

low-load policy. Most striking is the difference in returns during the early years. Because of its higher distribution costs, the agent-sold policy has much lower early cash values and therefore a lower—in fact, negative—rate of return. (In other words, during the first few years you would be better off if you bought term insurance and kept the difference under your mattress.) It's also worth noting that the gross interest rate of the agent-sold policy—9.5 percent—is higher than the 9 percent gross interest rate of the low-load product. This simply confirms the foolishness of looking at the interest rate by itself while ignoring the various policy loads.

Figure 5.2. Linton Yields for Two Products

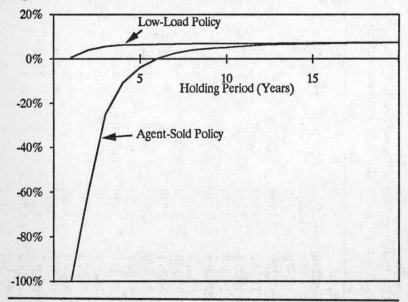

The usual interpretation of the Linton yield is that it is the average annual rate of return you would have to earn to match the whole life policy's cash value if you bought term insurance and invested on your own. It can also be interpreted as the internal rate of return for the investment project with cash flows as shown in Figure 5.3. At the beginning of each year you invest $3,750, and you receive a series of benefits in return.

First, you save what you would otherwise have to spend on term insurance each year if you didn't buy the whole life policy. Second, at the end of twenty years you receive an after-tax cash surrender value.

Figure 5.3. Cash Flow Diagram for a Whole Life Product

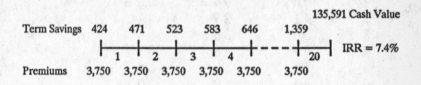

This IRR calculation is just like any other, with one exception: There is a peculiar interdependence between the cash flows and the rate of return. The rate of return affects the side fund balance, which affects the face amount of the term policy, which affects the term premium, which affects the rate of return, which affects the side fund balance, which. . .well, you get the idea. Through trial and error, you can eventually find one rate of return that makes everything come out right, and that number is the Linton yield.

Technical Considerations

Although a "buy term and invest the difference" analysis is not conceptually difficult, some questions arise when you actually sit down to do it. Let's look at each one briefly.

Choosing a tax rate. One possibility is to use 0 percent; that is, just ignore the income tax due upon surrender of the cash value policy. Unfortunately, this simple approach makes it harder to use the results, because there is no direct way of converting the before-tax rates of return into after-tax rates of return. Here's what happens if you compute the Linton yield on a before-tax basis for the low-load policy in Figure 5.2 and then multiply by one minus the marginal tax rate (1.00 − 0.30, or 0.70):

Year	Before-Tax Linton Yield	Multiplied by 0.70	Correct After-Tax Linton Yield
1	0.6%	0.4%	0.6%
2	4.1	2.9	4.1
3	5.6	3.9	5.6
4	6.5	4.6	6.3
5	7.1	5.0	6.5
10	8.3	5.8	7.0
15	8.6	6.0	7.2
20	8.8	6.2	7.4

The correct after-tax rates of return are always higher than what you might think, because of the impact of tax deferral and the tax shelter provided by the cost basis. To compare a cash value policy with another investment alternative, either compute the Linton yield using after-tax cash surrender values or be prepared to make a mental adjustment to the before-tax yield. (Above all, don't do what some agents do—compute the before-tax rate of return and then *divide* by 0.70 to get an "equivalent before-tax return" that is truly impressive—*and truly meaningless*.)

Once you take taxes into account, you may still wonder what tax rate to use. Your marginal tax rate is appropriate if you plan to surrender the policy for a lump-sum payment. However, you might want to use a lower rate—perhaps 10 percent less—to reflect the continued benefits of tax deferral if you plan to annuitize the cash value or exchange the policy for an annuity contract.

Choosing a term policy. As shown in Table 5.4 and Figure 5.3, a cash value policy does not have a rate of return by itself, but only in relation to an alternative insurance plan. There is nothing remarkable about this; corporate financial analysts encounter a similar situation whenever they do a "buy versus lease" or "make versus buy" analysis.

Higher term rates will cause the rate of return to go up, because less money is available for investment in the side fund; lower term rates will have the opposite effect. The type of term policy—annual renewable term or n-year level term—can also make a difference. Table 5.5 shows the results you'd get for the low-load policy in Figure 5.2 if you used three other sets of term rates.

Table 5.5. The Linton Yield Depends on the Term Policy

| | Annual Renewable Term | | | 10-Year |
Year	Benchmark	20% Less Expensive	1980 CSO Basic	Level Term
1	0.6%	(1.9)%	12.9%	4.6%
2	4.1	2.3	12.5	6.2
3	5.6	4.1	12.0	6.7
4	6.3	5.0	11.5	6.8
5	6.5	5.4	10.8	6.6
10	7.0	6.3	9.6	6.3
15	7.2	6.7	9.3	6.8
20	7.4	7.0	9.2	7.0

One New York company that sells through agents uses the 1980 CSO Basic mortality table to come up with "comparative rates of return," which it includes on its policy illustrations. Although a footnote makes the whole thing sound scientific, the effect is to overstate the rates of return by using unreasonably high term rates. This shows the danger of relying on rate-of-return information supplied by insurance companies.

Banded term rates. Many companies charge different rates per $1,000 of coverage, depending on the face amount of the policy. In such cases, it is possible that a smaller policy will actually be more expensive than a larger one, so a sensible consumer would not reduce the face amount of the term policy as called for in the Linton yield analysis.

Timing of term face amount adjustments. Most Linton yield analyses assume that the face amount of the term policy will be adjusted at the beginning of each year. However, it would be more correct to make the adjustment in the middle of the year, to reflect the fact that deaths occur throughout the period. On the other hand, it might be more realistic to adjust the death benefit once every few years.

Evidence of insurability. In some cases, the death benefit of the cash value policy may increase so quickly that the face amount of the term policy will also have to increase to keep the death benefits of the two alternatives the same. In the real world, this requires evidence of insurability.

Refund of unearned premium. With term and fixed premium cash value policies, many companies increase the death benefit by the unearned portion of the premium. Ideally, you should take this into account in determining the face amount of the term policy, although it will not affect the results significantly.

Value of unused cost basis. If a cash value policy is surrendered within several years of purchase, the cost basis will often be less than the cash surrender value. This excess cost basis can be used to shelter future investment income by exchanging the cash value policy for another cash value policy or a deferred annuity. Ideally, you should take this into account, perhaps by estimating the present value of the future tax savings.

State inheritance taxes. In some states, life insurance proceeds are exempt from state inheritance taxes. Because a portion of the term-plus-side-fund death benefit consists of an estate-taxable side fund balance, state death taxes will be higher for the term alternative than for the cash value policy.

Tax-deferred investments. The Linton yield is easiest to interpret when the alternative investments are fully taxable each year. When taxes are deferred on a portion or all of the returns, as with annuities and many mutual funds, the analysis may have to be modified.

Criticisms of the Linton Yield Method

Aside from the subtle complexities of the calculation, the Linton yield method has been criticized on several grounds.

Results depend on the assumed term rates. As we indicated earlier, this is a feature shared with analyses that take place every day throughout corporate America—without controversy, we might add. It's silly to criticize the Linton yield method for failing to deliver a unique rate of return when no such creature exists.

Term insurance is not a viable option for everyone. In these cases, you have to find some other way of assigning a value to the insurance protection provided by the policy. One possibility is to use a standard mortality table, with adjustments if necessary.

It's just an academic exercise. Many people will not actually invest the difference in premiums. Without the semi-compulsory savings feature of a whole life policy, "buy term and invest the difference" can become "buy term, spend the difference, and eventually have no insurance." However, there are hundreds of mutual funds that, on a preauthorized basis, will be happy to take money out of your checking account each month.

Results depend on illustrated values that may not come true. Obviously, this is a problem with every method of evaluating cash value policies. Nonetheless, the point is well taken; it's a mistake to focus on rates of return without also investigating the risk that actual results will turn out differently.

Linton yields can be misleading. In general, it can be dangerous to use internal rates of return to compare investment projects that have different patterns of cash flows. The Linton yield is no exception; it is best used to get an idea of whether a cash value policy provides good value for your money, and for that purpose it is quite effective.

RATES OF RETURN UPON DEATH AND SURRENDER

These two measures are widely used, and both can claim to be internal rates of return. The rate of return upon death is the rate that would have to be earned on the premiums to equal the death benefit. For example, if you pay $1,500 a year for a $100,000 policy, the ten-year rate of return on death would be 33.2 percent.

The rate of return upon surrender is the rate that would have to be earned on the premiums to equal the cash surrender value. In the same example, if the cash value were $20,000, the ten-year rate of return on surrender would be 5.2 percent.

Just as the interest-adjusted cost indexes are interesting because of what they reveal about the regulatory process, these two rates of return are interesting for what they reveal about the training of insurance professionals. Consider the following:

- You can look long and hard through the voluminous academic literature on methods of life insurance cost disclosure, and you will not find one serious researcher who has proposed that these measures should be used to compare policies.
- In 1974 a committee of actuaries prepared a comprehensive report on cost comparison methods. The rates of return upon death and surrender were not among the methods considered.
- In 1986, another committee of actuaries prepared a list of what *not* to do, entitled, "Improper Methods of Communicating Yield Information to Life Insurance Consumers." The rates of return upon death and surrender were both included.

The rate of return on death is not useful in comparing policies because it ignores cash surrender values. The rate of return on surrender is not useful in comparing policies because it ignores the value of the insurance protection. So what accounts for the strange persistence of these numbers? Perhaps the advisors who use them know something that academics and actuaries don't. Or perhaps they should just spend more time in the library.

NEEDS-BASED SELLING

This is a method of selling, not buying, but it deserves a quick mention anyway. "It's time to get back to needs-based selling" is what agents and companies say when they get tired of competing on price. Apparently the idea is that once the salesperson identifies a need for insurance (or just makes one up), the client should buy whatever product is recommended without worrying about its cost. Obviously, you should buy an insurance product only if you have a need for it, and you should also worry about the competitiveness of the products you buy. Needs-based selling is just a clever way of getting you to buy what the salesman wants to sell.

"BUY THE COMPANY"

This is what agents, advisors, and consumers fall back on when they decide they can't form an opinion about the product itself. The idea is that if a company has a good reputation for past performance and for treating its policyholders fairly, you can assume you'll be happy with whatever purchase you make from them today. Given the fact that product performance is ultimately determined by the issuer, this approach makes some sense. There are practical problems in implementing it, however. As we noted earlier, it's hard to get solid information about the past performance of insurance products, and it may be equally difficult to measure fairness. The best solution would be to have an actuarial consulting firm conduct a thorough audit, in which it would examine the company's pricing practices from the policyholder's point of view and offer some commentary. To our knowledge, this has never been done, although at least one company does have an oversight committee of policyholders, and some state insurance departments briefly discuss policyholder treatment in their periodic examination reports. Without a systematic review, you are forced to rely on whatever anecdotal evidence you can dig up.

Many financial advisors carry the "buy the company" approach too far by using easy-to-obtain company-wide information as a proxy for hard-to-obtain information about the product itself. For example, comments in *Best's Insurance Reports* about the company's overall net investment yield, mortality experience, lapse rates, and expenses are often used to make inferences about future product performance.

It would be nice if due diligence were that simple, but it isn't. Company-wide performance measures are affected by the company's product mix, age distribution of insureds, and other factors that make them unreliable for evaluating a specific product. As financial planners become more more knowledgeable about insurance product pricing, they will turn to *Best's Insurance Reports* as a source of questions rather than a source of answers. These comments notwithstanding, clearly you should not buy a product—no matter how competitive it looks on paper—if you don't have some confidence in the company behind it. When an obscure company suddenly has the "best" product, you are justified in being more than a little suspicious.

PRICING ASSUMPTIONS AND PROFIT TESTS

Here's a common occurrence: You receive a policy illustration from a low-load company and show it to an agent who says: "Oh, I can beat that." Then the agent pulls out a fully-loaded product that has higher illustrated twenty-year cash values. Should you believe him?

The most reliable way of answering that question is to do what insurance companies do: run a profit test on each product. Unfortunately, this approach rarely will be practical, because it requires some actuarial training, a computer, pricing software, and the disclosure of proprietary information. Nevertheless, profit testing can be such a powerful tool for countering the unsubstantiated claims of insurance salespeople, or simply for getting to the bottom of things, that it's worth a closer look. There are many ways to test the profitability of a product. One common approach is to treat each block of policies as a separate business with its own assets, liabilities, and net worth. The analysis outlined here is representative of what of a reasonably sophisticated company might do, and it will help you draw parallels between life insurance and manufacturing enterprises.

A Case Study: Universal Life

For our example, we'll compare two similar universal life products—one load and one low-load—with the same illustrated twenty-year cash values. We assume that policy purchases, deaths, and lapses all take place near the end of the calendar year. (In practice, a pricing actuary would assume that these events take place each month, but this simplified model is more than adequate for our purposes.)

Table 5.6 shows how the assets, liabilities, and net worth of a block of one thousand low-load policies might develop over a twenty-year period. The column labeled "Policies in Force" shows how many of the original one thousand policies remain at the end of each year, taking into account deaths and surrenders. Following a common practice, we cut off the analysis after twenty years by assuming that all outstanding policies are surrendered.

Table 5.6. Universal Life Profit Test: Assets, Liabilities, Net Worth, and Cash Flows

For a block of 1,000 low-load policies: $250,000 face amount, $1,500 annual premium, issued to 35-year-old male nonsmokers

	Year-End				Cash Flows	
	Policies	Year-End	Year-End	Target	Without	With [b]
Year	In-Force	Assets [a]	Reserves	Surplus	TS	TS
0	1,000	812,500	1,471,973	424,269	(659,473)	(1,083,742)
1	850	1,452,793	1,077,632	354,700	375,161	472,732
2	747	2,048,040	1,967,656	346,124	80,384	112,370
3	672	2,821,166	2,754,721	344,283	66,445	91,130
4	611	3,530,235	3,466,162	345,240	64,073	85,838
5	562	4,198,333	4,133,285	349,056	65,047	84,017
6	522	4,852,265	4,783,498	355,891	68,767	84,970
7	490	5,510,229	5,439,436	365,909	70,793	84,265
8	465	6,197,235	6,125,116	379,462	72,119	82,716
9	441	6,864,161	6,790,053	392,774	74,108	85,840
10	418	7,512,664	7,436,227	405,892	76,437	89,243
11	396	8,140,915	8,063,582	418,787	77,333	91,227
12	376	8,753,781	8,674,234	431,514	79,547	94,459
13	356	9,348,961	9,268,785	444,071	80,177	96,100
14	337	9,927,511	9,848,297	456,471	79,214	96,122
15	320	10,491,713	10,412,748	468,697	78,965	96,866
16	303	11,039,357	10,962,598	480,744	76,759	95,647
17	286	11,575,859	11,497,196	492,580	78,663	98,556
18	271	12,097,073	12,016,298	504,182	80,775	101,683
19	256	12,603,125	12,519,364	515,519	83,761	105,700
20	0	75,250	0	0	75,250	624,793

[a] Before capital transfers; does not include assets supporting target surplus.
[b] Includes capital transfers and after-tax investment income from assets supporting target surplus (TS).

As with any other business, the assets at the end of the year will be equal to the assets at the beginning of the year plus receipts and minus expenditures. The insurance company receives premiums and investment income. It pays out acquisition costs when the policies are issued, death claims when policyholders die, and cash surrender values when policyholders drop their policies. It also has to pay income taxes each year. In our example, the company receives $1,500,000 in premiums and pays out $687,500 for the distribution, underwriting, and administrative costs of acquiring the business. This includes the general overhead that the company allocates to its new business, based on its own cost studies.

The company also has to recognize its obligations to its policyholders by setting up a reserve, in accordance with regulatory and accounting requirements. We assume that the reserve is equal to the cash surrender value of the policies. Year-to-year increases in the reserve reduce the insurer's reported income for tax purposes. Following these initial transactions, the balance sheet of the block of policies looks like this:

Assets $812,500
Reserves   1,471,973
Surplus $(659,473)

You might say that the business is now insolvent, because it doesn't have enough assets on hand to meet its obligations. To bring assets and reserves back into balance, the company has to invest $659,473 of its own capital. This is the initial surplus strain that is characteristic of most insurance products.

Some companies take this one step further by recognizing that additional capital must be allocated to support the policies so as to reduce the risks of insolvency and to maintain favorable ratings from A.M. Best and other organizations. This tied-up capital is called *target surplus* (or sometimes *benchmark* or *required* surplus), and there are many formulas that companies use to determine how much target surplus is needed for each line of business. In our example, the initial target surplus is about $424,000, so the company's total investment is almost $1,084,000. The assets at the end of the first year are $1,452,793, determined as follows:

Assets at beginning of Year 1:	$1,471,973
plus: Investment income	147,197
less: Death claims paid	(118,172)
less: Cash surrender values paid	(194,668)
plus: Income tax savings from	
operating taxable loss	146,463
Assets at end of Year 1:	$1,452,793

The reserves at the end of the year are now $1,077,632, so the new balance sheet, excluding target surplus, looks like this:

Assets	$1,452,793
Reserves	1,077,632
Surplus	$375,161

This means that during the first year the block of policies has generated $375,000 of surplus that can be transferred back to the company for use in other areas, such as underwriting new business. In addition, several transactions related to target surplus also take place, generating another $98,000 of surplus that can be released for the company's use.

This process continues for twenty years, at which time the block of policies is assumed to be closed out, and all of the target surplus is released. The top part of Figure 5.4 diagrams the cash flows for several years; the cash flows related to target surplus are shown separately from those related to keeping assets and reserves in balance. Once these cash flows have been determined, the company can compute an appropriate profit measure such as internal rate of return or net present value. In our example, the IRR, including target surplus, is 12 percent after tax, and it takes the company nine years to break even by recovering its initial investment.

The bottom part of Figure 5.4 diagrams the cash flows for a similar agent-sold policy with higher distribution costs. In this example, the pattern of cash flows is irregular; the initial outlay is followed by two years of returns, six years of additional investments, and twelve more years of returns. The required investment is less than for the low-load product, due to lower reserves. However, the internal rate of return is only 4.6 percent, and it takes the company nineteen years just to break even.

Figure 5.4. **Universal Life Profit Test: Cash Flows from the Insurance Company's Point of View**

For a block of 1,000 policies issued to 35-year-old male nonsmokers, $250,000 face amount, $1,500 annual premium

Amounts are in thousands of dollars

Low-Load Product:

Generated Surplus:

Target Surplus ⟶ 98 32 25 21 22 550
Solvency Only ⟶ 375 80 66 81 84 75

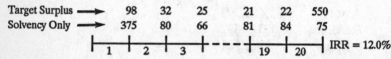

IRR = 12.0%

Invested Surplus:

Solvency Only 660
Target Surplus 424

Load Product:

Generated Surplus:

Target Surplus ⟶ 98 21 10 21 22 550
Solvency Only ⟶ 129 369 68 72 64

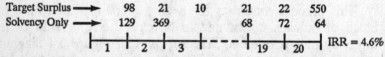

IRR = 4.6%

Invested Surplus:

Solvency Only 388 184
Target Surplus 373

Now let's take a closer look at the assumptions we've used to come up with these cash flows. All of the pricing assumptions are the same for both the load and low-load products, with two exceptions:

1. Distribution costs for the low-load product are assumed to be 25 percent of the first-year premium, versus 105 percent for the load product. In subsequent years, distribution costs are 2 percent of renewal premiums for

the low-load product, versus 6 percent for the load product. In dollar terms, sales costs for each load policy are $1,200 higher (80 percent of $1,500) in the first year and $60 higher in each renewal year.

2. The low-load product has no surrender charges; the load product has a declining surrender charge that disappears after fifteen years. As a result, the load product has lower illustrated cash values than the low-load product during the first fifteen years, and the same cash values after that.

Each of the initial pricing assumptions is in line with typical industry experience. *We assume that the low-load company enjoys no competitive advantages other than lower distribution costs.*

Table 5.7 summarizes the baseline assumptions. Expenses cover several categories, as outlined below.

- *Product development.* Costs incurred for actuarial design work and purchase or upgrade of administrative systems, to be amortized over all policies sold.
- *Distribution.* Commissions, expense allowances, field and home office marketing.
- *State premium tax.* Percent-of-premium tax levied by many states.
- *Per policy and per $1,000 face amount.* Underwriting, administrative, and general overhead expenses.
- *Per death claim.* Administrative and investigative costs.
- *Per lapse*: Administrative costs.
- *Expense inflation.* After the first year expenses are assumed to increase due to inflation, with some offsetting impact from increasing sales volume and, therefore, lower unit costs.
- *Interest earned.* The net yield, after investment-related expenses, on the insurer's portfolio.
- *Interest credited.* The gross interest rate credited on the universal life policy.
- *Mortality.* Mortality experience is often expressed as a percentage of the rates found in some standard pricing table, such as the 1975-80 Select & Ultimate Basic Table derived from the actual death claims of twenty-one large companies from 1975 to 1980. We have implicitly assumed

that (1) current aggregate (nonsmoker and smoker combined) mortality is 90 percent of the 1975-80 rates; (2) smoker mortality rates are double those of nonsmokers at all ages; (3) 80 percent of policyholders are nonsmokers; and (4) no future improvement in mortality will occur.

- *COI rates:* The cost of insurance (COI) rates on the universal life policy, expressed as a percentage of the 1980 Commissioners Standard Ordinary Mortality Table.
- *Policy loads:* Premium loads and policy fees.
- *Surrender charge:* A declining percentage of an assumed target premium that would keep the policy in force until maturity, based on current assumptions. The surrender charge can never exceed the account value of the policy.
- *Illustrated cash values:* For simplicity, we assume that premium loads, policy fees, and insurance charges are deducted at the beginning of the year, and that interest is credited at year-end.
- *Lapse rate:* The percentage of remaining policies that are dropped each year. Our assumed rates are in line with the lapse rates used in pricing agent-sold universal life policies; they may be too high for low-load products.
- *Commission chargeback:* The percentage of first-year commissions that is recovered from the agent when a policy is dropped or when death occurs during the first year. The chargeback typically starts at 100 percent and declines during the year.
- *Statutory reserves:* The reserve balance that must be established by the company in accordance with statutory accounting procedures. Under the Commissioners' Reserve Valuation Method, reserves for the load product start at $0 and grade into the cash value; reserves for the low-load product are equal to the cash value.
- *Tax reserves:* The reserve balance used to determine a company's taxable income.
- *Target surplus:* The additional capital that is allocated to support the block of policies. We assume that target surplus is equal to a percentage of statutory reserves plus a dollar amount per $1,000 of net amount at risk (policy face amount minus account value).

Table 5.7. Universal Life Profit Test: Initial Assumptions

Issued to: Male nonsmoker, age 35   Face amount: $250,000
Annual premium: $1,500   Number of policies: 1,000

Expenses:	Low-Load		Load	
	First-Yr.	Renewal	First-Yr.	Renewal
Product development (per policy) $30		—	$30	—
Distribution (% of premium)	25%	2%	105%	6%
State premium tax (% of premium) 2%		2%	2%	2%
Per policy	$130	$50	$130	$50
Per $1,000 —first $100,000	$0.70	—	$0.70	—
—thereafter	$0.35	—	$0.35	—
Per death claim: $100				
Per lapse: $30				
Renewal-year expenses inflated at 5%				

Interest earned: 10%
Interest credited: 9%
Mortality: 75% of 1975-80 Select & Ultimate Table
COI rates: 55% of 1980 CSO Table (Male Aggregate)

Policy loads:	Annual policy fee	$48	$48	$48	$48
	Premium load	None	None	None	None
Surrender charge		None	None	150% of $1,500 target premium, declining by 10% a year	

Illustrated cash values:	Year 1	$1,268	$0
	5	7,360	5,710
	10	17,787	16,887
	20	53,677	53,677

Lapse rate: 15,12,10,9,8,7,6,5,5%...

Commission chargeback	N/A	N/A	50%	—
Statutory reserves	Cash value		Approx of CRVM	
Tax reserves	Cash value		Approx of CRVM	
Target surplus — % of stat reserves	3.50%		3.50%	
—$/$1,000 at risk	$1.50		$1.50	

Tax rate: 34%
Profit objective: 12% IRR after tax, including target surplus

- *Tax rate:* The company's marginal income tax rate.
- *Profit objective:* The measure the company uses to decide if it is receiving an adequate return on its investment.

With these baseline assumptions, we saw earlier that the low-load product would have a 12 percent IRR, but the agent-sold product would have only a 4.6 percent IRR—well below the desired goal. Now we're ready to ask two questions—which is really the whole purpose of this exercise: What pricing assumptions would be necessary to make the agent-sold policy a viable product? Are these assumptions realistic?

Let's begin by taking one pricing assumption at a time and seeing what impact it has on the profitability of the fully loaded product, all other things being equal. Later we can see what happens if we change several assumptions together.

Table 5.8 summarizes the results of this series of what-ifs. For each pricing assumption, we have shown what it takes to achieve the profit objective of a 12 percent after-tax internal rate of return on invested capital (including target surplus). Following are some comments on each factor:

- *Net investment yield:* It is very difficult for a fixed-income portfolio manager to significantly outperform peers over the long run. A 1.50 percent above-average annual return over a twenty-year period would probably correspond to the top 5 percent of all bond managers. Without such talented employees, a company would have to invest in below-investment-grade securities or in other types of assets, such as common stocks, that tend to outperform fixed-income investments over time and are generally not appropriate for insurance companies. If the manager achieved an 11 percent yield, rather than 11.5 percent, the IRR would be 9.9 percent.
- *Mortality experience:* Studies of mortality experience published by the Society of Actuaries suggest that there is a wide range of experience among companies during the early policy years. After that, however, most companies fall within 15 percentage points of the average. Mortality experience of 60 percent of the 1975-80 Table would produce a 7.8 percent IRR.

Table 5.8. Universal Life Profit Test: How to Beat a Low-Load Product

- Baseline IRR: 4.6%

Pricing Assumption	Baseline Case	Assumption Needed for 12% IRR	Comments
Net investment yield	10.00%	11.50%	Unlikely
Mortality experience	75% of 1975-80 Table	40% of 1975-80 Table	Very unlikely
Administrative expenses	$130/50 per policy; $.70/.35 per $1,000; $100 per death; $30 per lapse	$0 in all categories	Impossible
Termination rates	15,12,10,9,8,7,6, 5,5,5%...	Not possible	See text
Reinsurance	N/A	N/A	See text
Reserving method	Approx of CRVM	Not possible	See text
Corporate taxes	34%	Not possible	See text
Target market	Age 35; $250,000 face; $1,500 premium	N/A	See text
Service	N/A	N/A	See text
Profit objective	12% aftertax IRR, including target surplus	N/A	See text

- *Administrative expenses:* The company would just barely meet its profit objective if it had no administrative expenses whatsoever. Companies do vary in efficiency; a 20 percent difference in unit costs is possible and that would raise the IRR to 5.7 percent.
- *Termination rates:* Because of the high surrender charges, the load product is relatively insensitive to lapse rates. If there were no lapses at all, the IRR would be 6.0 percent.
- *Reinsurance:* Product pricing is generally done before reinsurance is considered. A particularly favorable reinsurance agreement would be a competitive advantage, but reinsurance adds to costs more often than it reduces them.
- *Reserving method:* Companies have some latitude in how they compute reserves. This can affect profitability, although the impact would be small in this example.
- *Corporate taxes rate:* Companies in different tax situations will have different after-tax returns on their products. The most extreme case would be a tax-exempt institution that pays no taxes; the IRR in that case would be 5.7 percent.
- *Target market:* In designing a product, actuaries have to make assumptions about the likely issue ages, face amounts, and premium payment patterns. This means that a low-load product that is competitive in one case may have a load structure that makes it uncompetitive in another. Similarly, differences between the target and actual markets can affect the product's profitability.
- *Service:* In theory, commissionable products provide agent services you will not get with a low-load product. In our example, these additional services cost 80 percent of the first-year premium ($1,200) and 4 percent of renewal premiums ($60 a year). However, two reasons explain why you would be better off paying these same amounts for fee-for-service advice and buying a low-load product. First, the fees may be tax-deductible. Second, the insurance company's cost of capital is probably higher than yours, so in effect you are borrowing money to pay agent compensation at a higher cost than if you simply paid the same expenses out of your own pocket. This may be true even if the expenses are tax-deductible for the company but not for you. For example, it would cost a company $792 after

tax to pay $1,200 in agent compensation, assuming a 34 percent corporate tax rate. If the company wants to earn 12 percent after tax on its investment, it will have to earn an additional $95 a year—or $144 before tax. To do this, it gives you $144 less. So by letting the company pay for the agent's advice, you are losing $144 a year, before tax—or 12 percent of $1,200. Unless you can earn more than 12 percent on your investments, you would be better off paying the $1,200 yourself and having the agent work directly for you.

Profit objective: This, more than anything else, is what makes it hard to evaluate an insurance product. All other things being equal, the load product in this example would produce an IRR of 4.6 percent. Few companies would knowingly accept such a low overall rate of return. However, because some companies do not have the necessary accounting systems in place to determine the profitability of each product line, consumers can benefit from their pricing mistakes. (But do you really want to invest your money on the premise that the company will continue to be badly managed?) Even among well-run companies, profit objectives vary widely in several respects:

—*Varying formulas.* Companies use different target surplus formulas. Things that can be tossed into a formula include reserves, insurance in force, mortality charges, expenses, premium income, assets, and cash values. Using a target surplus formula of 5 percent of reserves, the after-tax IRR for the load product would be 4.2 percent.

—*Ignoring target surplus.* Some companies ignore target surplus in setting the profit objective. Without target surplus, the after-tax IRR for the load product would be 2.0 percent. (The rate of return is lower in this case because the assets supporting target surplus are assumed to be invested at 10 percent; therefore target surplus is more profitable than the product itself.)

—*Ignoring taxes.* Some companies set their profit objectives on a before-tax basis. Ignoring target surplus and taxes, the IRR for the load product would be 2.1 percent.

—*Averaging results.* Some companies determine the profitability of a product by averaging the results for various issue ages, face amounts, and premium payment patterns. It is therefore possible that in some cases the product could be unprofitable but still satisfy the overall goal.

—*Subsidizing products.* One line of business may sometimes be subsidized by another line of business.

—*Marginal Pricing.* In some cases, a company may use marginal rather than full cost pricing; that is, it chooses not to recover general overhead expenses. Obviously, a company cannot use marginal pricing for all of its products or it will eventually go bankrupt. Marginal pricing may be appropriate, however, in highly competitive situations—with large corporation buyers for example—where the choice is between a marginally profitable sale or no sale at all. If the load company in our example chose not to recover the product development costs ($30 per policy), one-fourth of the first-year distribution costs (26 percent of the premium), one-third of the first-year per policy cost ($43), and one-half of the per $1,000 cost ($0.35 for the first $100,000 and $0.18 thereafter), the after-tax IRR including target surplus would be 11.4 percent.

—*Using other measures.* Many companies use profit measures other than IRR, including break-even year and present value of profits as a percent of premium. Also, most companies look at profitability for more than one set of assumptions in order to estimate their potential losses or gains. It is possible—but not likely—that a product with a mediocre IRR for the baseline case would still be judged acceptable using some other profit goal.

These results suggest that it will generally take a combination of competitive advantages to beat a low-load product over the long run. Here are a few of the infinite number of possibilities:

- Excellent investment performance (11 percent), very good mortality experience (65 percent of 1975-80 Table), 12 percent IRR.

- Excellent investment performance (11 percent), accept a 9.9 percent IRR.
- Excellent investment performance (11 percent), very good mortality experience (65 percent of 1975-80 Table), efficient administration (20 percent below-average unit costs), accept a 10.5 percent IRR.
- Very good investment performance (10.5 percent), very good mortality experience (65 percent of 1975-80 Table), efficient administration (20 percent below-average unit costs), accept a 10.0 percent IRR.
- Very good investment performance (10.5 percent), very good mortality experience (65 percent of 1975-80 Table), efficient administration (20 percent below-average unit costs), greater leveraging of capital (target surplus equal to 3.5 percent of reserves and $0.40 per $1,000 at risk), 12 percent IRR.

If you can't come up with a plausible set of assumptions, you can reasonably conclude that the agent's product will not in fact perform as well as you're being led to believe. This detailed analysis should give you an idea of what is possible on the planet Earth—as opposed to the fantasyworld of policy illustrations, where anything seems possible. In fantasyworld, companies can shower salespeople with high commissions and trips to exotic places and still provide superior values for consumers. In contrast, on Earth there are trade-offs; every dollar paid to a salesperson is a dollar less for you or the company.

Remember, there is no better way to slice through baloney than to ask specific questions about the company's pricing assumptions. You may not get any answers, but at least you'll learn two things: (1) Many agents (and other advisors) really know little of interest about the products they recommend; and (2) insurance companies have a lot to learn about how to deal with consumers who are also serious investors.

THE BOTTOM LINE

Use policy illustrations as a tool for comparing policies with different load structures. Ask for illustrations with similar premiums and death benefits, and then put the cash values side by side. If you are comparing fixed premium and flexible premium products, get illustrations for the fixed premium products first. Always ask about the underlying assumptions.

When you run across a superior illustration, try to determine if the company has a legitimate competitive advantage or if its only real advantage is just a greater willingness to dupe the public. Use the "buy term and invest the difference" approach to convince yourself that a proposed cash value policy offers good value over your intended holding period.

Predicting Future Performance

The life insurance bazaar is a surrealistic place where every product is one of the best and every vendor knows why all other products are not as good as his or hers. Sooner or late, you'll have to peer into the future and decide whom to believe. Of course, a few products really *will* turn out to be "one of the best," and it will be for one or more of these reasons:

- lower profit objective
- lower distribution costs
- higher investment returns
- better mortality experience
- better persistency
- lower administrative costs
- lower reinsurance costs
- lower corporate taxes
- lower reserves

Keep this list in mind as you listen to the sales pitches.

6

LIFE INSURANCE: OTHER DECISIONS

After you've decided how much insurance, what type of policy, and which particular product to buy, you have a few more choices to make before you can sign the application and send it in.

PREMIUMS

How much money should you put into the policy? With fixed-premium policies, the premium will likely be dictated by the face amount you want. If the policy pays dividends, you can exercise some control over the outlay through the dividend option. To minimize the outlay, use dividends to reduce the premium; to maximize the outlay, use dividends to buy paid-up additions.

With flexible-premium policies, you can choose how much you want to invest within a broad range. The insurance company will probably require a minimum premium that is at least equal to the insurance and expense charges during the first year, maybe higher.

The maximum amount you can invest is governed by federal tax laws. In recent years, Congress has reacted to the growing use of life insurance contracts for investment purposes by enacting layer upon layer of legislation, each with its own "grandfathering" rules. The inevitable ambiguities will keep actuaries and lawyers busy for years to come, and each new wave of aggressively promoted products may well beget further congressional counter-moves.

Figure 6.1 summarizes the important provisions of two relevant sections of the Internal Revenue Code, and Figure 6.2 shows how these provisions would translate into premium limitations for one low-load universal life policy.

Figure 6.1. Sections 7702 and 7702A of the Internal Revenue Code

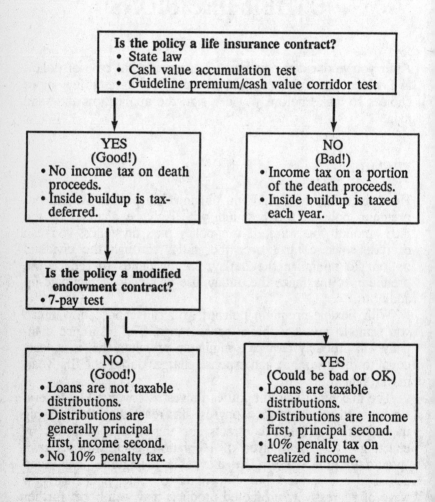

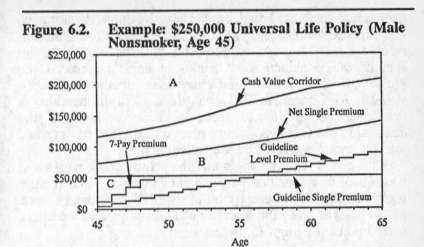

Figure 6.2. Example: $250,000 Universal Life Policy (Male Nonsmoker, Age 45)

Chart labels:
- A — Cash Value Corridor
- Net Single Premium
- 7-Pay Premium
- B — Guideline Level Premium
- C
- Guideline Single Premium

Y-axis: $0, $50,000, $100,000, $150,000, $200,000, $250,000
X-axis: Age — 45, 50, 55, 60, 65

TRA '84 and Section 7702

The Tax Reform Act (TRA) of 1984 set down a formal definition of a life insurance contract. To qualify under this definition, a contract must be a life insurance contract under state law and must also pass one of two tests: *a cash value accumulation test* or a *guideline premium/cash value corridor test*. If a contract does not qualify as a life insurance contract, the policyholder will have to pay tax on the investment earnings each year, and the beneficiary will have to pay tax on a small portion of the death proceeds (corresponding to any untaxed investment earnings). If at any time a life insurance contract fails to qualify as life insurance, all of the tax-deferred inside buildup becomes taxable income. Obviously this is a serious matter, and insurance companies have been careful to design their products so that they comply with the law.

The provisions of the 1984 law apply to all policies issued after December 31, 1984. However, even a grandfathered policy issued before 1985 can become subject to these provisions if it is exchanged for a new contract or if there is a change in policy terms.

To meet the cash value accumulation test, the cash value—computed without taking into account any surrender charges—cannot exceed the *net single premium* that would fund all future contractual benefits, based on conservative interest, mortality, and expense assumptions. To meet the guideline premium/cash value corridor test, two requirements must be met. First, the sum of the premiums paid cannot at any time exceed the greater of the *guideline single premium* or the cumulative *guideline level premiums* that would fund all future benefits, as determined at the time of issue. As in the previous test, the calculation of these hypothetical premiums is based on specified interest, mortality, and expense assumptions.

The second requirement is that the death benefit must be at least equal to a specified percentage of the cash value (before surrender charges) at each point in time. The percentage starts at 250 percent up to the insured's age 40 and gradually declines to 100 percent by age 95, as follows:

Age	40	45	50	55	60	65	70	75	90	95
% Required	250	215	185	150	130	120	115	105	105	100

For example, a policy with a cash value of $50,000 would have to have a death benefit of at least $125,000 if the insured is age 35, but only $60,000 if the insured is age 65. Viewed another way, a policy with a death benefit of $100,000 could have a cash value of up to $40,000 if the insured is age 35, and as much as $83,333 if the insured is age 65. In order to maintain the required relationship between cash values and death benefits, a company will automatically raise the death benefit of supposedly level-benefit policies in the later years, as the cash value approaches the allowable maximum.

TAMRA and Section 7702A

The Technical and Miscellaneous Revenue Act (TAMRA) of 1988 created a new class of life insurance policies, *modified endowment contract* (MEC). A life insurance policy is a MEC if at any time during the first seven years, the premiums paid exceed the cumulative *seven-pay net level premiums*; that is, level premiums that would produce a paid-up policy in seven years, based on certain interest and mortality assumptions but ignoring expenses. This does not mean that you actually have to pay premiums for seven years; it simply limits the amount that you can put into the policy during this period. If the limit is exceeded, the general rule is "once a MEC, always a MEC"; however, a company has at least sixty days to return excess premiums in order to preserve the policy's non-MEC status.

If a life insurance policy is a MEC, the tax treatment will be similar to that of deferred annuities. Amounts received—loans, withdrawals, and, in some cases, dividends—will be treated as income first, principal second, and any income will be subject to a 10 percent penalty tax if the policyholder is under age 59 1/2, with certain exemptions in cases of disability or annuitization. The seven-pay test applies to policies issued after June 20, 1988, and to any policy, regardless of issue date, whenever there is a *material change*, such as an increase in the death benefit, the addition of a rider, or an exchange for a new policy. For policies that are not grandfathered, the seven-pay test can also be triggered by a decrease in the death benefit during the first seven years (or until maturity, for second-to-die policies issued or materially changed after September 14, 1989) a new seven-pay premium will be computed and applied retroactively, as if the lower benefit had been in effect since issue.

The insurance industry has been quick to point out that the provisions of the 1988 tax law are not as unfavorable as they might seem. In reality the seven-pay test sets a generous ceiling on allowable premium payments, because it uses conservative interest and mortality assumptions. Single-premium policies will fail the test, but you still may be able to fully fund the policy—based on current interest, mortality, and expense assumptions—in two or three years without causing it to become a modified endowment contract. In addition, MECs continue to enjoy the other important advantages of life insurance: tax-deferred inside buildup and tax-exempt death benefits.

Figure 6.2 displays the various premium and cash value limitations during the first twenty years for one $250,000 level death benefit universal life policy issued to a 45-year-old male nonsmoker. Note in particular that:

- The cash value corridor test would permit higher cash values (as shown by the line labeled "cash value corridor") than would the cash value accumulation test (as shown by the line labeled "net single premium").

- Under the guideline premium test, total premiums would be limited by the guideline single premium during the first eleven years and by the cumulative guideline level premiums after that (as shown by the crossover point of the two lines). There is no explicit premium limitation under the cash value accumulation test, but the limit on cash values effectively serves to limit premiums as well.

- The seven-pay cumulative premium actually reaches the maximum allowable premium under the guideline premium test in the fifth year. This demonstrates that, for many investors, the seven-pay test will have more bark than bite. In fact, on a current (rather than guaranteed) basis, it would take only *two* seven-pay premiums to keep the policy in force until age 95.

- Contracts in region A would not qualify as life insurance contracts because the cash value exceeds the allowable limits under the cash accumulation and cash value corridor tests. Contracts in region B would not qualify as life insurance contracts under the guideline premium test because the cumulative premiums exceed the allowable limit. Contracts in region C would be modified endowment contracts, because they qualify as life insurance contracts but fail the seven-pay test.

Choosing the Outlay

Within the constraints set by the insurance company and the federal government, you have a decision to make, and you may have to balance several considerations:

- Obviously, you have to put enough money into the policy to keep it going for as long as you need it. In general, you should pay the required premiums sooner rather than later, since this lets you prefund the future insurance charges at a favorable discount rate. For example, if the credited interest rate is 8 percent and the policy has a 2 percent premium load, you would have to deposit $694 today to prefund a $1,000 charge to be deducted in five years. Unless you can earn more than 8 percent after-tax each year on your money, paying a $694 premium now is better than the alternative of investing the $694 on your own outside the policy and paying a $1,020 premium in five years. (These two choices are not perfectly comparable, however, because there would be a difference in cost basis if you surrendered the policy.)

- You should generally invest enough to make the cash value at the end of the holding period at least equal to the sum of the premiums (the cost basis), because this makes efficient use of the tax shelter aspects of the policy. For example, suppose the cost basis is $10,000 and the cash value is projected to be $8,000 in five years, assuming 9 percent interest. If the contract has no premium load, this gives you an opportunity to earn 9 percent a year after tax, risk free, by investing an additional $3,700. (With this additional premium, the projected cash value would be about $13,700, the same as the new cost basis.) Of course, this opportunity would be less attractive if there is a premium load. Also, if you decide not to make the additional investment now, you can still make use of the excess cost basis later on by exchanging the life insurance policy for an annuity.

- Once you have purchased it, the policy may be an attractive alternative to certificates of deposit or deferred annuities for additional amounts you want to invest. For example, it might well make sense to put an additional $1,000 into an existing low-load universal life policy with no premium load, no surrender charge, and a 9 percent tax-deferred interest rate, if the alternatives are a 9 percent taxable CD or a deferred annuity that also pays 9 percent, but with declining surrender charges and a 10 percent penalty tax.

- In a sense, this is an asset allocation decision, and the amount you invest in the cash value policy should be appropriate in the context of your overall portfolio. For example, you might choose the premiums so that the policy's cash value is about 10 percent of your investable assets.

Use the following list to help you decide how much to invest in the policy:

	First Year	Renewal Years
Maximum: life insurance		
modified endowment		
Future cost basis = future cash value		
Good investment for incremental dollars		
Desired asset allocation		
Amount needed to keep policy in force		
Minimum set by company		

OWNER/BENEFICIARY/PREMIUM PAYER

Who will own the policy? Who will receive the proceeds at death? Who will pay the premiums? Table 6.1 summarizes the possibilities.

This decision is complicated by the fact that you can choose more than one from each category. For example, a *split-dollar* plan will typically involve one owner (with some ownership rights shared with a second party), two beneficiaries, and two premium payers. Agents compete in the *advanced underwriting* markets by developing elaborate configurations of owners, beneficiaries, and premium payers. Sometimes the schemes are given fancy names—like "wealth accumulation plan"—that deliberately make no mention of life insurance.

Table 6.1. Owner, Beneficiary, Premium Payer: The Choices

Owner	Beneficiary	Premium Payer
Insured	Estate	Insured
Spouse	Spouse	Spouse
Other relative or associate	Other relative or associate	Other relative or associate
Business	Business	Business
• sole proprietorship	• sole proprietorship	• sole proprietorship
• partnership	• partnership	• partnership
• S-corp	• S-corp	• S-corp
• C-corp	• C-corp	• C-corp
• professional corp	• professional corp	• professional corp
Retirement plan	Retirement plan	Retirement plan
• defined benefit	• defined benefit	• defined benefit
• defined contribution	• defined contribution	• defined contribution
Trust	Trust	Trust
• revocable	• revocable	• revocable
• irrevocable	• irrevocable	• irrevocable
Tax-exempt organization	Tax-exempt organization	Tax-exempt organization

---

Issues to Address

There are many things to consider when setting up your insurance program. Keep in mind that mistakes can be costly, so it may be worthwhile to get professional advice. Following are the important issues that must be addressed.

Estate and inheritance tax. What taxes will be due upon the death of the insured, the policyowner, and the beneficiary? Under current law, you don't have to worry about Federal estate taxes if your taxable estate is less than $600,000. State exemptions vary.

Gift tax. Will premiums be taxable gifts? Will the death proceeds be a taxable gift? The $600,000 Federal exemption applies to gifts as well as to transfers at death. A $10,000 annual exclusion may also be available. State gift taxes vary.

Generation-skipping transfer tax. Will the death proceeds be subject to the generation-skipping transfer tax? Under current law, you don't have to worry about this if the proposed plan does not involve anyone who is two or more generations below you—for example, a grandchild—or if the amounts involved total less than $1 million.

Income tax. Will premiums and/or policy loan interest be tax-deductible? Will loans be taxable distributions? Will the proposal result in any imputed taxable income? The answers to all of these questions will depend on the particular situation.

15 percent additional income or estate tax. Under current law, there is a 15 percent additional income or estate tax on "excess" retirement distributions and accumulations. This is probably not an issue unless you have more than $1 million in your retirement plans. In that case, it can sometimes make sense to use heavily-taxed retirement plan assets to buy life insurance, since a portion of the death proceeds will be exempt from the 15 percent additional tax. (Note that life insurance cannot be purchased within an IRA.)

Corporate book income and taxable income. This is only of interest if a corporation is involved in the insurance program as the policyowner or beneficiary. Under current law, life insurance death benefits and cash values enter into the calculation of the corporate alternative minimum income tax.

Transfer for value. Does the proposal run afoul of the "transfer for value rule"? When an interest in a life insurance policy is exchanged for something of value, a portion of the death benefits may be taxable.

Simultaneous death. What happens if you and your beneficiary die within a short time of each other? Settlement options, beneficiary designations, and trusts can be used to produce any desired result, in the context of your overall estate plan.

Contestability period. If the proposal involves the replacement of existing coverage, will there be a new contestability period?

Protection from creditors. Will the policy's cash value be protected from your creditors? Will the death proceeds be protected from your beneficiary's creditors? State exemption laws vary, so you may need to consult an attorney.

Avoidance of probate. Will the cash value or death proceeds pass to your heirs without going through the expense, delay, and publicity of probate?

Financial astuteness. Does the proposal make financial sense? This may be the most difficult issue to address, because good salesmen are persuasive, even when they're wrong. Nature is also on the salesman's side: Whereas it can take only a few minutes to present a sales idea, it might take hours or even days to evaluate it properly. Because many people are not willing to spend that much time (or money), superficially appealing proposals can be effective.

The first—and most important—step in evaluating a complicated proposal is to understand what makes it work. Magicians often create their illusions through misdirection: While the magician's left hand captures your attention, his right hand does the "magic." Insurance agents, who like to think of themselves as financial magicians, use a different technique—misattribution. Their proposals draw upon the tax advantages of life insurance as well as other tax benefits that really have nothing to do with life insurance but are attributed to it anyway.

Consider a simple executive bonus plan. The agent suggests that as the owner of a small corporation, you can benefit by having the corporation give you a taxable bonus of $1,000 a year. The bonus only costs your company $660 because it's in the 34 percent tax bracket, but since your personal tax rate is 28 percent, you'll have $720 that you can use to pay the premium on a whole life policy. That means you can buy the whole life policy at an 8.3 percent discount (660/720 − 1).

What goes unsaid, of course, is that the "discount" depends upon a difference in tax rates that is unrelated to life insurance. The $1,000 bonus lets you buy anything at an 8.3 percent discount; the policy actually costs the same as it did before, even though the agent's proposal makes it look 8.3 percent cheaper. The decision to buy the policy is separate from the decision to make and receive the $1,000 bonus, and the illusion of a discount disappears when you unlink the two transactions.

If you look for it, you can see misattribution in proposals for split-dollar plans, deferred compensation, charitable gifts, irrevocable trusts, and purchases through qualified plans. That doesn't mean that the advanced underwriter's ideas are hokum. It simply means that you should always set up a simpler alternative as a point of reference, in order to determine which of the illustrated benefits are properly attributable to the purchase of the policy and which are not. With a few exceptions, you will find that the policy is really contributing nothing more than the usual advantages of life insurance: income-tax free death proceeds, tax-deferred investment income, a favorably-computed cost basis, and nontaxably withdrawals and policy loans.

Clearly, setting up an insurance program requires some thought. You have three courses of action:

- Keep it simple by being the owner and insured and naming your spouse or other relative as the beneficiary. The death proceeds will be included in your estate, but you won't have to worry about gift or income taxes. You should generally avoid naming your estate as the beneficiary, since this can make the proceeds subject to state death taxes.

- Learn about other techniques on your own. Start by looking through *Tax Facts 1*, mentioned earlier in this chapter (also see Appendix J).

- Work with a professional to design an appropriate program, such as an irrevocable life insurance trust to keep the death proceeds out of your taxable estate. Bear in mind, however, that if you want professional advice, you have to pay for it. You can buy a commission-paying product, with its hidden compensation to the selling agent, or you can buy a low-load product and pay a separate fee to a planner, consultant, attorney, or accountant.

OTHER DECISIONS

The additional choices you face depend on the contract. Here are the more common ones.

Option A/Option B

With universal life and variable universal life, you can choose between a level death benefit (Option A) or an increasing death benefit that is equal to the initial face amount plus the account value (Option B).

Option A produces lower insurance charges, because the net amount at risk decreases as the accumulation account builds; you're buying less insurance protection and therefore paying less. On the other hand, Option B allows you to make a larger investment, because the guideline annual premium is generally much higher. If you're looking for an accumulation vehicle, it might be worthwhile to pay for more insurance in order to enjoy the benefits of tax deferral. It's also a little easier to keep track of what you're paying for insurance under Option B, because the net amount at risk remains level.

Settlement Options

Instead of a lump-sum payment, your beneficiaries can receive the proceeds in various forms of a life income or in installments. In general, this is a decision that should be left to the beneficiary, since it is always a good idea to shop around for competitive annuity rates (see Chapter 8, "Annuities"). However, it may make sense to choose a settlement option when the beneficiary needs to be protected from creditors or from his or her own extravagance. Discuss this with a local attorney.

Waiver of Premium Rider

This rider keeps the policy from lapsing if you become disabled. It can be a helpful *supplement* to a quality disability income insurance policy, but it is not a *substitute* for one. In general, the definition of the term *disability* will be less favorable than under a stand-alone contract, and partial disability may not be covered at all.

Agents who sell traditional whole life policies like to point out that the waiver-of-premium benefit pays the entire premium, whereas for universal life it typically pays only the cost of insurance charges. They forget to add that the cost of the rider for universal life may also be less. To do a careful comparison, you really need to know how much individual disability income insurance you could buy with the difference in rider premiums. In the absence of this type of analysis, you should ignore any claims that one type of rider is better than another.

Accidental Death Benefit Rider

This rider increases the death benefit—if your number comes up in an airplane crash, drowning, or other mishap. Unless you're accident prone, forget it; Las Vegas and Atlantic City will give you better odds.

The most interesting thing about this rider is that although financial advisors seem to agree that it's a waste of money, insurance companies continue to offer it and consumers continue to buy it.

Premium Payment Mode

With fixed-premium policies, you often have the option of paying the premiums semi-annually, quarterly, or monthly, rather than annually. Embedded in these "fractional premiums" is an implicit charge to compensate the insurer for the time value of money, higher administrative costs, and higher expected lapse rates. The charges are generally lowest for monthly premiums paid automatically from your checking account, because this reduces administrative costs and lapse rates.

To compute the fractional premium, multiply the annual premium by a modal factor, as shown in the example below.

Frequency	Modal Factor	Premium
Annual	—	$1,000
Semi-annual	0.510	510
Quarterly	0.260	260
Monthly	0.085	85

Some companies also charge a small service fee—for example, $0.50—in addition to the modal factor.

The choice between annual and semi-annual payment modes can be described by a cash flow diagram, as shown in Figure 6.3. By paying the $1,000 annual premium at the beginning of the year, you avoid having to pay the two $510 semi-annual premiums. The six-month rate of return on this "investment" of $1,000 is 4.08 percent (510/490 − 1), which is equivalent to an annual rate of 8.33 percent.

Figure 6.3. Cash Flow Diagram for Fractional Premiums

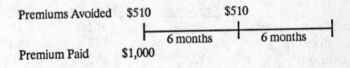

Another way of looking at this is that if you start with $1,000 and pay the first semi-annual premium, you would have to earn 4.08 percent on the remaining $490 to have enough to pay the second semi-annual premium.

Either way, 8.33 percent is the company's implicit charge for the privilege of spreading the premiums throughout the year.

Because this charge is not tax-deductible (although it does increase the cost basis of the policy and therefore reduces the taxable income upon surrender), you should pay the premium annually unless you can earn more than 8.33 percent after tax on your money.

The charge for quarterly and monthly premiums is computed in a similar manner. For example, the implicit charge for quarterly premiums would be the annualized internal rate of return for these four cash flows: −740, 260, 260, 260. (You can determine the answer by trial and error or by using a calculator with an IRR function.)

Table 6.2 shows the implicit charges levied by several well-known companies. As a general rule, you should avoid paying premiums semi-annually or quarterly. Automatic monthly payments may or may not make sense, depending on the company. To eliminate the need for arithmetic, Table 6.3 shows the modal factors that correspond to various annualized carrying charges. If you know the modal factor, you can quickly get an idea of what it costs you to pay the premiums in installments. (If there is a service fee, you will have to adjust the modal factor.)

Table 6.2. Implicit Annualized Charge for Fractional Premiums [a]

	Semi-annual	Quarterly	Monthly
Connecticut General	12.8%	17.1%	11.3%
Executive Life	17.4	17.1	18.6
Guardian	12.8	14.3	6.7
Lincoln National[b]	20.7	20.2	27.0
Massachusetts Mutual	12.8	13.5	13.1
New England Mutual	12.8	14.1	11.3
New York Life	5.8	5.5	5.8
Northwestern Mutual[b]	10.1	10.0	10.3
Phoenix Mutual	10.5	14.1	8.0
Principal Mutual	10.5	14.1	11.3

[a] Based on modal factors in *Best's Flitcraft Compend*, April 1989.
[b] Service fee is charged. Calculation assumes a $2,000 annual premium; implicit charge would be lower for higher premiums.

Table 6.3. Modal Factors Corresponding to Various Annualized Carrying Charges

Annualized Carrying Charge	Semi-Annual	Quarterly	Monthly
30%	0.5327	0.2751	0.0937
25	0.5279	0.2713	0.0921
20	0.5228	0.2673	0.0905
15	0.5175	0.2633	0.0888
12	0.5142	0.2607	0.0877
10	0.5119	0.2590	0.0870
8	0.5096	0.2573	0.0863
6	0.5073	0.2555	0.0856
4	0.5049	0.2537	0.0848
2	0.5025	0.2519	0.0841
0	0.5000	0.2500	0.0833

Finally, be aware that some companies do not refund unearned premiums if you cancel the contract in the middle of the policy year. Therefore if you're thinking of dropping the policy, you might want to pay fractional premiums even if the implicit charge is high.

7

LIFE INSURANCE:
AFTER THE PURCHASE

Your job as an insurance buyer is not done once you've made a purchase. In fact, it has only begun. You must now decide if you want to keep the policy in force, surrender it, exchange it for another policy, add money to it, take money out of it, borrow against it, or make other changes, as permitted by the contract.

TAKING STOCK OF WHAT YOU'VE GOT

A variety of measures can help you decide whether a cash value policy deserves your continued commitment:

- Cash accumulation method (net future value)
- Linton yield method (internal rate of return)
- Yearly rate of return (internal rate of return)
- Change in "asset value"
- Cost per $1,000 of protection
- Expected value/utility
- Emotional needs

Cash Accumulation Method

As with new policies, the idea here is to construct the alternatives so that they have the same outlays and the same death benefits, and then compare the cash values each year. In this case, the outlay is the current cash value of the existing policy and any additional premiums that will be paid. You can compare the existing policy against a proposed cash value policy (by assuming that the cash value is rolled over in a tax-free exchange) or against term insurance (by assuming that the policy is surrendered, income tax is paid, and the after-tax cash value is invested). In either case, you may need to create a hypothetical side fund to equalize the outlays, and you may also have to make adjustments for any differences in the death benefits.

Once you have set up the analysis properly, you can determine how many years it will take before the proposed policy produces a higher cash value. As always, be aware that the illustrated policy values may not be reliable.

Linton Yield Method

As with new policies, the idea here is to determine the rate of return that you would have to earn to produce the same cash values at some future time, given identical outlays and death benefits. The calculation is the same as for new policies, except that the beginning outlay includes the current cash value.

Yearly Rate of Return

The yearly rate of return (ROR) is the rate of return on your investment during each policy year. It is simply an application of the Linton yield method for a series of one-year holding periods. Figure 7.1 shows how the rate of return in the fifth policy year would be calculated for the agent-sold policy in Figure 5.2 on page 120. Here's the reasoning:

At the beginning of the year, the cash surrender value is $9,832. By keeping the policy in force, you are committing this amount plus the annual premium of $3,750. Therefore, your total investment is $13,582. What do you get in return? First, you immediately save the premium for the term insurance you would otherwise have to buy if you dropped the cash value policy. To produce the same total death benefit, you'd need a $236,418 term policy ($250,000 − $13,582). If the cost per

Figure 7.1. How to Calculate the Yearly Rate of Return

$250,000 policy issued to a 45-year-old male nonsmoker
$3,700 annual premium
Assumed term rate: $2.80 per $1,000

Calculations are for Policy Year 5

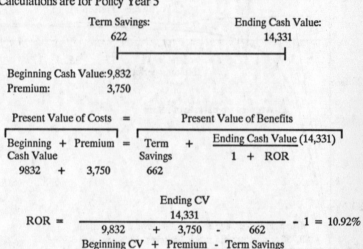

By definition, the yearly rate of return is the discount rate that makes the present value of the benefits (the term savings today and the cash value next year) equal to the present value of the costs (the cash value and premium committed today). By solving the present-value equation in Figure 7.1 for the ROR, you get 10.92 percent. You can interpret this in another way: If you surrendered the cash value policy, added the $3,750 premium, and spent $662 for term insurance, you would have to earn 10.92 percent on the remaining $12,290 (9,832 + 3,750 − 662) in order to have $14,331 at the end of the year. Either way, 10.92 percent represents the rate of return on your investment in the cash value policy during the fifth policy year.

$1,000 is $2.80, the savings would be $662 (2.80 x 236.4). Second, at the end of the year, you have the option to surrender the policy and receive $14,331.

Figure 7.2. **Prospective Buyers and Existing Policyholders Have Different Perspectives: Average Annual and Yearly Rates of Return For an Agent-Sold Universal Life Policy**

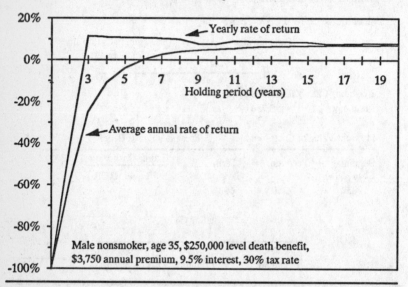

Figure 7.2 shows why it can be a good idea to keep a policy you shouldn't have bought in the first place. As a prospective buyer, you might find this agent-sold policy unattractive because of its low average returns during the first ten years. However, once you've bought it you would probably be ill-advised to drop it. That's especially true during the early years, when the yearly rates of return are boosted by a declining surrender charge.

Because the yearly rate of return is just a special case of the Linton yield, all of the subtleties mentioned earlier apply here as well. The before-tax rate of return, based on the before-tax cash values, can be used as a kind of index to let you know if the policy is competitive with other cash value policies. However, if you want to compare the existing policy with other types of investments, compute the *after-tax* rate of return, based on the *after-tax* cash values at the beginning and end of the year.

Evaluating an Existing Whole Life Policy

Calculating the rate of return on your investment in a participating whole life policy can be tricky because of the various ways in which dividends can be received. Here are some guidelines for avoiding the pitfalls:

- When dividends are received in cash or used to reduce the premium, the dividend received at the beginning of the year should be ignored, because it reflects last year's decision to renew the policy and will be received whether or not you keep the policy in force this year.

- When dividends are used to buy paid-up additions, the investment at the beginning of the year should include the cash value of the paid-up additions. It is appropriate to include the beginning-of-year dividend in this case because you are reinvesting it for one more year, and the total year-end cash value will reflect the growth of the paid-up additions as well as the increase in the guaranteed cash value.

- When dividends are accumulated at interest, you have a problem. Should you treat the dividend account as a separate investment or lump it together with the base policy? What if the interest rate on dividends is significantly above money market rates, as it sometimes is? In this case, the insurance policy is giving you a valuable option to invest some money at above-market rates, and that option exists only as long as you keep the policy in force. One possibility is to calculate the excess interest and treat it as an additional benefit of the base policy, thereby increasing the return. Different approaches are possible, but treating the base policy and dividend account as a unified whole is probably best.

- A similar problem arises if you use dividends to buy one-year term insurance. Do not elect this option if the cost per $1,000 of the company's one-year term will be higher than the cost of a competitive term policy purchased separately. If the one-year term rates are reasonable, the base policy and the one-year term amount should probably be examined together.

Policy loans can present another headache for the conscientious investor. If you can borrow money from the policy and invest it at a higher rate, you'll have to add any "arbitrage" profits to the base policy benefits and then compute the rate of return on the gross investment, ignoring the loan. This is appropriate because the loan transactions put you in the same position as if you told the company, "Let's avoid all the paperwork of this loan stuff, shall we? Just increase my dividend by the extra interest that I could earn." Note that the cost of borrowing is generally no bargain (see "Policy Loans and the Cost of Borrowing" later in this chapter), so arbitrage opportunities are probably rare.

By now it should be clear that traditional whole life policies are difficult to monitor and thus have a hidden cost. In fact, you may have to call the agent several times and write several letters to the company before you can assemble all of the information you need to do the analysis, especially if you want to take account of taxes or policy loans.

If you've gotten this far and still think this sounds like a piece of cake, here's a test using an actual policy issued in 1957 by a large mutual company. The ledger statement is reproduced below (see Figure 7.A). In addition, you need to know that the gross premium, excluding riders, is $189 and that a healthy 53-year-old might reasonably value the insurance protection at about $4.00 per $1,000. Ignoring taxes, what is the projected rate of return for the policy year starting in 1989 and ending in 1990?

For your convenience, here's a blank cash flow diagram. The answer is explained on the next page. No peeking.

Figure 7.A. Sample Policy Illustration, With Personal Information Deleted and Ending at Year 35

ILLUSTRATION FOR POLICY NUMBER: $12,000   65 LIFE

INSURED: MALE AGE 21   POLICY DATE 7-30-57

CURRENT ANNUAL PREMIUM $191.20 INCLUDING WAIVER OF PREMIUM

GROSS PREMIUM $189 EXCLUDING RIDERS

		1	2	3	4	5	6	7	8
								CASH	TOTAL
END	CAL-				CASH	PAYMENT		VALUES	
OF	ENDAR	INSUR-	DIVI-	ANNUAL	VALUE	LESS CV	----	----	PAID-UP
YEAR	YEAR	ANCE*	DEND*	PAYMENT*	INCR.*	INCREASE*	GUAR.	TOTAL*	INSUR.*
32	1989	14822	491	0	544	544CR	4989	6418	13662
33	1990	15506	546	0	609	609CR	5209	7028	14557
34	1991	16258	590	0	667	667CR	5432	7695	15521
35	1992	17082	639	0	729	729CR	5660	8425	16546

DIVIDENDS USED TO REDUCE PREMIUMS - EXCESS DIVIDENDS PURCHASE ADDITIONS

*Assumes no loans after 9-2-88

The most reasonable answer is 10.1 percent. Here's the explanation: At the beginning of the period, you are investing the gross premium, excluding riders, of $189. (Remember that the dividend received at the beginning of the year does not enter into the calculation, because it represents a benefit earned from last year's investment decision.)

You are also investing the cash value that would be available to you if you decided to surrender the policy. At first glance, it appears that this amount is $6,418. But wait! A closer inspection of the numbers in the total cash value column (column 7) reveals that the company is including the entire year-end dividend, even though a portion of it is used to reduce the premium. (You can deduce this by attempting to reconcile the increase in the total cash value ($7,028 - $6,418, or $610) with the increase in the guaranteed cash value ($220) and the year-end dividend of $546. The actual illustration provided no explanation of any of these amounts.) So in fact you are investing $6,418 less the $191 portion of the dividend used to pay the premium, or $6,227. It is only this amount that remains with the insurance company to earn interest.

In exchange for these invested amounts, you will receive about $8,500 of insurance protection (the total death benefit of almost $15,000 less the investment of almost $6,500). Valued at $4 per $1,000, this is worth $34 at the beginning of the year. At the end of the year, you will also have access to a cash value, including the year-end dividend, of $7,028.

As the cash flow diagram shows, the before-tax rate of return for this "investment" is 10.1 percent. It's worth noting that if you mistakenly use $6,418 rather than $6,227 in the calculation, you'll get a rate of return of 6.9 percent—and you might decide to drop the policy.

If you came close to the "right" answer, congratulations. If you didn't, that's even better because the point of this test is that there are many ways to make mistakes. Of course, insurance companies *could* help by providing the necessary information in a clear format, but don't count on it.

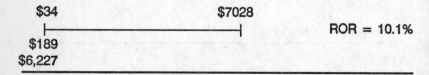

Table 7.1 reiterates what happens if you compute the yearly rate of return on a before-tax basis and then multiply by one minus the marginal tax rate (1 − 0.30, or 0.70). If you try to estimate the after-tax returns indirectly, your results will always be too low, and you might be misled into thinking that the policy should be dropped.

Again, don't do what some agents do: i.e., divide a 10.5 percent before-tax return by 0.70 and proudly announce that the "equivalent before-tax return" in the fifteenth policy year is 15 percent. What a deal—and virtually risk free, too! The fallacy, of course, is that investment gains within a life insurance policy are tax deferred, not tax exempt. Someone who has a $92,000 cash value with a potential tax bill of $10,000 is not in the same position as someone who has $92,000 free and clear.

In general, ROR calculations should exclude riders, fractional premiums, and policy loans. These should be evaluated separately.

Table 7.1. Before-Tax and After-Tax Yearly ROR

Year	Before-Tax Yearly ROR	Multiplied by 0.70	Correct After-Tax Yearly ROR
1	(100.0)%	(70.0)%	(100.0)%
2	(42.7)	(29.9)	(42.7)
3	11.6	8.1	11.6
4	11.1	7.8	11.1
5	10.9	7.6	10.9
10	9.9	6.9	7.8
15	10.5	7.4	8.7
20	9.4	6.6	8.2

For fixed-premium policies with fractional premiums, use the annual premium mode to compute the rate of return. Periodic payment modes can then be treated as a separate decision to borrow from the company. (This treatment might be inappropriate if the company offers a below-market carrying charge, but that's rare.) For flexible-premium policies with premiums paid throughout the year, take into account the timing of each premium in the internal rate of return calculation, and then annualize the result.

When there is an outstanding policy loan, it is usually more informative to examine the policy and the loan separately; in other words, look at the rate of return for the policy without a loan and then look at the effective cost of the loan. The problem with computing the rate of return for the combined policy and loan is that you may get ambiguous results; a low rate of return could mean the policy should be dropped, or it could mean you should repay the loan and keep the policy in force.

Finally, from time to time you may run across a "new method" for computing the yearly rate of return. These alternatives make different assumptions about the timing of the cash flows and may or may not produce significantly different results. The irony is that these so-called new methods—one of which seems to have been quietly dropped in favor of a newer method—are less defensible than what they are intended to replace. The problem of determining the rate of return on an investment in an existing policy was solved long ago, and there's no reason to keep fussing with it.

Change In "Asset Value"

This approach was hinted at in a 1982 article by Professor Ralph A. Winter in *The Journal of Risk and Insurance*:

> The belief that the asset-value of a policy is its cash value has caused an astonishing amount of confusion in life insurance economics. The economic asset represented by the policy at any time is not the cash value *per se* but rather (1) insurance coverage at a premium that is low relative to the cost of entering a new policy combined with (2) the option to withdraw and realize the cash value.

The idea of measuring the rate of return as the percentage change in a policy's economic asset value has never been elaborated, but it may become more relevant in the future. One insurance brokerage firm recently announced that it wanted to create a marketplace where insurance policies could be bought and sold. The prices would be determined through negotiation and would likely be different from the cash values.

Price of Protection

This is probably the most widely disseminated method of evaluating an existing policy. It is used in many financial planning courses and even shows up in the applications section of the owner's manual of some Hewlett-Packard business calculators. A cash value life insurance policy is a package of savings and protection, so the rate of return on the savings portion and the cost of the insurance portion are directly related. To compute the rate of return, you have to make an assumption about the value of the insurance protection. To compute the yearly price per $1,000 of protection, you have to make an assumption about the rate of return. The formula is the same in both cases. To get the rate of return, solve the present-value equation in Figure 7.1 for ROR; to get the price per $1,000 of protection, solve the equation for the term savings. You can then compare the result against term insurance rates or some other benchmark. For the policy in Figure 7.1, the yearly price per $1,000 of protection in the fifth policy year would be:

Assumed Rate of Return	Yearly Price per $1,000 of Protection
6.00%	$0.26
8.00	1.32
9.50	2.09
10.92	2.80

Clearly, the price per $1,000 depends on the assumed rate of return, just as the rate of return depends on the assumed value of the insurance protection. Most investors will probably feel more comfortable thinking in terms of a rate of return on investment rather than a price per $1,000 of protection, but the two approaches are equivalent.

Expected Value and Expected Utility

In discussing the reasons for buying life insurance, we suggested that consumers can "make money" on average by buying competitive policies, because the tax advantages more than offset the insurer's expenses. This is even more likely to be true for existing policies, because the acquisition costs have already been incurred and are reflected as a reduction in the cash surrender value. Given a choice between receiving the invested after-tax cash value and future premiums and receiving the death benefit, most informed beneficiaries would urge you to keep the policy in force. Of course, this argument will carry less weight if the choice is between having enough to eat in your retirement or leaving a larger estate for your heirs.

Emotional Needs

The same nonfinancial considerations that enter into the decision to buy a policy also affect the decision whether or not to keep it in force. The policy may have a personal meaning beyond premiums, cash values, and death benefits, and this should not be overlooked or dismissed.

"Quacky" Comparisons

Some poorly trained agents have their own ways of convincing you to keep a policy in force. Here, in his own words, is a financial quack at work:

> Two of my clients were loyal enough to inform me that someone was trying to replace policies I had sold to them... What I did was to break down, for just this year only, the current net cost of the policies. Both policies were in their fifth year and both were with good par companies. By adding up the increase in the cash value and the increase in dividends for this year only, I was able to show the clients that the net cost was less than 50 cents per $1,000. Why drop the policy at this point and start out with some term policy that is never going to have any cash value?

Quacky comparisons will often be some variation of "...exceeds the premium"; for example, "the dividend exceeds the premium" or "the increase in cash value exceeds the premium." The idea is that the existing policy must be a great deal because you're getting back more than you're putting in. In other words, the insurance is free! (In the example above, the argument is that you're getting back almost as much as you're putting in, so the insurance is very cheap.) The fallacy of such arguments is that the investment in the contract is not just this year's premium; it's the premium plus the cash value. It is just as meaningless to compare dividends with premiums as it is to compare interest earned on the entire balance in a bank account with the latest deposit.

Needless to say, you should not make any investment decisions on the basis of quacky comparisons. In fact, you might consider billing the agent for the time that you wasted listening to him.

The Bottom Line

Make a preliminary judgment about the competitiveness of an existing policy by comparing projected cash values and/or computing the yearly rate of return for the next policy year and several future years. If the policy appears to be uncompetitive, ask the insurance company if there is any way to salvage it; for example, by updating to a variable policy loan interest rate and a higher dividend scale.

Do not give up on an existing policy until you are convinced that it's a loser. If you don't want to spend the time or money required to do a credible analysis, one rule of thumb for old whole life policies is to keep participating (dividend-paying) policies and get rid of nonparticipating ones. However, we prefer credible analyses to rules of thumb.

ALTERNATIVES TO KEEPING THE POLICY IN FORCE

If you decide that your cash value policy no longer meets your needs, you can exchange your policy or select a *nonforfeiture option*.

Policy Exchange

Section 1035 of the Internal Revenue Code provides an option you should carefully consider: You can exchange the contract for another life insurance or annuity contract. A *Section 1035 exchange* offers two advantages. First, it allows you to defer paying taxes on any taxable gain in the policy. Second, if the cost basis exceeds the cash value, it allows you to use the excess cost basis to shield future investment income from taxation. For example, if the policy has a $10,000 cash value and a $15,000 cost basis, you can exchange it for a deferred annuity and let the cash value continue to grow. Because the original cost basis carries over to the annuity, you will not have to pay taxes on the next $5,000 of credited interest.

Although in some respects policy exchanges resemble IRA rollovers, the rules that govern them are more ambiguous and the range of permissible transactions is more limited. Insurance professionals, accountants, and attorneys have had to infer what is acceptable and what is not from IRS private letter rulings on individual cases—rulings that are not binding in future situations.

Most insurance companies have developed forms and procedures to handle Section 1035 exchanges, although delays are not uncommon. The recommended approach is to assign the existing contract to the new insurer, in exchange for a new contract. Keep a copy of all documentation, in case the IRS challenges the exchange.

Articles in trade publications sometimes raise questions about whether a particular transaction would qualify as a tax-free exchange. For example, can you roll over the proceeds from an existing contract into another existing contract? Can you exchange a universal life policy for a single premium whole life policy with a much smaller face amount? There is also some disagreement over the treatment of cash distributions or the elimination of a policy loan. The majority view is that any amounts received should be treated as taxable income, to the extent of the tax-deferred gains in the contract. The minority view is that amounts received should be treated as a tax-free recovery of the cost basis, and as taxable income thereafter.

Given the uncertainties in this area of the tax law, you should not try to be clever. Two taxpayers recently learned this lesson when they withdrew some money from an annuity, purchased a single premium whole life policy, and then exchanged the annuity for another annuity contract. They called this a 1035 exchange. The IRS disagreed, saying they had underreported their taxable incomes by $59,615.54.

Nonforfeiture Options

As an alternative to surrendering or exchanging a policy, you can elect one of the *nonforfeiture options*. The default option is usually *extended term insurance*—a term policy with the same face amount that uses the cash value as a single premium. Another option is to receive a paid-up whole life policy with a lower face amount. The problem in both cases is that it may be hard to determine if the option is reasonably priced.

MAKING ADDITIONAL INVESTMENTS

Flexible premium policies—and some fixed premium policies—allow you to deposit additional amounts. The considerations involved in making this decision were discussed in Chapter 6 ("Choosing the Outlay"). Additional deposits can make sense when the rate of return is attractive, taking into account all of the pricing features of the policy, the anticipated holding period, and income tax rates. For example, some companies pay a higher interest rate on larger account balances, so it may be advantageous to increase your investment.

At the extreme, additional deposits could make it worthwhile to keep a policy that you would otherwise drop. If a policy has high insurance charges, a high interest rate, and no premium load, the overall rate of return will improve with each dollar that you add.

GETTING CASH FROM YOUR POLICY

You can retrieve cash from your policy in two ways, through withdrawals and policy loans.

Withdrawals

Some policies allow you to withdraw a portion of the cash value, with a corresponding reduction in the death benefit. The issue here is: If you need money, should you get it from your life insurance policy or from some other asset you own? The general rule is that you should tap the asset with the lowest expected after-tax rate of return, since that will leave you with more money in the future. If you expect your stocks to go up by 12 percent and your money market account is earning 8 percent, the choice is clear. The *opportunity cost* of taking money out of a life insurance policy depends on the tax treatment of the withdrawal. Unfortunately, this area of the tax law is absurdly complicated, so you may have to ask the insurance company what taxes, if any, will be due before you can make a decision. Briefly, here are the rules:

- Withdrawals from contracts issued before January 1, 1985, are treated as a recovery of the cost basis first, and then as taxable income.

- Withdrawals from modified endowment contracts are treated as taxable income, to the extent of gains within the contract.

- For all other life insurance contracts, the tax treatment depends on the policy year of the withdrawal. During the first fifteen years, withdrawals can be entirely tax free, entirely taxable, or partially taxable, depending on the size of the withdrawal in relation to the face amount, cash value, and premiums paid. There are separate rules for years 1-5 and years 6-15; the rules for years 1-5 are more likely to result in taxable income than the rules for years 6-15. After year 15, withdrawals are treated as a recovery of the cost basis, and then as taxable income.

Suppose you own a universal life policy with a 9 percent gross interest rate, a $20,000 cash value, and a $15,000 cost basis. Your marginal tax rate is 30 percent. You are trying to decide if you should withdraw $1,000 from the policy or from a $20,000 tax-exempt bond fund account that yields 7 percent. One way to answer the question is to look at the change in the after-tax cash value as a result of the withdrawal. By leaving the $1,000 in the policy, you would have $1,090 a year from now, before taxes. If the withdrawal is tax free, the after-tax cost would be 6.3 percent, because you are losing $63 in after-tax cash value.

You might argue that the after-tax cost is really 9 percent, not 6.3 percent. By leaving the $1,000 in the policy, you would have $1,090 that could be withdrawn—we assume, again, tax free—in a year and used to replenish the bond fund. This is true in the short run, but it ignores the higher potential tax liability due to the $1,090 reduction in the cost basis. In fact, the effective cost is somewhere between 6.3 percent and 9 percent, depending on how long you keep the policy in force. If you surrender the policy after a year, you're better off making the withdrawal, since you give up $63 instead of $70. On the other hand, if you make the withdrawal and keep the policy in force for another twenty years, you would have $156,133 of total after-tax wealth ($78,739 in the policy and $77,394 in the bond fund), versus $156,486 ($82,962 in the policy and $73,524 in the bond fund) by using the tax-exempt money. So in that case, the effective cost of the withdrawal is a little above the 7 percent yield on the bond fund.

Nothing is ever simple, especially when you're dealing with tax-deferred investments. If the withdrawal is fully taxable, the after-tax cost is 9 percent. In order to net $1,000 after taxes, you will have to withdraw $1,429. By leaving that money in the policy for a year, the cash value would grow by $1,558, or $1,090 after taxes. If the withdrawal is partially tax free, the opportunity cost will depend on the situation, but the reasoning is the same.

Although rules of thumb are always risky, this example suggests that you should generally look to other assets before drawing on your life insurance cash values. In addition to having a significant opportunity cost, withdrawals and subsequent repayments increase your chances of running afoul of some arcane tax provision. If you need to access your cash values on a short-term basis, a policy loan may be preferable. For long-term needs, a withdrawal will often be the better choice, despite the complexity.

Policy Loans and the Cost of Borrowing

Question: When is 2 percent the same as 11 percent? *Answer:* When 2 percent is the *net cost of borrowing* and 11 percent is what it really costs.

No feature of today's life insurance products is more widely misunderstood than the cost of borrowing. After years of being told by insurance companies, agents, stockbrokers, and other financial advisors that they can borrow against a life insurance policy at a low cost, consumers can be forgiven for actually believing it. To sort out the confusion, let's look at what happens when you borrow against a typical universal life policy. In this example, the credited interest rate is 9 percent, and the policy loan interest rate is 8 percent. When you borrow money, the company sets aside an offsetting amount of your cash value as collateral. It pays 6 percent interest on the borrowed portion of your cash value and continues to credit 9 percent on the unborrowed portion.

What does it cost you to borrow? First, you have to pay the 8 percent policy loan interest. Second, you lose 3 percent interest—the difference between the 9 percent you would have earned if you hadn't borrowed and the 6 percent you actually get. Therefore, the cost of borrowing is 11 percent, ignoring taxes. But the insurance industry sees it differently. They say that the *net loan cost* is only 2 percent—the difference between the 8 percent they charge and the 6 percent they credit—and they highlight this supposedly valuable feature in their sales materials. You can't fault their arithmetic—8 minus 6 does indeed equal 2—but you can certainly question the relevance of it. The net loan cost doesn't tell you anything important, and it can easily mislead you into thinking that the cost of borrowing is far less than it really is.

The before-tax cost of borrowing is similar for other types of life insurance products. With traditional whole life products, many companies adjust dividends to reflect borrowing activity—a practice called *direct recognition*. In these cases, the cost of borrowing is equal to the policy loan interest rate plus any decrease in the dividend. This creates a problem for policy-owners, because you need to obtain two sets of dividend projections to figure out whether it makes sense to borrow. For universal life, as our example shows, the cost of borrowing is equal to the policy loan interest rate plus any reduction in the credited rate. Single premium whole life products that were issued before the 1988 tax law changes often contain a flam-boyant "zero net cost" loan provision—when you borrow accumulated interest, the loan interest rate is exactly matched by the credited rate—but the cost-of-borrowing calculation is the same as for universal life. If the credited rate on unborrowed amounts is 8 percent and the policy loan interest rate is 6 percent, the cost of borrowing is 6 percent plus the 2 percent reduction in the interest rate. When you borrow against variable life products, an offsetting portion of your cash value is transferred to the company's general account and is credited with a fixed rate of interest, such as 6 percent. The cost of borrowing is the policy loan interest rate plus the difference between what you would have earned on the selected funds and the fixed-account rate.

Note that all of these comments refer to policies that are not modified endowment contracts. As a result of the Technical and Miscellaneous Revenue Act of 1988, loans against modified endowment contracts are treated as taxable distributions, to the extent of any gains within the policy. This will generally make such loans prohibitively expensive whenever there are accumulated gains (i.e., whenever the cash value exceeds the cost basis).

The decision to borrow against a life insurance policy should be made in the context of your entire balance sheet. In general, you should borrow money only when the after-tax cost of borrowing is less than the after-tax rate of return on your assets. From a strictly financial point of view, it makes sense to prepay an 11 percent mortgage if your money is earning 8 percent in a certificate of deposit. Similarly, it makes little sense to borrow money at 10 percent from your broker to buy stocks on margin if your other assets are earning less than that. By taking a broader view, you avoid the common mistake of trying to double the return on your investment by putting only 50 percent down.

The reasoning is similar for life insurance. Should you pay back an outstanding loan? If the loan costs 8 percent after tax and you have some assets that are earning 7 percent, then the answer is yes. Unfortunately, the decision is rarely that easy. First, it's not always obvious what the cost of borrowing is on an after-tax basis. Is the policy loan interest tax deductible or not? And what is the after-tax cost of lost tax-deferred interest? Second, policy loans can affect future death benefits as well as cash values, so it may be hard to compare the alternatives properly.

Suppose you have $150,000—$50,000 in a single premium whole life policy and $100,000 in other assets—and you want to spend $4,000 a year to supplement your other sources of income. Should you borrow against the life insurance policy or draw on your other assets? Additional assumptions are:

1. The single premium whole life policy has a cost basis of $40,000, an 8 percent interest rate, and a "0 percent net

cost of borrowing" against accumulated interest; i.e., the company charges 6 percent on the loan but credits 6 percent on the borrowed portion of the cash value. It is grandfathered under the 1988 tax law, so loans are not taxable distributions. The policy matures at age 95.

2. The annual before-tax rate of return on other assets is 10 percent, and all gains are taxed each year.

3. You are 55 years old and in the 30 percent tax bracket.

Table 7.2 shows two scenarios: First, what happens if you borrow $4,000 a year against the single premium whole life policy and let your other assets grow. Second, what happens if you withdraw $4,000 a year from other assets and let the single premium whole life policy grow.

If you borrow against the life insurance policy, you'll leave less money to your heirs, and you'll also have less money for yourself if you decide to drop the policy. In the later years, the potential tax liability upon surrender actually exceeds the net cash value, so you would have to draw upon your other assets to pay the bill. It's clear from this example that the "zero net cost" loan provision is a misnomer. The opportunity cost of usingother assets is 7 percent after tax, while the cost of using a policy loan is the 6 percent nondeductible loan interest plus the after-tax portion of the 2 percent reduction in the credited interest rate.

The Bottom Line

In general, the after-tax cost of a policy loan against policies that are not modified endowment contracts should be reasonably close to the cost of a home equity loan or a margin loan. Because a policy loan may be faster and more convenient, it may be the preferred choice. Policy loans against modified endowment contracts are currently treated as taxable distributions, so they should generally be avoided.

Table 7.2. Two Distribution Scenarios

Scenario 1: A $4,000 annual loan from SPWL; let other assets grow

| | Other Assets | Single Premium Whole Life | | |
| | After-Tax | | Loan | Net CV | Net Death |
Age	Balance	Gross CV	Balance	After-Tax	Benefit
55	$100,000	$50,000	$0	$47,000	$75,000
65	196,715	102,723	52,723	31,183	70,545
75	386,968	197,142	147,142	2,857	59,857
85	761,226	366,233	316,233	(47,870)	68,312
95	1,497,446	669,048	619,048	(138,714)	(138,714)

Scenario 2: A $4,000 annual withdrawal from other assets; let SPWL grow

| | Other Assets | Single Premium Whole Life | | |
| | After-Tax | Gross | After-Tax | Death |
Age	Balance	Cash Value	Cash Value	Benefit
55	$100,000	$50,000	$47,000	$75,000
65	141,449	107,946	87,562	129,535
75	222,986	233,048	175,134	244,700
85	383,382	503,133	364,193	528,289
95	698,905	1,086,226	772,358	772,358

Summary: Scenarios 1 and 2

| | If You Borrow Against Your Life Insurance | | If You Withdraw Money From Your Other Assets | |
| | Total Living | Total Death | Total Living | Total Death |
Age	Benefit	Benefit	Benefit	Benefit
55	$147,000	$175,000	$147,000	$175,000
65	227,898	267,260	229,011	270,984
75	389,825	446,825	398,120	467,686
85	713,356	829,538	747,575	911,671
95	1,358,732	1,358,732	1,471,263	1,471,263

8

ANNUITIES

OVERVIEW

Consider investing in an annuity if you want to defer taxes on your savings and/or if you want to receive a series of payments that you cannot outlive.

A deferred annuity is a contract that provides a lump sum payment or a series of periodic payments, after an accumulation period. An immediate annuity is a contract that provides a series of periodic payments in exchange for a single premium.

An annuity purchase involves a series of choices. Figure 8.1 provides a checklist to help you in the decision-making process.

Table 8.1 shows the types of annuities available to individual investors.

Table 8.1. Types of Annuities

General Account	Separate Account
• Deferred	• Deferred
—Fixed:	—Variable:
Single premium	Single premium
Flexible premium	Flexible premium
	—Market-value-adjusted
• Immediate	• Immediate

Deferred Annuities

During the accumulation period, your money grows tax deferred. At the end of this period—often at or before age 85—you can

Figure 8.1. Annuities: A Checklist

I. BEFORE THE PURCHASE

1. What is your definition of a successful search?
   ____ the *best* product (sorry, this book can't help you)
   ____ top decile in expected performance
   ____ top quartile in expected performance
   ____ good value for your money
   ____ better than a taxable investment

2. Who will advise you?
   ____ do it yourself
   ____ commission-based agent or broker
   ____ fee-and-commission financial planner
   ____ fee-for-service consultant or financial planner
   ____ accountant
   ____ attorney
   ____ consulting actuary

3. What type of contract will you buy?
   ____ deferred annuity
   ____ fixed
   ____ variable
   ____ market value adjusted
   ____ immediate annuity

4. How will you decide how much to invest?
   ____ estimated value of tax deferral
   ____ minimum/maximum allowed by contract
   ____ liquidity constraints
   ____ asset allocation
   ____ rough guess
   ____ formalized decision-making techniques
   ____ optimization models

5. How will you choose among several companies?
   ____ ratings
   ____ analysis of financial statements
   ____ management quality
   ____ valuation actuary's report
   ____ reputation
   ____ quality of service to customers
   ____ other judgments

6. How will you choose among several products?
   ____ interest rate or fund performance
   ____ projected cash value, after all charges
   ____ company's reputation and track record
   ____ profit testing
   ____ other features

Continued

7. Who will own the contract?
   ____ investor
   ____ annuitant
   ____ other relative or associate
   ____ nonnatural person (e.g., corporation, etc.)

8. Who will the annuitant(s) be?
   ____ owner
   ____ spouse
   ____ other relative or associate

9. Who will the beneficiary(ies) be?
   ____ spouse
   ____ other relative or associate
   ____ estate or other entity

10. What other decisions might be required?
   ____ investment allocation (variable annuities)
   ____ settlement option
   ____ riders (if any)

_____

II. AFTER THE PURCHASE

1. ____ Will you keep the policy in force/ surrender it/exchange it?
2. ____ Will you add money/ withdraw money/ borrow?
3. ____ Will you annuitize?

---

surrender the contract for a lump-sum payment or elect one of the annuitization options. These options may include:

- Life income—an income for life, with nothing remaining upon your death

- Life income with 10 or 20 years certain—an income for life, with payments guaranteed to continue to your beneficiary until 10 or 20 years after the annuitization date

- Life income with installment refund—an income for life, with payments guaranteed to continue to your beneficiary until the total amount received equals the fund balance that was annuitized

- Life income with cash refund—an income for life, with a lump sum payment at death equal to the difference between the annuitized fund balance and the total payments received

- Joint-and-survivor life income—an income for your life, with payments continued at the same or a reduced level for the life of your survivor

- Fixed-period or fixed-amount installments—a series of payments for a specified period or amount (you tell them how much and they'll tell you how long, or you tell them how long and they'll tell you how much)

- Customized payments—a series of payments that matches your own needs. This is offered at the company's discretion and is generally only available for larger amounts.

Fixed deferred annuities credit interest based on the earnings of the company's general account, with no risk to principal. Variable annuities allow you to choose among several investment options, and the corresponding returns—positive or negative—are passed through to you.

Market-value-adjusted, or *modified guaranteed*, deferred annuities are a hybrid of fixed and variable. These products provide a guaranteed interest rate for up to ten years, but adjustments are made to the cash value if you decide to surrender the contract before the end of the guarantee period. The idea is to link the interim cash values to changes in the market value of the underlying investments caused by fluctuating interest rates. This reduces the insurer's risk and, in theory, allows the company to offer a higher interest rate. Market-value-adjusted annuities may become more important in the future, but they are sold by only a few companies today. For now, their main attraction is that they give you some flexibility in choosing a guarantee period.

Immediate Annuities

As the name implies, an immediate annuity provides a series of periodic payments as soon as you pay the premium (or *consideration*) to the company. The annuitization options are similar to those for deferred annuities.

With fixed immediate annuities, the payments are generally guaranteed to remain the same regardless of future changes in interest rates or mortality. In contrast, with variable immediate annuities, the payments can go up or down depending on the investment performance of the selected funds. Most stand-alone immediate annuities are of the fixed-interest variety. Variable immediate annuities are usually obtained by electing one of the annuitization options within a variable deferred annuity.

Split-funded annuities are a combination of immediate and deferred. A portion of your premium is annuitized, while the remainder grows at current interest rates to provide future income.

How a Modified Guaranteed Annuity Works

A modified guaranteed annuity offers guaranteed terminal values but allows interim values to vary up or down with changing interest rates. The market value adjustment formula is always stated in the contract. Here's a typical example:

Suppose you invest $10,000 in an annuity with a 9 percent interest rate, guaranteed for five years. Two years from now, interest rates move up to 11 percent and you decide to roll your money into a different product. Under one company's formula, you would take your expected account value at the end of year 5 ($10,000 x 1.09^5, or $15,386) and discount it back to the end of year 2 at 11.5 percent (11 percent plus a surcharge of 0.5 percent). The result would be $11,110 ($15,386/1.115^3)–or $771 less than the year 2 account value of $11,881 ($10,000 x 1.09^2). Any fixed surrender charges would then be subtracted to get the cash surrender value.

Market value adjustments can work in your favor if interest rates go down. In the example above, a drop in rates to 7 percent would cause your cash value to increase from $11,110 to $12,385 ($15,386/1.075^3). These swings are different from what they would be with zero-coupon bonds because the company uses a less favorable discount rate in the calculations; in this example, there is a surcharge of 0.5 percent, so the discount rates are 11.5 percent and 7.5 percent, instead of 11 and 7 percent. That means that you lose more when rates go up, and you make less when rates go down.

Tax Considerations

As with life insurance, the tax treatment of annuity products is complex, in part because the laws keep changing. You can probably find answers to most of your questions in *Tax Facts 1* (see Appendix I). Table 8.2 provides a brief overview and necessarily omits some details. If the tax treatment is not clear in your situation, you may have to request a private letter ruling from the IRS.

As indicated in Table 8.2, payments received during the annuity period are part income and part return of capital. In general, the amount you can exclude from taxable income is determined by dividing the total investment in the contract by the total *expected return* as of the annuity starting date. However, the actual steps in the calculation depend on the payment option you have chosen. To see how it's done, let's assume that a 65-year-old man pays $10,000 for a monthly life income of $93, with no survivor benefit. The taxable income each year would be computed as follows:

1. Determine the total annual payment: $93 x 12 = $1,116.
2. Look up the annuitant's life expectancy in the appropriate IRS table, using the age nearest the annuity starting date. Unisex Tables V - VII are used if some or all of the premiums were paid after 6/30/86. Gender-based Tables I-III are used if all of the premiums were paid before 7/1/86; however, you can also elect to use the unisex tables.
   Life expectancy at age 65 per IRS Table V: 20.0 years.
3. Determine the total expected return by multiplying the annual payment by the annuitant's life expectancy: $1,116 x 20 = $22,320.
4. Determine the exclusion ratio by dividing the investment in the contract ($10,000) by the total expected return. Round to the nearest tenth of a percent: 10,000/22,320 = 44.8%.
5. Determine how much of the annual payment is return of capital: $1,116 x .448 = $500.
6. Determine how much of the payment is taxable income: $1,116 - $500 = $616.

In this example, the annuitant can exclude $500 of the annuity payments from taxable income for twenty years, until the entire investment in the contract is recovered. After that, all of the payments will be taxable.

To determine the taxable portion of the payments for other annuity options, such as a life income with twenty years certain, you have to adjust the investment in the contract for the value of the survivor's benefits, in accordance with IRS tables. The exclusion ratio is then determined in the usual manner (see *Tax Facts 1* for examples.)

For variable annuities, the amount that can be excluded each year is equal to the total investment in the contract divided by the expected number of payments, based on IRS tables. As before, the total investment must be adjusted for the value of any survivor's benefits. All payments become taxable once the entire investment has been recovered.

Owner/Annuitant/Beneficiary

An annuity contract can have one or more owners, annuitants, and beneficiaries. Terminology can be a problem here, so make sure you understand who is entitled to what.

The *owner* pays money into the contract and retains the right to surrender it for cash, to determine how the payouts will be made, and to change the beneficiary.

The *annuitant* is the person who receives the annuity payments and whose life expectancy is used to determine the payment amounts. In some cases, however, the "measuring life" will be different from the payment recipient.

The *beneficiary* receives any death benefits due under the contract if the owner dies during the accumulation period or if the annuitant dies during the annuity period. If there is more than one owner, the death benefit is paid at the first death; if there is more than one annuitant, the death benefit is paid at the last death. The owner's beneficiary (also called the *contingent owner*) can be different from the annuitant's beneficiary. If the beneficiary is not alive, the benefits may be paid to a *contingent beneficiary*.

In many cases, the annuity contract will be purchased by an investor to provide an income in retirement, and the owner and

Table 8.2. Taxation of Annuities

General Rule	Exceptions

During the Accumulation Period

General Rule

- Investment gains within the contract are tax-deferred.
- Any taxable gains are treated as ordinary income, not capital gains.
- Losses from surrender of an annuity contract are ordinary losses, not capital losses, and are deductible against ordinary income.
- Withdrawals and loans are taxable distributions to the extent of income within the contract.
- Multiple contracts issued by same company to same owner during a calendar year are treated as one contract for purposes of determining amount of taxable income from distributions.
- There is a 10% penalty tax on taxable income realized from withdrawals, loans, or surrenders.

- Upon death of owner, accumulated value must be distributed within 5 years or annuitized over the beneficiary's lifetime.

- Upon death of annuitant, beneficiary is taxed on all accrued gains.

- Taxable portion of annuity death benefit is "income in respect of a decedent," so beneficiary is entitled to an income tax deduction for applicable portion of estate tax paid, if any.
- When an annuity is given from one person to another, donor realizes taxable income to the extent of gains within the contract.

Exceptions

- Contracts owned by non-natural persons, if issued after 2/28/86.

- Deductible loss is not allowed if annuity is purchased for personal reasons and not for profit.
- For contracts issued before 8/14/82, withdrawals and loans are treated as a return of principal first, income second.
- Does not apply to contracts issued before 10/22/88 or to immediate annuities.

- Distributions after age 59.5, or due to disability, owner's death, or annuitization over life expectancy; payments allocable to investment in contract before 8/14/82.
- Contracts issued before 1/19/85. For contracts issued after 1/19/85 where beneficiary is surviving spouse, distributions can be postponed by treating spouse as the contractholder.
- If beneficiary elects within 60 days to receive proceeds under a life income or installment option, payments are taxed according to annuity rules (see below). For variable annuity contracts issued 10/21/79, death proceeds are received income-tax-free.

- Transfers between spouses or as part of a divorce; gains allocable to investments made before 8/14/82. For contracts issued before 4/23/87, tax is deferred until maturity or surrender.

Table 8.2., Continued

- An annuity contract can be exchanged for another annuity contract in a tax-free exchange. Contracts issued before 8/14/82 will not lose their favorable tax treatment if exchanged.
- Annuity values are included in the gross estate of the deceased annuitant in the same proportion as the annuitant's premium payments (i.e., 100% includible if annuitant paid all premiums, 50% if only half paid, etc.)

- There are limitations on what transactions qualify as a tax-free exchange.

- All values payable to estate are includible, regardless of who paid the premiums.

During the Annuity Period

- A portion of each payment represents a tax-free return of capital, and the re-mainder is taxable income. The return-of-capital amount is based on the the ratio of the investment in the contract to the total expected return. This *exclusion ratio* applies until the entire investment in the contract has been recovered; after that, all payments are taxable.
- Upon death of annuitant, payments received by beneficiary are tax-free until the entire investment in the contract has been re-covered; after that, all payments are taxable. If the entire investment cannot be recovered, the beneficiary can claim a tax-deductible loss.
- Upon death of owner, remaining value must be distributed at least as rapidly as under the method in effect at the date of death.
- When an annuity is given from one person to another, the donor realizes taxable income. This increases the investment in the con-tract, and the exclusion ratio is then determined in the normal manner.
- Annuity values are included in the gross estate of the deceased annuitant in the same proportion as the annuitant's premium payments.
- Purchase of a joint-and-survivor annuity by one annuitant is a gift of a future interest to the other annuitant and does not qualify for the $10,000 annual exclusion.

- For variable annuities, divide total investment by life expectancy.

- If the annuity starting date is before 1/1/87, the exclusion applies to all pay-ments, even after the entire contract has been recovered.
- If the annuity starting date is before 7/2/86, a deductible loss is not allowed.

- Contracts issued before 1/19/85; con-tracts issued after 1/19/85 where the beneficiary is the surviving spouse.
- For contracts issued before 4/23/87, the exclusion ratio does not change.

- All values payable to estate are are includible, regardless of who paid the premiums.

- If transaction is between two spouses, marital deduction is allowed.

annuitant will be the same. The other spouse, if any, if often named as the contingent owner and beneficiary, in order to postpone taxes beyond the first death. Other configurations are possible, but make sure that you understand the income, estate, and gift tax consequences, or seek professional advice.

DEFERRED ANNUITIES

Advantages and Disadvantages

Deferred annuities offer general advantages, such as:

- Investment income within the contract is tax-deferred. The actual value of this benefit depends on several factors, including the length of the holding period, the rate of return, contract expenses, and future tax rates.

- Investment income within an annuity is not included in "modified adjusted gross income," which is used to determine the taxable portion of Social Security payments. (But, this can work to your disadvantage in later years as the deferred income is received. The overall impact depends on your own situation.)

- Death benefits can be paid directly to the beneficiary without going through probate. This saves time, legal costs, and publicity.

- In some states, cash values are protected from creditors, an important feature for likely targets of lawsuits. However, you have to plan ahead. If you put your assets into an annuity while the process server is knocking on your door, you may get an unwanted education in what fraudulent conveyance means.

Among the disadvantages are the following:

- Contract expenses or unfavorable changes in the tax laws can offset some or all of the gains from tax deferral.

What is the After-Tax Rate of Return on a Tax-Deferred Investment?

If a certificate of deposit yields 9 percent and your marginal tax rate is 30 percent, the after-tax rate of return is 6.3 percent [9 x (1-0.30)]. But what if the 9 percent is tax deferred, as with a single premium deferred annuity or an Individual Retirement Account? For tax-deferred investments, the after-tax rate of return is generally taken to be the percentage change in after-tax liquidation value from one year to the next.

Example 1: Deductible Individual Retirement Account

Suppose the beginning balance in your deductible IRA is $10,000, the ending balance is $11,000, and tax rates remain constant at 30 percent. The after-tax rate of return would be calculated as follows:

Proceeds from IRA after paying taxes:
```
Beginning   $7,000  (10,000 x 0.70)
Ending       7,700  (11,000 x 0.70)
% increase:    10%
```

This shows that the after-tax rate of return on a deductible IRA (or any other qualified retirement plan) is the same as the before-tax rate of return, as long as tax rates do not change.

On the other hand, if taxes increase from 30 to 35 percent during the period, the aftertax rate of return would be:

```
Beginning   $7,000  (10,000 x 0.70)
Ending       7,150  (11,000 x 0.65)
% increase   2.14%
```

Example 2: Single Premium Deferred Annuity

Suppose you put $10,000 into an SPDA yielding 9 percent, guaranteed for five years. What is the after-tax rate of return in the fifth year, if tax rates are constant at 30 percent?

Year 5	Surrender Value		
	Before Tax	After Tax	
Begin	$14,116	$12,881	[14,116 - (4,116 gain x 30% tax)]
End	15,386	13,770	[15,386 - (5,386 gain x 30% tax)]
% increase in after-tax surrender value:	6.9%		

Note that, the after-tax rate of return (6.9 percent) is less than the after-tax rate of return on an IRA (9.0 percent) and more than the after-tax rate of return on a taxable CD (6.3 percent). The SPDA beats the CD because taxes have been postponed on past earnings, and the postponed taxes have remained invested within the contract to earn additional interest.

- For fixed annuities, the credited interest rate may not keep pace with taxable yields on certificate of deposits, especially during periods of rising interest rates.

- Liquidity is limited, because:

  - There is usually a surrender charge during the early years.

  - There is a 10 percent penalty tax (with some exceptions) for withdrawals, loans, and surrenders before age 59 1/2.

  - The after-tax cost of accessing your money in an annuity, even without the penalty tax, is probably higher than the cost of using your other funds. If the amount withdrawn is fully taxable, the after-tax cost is the same as the investment yield; that is, it effectively costs 8 percent after tax to remove money from a fixed annuity paying 8 percent interest.

Fixed Deferred Annuities

Fixed annuities are classified as *single premium deferred annuities* (SPDA) or *flexible premium deferred annuities* (FPDA), in accordance with the number of deposits that are allowed.

Product features. Some important features are:

Credited interest rate. All fixed annuities have a minimum guaranteed interest rate—usually 3-6 percent—but current rates are structured in a variety of ways. As with CDs, there may be different guarantee periods, ranging from less than one year to as many as ten years. Some companies pay higher interest on larger account balances while others promise to pay bonus interest after some number of years. As with life insurance, there are different ways of apportioning investment income among contractholders. Under the *portfolio-average* approach, the same rate is paid on all contracts, regardless of when the money was deposited. Under the *investment-year* (or *investment generation*) method, deposits are grouped by the period of receipt, and the credited rate for each pool is determined separately. *Two-tiered* annuities have a dual interest rate; you get a higher rate if you annuitize the account balance and a lower rate if you surrender the contract for a lump sum. This requires the company to maintain two parallel series of account balances, and is designed to lock you into the company's own annuity options.

No interest-rate risk. The surrender value is based on the book value of the company's assets, so the company bears the investment risk if interest rates go up and the market value of its portfolio drops.

Contract loads. Most SPDAs have no front-end load or annual maintenance fee, but they do have a surrender charge. This ranges from 4 percent to 10 percent of either the initial premium or the account balance, and it often declines by 1 percent a year. The surrender charge is usually waived in the event of death or annuitization, and it will be limited to the amount of accumulated interest if the contract has a money-back guarantee. With FPDAs, the surrender charge may be made on a *premium-year* basis (there is a separate measuring period for each deposit) or on a *contract-year* basis (the measuring period is based on the date of issue). There may also be an annual maintenance fee.

Penalty-free withdrawals. Although there may be a small processing fee, some contracts allow you to withdraw up to 10 percent of the account balance each year without a surrender charge. This is of little value, since you should generally not make withdrawals from an annuity except as a last resort.

Bailout provision. Some companies waive the surrender charge for a specified window period (typically 30-90 days) if the credited rate drops below some a predetermined threshold—for example, one percent below the initial rate. This provision eliminates the possibility of a bait-and-switch; i.e., the company lures you in with a high rate and then drops it the following year. However, the provision is of no value if interest rates go up and the company lags behind, if interest rates fall and you have no better place to put your money, or if interest rates remain the same and the company lowers its rate to just above the threshold.

Guaranteed and current settlement options. Although many policyholders choose a lump-sum payment, you do have other options, such as monthly payments for life. Annuitization should be viewed as a separate investment decision, and you should shop around for the best rates when you're ready. Note that some contracts require you to annuitize the balance, or receive a lump-sum payment, by age 85.

Death benefit. If the owner or annuitant dies, most contracts pay the entire account value to the beneficiary, without surrender charges.

Special situations. Two types of SPDAs have features that are different from the traditional product.

CD annuities. Also called *certificates of annuity*, these mimic certificates of deposit by allowing contractholders to surrender without penalty at the end of each interest rate guarantee period. The length of the guarantee can vary from one to ten years, and there is usually a window of 30-60 days during which you can elect to withdraw your money or renew at the current rate. If you surrender the contract at any other time, you have to pay a surrender charge. CD annuities pay an ongoing commission to the selling agent of 0.5-1.0 percent a year, and the interest rate tends to follow taxable CD yields more closely than with other annuities.

Tontines. Tontines have been around since the seventeenth century, when they were popular in several European countries. In the early versions, each investor bought a share, and the collected funds provided a pool of income that was divided among the surviving shareholders each year. As shareholders died, each survivor's share of the total income would grow, and upon the last death the principal would revert to the state. The shareholders' heirs received nothing, but the chance to have a fabulous income in old age kept tontines alive despite exaggerated projections and an occasional default.

A Minnesota company has come up with an SPDA tontine for the twenty-first century. Upon death or surrender, the company returns only your principal; the accumulated interest is divided among the remaining contractholders. This is bad news if you die or drop out, but it's good news if you live. Assuming reasonable mortality and no lapses, a 55-year-old man might receive 20 percent more income at age 75 than with a traditional product. And if just 2 percent of the contractholders drop out each year, his income could be 50 percent higher. (The flip side, of course, is that those who drop out will wish they'd never heard of the product.)   At a time when so many

Are Guaranteed Annuity Rates Worth Anything?

When you elect an annuity option, your monthly payments are based on the company's current annuity rates, but these can never be less than the guaranteed rates specified in the contract. These guaranteed rates are computed using a low interest rate, such as 4 percent, and low death rates. If mortality continues to improve during the next few decades, what are the chances that this guarantee will actually be of value to you someday?

Let's say the guaranteed monthly life income for a 65-year-old man is $6.84 per $1000 account balance, based on 4 percent interest and the 1983 Individual Annuity Mortality Table. Assume, also, that mortality improves by 2 percent a year–an optimistic projection.

If future interest rates are 8 percent, it would take 130 years for mortality rates to improve to the point where then-current annuity rates–based on 8 percent interest would be less than the guaranteed rate in the contract. If interest rates are only 6 percent, it would still take 35 years before the guaranteed rates were "in the money," as options traders would say.

In short, you can pretty much forget about the guaranteed annuity rates.

---

people are wondering how they're going to pay their bills in old age, this idea is bound to be attractive. In theory, it lets the elderly keep more of their money, with reduced transfers to succeeding generations who might not need the funds so urgently. The obvious problem is that you're locked into one company's contract for life and cannot leave without an onerous penalty if your circumstances or tax laws change or if the product does not live up to your expectations. Until this problem is resolved, SPDA tontines are most appropriate for people who trust insurance companies and don't know very much about the scandal-ridden history of tontines.

Pricing considerations. Many of the problems that confront the manufacturer of life insurance products also apply to fixed annuities. From the company's point of view, an annuity contract is an investment project, just like a factory or other enterprise. When the contract is issued, the insurer has to invest some of its own capital, because the money that it receives is less than the acquisition costs that are paid out, the reserve that must be established, and the *target surplus* that the insurer keeps as a cushion against future risks. For a $20,000 SPDA contract, the numbers might look like this:

Premium received	$20,000
Agent's commission (4%)	(800)
Other acquisition costs	(200)
Reserve	(19,020)
Target surplus	(950)
Insurer's investment	$970

The company recovers its investment and makes a profit from the spread between what it earns on its assets and what it credits to its contractholders. A typical spread might be 1-2 percent. For low-load products, the spread should naturally be less, because the acquisition costs are lower. All other things being equal, the interest rate on a low-load annuity should be about 0.25-0.75 percent higher than the rate on an agent-sold product.

In general, the longer the guarantee period, the higher the reserve that must be held by the company. This is one reason why the interest rate is often lower for longer guarantee periods; for example, a company might pay 8.5 percent for one year and 8.25 percent for three years. This pattern is different from the usual yield curve for CDs, Treasury securities, and other fixed-income investments, where the issuer does not have the same reserve requirements that insurance companies do.

Early lapses are not as important for annuities as they are for life insurance, because the company can recover its acquisition costs—and sometimes even make money—from the declining surrender charge. At worst, the cost to consumers is probably about 0.25 percent; that is, a company might be able to pay 0.25 percent more each year if it knew in advance that the contracts would stay in force, instead of being churned every few years by stockbrokers and agents seeking more commission income. Persistency tends to be worse for contracts with multi-year guarantee periods. This means that companies have to recover their initial investment over a shorter period, which also explains why the credited interest rates on these products are often lower.

As with life insurance, book-value-based cash surrender values expose the insurer to considerable investment risk. If contract-holders decide to cash out during a period of rising interest rates, the company may experience losses on its investment portfolio. In order to estimate potential profits and losses more reliably, many insurers have been incorporating asset/liability analysis into the pricing process.

The most sophisticated pricing methodology couples an economic scenario generator with a dynamic cash flow model for projecting profits on a group of contracts. The cash flow model links together various pricing assumptions, such as lapse rates and the credited rate on competing products, so that a change in one factor is reflected logically throughout the model. The scenario generator spews out hundreds of sets of economic assumptions, in accordance with predetermined probabilities of occurrence. These scenarios are then run through the cash flow model, and the results are tabulated to show the probability distribution of profits and losses. In this way, the insurer can test various pricing strategies, such as:

- constant spread—the credited interest rate is always X percent less than the insurer's portfolio yield

- targeted spread with constraints—the company tries to credit X percent less than its portfolio yield, but it will never credit much more or much less than its competitors

- bait-and-switch—the company lures buyers in with a high rate and then lowers it after the initial guarantee period

Some companies will not put an annuity product on the market without careful analysis. When it comes time to sell the product to *you*, however, careful analysis just gets in the way, so they'll show you numbers like those in Table 8.3.

More likely than not, the comparison will conveniently ignore any taxes due on the annuity proceeds, except perhaps in a footnote. And don't expect the company to tell you much about its pricing strategy.

Table 8.3. Taxable Versus Tax-Deferred Investment

End of Year	Taxable CD 8% Interest 33% Tax Rate	Tax-Deferred SPDA 8% Interest
0	$10,000	$10,000
5	12,983	14,693
10	16,856	21,589
20	28,413	46,610
30	47,893	100,627

Should you buy it? There are several ways you can decide how much to invest in a fixed annuity.

Estimated value of tax deferral. The primary attraction of fixed annuities is that interest grows tax-deferred. Table 8.4 provides several perspectives on what this benefit is worth in terms of annual after-tax returns. From these numbers, you can see that:

- As you might expect, tax deferral is more valuable for longer holding periods. For example, if you invest $10,000 in a CD earning 8 percent and are in the 33 percent bracket, you'll have $16,856 in ten years; the annual after tax return is 5.36 percent. On the other hand, if you invest $10,000 for ten years in an SPDA yielding 8 percent, upon surrender you'll have $17,765 after paying taxes. The equivalent annual after-tax return is 5.91 percent, or an increase of about 0.6 percent. But if you can keep the annuity going for thirty years, the difference in after-tax returns grows to 1.4 percent a year.
- Tax deferral is more valuable for investors in higher tax brackets (Table 8.4., part A).
- Tax deferral is more valuable at higher interest rates (Table 8.4., part B).
- The benefits of tax deferral are reduced or eliminated if the annuity proceeds are subject to a higher tax rate (Table 8.4, part C). A future jump in tax rates by 10 percent has the same effect as the current 10 percent penalty tax; i.e., it erases the benefits of years of tax deferral. This is also

relevant for people who live in high tax states, since annuity proceeds will be taxed at a higher rate than U.S. Treasury securities.

- A fixed annuity can give you greater after-tax wealth even if the credited interest rate is somewhat below the yield on CDs or other taxable alternatives (Table 8.4, part D). This is reassuring during periods of rising interest rates, when annuity yields tend to lag behind taxable yields. At other times, annuities tend to pay at least as much as the taxable alternatives.
- These tables do not compare annuities and tax-free municipal bonds; however, you might expect the results to be somewhere between those in parts B and C in Table 8.4.

Liquidity constraints. It is not advisable to put any money that you might need before age 60 into a deferred annuity, because the 10 percent penalty tax will offset all or most of the gains from tax deferral. The maximum you should consider putting into an annuity is the amount you won't need for near-term financial goals.

Asset allocation. Asset allocation has become a popular topic in the financial planning community and the financial press—and rightfully so. Many researchers have found that total returns are determined more by the selection of asset classes, such as stocks or bonds, than by the selection of individual securities within those classes. Taking into account your total investment portfolio, how much belongs in fixed annuities? Rough guessing, formalized methods, and optimization models provide three decision-making approaches (there's rarely only *one* way to decide *anything*).

Rough guess. This is probably adequate in many cases, and it's certainly better than investing helter-skelter. You might decide that 10 percent "feels right" because you don't want to put too much in any one place, and you're happy with most of the other investments you have. Other people in a similar situation might choose 50 percent or nothing at all.

Formalized decision-making techniques. Various procedures have been developed over the years to help people rank alternatives that differ along several dimensions. In general, the idea is to identify a set of important features, assign weights,

Table 8.4. Taxable CD Versus Tax-Deferred SPDA: Revisited

A. Tax deferral is more valuable at higher tax rates
   8% pretax interest rate for CD and SPDA

Difference in Annual After-Tax Returns[a]

Holding Period in Years	Tax Rate			
	23%	33%	43%	53%
5	0.2%	0.3%	0.3%	0.3%
10	0.4	0.6	0.6	0.7
20	0.8	1.0	1.2	1.4
30	1.0	1.4	1.7	1.9

B. Tax deferral is more valuable at higher interest rates
   33% tax rate for CD and SPDA

Difference in Annual After-Tax Returns[a]

Holding Period, in Years	Interest Rate			
	6%	8%	10%	12%
5	0.1%	0.3%	0.4%	0.6%
10	0.3	0.6	0.8	1.2
20	0.6	1.0	1.5	2.0
30	0.9	1.4	1.9	2.5

and then score the responses to a series of questions. Some techniques have been computerized, and programs may be available through online information services or shareware distributors. (For an inexpensive look at this genre, try "Decision Analysis System," available from The Software Labs, 800/359-9998.)

Optimization models. Optimization models are widely used among institutional investors, such as pension funds, to construct portfolios that have the highest expected return for a given level

Table 8.4., Continued

C. The benefits of tax deferral are greatly reduced by a 10% penalty tax or a future increase in tax rates

33% tax rate for CD; 43% tax rate upon surrender of SPDA

Difference in Annual After-Tax Returns[a]

Holding Period, in Years	Interest Rate			
	6%	8%	10%	12%
5	(0.4)%	(0.5)%	(0.5)%	(0.6)%
10	(0.2)	(0.2)	0.0	0.2
20	0.1	0.4	0.8	1.3
30	0.4	0.9	1.4	2.0

D. Annuities can be advantageous even if the credited interest rate is less than the yield on taxable investments

33% tax rate for CD and SPDA

Annuity Interest Rate Needed to Produce the Same After-tax Wealth as with a CD

Holding Period, in Years	CD Interest Rate			
	6%	8%	10%	12%
5	5.8%	7.6%	9.5%	11.3%
10	5.6	7.3	9.0	10.6
20	5.3	6.8	8.4	9.8
30	5.1	6.5	8.0	9.4

[a] All calculations assume that the SPDA is surrendered at the end of the holding period. If the balance is annuitized, taxes can be postponed for a longer period, and the equivalent difference in after-tax returns would be several tenths of a percent higher.

of risk or the lowest risk for a given expected return. The usefulness of any computerized optimization program depends on the validity of the underlying theory of how assets are priced, as well as on the definition of risk. Different models produce different *efficient frontiers*; that is, sets of optimal portfolios that offer the best return for any level of risk.

Figure 8.2 shows the efficient frontier with and without SPDAs, based on the results from a commercially available optimization program. Risk is defined as *standard deviation*, a widely used measure of volatility. The ABC curve ("without SPDAs") shows the highest expected return you could achieve by allocating your assets among stocks, bonds, and "cash" (money market instruments); the DEF curve ("with SPDAs") adds SPDAs to the investment mix. Given the following assumptions, the graph shows that SPDAs let you increase your return with no increase in risk. The key assumptions are:

- SPDAs have the same risk as cash.
- Annual rates of return for SPDAs are correlated with other asset returns in the same manner as rates of return for cash are.
- The expected annual return for SPDAs is the same as the expected return for intermediate-term bonds (8.0 percent), plus 0.5 percent to take into account the benefits of tax deferral. (Optimization models have been developed with tax-exempt investors in mind, so variations in the tax treatment of different asset classes have not mattered. To obtain a set of optimal portfolios for individual investors, you either have to make an *ad hoc* adjustment or use a different model altogether.) Table 8.5 shows optimal asset mixes for three pairs of points (labeled A through F) along each of the two curves shown in Figure 8.2. Each pair of portfolios has the same risk (standard deviation). You can see that:

  —When SPDAs are added to the choice of investments, they drive out cash from the portfolio, and they make up more than half of the portfolio at low-to-moderate levels of risk.

  —At any given level of risk, the rate of return with SPDAs is higher than without them.

  —If risk is defined as the probability that the compound annual return over a twenty-year period will be less than 8.21 percent (the pretax equivalent of a 5.5 percent inflation rate, assuming a 33 percent tax rate), the portfolio is much less risky with SPDAs than without them. With cash, there's a good chance that you won't keep up with inflation over the long run.

Figure 8.2. Return Versus Risk With and Without SPDAs

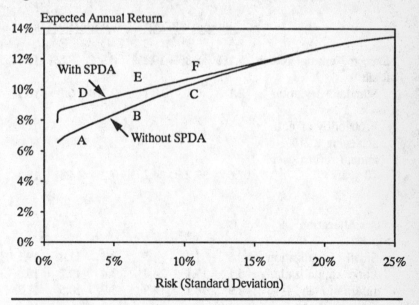

Optimization models are very sensitive to small changes in the assumptions, so this example is intended merely to illustrate one high-tech approach to the asset allocation problem. Needless to say, we do not recommend that you rush out and put all of your money into SPDAs.

Choosing a product. Various types of information can help you choose among competing products.

Current interest rate and surrender charges. Is the interest rate competitive in relation to other annuities and other investment alternatives, such as certificates of deposit? What is the guarantee period? Are you comfortable with the surrender charges and expense loads (if any)?

Interest rate forecasts. If you are comparing products with different guarantee periods, your decision may depend on your opinion about interest rate trends. If you think rates will go down over time, look for products with longer-term guarantees. If you think rates will go up, you might want to postpone your purchase altogether and park the money in a short-term investment.

Table 8.5. Optimal Portfolio Mixes

	Without SPDAs			With SPDAs		
	A	B	C	D	E	F
Expected annual return	7.2%	8.8%	10.2%	8.9%	9.8%	10.7%
Risk:						
Standard deviation	2.1	6.1	10.1	2.1	6.1	10.1
Probability of not achieving 8.21% annual return over 20 years	97.6	37.2	24.2	7.2	14.5	18.5
Asset Allocation						
Stocks:						
Small capitalization	0.6	1.4	8.5	3.4	11.4	19.1
Large capitalization	5.1	17.1	24.4	3.4	10.2	16.8
International	2.9	8.1	14.9	3.7	10.5	17.2
Bonds:						
Intermediate-term	12.2	53.2	31.2	—	—	—
Long-term	2.5	—	21.0	—	—	—
Cash	76.8	20.2	—	—	—	—
SPDA	—	—	—	89.5	67.9	46.9
Total	100	100	100	100	100	100

Interest-crediting strategy. You should certainly take into account any information that the company provides about what rates it might credit in the future. For regulatory and other reasons, insurance companies are reluctant to commit in advance to a particular course of action, but you may be able to make some inferences by looking at the investment portfolio. A high proportion of long-term bonds would suggest that the company may be able to maintain its current rate for a while but might not be able to respond quickly to rising market rates. A change in the asset mix—for example, from high-grade bonds to junk bonds—might suggest that the company is struggling to support its credited interest rate.

Many companies divide their general account into various *segments* for internal management purposes, in order to keep track of cash flows by product line and tailor appropriate investment strategies. If you are trying to guess at future credited rates, the only investments that matter are those in the fixed-annuity segment; the rest of the company's investments are relevant only when your concern is overall solvency.

Interest-crediting history. You should not buy a fixed annuity without knowing what rates the company has credited in the past on that annuity and on similar products. The interest-crediting history may be presented in various formats, depending upon the crediting method used by the company. Table 8.6 uses a matrix format to show the interest-rate histories for three different products with one-year guarantees. Each row represents the experience of those investors who purchased the product in the year shown; for example, the first row tells you what rates were paid each year from 1984 to 1989 on contracts issued in 1984. Each column tells you what rates were being paid to the various groups of contractholders in any given year.

Company A credits the same rate to everyone after the first year, but it sometimes credits a different rate initially. In general, the credited rates have moved as you might expect in relation to yields on one-year CDs. As market rates go down, the credited rate also falls, but with a slight lag.

Company B credits different rates to each group of contractholders, depending on the year of issue. The pattern of rates is not closely related to market interest rates. Instead, it appears that the company tries to attract new buyers with a high initial rate and then lowers it in the following years. This is a good example of why it's important to look at the past as well as the present. If you had invested $10,000 in this SPDA in 1984, your 1989 account balance would be $16,715, versus $17,615 for company A—which was crediting 2 percent less at the time.

Company C also uses a new-money approach, but it has maintained a reasonable degree of equity between new and old

Table 8.6. Three Interest-Crediting Histories

	1985	1986	1987	1988	1989	1990
Benchmark: One-year CDs	9.91	8.55	6.92	6.92	7.66	8.67

Company A: Modified portfolio-average approach

Deposited on 1/1	Declared rate at 1/1					
	1984	1985	1986	1987	1988	1989
1984	10.00	11.25	11.00	9.25	9.10	8.80
1985		9.00	11.00	9.25	9.10	8.80
1986			10.00	9.25	9.10	8.80
1987				8.00	9.10	8.80
1988					8.80	8.80
1989						8.80

Company B: Investment-generation approach

Deposited on 1/1	Declared rate at 1/1					
	1984	1985	1986	1987	1988	1989
1984	12.00	11.00	9.75	7.00	7.00	7.00
1985		12.25	10.00	8.00	8.00	8.00
1986			10.50	8.00	8.00	8.00
1987				9.50	9.00	8.50
1988					9.50	9.00
1989						10.00

Company C: Investment-generation approach

Deposited on 1/1	Declared rate at 1/1					
	1984	1985	1986	1987	1988	1989
1984	10.00	10.00	10.00	10.00	9.50	9.00
1985		10.25	10.25	10.25	9.50	9.25
1986			9.50	9.50	8.50	8.50
1987				7.50	7.50	7.50
1988					9.50	9.00
1989						9.50

policyholders. Changes in credited rates are more clearly related to the economic environment.

Agent's commission and other compensation. Some companies offer a selection of annuity products with different interest rates, surrender charges, and commission levels ranging from 3 percent to 10 percent of the premium. As you might expect, the products with higher commissions generally have lower interest rates or higher surrender charges. If you decide on an agent-sold product, make sure you buy the version with the greatest benefits for *you*, not the greatest compensation for the agent. Annuities that pay commissions higher than 5 percent will rarely be attractive to an informed buyer.

Profit testing. When presented with a product that seems to outshine the competition, a prudent investor should ask, "It looks great, but how are you doing it?" As with life insurance, the most reliable way to make predictions about the future performance of annuities is to examine the company's own pricing assumptions. When the product contains unusual features, such as a promised interest rate bonus after ten years, profit testing is probably the only way that you can determine if there are real competitive advantages or just empty claims. Unfortunately, this level of analysis is rarely practical. (For a detailed explanation of profit testing, see Chapter 5).

Shopping for fixed deferred annuities. Here are some suggestions for finding a reasonably priced product.

- Focus on the interest rate and the surrender charges. If the contract has other features that make it "unique" or "special," ask yourself how much you would be willing to pay for them if they were offered as an option.

- Ask for an interest-rate history of the company's fixed-interest annuity products, including those that are no longer being sold.

- Ignore the annuitization options, since you can always shop around for the best rates when you decide to annuitize the proceeds.

- Investigate the financial stability of the issuer (see Chapter 10).

Variable Deferred Annuities

Variable annuities were first developed in the 1950s to take advantage of the superior long-term performance of common stocks in relation to fixed-income investments. The goal was to provide retirees with a monthly income whose purchasing power would not be eroded by inflation. Today, variable annuities are marketed as tax-advantaged accumulation vehicles; they allow you to invest in a family of funds without having to pay taxes each year on the gains. As with fixed annuities, there are single premium and flexible premium versions.

Product features. Some important product features are:

Investment choice. Almost all contracts offer at least three funds—common stocks, bonds, and money market—and some offer ten or more, including real estate, gold, and asset allocation. The funds may be managed by an outside organization (often a big-name advisor, to attract customers) or by an affiliate of the insurance company, in order to keep the investment management fees "in the family."

Because of consumer demand for guarantees, some contracts also offer one or more fixed-interest options, similar to fixed annuities. However, as with variable life insurance, you should generally avoid the guaranteed-interest accounts, since (1) there are likely to be restrictions on getting your money out; (2) the interest rate may not be as high as on fixed annuities; and (3) the supporting assets are held in the company's general account, where there is less protection in the event of insolvency. (If you really want a fixed interest rate, why buy a variable annuity?)

Transfers between funds may be limited as to frequency, timing, and amount. Most contracts have liberal transfer provisions for the variable funds and more severe restrictions for the guaranteed-interest account.

Contract expenses. These may include:
- a front-end sales load
- an ongoing mortality and expense risk charge (up to 1.25 percent a year, or higher with SEC approval)
- an ongoing administrative fee (often $20-40 a year)
- fund operating expenses (investment advisory fee and administrative costs)

- surrender charge (usually a declining percentage of the premium or account balance, on a premium-year or contract-year basis)
- state premium tax (usually deducted when incurred, either when premiums are received or upon annuitization)
- nominal fees ($5-25) for transfers and withdrawals

Total contract expenses are generally 1.5-3.0 percent of the account balance each year, depending on the investment option (some funds have higher expenses than others) and the amount invested (a $30 charge is 0.6 percent of $5,000 but only 0.06 percent of $50,000). The total expense ratio for variable annuities is usually higher than for taxable mutual funds because annuities have some additional charges that mutual funds don't. In addition, the annuity funds may be relatively small, which increases each investor's share of the operating costs.

Accumulation units and annuity units. To keep track of contract values more easily, companies use *accumulation units* during the accumulation period and *annuity units* during the annuity period.

Table 8.7 shows the relationship between *net asset value*—a measure of per-share value that is familiar to mutual fund shareholders—and *accumulation unit value*. In this example, each share of the variable fund and each accumulation unit is worth $10 at inception, but their values diverge over time. That's because the accumulation unit value takes into account some asset-based contract charges, such as the mortality and expense risk charge, in addition to the total return of the fund's investments. The formula for the accumulation unit value at the end of any measuring period is:

$$\text{Unit value at end} = \text{Unit value at beginning} \times \left[\frac{\text{Net asset value at end} + \text{Dividends}}{\text{Net asset value at beginning}} - \text{Contract charges} \right]$$

The calculation is done each business day, as it is for the net asset value of the variable funds.

As shown in Table 8.7, contract expenses are deducted at several levels. Fund operating expenses are incurred at the fund level and are reflected in net asset value (and therefore in accumulation unit value). Asset-based contract charges are incurred at the subaccount level, by liquidating fund shares; these expenses are reflected in the accumulation unit value. Other charges, such as annual maintenance fees, are incurred at the contract level by liquidating accumulation units. Upon annuitization (discussed later), the accumulation units are converted to annuity units, whose value depends on the net rate of return for the variable funds, relative to an assumed investment return.

Table 8.7. Relationship Between Net Asset Value and Accumulation Unit Value

Event	Net Asset Value	Accum. Unit Value	Units Owned
Fund starts up and you invest $1,000	$10.00	$10.00	100.000
15% total return during the year	11.50	11.50	100.000
$1.00/share dividend is paid and reinvested	10.50	11.50	100.000
1% mortality & expense risk charge	10.50	11.39	100.000
$30 annual maintenance fee	10.50	11.39	97.366

Penalty-free withdrawals. As with fixed annuities, some contracts allow you to withdraw up to 10 percent of the account balance each year without a surrender charge. Withdrawals are taxable distributions, however, so you should not take money out unless you really need to.

Death benefit. If the owner or annuitant dies, most contracts pay the greater of the premiums or the account value. This means that your beneficiaries will get back at least what you put into the contract, regardless of investment performance. To make their products stand out from the crowd, some companies raise the minimum death benefit by compounding the premium (for example, at 5 percent), or by resetting the minimum at the then-current account value every few years. These variations —and others that will surely be invented—should be seen for what they are: gimmicks. If you're worried about the death benefit, buy life insurance, not an annuity; if you're worried about loss of principal, buy a fixed annuity, not a variable one.

Guaranteed and current settlement options. Variable annuities generally offer the same fixed-payment options that fixed annuities do. In addition, many contracts offer variable-payment options, with a choice of funds. Instead of a fixed number of dollars, the monthly benefit is expressed as a fixed number of annuity units, whose value moves up or down with the performance of the selected funds.

For variable-payment options, the first payment is computed using a table of guaranteed purchase rates contained in the contract. For example, a 65-year-old man might be entitled to receive a first payment of $6.50 for each $1,000 of accumulated values. These purchase rates are based on an appropriate mortality table and an *assumed investment return*, such as 4 percent. In subsequent months, the annuity payment will increase if the fund's annualized net rate of return is greater than 4 percent, and decrease if the net rate of return is below 4 percent.

The assumed investment return affects both the initial payment and the rate at which future payments will change. Figure 8.3 shows the trade-off, assuming an actual net rate of return of 8 percent. A lower assumed investment return (AIR) produces a lower initial payment, but the payments increase more quickly. A higher assumed return produces a higher first payment, but slower growth. If the assumed return and the actual net return are the same, the payments remain constant. In this sense, a fixed payment option is just a special type of variable payment option, where the actual return is guaranteed to be equal to the assumed return.

Of course, Figure 8.3 paints a too-rosy picture of variable payment options, because it ignores the variability of the payments. Instead of a predictable 4 percent increase each year,

Figure 8.3. Variable Annuity Payments (Monthly Income per $100,000)

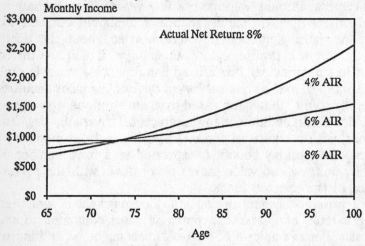

your income could go up by 20 percent one year and down by 10 percent the next. This uncertainty makes variable settlement options unsuitable as the foundation of a retirement plan; you should use them only to supplement other sources of income.

Pricing considerations. With fixed annuities, product pricing centers on the spread between the earned and credited interest rates. With variable annuities, the most important element is the mortality and expense risk charge. Here's the explanation of the m&e charge in one company's prospectus:

The mortality risk assumed by the Company arises from its promised death benefit proceeds and from its contractual obligation to continue to make annuity payments to each annuitant regardless of how long he or she lives and regardless of how long all annuitants as a group live. This assures each annuitant that neither his own longevity nor an improvement in life expectancy generally will have an adverse effect on the annuity payments he will receive under a Contract and relieves the annuitant from the risk that he will outlive the amounts actually accumulated for retirement. The Company also assumes the risk that the amounts deducted for sales and administrative expenses may be insufficient to cover the actual cost of such items...If [the mortality and expense risk charge] is insufficient to cover the actual cost of these mortality and expense risks, the loss will fall on the Company. Conversely, if the charge proves more than sufficient, any excess may be retained by the Company for profit or otherwise used by it to meet any operational expense, including that of distribution of the Contracts.

So that's what the prospectus says. Now let's see what the mortality and expense risk charge is really for. Table 8.8. shows the results of a profit test of a typical agent-sold flexible-premium variable annuity. The pricing assumptions are listed in the top section of the table. For this baseline set of assumptions, the components of the 1.25 percent m&e charge are shown in the middle section. In the bottom section, you can see how the m&e charge would be affected by various hypothetical, or what-if, changes in the pricing assumptions. Notice that:

- Most of the mortality and expense risk charge represents a return on the insurer's invested capital; in other words, it is profit. In this example, the invested capital consists of the initial distribution costs ($200), other acquisition costs ($150), and target surplus (0.75 percent of reserves). Presumably, insurance companies downplay the profit-making aspects of the m&e charge because they don't want to argue with consumers over what level of profit is reasonable. ("What?! I'm getting a measly 8-12 percent tax-deferred and you're getting 15 percent after tax?"). However, if you accept the premise that a 15 percent after-tax rate of return is reasonable, then it appears that an insurer really does need to charge 1.25 percent—or even more.

- Some of the m&e charge offsets the ongoing administrative expenses that exceed the $30 maintenance fee. For many companies, these expenses are more than $30 to begin with, and they can be expected to increase over time due to inflation.

Table 8.8. What the Mortality & Expense Risk Charge is Really For

Pricing assumptions for a typical agent-sold flexible premium product:

Premium: First year $5,000
         Renewal years $2,000

Issue age: 55

Expenses:
   Distribution   4% of all premiums
   Administrative: First year $150
                 Renewal years $50
   Per death claim or surrender $30
   Renewal-year expenses are inflated at 4%

Gross rate of return (after fund expenses): 9%

Contract loads:
   Front-end load   None
   Annual maintenance fee $30
   Surrender charge   8% of premium in Year 1, declining by 1% a year, waived upon death

10% penalty-free withdrawal; 8% utilization

Lapse rate: 5, 5, 6, 6, 7, 7, 8, 9, 10, 10, 9, 9, 8, 8, 8%...

Mortality: 75% of 1975-80 Ultimate Table

Statutory and tax reserves: Account value

Tax rate: 34%

Target surplus: 0.75% of reserve

Profit objective: 15% IRR after tax, including target surplus; 20-year pricing horizon

Breakdown of mortality and expense risk charge (in basis points):

Return on investment:	
Acquisition costs	78
Target surplus	10
Administrative expenses	16
All other	21
	125

Table 8.8., Continued

What if...? [a]

	Required Charge [b]	Change from Base Case
Gross rate of return is 6%	138	+13
Gross rate of return is 12%	113	-12
Lapse rate increases to 15% in Year 9	132	+7
Lapse rate is 2% level	110	-15
Annual maintenance fee is $50	111	-14
Commissions are 5%	144	+19
Commissions are 3%	106	-19
Product is low-load; distribution costs are $200 in Year 1 only	81	-44
First-year issuing expense is $200	133	+8
First-year issuing expense is $100	117	-8
No surrender charge	140	+15
Surrender charge is not waived at death	123	-2
No penalty-free withdrawal	123	-2
Average premium is $10,000 in the first year and $4,000 thereafter	106	-19
Profit objective is 12% after-tax IRR	110	-15
$150 front-end load and 4% premium load	49	-76

[a] All pricing assumptions are the same as in the base case except for the indicated assumption.
[b] All results are in basis points. The "all other" component of the m&e charge is assumed to remain constant at 21.

- A small portion of the charge covers all other risks, including the guaranteed minimum death benefit, the risk of better-than-expected mortality, the risk of higher-than-expected lapses, and the risk of lower-than-expected fund performance.

- Every little benefit costs money. For example, it costs a few basis points to waive the surrender charge at death and to provide a 10 percent penalty-free withdrawal.

- A company could do away with surrender charges if it wanted to, but then it would have to increase the m&e charge.

- The m&e charge can be significantly reduced by lowering distribution costs. Each 1 percent agent's commission costs about 0.2 percent a year, so a product with very low distribution costs can have a much lower m&e charge—and therefore higher cash values.

- The required m&e charge is also affected by the average contract size, persistency, administrative expenses (first year and renewal), and the company's profit objective.

- Front-end loads and ongoing premium loads can result in better long-term performance. Using the numbers in Table 8.8, you would have $113,459 after twenty years with a front-end-load version of the agent-sold product, versus $107,839 with the typical back-end-load design. This is not surprising, since the product is priced to yield a 15 percent return on the company's investment, while the variable funds are only earning 9 percent. Many people would probably refuse to pay an insurance agent $400 for "services rendered" in selling them a $10,000 variable annuity, but they are quite willing to let the insurance company pay the same $400 on their behalf, while they repay the "loan" over time—at 15 percent interest. This is strange behavior indeed, but it happens every time someone buys a so-called no load—that is, no front-end load—deferred annuity.

To sum up, you can expect the total expenses for a variable annuity to be greater than those for no-load mutual funds because of:

- higher distribution costs, even for low-load annuities
- higher first-year and renewal-year administrative expenses
- target surplus

• other risks borne by the insurance company

Should you buy it? The main considerations in deciding whether or not to invest your money in a variable annuity instead of a portfolio of taxable mutual funds are liquidity and the value of tax deferral. As with fixed annuities, withdrawals and loans are taxable distributions, and a 10 percent penalty tax falls on income realized before age 59 1/2 (with a few exceptions). Most contracts also have a declining surrender charge. In general, you should view variable annuities as long-term investments; money that might be needed in a few years doesn't belong there.

The value of tax deferral is harder to assess because it depends on a variety of factors. To compare variable annuities with taxable mutual funds on an after-tax basis, you need to take into account all the factors represented in Table 8.9.

From the individual investor's point of view, the breakdown of total return for a portfolio of taxable mutual funds depends on the funds' investments (stocks, bonds, etc.) and on two levels of portfolio turnover. At the mutual fund level, fund managers buy and sell securities, and this increases the taxable distributions that have to be made each year. At the individual investor level, investors buy and sell mutual fund shares, thereby realizing any unrealized capital gains.

Table 8.10 shows how some taxable mutual funds allow you to defer taxes on a significant portion of the total return. If you had invested $10,000 at the beginning of 1982 in the Vanguard Index Trust-500 Portfolio (a no-load fund that mirrors the S&P 500) and reinvested the income and capital gains distributions at the end of each year, more than half of the appreciation in your account through 1989 would have been tax-deferred. In addition, under current law no income tax would be due if you died, because your heirs would receive a stepped-up basis. The problem with deferring taxes in this way, however, is that it doesn't always work. A fund might have samll distributions for a few years, but then you might suddenly be hit with a big tax bill. Also, you have to buy and hold, since all of the unrealized appreciation is taxed when you sell your shares. With variable annuities, on the other hand, tax deferral is more reliable.

Table 8.9. Comparing Variable Annuities with Taxable Mutual Funds: Things to Consider

Factor	Explanation
Total expenses	Higher expenses offset some or all of the value of tax deferral.
Holding period	Tax deferral becomes more valuable as the holding period increases.
Your current tax rate	Tax deferral is more valuable for people in higher tax brackets.
Your future tax rate	An increase in tax rates can wipe out the benefits of years of tax deferral.
Tax treatment of capital	Preferential tax rates for capital gains will favor taxable mutual funds over variable annuities.
Deductibility of expenses for taxable funds	Under current law, fund operating expenses are effectively tax-deductible, because they are not added back in determining the amount of taxable distributions.
Fund performance	Tax deferral is more valuable when rates of return are higher. Also, superior fund performance can offset the higher expenses.
Fund volatility	For taxable funds, capital losses can be used to offset capital gains or, to some extent, ordinary income. For variable annuities, a capital loss on one fund can only be realized by surrendering the entire contract.
Breakdown of total return (ordinary income, realized long-term capital gains, unrealized gains)	This determines the taxes that you have to pay on your mutual fund investments.

Table 8.10. You Can Also Defer Taxes with Taxable Funds

Vanguard Index Trust — 500 Portfolio: 1982-1989

Year	Rate of Return [a]	Ending Balance	Taxable Distributions
		$10,000	
1982	22.1%	12,210	$896
1983	21.2	14,797	1,099
1984	6.0	15,683	1,021
1985	30.7	20,496	2,025
1986	18.2	24,231	2,594
1987	5.1	25,469	859
1988	16.0	29,550	1,467
1989	30.9	38,693	2,120

Total distributions:	$12,080	42%
Unrealized appreciation:	16,613	58
Total gain:	$28,693	

[a] These rates of return assume end-of-year reinvestment of distributions and may therefore be different from published figures.

Table 8.11 shows the value of tax deferral expressed as the difference in annual after-tax returns in relation to taxable funds. The calculations take into account all factors in Table 8.11 except fund volatility, which is generally of less importance. You can see that:

- With a moderate level of extra expenses—for example, 1 percent a year—a variable annuity can provide a significant increase in after-tax returns if (1) you hold it for a long time and (2) you invest in higher-risk funds that have a greater potential for appreciation. To match the after-tax returns of the annuity over a twenty-year period, you might have to choose taxable funds that yield an extra 1-2 percent each year. That may not sound like much, but it's probably equivalent to picking a fund among the top 25 percent of its peers. In a sense, tax deferral produces the same results as superior fund-picking ability.

Table 8.11. Variable Annuities Versus Taxable Mutual Funds

Assumptions (unless otherwise noted):

1. Similar annuity and taxable funds have the same gross rate of return, before operating expenses.
2. Gross rate of return (before all expenses) is 8 percent for money market and bond funds, 12 percent for growth and income funds, and 15 percent for aggressive growth funds.
3. Breakdown of gross returns for taxable funds: for money market and bond funds, 100 percent income; for growth and income funds, 30 percent income, 30 percent realized capital gains, 40 percent unrealized capital gains; for aggressive growth funds, 10 percent income, 20 percent realized capital gains, 70 percent unrealized capital gains.
4. *Portfolio turnover* means the percent of accumulated unrealized capital gains that the individual investor realizes each year, as a result of selling fund shares.
5. Expense ratio for all taxable funds is 1 percent.
6. Tax on ordinary income and capital gains is 33 percent. Fund operating expenses are deductible.

A. Higher annuity expenses offset some or all of the benefits of tax deferral (assumes that all gains are realized each year).

Difference in Annual After-tax Returns [a]

Holding Period in Years	Money Market/Bonds (8%) Additional Expenses			Aggressive Growth (15%) Additional Expenses		
	0.5%	1.0%	1.5%	0.5%	1.0%	1.5%
5	(0.16)	(0.52)	(0.88)	0.37	0.02	(0.40)
10	0.04	(0.35)	(0.73)	1.09	0.66	0.24
20	0.38	(0.05)	(0.47)	2.08	1.61	1.14
30	0.65	0.19	(0.26)	2.66	2.17	1.68

Table 8.11., Continued

B. Variable annuities provide greater benefits to market timers than to buy-and-hold investors (assumes that total annuity expenses are 1% greater than for a portfolio of taxable funds).

Difference in Annual After-tax Returns [a]

Holding Period, in Years	Market Timer (100% portfolio turnover)		Buy-and-Hold Investor (20% portfolio turnover)	
	Growth & Income (12%)	Aggressive Growth (15%)	Growth & Income (12%)	Aggressive Growth (15%)
5	(0.27)%	(0.02)%	(0.41)%	(0.39)%
10	0.17	0.66	(0.05)	0.07
20	0.83	1.61	0.55	0.85
30	1.27	2.17	0.97	1.35

C. Preferential tax treatment for capital gains can erase the benefits of a variable annuity (assumes (1) 40% portfolio turnover; (2) "Current Tax Law" is 33% rate for ordinary income and capital gains; (3) "What-if scenario" is 33% tax rate for ordinary income and 19.8% tax rate for capital gains, starting in Year 3).

Difference in Annual After-Tax Returns [a]

Holding Period, in Years	Current Tax Law		A What if Scenario	
	Growth & Income (12%)	Aggressive Growth (15%)	Growth & Income (12%)	Aggressive Growth (15%)
5	(0.36)%	(0.25)%	(1.12)%	(1.52)%
10	0.05	0.35	(0.86)	(1.11)
20	0.70	1.25	(0.29)	(0.31)
30	1.13	1.79	0.12	0.21

[a] All calculations assume that the annuity contract is surrendered at the end of the holding period. If the balance is annuitized, taxes can be postponed for a longer period, and the equivalent difference in after-tax returns would be several tenths of a percent higher.

- Because of the higher expenses within a variable annuity contract, you will probably have to hold it for five years or more before it can outperform a portfolio of taxable funds (assuming similar fund performance). The breakeven point can be more than twenty years if you decide to play it safe by investing in low-risk funds with a relatively low rate of return.

- For investments of $5,000 or less, a $30 annual administrative fee "costs" several years of tax deferral benefits. For example, if you invest $5,000 the first year, $2,000 each year after that, and the annuity funds grow at 10 percent, the administrative fee is about 0.4 percent of your account balance, on average, during the first five years. That seemingly-small charge erases three to four years of tax savings.

- Not surprisingly, variable annuities are most appropriate for market timers, whose trading activity leads to more realized capital gains. It's worth noting, though, that the number of people who believe they can successfully time the market greatly exceeds the number who can actually do it. By allowing you to move in and out of the market painlessly, a variable annuity may make it harder for you to be a successful long-term investor.

- A future reduction in tax rates on capital gains could wipe out the benefits of tax deferral, unless the gains within an annuity are treated as capital gains rather than ordinary income. The possibility that tax laws will change is one of the biggest risks of investing in a variable annuity.

To sum up, variable annuities provide four dimensions of tax-deferred portfolio diversification. First, you can diversify across asset classes by choosing more than one type of fund. Second, you can diversify across time by gradually adding to your investment and remaining invested throughout up and down markets. Third, as with taxable mutual funds, you can diversify across individual securities. And fourth, you can diversify across tax laws, since variable annuities and taxable funds will probably be affected differently by whatever legislation is enacted in the years to come.

These rewards are accompanied by risks, however. Investing in a variable annuity may turn out to be a bad decision if you don't hold the contract long enough to compensate for the higher expenses; if the annuity funds do not perform as well as similar taxable funds; if you have to pay a 10 percent penalty tax or a surrender charge; or if unfavorable changes occur in the tax laws.

Shopping for variable deferred annuities. Here are some suggestions for finding a reasonably priced product.

- To compare variable annuities, look at total contract expenses, the variety of funds, fund performance, transfer restrictions, and customer service capabilities.

- Fund operating expenses can be determined by looking at the latest annual report; the prospectus lists all other expenses.

- Look for products that have a range of investment options, so that you can respond to future economic changes.

- To evaluate the performance of annuity funds, you can use the same methods as for taxable mutual funds. However, annuity fund performance figures may be based on changes in net asset value (after fund operating expenses, but before other contract expenses) or accumulation unit value (after expenses at both the fund and accumulation unit levels). If you're comparing annuity funds with similar taxable funds, you may have to adjust the performance figures by adding back the mortality and expense risk charge.

- The transfer provisions should match your investment style; if you intend to time the market, you might want more than four free switches a year. Frequent transfers can impair fund performance, however, so buy-and-hold investors might want a contract that offers only a few free switches.

- To reduce the risk of service problems, choose a company that has some experience with variable annuities.

By doing your homework at the beginning, you'll increase your chances of finding a product you can stick with until you're ready to receive annuity payments.

After the purchase. Here are some suggestions for getting the maximum value out of a contract you already own:

- Don't make withdrawals except as a last resort.

- Make your investment decisions in the context of your overall portfolio. You can use the variable annuity to periodically adjust your asset allocation; for example, to shift 5 percent of your assets from common stocks to cash. However, unless you have a disciplined market-timing strategy, you should resist the temptation to move everything from one fund to another.

- If you become unhappy with your purchase, consider rolling your money over into another deferred annuity contract (fixed or variable) in a tax-free exchange.

- At the end of the accumulation period, shop around for the best annuity rates. Annuitization is a separate purchase decision.

IMMEDIATE ANNUITIES

Immediate annuities are the easiest insurance products to compare, because the benefits are fixed at issue and are not affected by the insurer's subsequent investment or mortality experience. Price is typically expressed as (1) monthly life income per $1,000 invested, (2) monthly life income per $10,000 invested, or (3) purchase price of a $10 monthly life income. Of course, these are just different ways of looking at the same transaction. Because of the surprisingly large differences in price among products, comparison shopping is likely to be worth the time spent. For example, in early 1989 a diligent 65-year-old man could have increased his before-tax monthly income by at least $5 for each $10,000 invested in a straight-life annuity—that was the difference in rates between the average product and products in the top decile. If he invests $30,000 and is in the 30 percent tax bracket, the present value at 6 percent of the additional after-tax payments over twenty years would be almost $1,400. If it takes ten hours to do the shopping, that's $140 an hour. Not a bad hourly wage for someone in retirement.

Finding a Competitive Product

You should be able to find a competitive product if you follow these steps:

1. Get a copy of *Best's Retirement Income Guide* or *Best's Flitcraft Compend*, available in libraries or from the A.M. Best Company (see Appendix D).

2. Decide what annuitization option you want; for example, life only or life income with ten years certain. You might want to look at the rates for several options to get a feel for the trade-offs between monthly payment and guarantee period. Here are one company's rates as of February 1989 for a 70-year-old woman:

   Monthly Life Income per $10,000 Single Premium

Life only (no refund)	$97.40
Life income—10 years certain	92.60
Life income—20 years certain	84.30

   Choose the level of guarantee that is appropriate for your situation. Don't try to outsmart the insurance company by guessing which option is the "best deal." Unless you have some actuarial evidence to the contrary, you can assume that all of the options have been priced consistently.

3. Using *Best's Retirement Income Guide* or *Best's Flitcraft Compend*, make a list of the twenty or so companies with the highest monthly incomes for the age and plan that are closest to your own situation. (These publications do not contain rates for joint and survivor options, so you will have to use a single life option in this step.)

4. Starting at the top of your list, investigate the financial stability of each company (see Chapter 10). This is especially important for immediate annuities, because you cannot take your money and run if the company's condition deteriorates; you are committed for life.

5. When you have found five to ten companies you feel comfortable with, contact them to obtain the current rates for your own situation. If you are annuitizing a deferred annuity contract or a life insurance settlement, be sure to obtain a comparable quote from your own company as well; insurers sometimes give policyholders a preferred rate. In each case, ask if there is an initial policy fee and if state premium taxes will be deducted from the premium before annuitization. Based on this information, you can adjust the quoted payment as in this example:

Assumed investment:	$50,000
Quoted monthly payment per $10,000:	$95.00
Unadjusted total monthly payment:	$475.00 ($95 x 5)
Assumed investment:	$50,000
less: Policy fee	(300)
less: State premium tax (2%)	(600)
Amount available for annuitization	$49,100
Adjusted total monthly payment	$466.45 ($95 x 4.91)

6. Obtain similar information from companies with low-load products. Note that commissions on immediate annuities are typically only 1-3 percent, so differences in marketing costs are not as significant as with other types of products. Nevertheless, you should check the low-load rates just to be sure.

7. Take your list of tentative choices to a knowledgeable agent to see if he or she can come up with anything better. (If you already have a working relationship with an agent, you may be able to skip or delegate some of the earlier steps.)

8. Consider spreading out your purchases over several years, or over one or more interest-rate cycles, in order to avoid locking in a low rate on all of your money. This approach is similar to dollar-cost averaging. In fact, unless you believe that interest rates (and therefore annuity payment rates) have nowhere to go but down, you should never commit all of your earmarked capital at once. Also, remember that annuity payments remain fixed for life, so you need to have other investments on hand to offset the effects of inflation.

Should You Buy It?

Whereas it is relatively easy to shop for an immediate annuity, it's much harder to decide whether you should want one. Can you duplicate the immediate annuity on your own? Can money be made, on average, by buying immediate annuities?

Duplicating the annuity. Insurance companies provide a practical way to share the risk of living longer than expected. Without insurance products, the only way you can pay yourself a guaranteed income for life is to invest in very long-term securities and not spend any of the principal. Even though there is no real substitute for immediate annuities, it may sometimes be helpful to compare the after-tax annuity payments with what you could have if you accepted various levels of risk.

Suppose the monthly life income per $10,000 for a 65-year-old woman is $90, at the same time that long-term Treasury bonds are yielding about 9 percent. Based on an exclusion ratio of 46.3 percent and a tax rate of 32 percent, the after-tax annuity income would be $894 a year for the first twenty years and $734 after that. Compare that with the after-tax payments provided by a portfolio of Treasury bonds, assuming a 28 percent tax rate (Treasuries are exempt from state income tax) and no withdrawals from principal: $648. Of course, you can increase the payments if you're willing to take a chance on outliving your money. Table 8.12 shows several payment schedules, the projected age at which principal would be exhausted, and the probability that a woman age 65 today would still be alive, based on two different mortality tables.

Any comparison between annuities and non-annuities inevitably suffers from several deficiencies. For one thing, it ignores the money that will be left to the do-it-yourselfer's survivors if she dies sooner rather than later. It also ignores the practicality of doing it yourself; it may be difficult to sell investments in the quantity required with reasonable transaction costs. Finally, the conclusions may well depend on what investment you select; for example, tax-exempt municipal bonds yielding 7 percent, rather than Treasury bonds yielding 9 percent.

Table 8.12. Immediate Annuity Versus Do-It-Yourself

Annual Aftertax Payment [a]	Age at Which Money Runs Out	Probability of Outliving Payments
Annuity:		
$894 for 20 years, then $734	Never	0%
Do-it-yourself:		
$1,361	Age 75	80-90%
893	Age 85	45-67
757	Age 95	9-31
701	Age 105	0-7
648	Never	0

a   Per $10,000 invested by a 65-year-old woman. Tax rate is 32 percent for the annuity and 28 percent for the do-it-yourself alternative.

Expected value. The second question—can annuity buyers make money on average?—is more interesting. You'll recall that when we wanted to know if cash value life insurance was a good deal for the average buyer, we got 50,000 people together in a football stadium, formed an association with no tax advantages and no expenses, computed what premium we would have to charge, and then compared this hypothetical premium with what companies actually charge in the marketplace. We can do the same thing for immediate annuities, but it requires a lengthier explanation.

To decide what annuity rates to offer, companies make assumptions about expenses, mortality, and the investment yields to be earned and credited. The spread between earned and credited rates is especially important, since this is used to recover the distribution costs and annual maintenance expenses, and to generate a return on the insurer's invested capital. A typical interest spread might typically be 1-1.25 percent. To simplify things, let's assume the following:

1. The annuity is life-only and provides annual payments at the end of each year to all survivors, with nothing paid at death.

2. All deaths occur at the end of each year, just before payments are made.

3. Mortality rates follow the 1983 Individual Annuity Mortality Table (a standard table used in calculating annuity reserves).

4. The assumed credited interest rate is 8.5 percent.

5. You are a 65-year-old man.

Based on these assumptions, an actuary could calculate that a single premium of $8,286 would be sufficient to provide you with a $1,000 annual income for life. Table 8.13 shows how the funds would be gradually depleted, if you live until a maximum age of 115 (the age at which the 1983 IAM Table stops). Note that the annual payment is always greater than the 8.5 percent interest that is credited each year, so the company has to draw upon principal. The column labeled "Survivorship benefit" is your share of the funds that have been lost by the annuitants who died during the year; as death rates increase and the number of survivors diminishes, this becomes an increasingly important part of the annuity payment. If mortality and interest rates behave as assumed, there would be just enough money to keep the annual payments going until the last annuitant died.

Table 8.13. $8,286 Is Just Enough to Provide an Annual Payment for Life

	Development of Fund Balance Per Survivor				
Age	Beginning Balance	Interest	Survivorhip Benefit	Payments	Ending Balance
65	$8,286	$704	$117	$(1,000)	8,108
66	8,108	689	127	(1,000)	7,923
67	7,923	673	137	(1,000)	7,734
68	7,734	657	149	(1,000)	7,540
69	7,540	641	161	(1,000)	7,342
.	.	.	.	.	.
.	.	.	.	.	.
.	.	.	.	.	.
110	455	39	858	(1,000)	352
111	352	30	873	(1,000)	255
112	255	22	887	(1,000)	164
113	164	14	901	(1,000)	79
114	79	7	914	(1,000)	0

Now let's look at the annual payments more closely. We'll need to make two further assumptions:

6. Each payment consists of three parts: interest, your principal, and principal from deceased annuitants that is redistributed among the survivors.

7. Interest is paid out first, then your principal, and finally your share of the principal from others.

Figure 8.4 shows the breakdown of the $1,000 annuity payments from age 65 to age 115. All of the credited interest is paid out each year, along with enough principal to complete the $1,000 payments. As time goes on, an increasing proportion of each payment is principal, both yours and others'.

Figure 8.4. Immediate Annuity Payments Have Three Parts

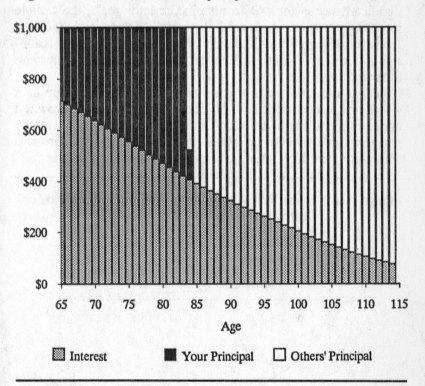

The next step is to look at the amounts you would receive after taxes. Recall that annuity payments are taxed according to these rules:

- While alive, you can exclude a portion of the payments from taxable income, based on a prescribed exclusion ratio. However, once you have recovered your cost basis, all payments become taxable.

- At death, any unrecovered basis can be deducted on your final income tax return, producing a tax savings for your estate.

This tax treatment is shown in Figure 8.5A. During the early years, the taxable income is less than the actuarially-determined interest component, because of the way the exclusion ratio is computed. In addition, the decedents' beneficiaries realize a significant tax savings. Of course in the later years, the taxable income greatly exceeds the actuarially-determined interest. However, Figure 8.5A gives a distorted picture of these relationships, because it presents the extreme case of someone who lives until age 115.

To get the true picture, you have to look at the group as a whole and keep track of how quickly the cost basis is recovered under current tax laws—taking into account both the annuity payments and the tax savings at death—and then compare this with the actuarially-determined principal that is paid out.

Figure 8.5A. Immediate Annuities are Taxed in Your Favor (Individual Investor's Perspective)

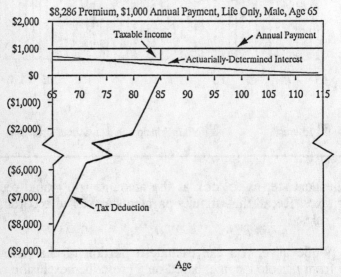

This comparison is shown in Figure 8.5B. In both cases, 100 percent of the principal, or cost basis, is eventually recovered. However, current tax law permits the cost basis to be recovered more quickly than it "should" be, and this translates into greater after-tax benefits for the annuity buyers and their beneficiaries. The tax advantage of immediate annuities arises from the fact that the government ignores actuarial reality in favor of the principle that each individual should be able to deduct his own investment in the contract, either during life or at death.

But the picture is still not complete, because we have quietly lumped together the annuity buyers, who receive after-tax payments while they are alive, and their beneficiaries, who receive tax savings when the contractholders die. Purchasers of immediate annuities are generally thinking of themselves, not their beneficiaries, so you might argue that it is only the annuity payments that really matter and that post-death tax savings are worthless.

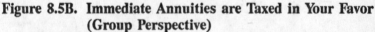

Figure 8.5B. Immediate Annuities are Taxed in Your Favor (Group Perspective)

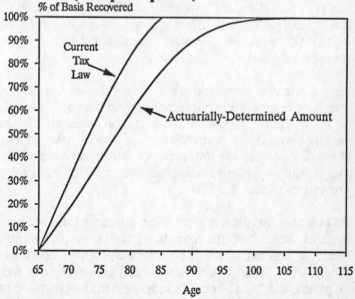

In this example, 77 percent of the total cost basis is recovered by the annuitants, and the remaining 23 percent is recovered by the annuitants' beneficiaries. So how you choose to characterize the tax treatment of immediate annuities depends on your point of view. In a sense, when you buy an immediate annuity you are also buying a decreasing term insurance policy for your heirs, with a face amount equal to the remaining tax savings each year. Altruistic annuity buyers might look at the combined package and conclude that it's a good deal. Selfish annuity buyers might ignore the tax savings at death and grumble that the government has given some of their benefits away. Both perspectives are valid.

We can use our imaginary taxable association of 65-year-olds to get some idea of the impact of current tax laws. Table 8.14 shows the annual rate of return the association would have to earn on its investments, for several assumed tax rates, to provide the same after-tax benefits as the immediate annuity. (This is equivalent to finding the discount rate that makes the present expected value of the benefits equal to the $8,286 single premium.) These results suggest that:

- For tax-exempt institutions and qualified retirement plans, the immediate annuity offers no tax advantages over a do-it-yourself approach, because there is no cost basis to recover.

- As tax rates increase, the annuity provides an increasingly attractive combination of after-tax payments and tax savings at death. For example, an association with no tax advantages and a 30 percent tax rate would have to earn about 9.1 percent on its assets—or 0.6 percent more than the annuity's assumed credited rate of 8.5 percent—to provide the same benefits.

- As tax rates increase, a greater proportion of the annuity's benefits consist of tax savings at death, so the annuity becomes less attractive for those buyers who don't care about what their beneficiaries get. However, for most taxpayers, the "lost" benefits simply erase the favorable tax treatment and do not constitute a real penalty. These buyers are effectively in the same position they would be in if they earned the implicit credited rate on their own.

These results ignore the value of the annuity's most important feature; namely, that it provides a guaranteed income for life. For most people this guarantee has some value, so all of the required rates of return in Table 8.14 probably represent a "worst case"—and that's how you should interpret them.

So that's the theory, but what about the *real* world? After all, even favorable tax treatment is of no value if it is offset by an insurer's high expenses and profit margins. Do immediate annuities in the marketplace seem to be reasonably priced? The left side of Figure 8.6 shows the distribution of monthly life incomes per $10,000 invested for the 122 products listed in *Best's Retirement Income Guide*, as of February 1989. The right side shows the monthly incomes that correspond to various assumptions about mortality and credited interest, assuming annual payments at mid-year (a reasonable approximation of monthly payments).

Table 8.14. Before-Tax Rate of Return that a Taxable Association Must Earn to Match the After-Tax Benefits of an Immediate Annuity

Immediate annuity: 8.5% implicit credited rate

| | Required Rate of Return (Before Tax) | |
Tax Rate	Living and Death Benefits Combined	Living Benefits Only
0%	8.5%	8.5%
15	8.8	8.5
30	9.1	8.4
50	9.7	7.8

In early 1989, long-term Treasury bond yields were about 9 percent, while the implicit credited rate for competitive annuities seems to have been about 8.5-10.0 percent. This suggests that a careful shopper could have found a contract that provided good—perhaps excellent—value for the money. As before, this comparison ignores the potentially significant value of the annuity's long-term guarantees. In short, it appears that investors had to give up little or nothing in investment performance to obtain an income that they could not outlive.

Figure 8.6.   Implicit Mortality and Interest Assumptions for Immediate Annuities: February 1989

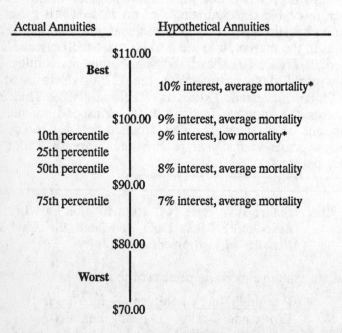

Actual Annuities	Hypothetical Annuities
$110.00	
Best	
	10% interest, average mortality*
$100.00	9% interest, average mortality
10th percentile	9% interest, low mortality*
25th percentile	
50th percentile	8% interest, average mortality
$90.00	
75th percentile	7% interest, average mortality
$80.00	
Worst	
$70.00	

* "Average mortality" is the 1983 IAM Table. "Low mortality" is the 1983 IAM Table with a projected 1.25% annual improvement.

Immediate annuities are boring, but they probably deserve to be used more than they are. They provide a solid foundation that you can build on with income and appreciation from mutual funds, real estate, and other sources.

9

DISABILITY INCOME INSURANCE

For most people, the risk of becoming disabled is greater than the risk of dying; and the financial consequences of a long-term disability may be more onerous than the hardships caused by a premature death. In spite of this, many people insure their homes, their cars, and their lives but overlook the need to insure their incomes.

Disability is a much more complicated condition than death. After all, you're either dead or you're not—and once you're dead, you stay dead. In contrast, you can be disabled for a day or for the rest of your life. You can be unable to work at all, unable to work at what you were doing, or simply unable to do *some* of what you were doing. You can be disabled, recover, and then become disabled again. And you can call yourself disabled when another person in the same situation goes to work every day. All of these complications are reflected in the contractual provisions of a disability income policy. Companies compete on contract language as well as price, so you should not assume that once you've read one disability income contract, you've read them all. The proof of this is that the National Underwriter Company's *Disability Income & Health Insurance Time Saver*, a reference tool for agents, has more than one thousand explanatory footnotes.

Figure 9.1 provides a checklist to help you select an appropriate contract.

Figure 9.1. Disability Income Insurance: A Checklist

I. BEFORE THE PURCHASE

1. What is your definition of a successful search?
   ___ the *best* product (sorry, this book can't help you)
   ___ good price/benefit relationship

2. Who will advise you?
   ___ do it yourself
   ___ commission-based agent or broker
   ___ fee-and-commission financial planner
   ___ fee-for-service consultant or financial planner
   ___ consulting actuary
   ___ employee benefits or health care specialist

3. How much coverage?
   ___ enough to replace income
   ___ minimum/maximum limits
   ___ affordable amount

4. What type of policy?
   A.___ level or step-rate premium
   ___ yearly renewable term universal
   B.___ Participating
   ___ Nonparticipating

5. How will you choose among several companies?
   ___ ratings
   ___ financial analysis
   ___ management quality
   ___ valuation actuary's report
   ___ experience/commitment to disability income business
   ___ other judgments

6. How will you choose among several products?
   ___ product features
   ___ price
   ___ company's reputation and track record

7. Who will pay the premiums?
   ___ you
   ___ employer
   ___ both

8. Other decisions?
   ___ definition of disability
   ___ benefit period
   ___ waiting period
   ___ residual disability benefit
   ___ cost-of-living benefit
   ___ future increase options
   ___ other optional provisions
   ___ level/step-rate premium
   ___ premium payment mode

II. AFTER THE PURCHASE

1.___ Will you keep the policy in force?
2.___ Will you change the monthly benefit?
3.___ Will you change the waiting and/or benefit period (if applicable)?
4.___ Will you add or remove riders?

PRODUCT FEATURES

All disability income insurance policies pay a monthly income while you are disabled; all have a *waiting period* before payments begin; and all have a maximum *benefit period*. But that's where the similarity ends. The only reliable way to compare the provisions of different contracts is to get specimen copies, read them, and ask questions. Some provisions will be part of the base policy, while others are added as riders.

Table 9.1 highlights some of the contract differences you should be aware of. Here's a brief explanation of the features you will likely run across as you go shopping:

Type of Policy

Disability income insurance comes in three forms that are analogous to whole life, annual renewable term, and universal life. The whole life form is by far the most common. Premiums remain level to age 65, although many companies also offer a "step-rate" version that has a lower initial premium and then a higher level premium after several years. Unlike whole life insurance, there is no cash surrender value, so you wind up overpaying for your coverage if you buy a level-premium policy and then drop it after a few years.

To solve this problem, some companies offer a yearly renewable term form of disability income insurance, either on a stand-alone basis or as an addition to a level-premium base policy. Premiums increase annually and may become level at a later age. The main advantage of the yearly renewable term (YRT) form is that it is as much as 50 percent cheaper than traditional contracts during the early years. At least one company offers a *universal disability* contract. As with universal life, the premium is deposited into an interest-earning account, and charges are made for expenses and the annually increasing cost of insurance.

Table 9.1. A Comparison of Different Levels of Coverage

Feature	More Protection	Less Protection	Recommendation
• Policy form			Level- or step-rate premium if you think you'll keep the policy for a long time; YRT if you're not sure.
• Premium guarantee	Noncancellable and guaranteed renewable.	Guaranteed renewable, conditionally renewable.	Non-cancellable and guaranteed renewable.
• Definition of total disability	Own occupation.	Any income, occupation replacement.	Depends. If you couldn't do your current job, what could you do?
• Exclusions	None, except for pre-existing conditions during the contestable period.	Acts of war, normal pregnancy, pre-existing conditions, self-inflicted injuries.	The fewer, the better.
• Waiting period	One month.	One year.	Depends on your other resources. Compare prices for several waiting periods.
• Benefit period	Lifetime, for both sickness and accident.	Two years.	Depends on what you can afford. Compare prices for several benefit periods.
• Social Security	Yes.	No.	Yes. Good way to supplement and increase your coverage.
• Residual disability benefit	Yes, with zero-day qualification period.	No.	Depends. What will your income be if you return to work part-time?
• Future increase options	Yes.	No.	Yes. This will help you keep your coverage up-to-date.
• Cost-of-living adjustments	Yes. No cap, with compounded rate.	No.	Depends on what you can afford. Nice to have, but it isn't cheap.
• Full recovery benefit	Same benefit period as for total disability.	For three months after disability ends.	Depends. Will you have to rebuild your business?
• Post-issue			
–flexibility			Good to have; needs may change.
–enhancements			Good to have, to keep coverage up-to-date.

Guarantees

There are several kinds of renewal and rate guarantees. *Conditionally renewable* means that the company cannot cancel your coverage because of your health, but it reserves the right to increase premiums and to refuse to continue offering the coverage to all insureds of the same class. *Guaranteed renewable* means that the company cannot refuse to renew the coverage, but it can increase the premiums for all insureds of the same class. *Noncancellable and guaranteed renewable* (*noncan* for short) means that the company cannot refuse to renew your coverage and cannot increase the premium.

All quality individual disability income insurance policies are noncancellable and guaranteed renewable to at least age 65, and you should not consider buying anything else. Policies are typically guaranteed renewable beyond age 65 if you are actively working, and premiums are based on then-current rates set by the company.

Premium Rate Structure

Some companies charge men and women the same rate; others charge different rates. At most ages, morbidity rates are higher for women than for men, so unisex pricing creates a subsidy from men to women. A general rule is that women should buy policies with unisex rates, and men should buy policies with sex-distinct rates. However, prices vary from one company to another, so you can't rely on general rules.

Nonsmoker/smoker distinctions are also common; for level-premium policies, nonsmoker rates might be 10-15 percent less than smoker rates.

In addition to a rate per $100 of monthly income, many companies charge an annual policy fee of $15-$50. Banding—that is, charging a lower rate for larger policy sizes—is not as common for disability income insurance as it is for life insurance. As with life insurance, premiums can be paid annually, semi-annually, quarterly, or monthly. The least expensive payment modes are annually or monthly, through preauthorized withdrawals from your checking account. Nonparticipating contracts charge a guaranteed premium and pay no dividends. Participating contracts charge a somewhat higher guaranteed premium and pay a dividend each year, based on actual experience.

Issue and Participation Limits

Experience has shown that claims occur more frequently and last longer when people have so much disability income insurance that they have little or no incentive to return to work. To prevent overinsurance, companies set limits on the amount of coverage they will issue (the *issue limit*), as well as on the total amount of disability income insurance from all sources (the *participation limit*). The higher your income, the lower the percentage you will be able to replace. For any given income level, the maximum replacement ratio is higher when the disability benefits will be taxable (see "Tax Considerations" later in this chapter), since your spendable income will be reduced by taxes.

The issue limit is also affected by the company's calculation of your insurable income. In addition to salary and bonuses, your insurable income may include pension plan contributions and the imputed value of some perquisites. When you apply for coverage, list every item of compensation that is job-related, even if it is not reportable as taxable income.

Once the contract is issued, the maximum monthly benefit usually cannot be reduced if your income drops. This is a peculiar feature that promotes fraudulent claims, since under-employed insureds can "earn" more from disability than by working. Australian insurance companies are smarter; they set limits on what they'll pay.

Definition of Total Disability

This is one of the most important features of the policy. The actual language varies from one contract to another, but the main distinction is between *any-occupation* and *own-occupation*. Here's one *any-occ* definition of total disability: "Total disability means your inability to engage in any gainful occupation in which you might reasonably be expected to engage, with due regard for your education, training, experience, and prior economic status." Under this definition, a surgeon who injures a hand and can no longer operate would not be considered disabled if he was able to work as a hospital administrator.

In contrast, an *own-occ* definition might say that "total disability means your inability to perform the material and substantial duties of your occupation." With this policy, the injured surgeon would collect full disability benefits in addition to any salary as an administrator.

The insured occupation is the occupation at the time of claim, not the occupation at the date of issue. If you take out the policy as an accountant and then become a professional stock car driver, that's the company's problem. (Wait until the contestable period ends before you change careers, though.) Contracts sometimes contain a *split definition*; disability is defined as own-occ during an initial period, such as two years, and any-occ thereafter.

Income replacement contracts are designed to indemnify you against a loss of income. A typical definition might be "total disability means that due to sickness or injury you are unable to perform the material and substantial duties of your occupation and you are not engaged in any occupation."

Definitions of *injury* and *sickness* are also worth reading. The policy might say that "*sickness* means disease which first manifests itself after the date of issue and while your policy is in force." Or it might simply say that "*sickness* means illness or disease."

An own-occ definition results in more claims and is therefore more expensive, but it does not necessarily offer more protection to every policyholder. You have to ask yourself what jobs you could do if you couldn't perform the duties of your current job. For example, if you work at a desk all day, you might not need own-occ coverage, since a total disability in your own job would probably keep you from doing anything else. In contrast, dentists, TV reporters, and symphony orchestra conductors might want to insure their earnings in their own occupations.

Exclusions

A quality policy will cover occupational and nonoccupational disabilities due to sickness or accident, but there may be exclusions for acts of war, normal pregnancy, self-inflicted injuries, and pre-existing conditions. The meaning of "acts of war" has become fuzzy in an age of state-sponsored terrorism, so you might have to ask the company for an explanation. Companies also add exclusions at the time of issue for specific impairments, in lieu of charging an extra premium or rejecting the application altogether.

Waiting Period

Also called the *elimination period*, a waiting period is the number of days of disability that must elapse before benefits begin. Typical waiting periods are 30, 60, 90, 180, and 360 days. The longer the waiting period, the lower the premium. For example, here's one rate schedule for a policy with a $3,000 monthly benefit to age 65, issued to a 40-year-old nonsmoker:

Waiting Period	Annual Premium	As % of 90-Day
30 days	$1,567	135
60	1,309	113
90	1,161	—
180	1,013	87
360	886	76

You should generally choose the longest possible waiting period, in accordance with your available assets and your other sources of protection, such as employer-provided sick pay. Note that if benefit payments are made at the end of each month, the actual waiting period is one month longer than the stated period. Some companies allow you to increase the waiting period after issue, with a premium adjustment based on the issue-age rates.

Benefit Period

This is the maximum period for which benefits are payable for a disability. The most common benefit periods are two years, five years, to age 65, and lifetime. The benefit period for sickness may be less than the benefit period for accidents. Also, the benefit period and/or the benefit amount may be reduced for disabilities that begin at age 55 or later.

The longer the benefit period, the higher the premium. Here's the rate schedule for the earlier example of a policy issued to a 40-year-old, with a 90-day waiting period:

Benefit Period	Annual Premium	As % of Age 65
2 years	$448	39
5 years	757	65
Age 65	1,161	—
Lifetime	1,617	139

You should generally choose the longest benefit period that you can afford and might need, taking into account your Social Security retirement benefits, employer-provided pension, and other assets, as well as your other financial planning goals.

In order to make an informed decision, it's helpful to know something about the probability of being disabled for a long time. Table 9.2 shows the probability that a 35-year-old professional who has been disabled for ninety days will continue to be disabled for a longer period, based on the actual claims of 20 companies from 1973 to 1979. (This is the most recent published data that is available in sufficient detail.) A few observations:

- The odds of being disabled for at least ninety days at age 35 seem small (0.16 percent), but they're actually about three times as great as the chances of dying.

- Almost 75 percent of the people who are disabled for three months will recover within the first year, and almost 90 percent of them will recover within 5 years. That's the good news.

- 50 percent of the people who are disabled for two years will still be disabled after fifteen years, and 25 percent will remain disabled until age 65. That's the bad news.

This pattern is the same at other ages; most people recover after a short time, but those who don't are likely to remain disabled for years.

Table 9.2. If You're Disabled for Ninety Days, How Long Will Your Disability Last?

Male, age 35, professional class, 90-day waiting period
Probability of 90-day disability at age 35: 0.16%

		Probability of Continued Disability
Month:	4	79%
	5	63
	6	51
	9	33
	12	26
Year:	2	16
	3	14
	4	12
	5	11
	10	9
	15	8
	20	7
	30	4

Source: Continuance table derived from 1985 Disability Table Study (DTS) Basic Table

---

The general rule that you should buy insurance to cover catastrophes would seem to argue in favor of lifetime benefits. However, most people have limited resources, so you may have to answer this question: Which is the more likely catastrophe, being permanently disabled and seeing your benefits stop because you were too cheap to buy adequate coverage, or living a healthy life and running out of money in retirement because you spent too much on disability income insurance?

Recurrent Disability

If you return to work on a full-time basis and then become disabled again from a related cause, companies will generally treat this as a continuation of the prior disability for the purpose of satisfying the waiting period. The maximum allowable period between such disabilities is often six or twelve months.

Presumptive Total Disability

You are generally considered to be totally disabled, whether or not you can work, if you suffer a permanent loss of sight, speech, hearing, or use of hands or feet. The list of included conditions varies from one company to another.

Residual Disability Benefit

This pays a partial benefit if you are not totally disabled but suffer a loss of income because of an injury or sickness. Typically, no benefits will be paid unless your loss exceeds 20-25 percent of prior earnings, and total disability benefits will be paid if your loss exceeds 80 percent. The definition of residual disability must be congruent with the definition of total disability in the contract. For example, under a *dual definition* in an own-occ contract, you would receive total disability benefits if you could not work in your own occupation, and you would receive residual disability benefits if you could continue to work in your own occupation at reduced earnings.

The *qualification period* is the number of days that total disability must continue before residual disability benefits are payable. A *zero-day qualification period* means that residual benefits can begin as soon as the waiting period ends, even if you have not been totally disabled. The benefit payment is usually computed using this formula:

$$\begin{matrix} \text{Residual} \\ \text{disability} \\ \text{benefit} \end{matrix} = \frac{\text{Loss of earnings}}{\text{Prior earnings}} \times \text{Maximum benefit}$$

For example, if your prior earnings were $80,000, your current earnings are $40,000, and the maximum benefit is $3,000 a month, the company would pay you 50 percent of the maximum benefit, or $1,500.

Prior earnings are often indexed to inflation; otherwise, the residual disability benefit will gradually drop even if your degree of disability remains the same. There may also be a minimum benefit, such as 50 percent, for a short period. The definition of prior earnings varies from one company to another. It can be based on one year's earnings or an average of several years. Self-employed professionals and business owners also need to know how the company treats accounts receivable. If you become disabled but are continuing to collect amounts previously billed, are you entitled to receive benefits?

With income replacement contracts, residual disability benefits are automatically included as part of the base policy, since the purpose of the policy is to indemnify you against the loss of income due to sickness or accident.

As with the own-occ definition of total disability, the usefulness of residual disability benefits depends on your situation. You have to ask yourself what your income would be if you returned to work on a part-time basis. If your employer would pay you a full salary, this provision may be not needed. (But what if you change jobs?)

Partial Disability

Partial and *residual* are often used interchangeably, but some contracts that do not pay residual benefits have a limited benefit for partial disabilities, based on loss of ability to perform significant duties.

Social Security Supplement

This pays an additional monthly benefit if you are not eligible to receive Social Security disability benefits. Most applications for Social Security benefits are rejected, so this is a good way to increase your available coverage. Questions to ask: When do the benefits begin? Are benefits paid for both total and residual disability? Is the benefit coordinated with government programs other than Social Security?

Cost-of-Living Benefit

During a period of disability, this increases your monthly benefit once a year, to offset the impact of inflation. Some questions to ask: Is the increase based on the Consumer Price Index, a constant rate, or some combination of the two? Are the increases based on simple interest (that is, a fixed dollar amount each year) or compound interest? Is there a cap on the total accumulated increases? Can benefits go down as well as up?

Adjustments are made only once you become disabled; this provision does not index the pre-disability maximum monthly benefit to inflation. However, after a period of disability, some companies will allow you to increase your base coverage to the new inflation-adjusted amount, without evidence of good health. You'll have to pay an additional premium, but you'll qualify for standard rates even though you've just been disabled. Despite this favorable aspect, the cost-of-living benefit is not for everyone. It's an expensive option that is of real value only during long periods of disability. If you have limited money to spend on disability income insurance, you should probably pass this up.

Future Increase Option

This gives you the right to purchase additional insurance at one or more policy anniversary dates. Evidence of good health is not required; however, your income must be sufficient to justify the increase. The additional premium is based on the rate for your attained age. Questions to ask: Does the company use the rate schedule at the date of issue or the date of increase? Can an option be carried over if it is not exercised? Can an option be exercised while you are disabled? (If so, this is a partial—and much cheaper—substitute for the cost-of-living benefit.)

Full Recovery Benefit

Some companies will pay a partial benefit after you are no longer disabled if you continue to suffer a loss of income. The maximum benefit period varies. This provision is especially useful for self-employed professionals who must re-establish contacts and build up their business again.

Rehabilitation

To help you return to work, a company will often pay the cost of a pre-approved rehabilitation program, in addition to the normal disability benefits. Limitations vary.

Hospital Benefits

Some contracts provide that benefits will be paid during the waiting period if you are confined in a hospital.

Short-Term Benefits

You can sometimes receive an additional monthly income for a short time after the waiting period ends, to cover short-term financial needs.

Survivor Benefit

Some companies pay a small benefit to your estate—for example, three times the monthly benefit—if you die before the end of the benefit period. Your estate may also receive a pro rata refund of premiums paid for a period beyond the date of death.

Benefit Payment Mode

Disability income policies usually pay a monthly income, but some companies will make a lump-sum payment if the length of the disability can be reasonably determined.

Waiver of Premium

Insurance companies typically waive the premium while you're disabled. Some questions to ask: Is the waiver for both total and residual disability? When does it start? How long does it stay in force? Does it include a refund of premiums for the waiting period?

Return-of-Premium Rider

This rider refunds a portion or all of the premiums you have paid over a certain period, but the refund is reduced dollar for dollar by any claims that you file. In theory, this allows the company to offer lower-cost coverage, because it encourages persistency and discourages small claims.

Figure 9.2A shows one common way of evaluating the investment merits of the rider. In this case, the rider costs 51 percent of the base policy premium (P) each year, and it provides a refund of three years' total premiums (3 x 151 percent of the base policy premium, or 4.53P) at the end of the sixth year, assuming that you have no claims during that period. The internal rate of return on the "investment" in the rider is therefore 11.3 percent. However, this does not take into account any claims that will reduce, or even eliminate, the refund, so the true rate of return must be less than 11.3 percent.

Figure 9.2B presents another approach, which starts with the observation that by electing the return-of-premium rider, you are in effect choosing a longer waiting period, since you are on the hook for up to three years' worth of premiums if you file any claims. You can duplicate the results of the return-of-premium rider by imagining a policy with a special kind of waiting period, one where the company pays the claim but then demands a reimbursement (without interest) at the end of six years.

Let's suppose that a 40-year-old would have to pay $920 a year for a policy with a $2,000 monthly benefit and a 90-day waiting period. Add $469 (51 percent of $920) for the return-of-premium rider, so the total premium is $1,389 a year, and the maximum refund that you can get at the end of six years is $4,167 (3 x $1,389).

Figure 9.2. Two Ways of Looking at the Return-of-Premium Rider

Figure 9.2A   A. If you ignore potential claims

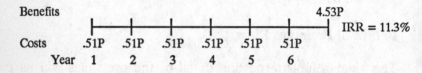

Figure 9.2B   B. If you take into account potential claims

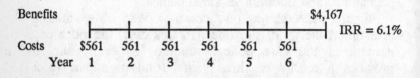

Now suppose that, instead of buying the rider, you ask the company to give you a base policy with a waiting period that would put you at risk for the same amount—$4,167—as with the rider. With a $2,000 monthly benefit, that translates into about two months, in addition to the original 90-day period. Let's assume that a policy with a five-month waiting period (and an appropriate stop-loss provision for multiple claims) would cost $828 a year, or 10 percent less than the ninety-day base policy. You will be better off with this alternative if you can invest the difference in premiums ($1,389 less $828, or $561) so that you have more than the maximum refund ($4,167) at the end of the sixth year. That implies an annual rate of return of 6.1 percent.

Clearly, a lot depends on what the actual premiums are. If the alternative policy costs $874, rather than $828, the implied rate of return would be 8.6 percent. Leaving aside the irony of giving insurance buyers another way to gamble, the return-of-premium rider is a good example of what consumer advocate Ralph Nader has called "contrived complexity." Is the rider a good deal or just a marketing gimmick? How much time are you willing to spend to figure it all out?

Enhancement of Existing Contracts

Some companies try to keep their existing contracts up-to-date by adding improvements as they are made to new products. This is practical, however, only if the new policy provision is not likely to significantly increase claims costs. For example, a company might be able to remove an "act of war" exclusion from existing policies, but it would probably not be able to add an automatic cost-of-living adjustment or future increase option without charging an extra premium and requesting evidence of insurability. The practice of enhancing existing contracts is especially important for level-premium products. Because you are overpaying for your coverage during the early years, you don't want to have to replace an obsolete contract with a new one every few years. Planned obsolescence is fine for insurance salespeople—who pocket a new first-year commission each time—but it's not very good for the people who have to pay the premiums.

Other Types of Disability Income Policies

In addition to policies that replace a worker's lost earnings, there are several types of disability income policies for business needs. *Overhead expense* policies reimburse a disabled business owner for normal operating expenses, such as employee salaries, rent, and utilities. The benefit period generally does not exceed two years.

Disability buy-out policies provide a funding vehicle for business buy-sell agreements. If an owner is disabled for an extended period, such as one year, the other owners can buy him out with the money received from the insurance company.

Key person disability policies protect businesses against economic losses caused by the disability of a key employee. A monthly benefit is paid for a relatively short period, such as eighteen months, to cover the salary of a replacement employee and any other expenses that may arise.

TAX CONSIDERATIONS

In most cases, the tax treatment of disability income insurance is mercifully simple. If you pay the premiums with your own after-tax dollars, the benefits are tax free. If your employer pays the premiums and takes a tax deduction for them, you will have to pay income tax on any benefits you receive. You and your employer can also arrange to split the premiums. Here are some of the possibilities:

- Your employer pays the portion of the premium that corresponds to the first two years of benefits, and you pay the rest. Result: The first two years of benefits are taxable, and the rest are tax free.

- Your employer pays the portion of the premium that corresponds to benefits for total disability, and you pay the portion that corresponds to residual disability. Result: Total disability benefits are taxable, and residual disability benefits are tax free.

- You and your employer each pay 50 percent of the premium. Result: 50 percent of the benefits are taxable, and 50 percent are tax free.

One planning approach is to split the premiums so that the taxable portion of the benefits received will offset your tax-deductible expenses (mortgage interest, state taxes, medical expenses, miscellaneous deductions) while you are disabled.

PRICING CONSIDERATIONS

As with life insurance and annuities, individual disability income insurance requires the insurer to make an initial investment of its capital, with the expectation of realizing an adequate rate of return over time. To set a price for its product, the company has to take account of anticipated marketing, underwriting, and administrative expenses; morbidity, mortality and recovery rates; lapse rates; investment income; and the prices charged by competitors. A prudent company will perform profit tests and sensitivity analyses before a product is offered for sale to the public.

For agent-sold contracts, the base commission might be 50 percent or more of the premium in the first year, 10-15 percent for the next nine years, and 5-10 percent thereafter. Other agent-related compensation can raise the distribution costs to 90 percent or more of the first-year premium.

Underwriting costs are generally higher for disability income insurance than for life insurance, because of the need to assess the applicant's financial status and propensity to work, in addition to his or her health.

Ongoing administrative expenses are also higher, because of the subjective nature and complexity of the claims. Some actuaries believe that in order to evaluate claims and service them properly, claims administration expenses need to be at least 7 percent of claims costs. In contrast, the administrative costs for a $100,000 life insurance claim are generally less than 0.5 percent.

Morbidity rates—that is, the incidence of sickness and injuries—are a major determinant of price. Morbidity experience has been deteriorating in recent years. Possible contributing factors include medical advances that have converted deaths into long-term disabilities, a higher incidence of subjective claims that are hard to challenge (back problems, mental and nervous disorders), a growing entitlement mentality among Americans, an oversupply of professionals (who then use their disability income policies as a kind of unemployment insurance), liberalized pregnancy coverage, unisex pricing, AIDS, and overinsurance. By one estimate, 20-25 percent of all claims paid are fraudulent.

High expected lapse rates increase the cost of disability income insurance, because the company has to recover its acquisition costs from a smaller number of remaining policyholders, who also tend to be poorer health risks. In contrast to life insurance, however, high lapse rates can benefit the company after a level-premium contract has been in force for many years, since there is no cash surrender value to pay out. If past experience is any indication of the future, fewer than half of the contracts sold today will still be in force ten years from now.

Investment income, although not as important for disability income insurance as it is for cash value life insurance, is still a significant source of revenue. A high portfolio yield can partially offset unfavorable morbidity, expense, and lapse experience. Assets supporting disability income policies are usually invested in short- to medium-term instruments.

Load Versus Low-Load

All other things being equal, a low-load product should cost about 15-25 percent less than an agent-sold product, because of the lower distribution costs. However, this theoretical difference may overstate the actual cost savings, because agents are often able to offer 5-15 percent discounts to small groups of individuals whose premiums are billed together. For years, actuaries have criticized these discounts as being economically unjustified, but they still persist.

You may also be able to obtain individual disability income insurance at a discount through a professional or special-interest association.

The Past and the Future

The 1980s were a wonderful time for disability income insurance buyers. In their scramble for market share, insurers competed by expanding benefits and lowering prices, while agents, financial planners, and journalists upgraded their lists of "things to look for" in a quality disability income policy. Pricing actuaries, the people who design these products, had a different perspective. To them, the previous decade was the "silly period" in the history of disability income insurance. In 1985, Monte J. Hopper, of Connecticut Mutual Life Insurance Company, had this to say about the own-occupation definition of disability: "If there is a good reason to pay an insured a full benefit when he or she is unable to work at his or her regular occupation, but is actually working at another, I certainly haven't heard one." He went on to ridicule cost-of-living adjustments that exceed inflation, guaranteed insurability options that can be exercised while an insured is disabled, unreduced lifetime benefits for older insureds, unisex pricing, normal pregnancy benefits with no increase in premium, presumptive disability, and small-group discounts.

It's clear that product design has been driven more by marketing than by actuarial considerations and that many insurers are now suffering the consequences. In addition, rating organizations, such as Standard & Poor's, take a dim view of companies that value growth over profitability, so insurers that want to maintain a favorable claims-paying rating will have to change their focus. Industry observers generally make these predictions about the future:

- Premiums will go up, and dividends (if any) will go down. Some companies have already raised their prices.

- The trend toward more liberal contractual provisions will slow or stop and may even reverse itself.

- Follow-up procedures used to detect malingering will be strengthened.

- Underwriting will become more stringent. Insurers have found that full medical testing can be economically justified even for low levels of coverage, since substance abuse and other disorders are more common than was previously thought.

For consumers, the obvious implication is that you should buy a quality policy now and lock in today's prices and contractual provisions.

HOW MUCH COVERAGE DO YOU NEED?

The amount of disability income insurance that you need is the difference between your required income and the resources available if you become disabled. Figure 9.3 is a "quick and dirty" outline of the calculation.

If you become disabled, some of your living expenses will probably go up (medical care, electricity) and some will probably go down (vacations, clothing). Your financial goals may change as well. You might need to remodel your home to allow wheelchair access, or you might cancel your plans to buy a boat or a new house. However, you might still want to set aside some money each month for your children's education. You will need enough spendable income each month to take care of your living expenses and your other goals. Some of your disability income needs may be satisfied by coverage that you already have—or think you have. Before you include these potential sources in your calculation, however, it's important to understand their limitations, discussed below.

Social Security

The Social Security Administration's definition of *disability* is very restrictive: "An individual is permanently and totally disabled if he is unable to engage in any substantial gainful activity by reason of medically determinable physical or mental impairment which can be expected to result in death or which has lasted or can be expected to last for a continuous period of not less than twelve months." Not surprisingly, most applications for benefits are rejected. To qualify for benefits, you must have worked for up to ten years, depending on your age. If you pass both of these hurdles, there is still a five-month waiting period, and the benefits will probably satisfy only part of your monthly income need.

Other Government Programs

These include workers' compensation, state cash sickness programs, and a variety of other programs targeted at specific groups. As with Social Security, the provisions are restrictive.

Figure 9.3. How Much Disability Income Insurance Do You Need?

Required Monthly Income:

Current living expenses _____

  —Increases due to disability _____

  —Decreases due to disability _____

Savings for other goals _____

  —Increases due to disability _____

  —Decreases due to disability _____

Total Income Needed _____

Available Monthly Income:

Social Security _____

Other government programs _____

Employer/group/association benefits _____

Waiver-of-premium benefits _____

Credit disability benefits _____

Income from investable assets not
    allocated to other goals _____

Spouse's income _____

Total Income Available _____

Additional Coverage Needed _____

Group Coverage

These plans are often sponsored by employers and professional associations. Before you include them in your calculations, some questions need to be asked. What is the definition of *disability*? What are the exclusions? What is the waiting period? What is the benefit period for accident and sickness? Is there any reduction in benefits at later ages? Are benefits offset by Social Security or other payments? Is there a residual disability benefit? Are benefits taxable? What happens if you leave the employer or association? What are the rate and renewal guarantees—can the insurer stop offering the plan or raise rates without limit?

Employer- and association-sponsored coverage is popular because of its low cost and simplified underwriting. However, in many cases your employer or association would be doing you a bigger favor if it helped you obtain a quality, individually-owned policy at a discount.

Waiver-of-Premium Provisions

The waiver-of-premium provision on life insurance contracts typically contains an any-occupation or split definition of disability. Depending on the product, it may cover either the entire premium or only the cost-of-insurance deductions.

The waiver-of-premium provision on disability income contracts uses the same definition of *disability* as the contract itself, so it's probably appropriate to include it as a resource.

Credit Disability Income

These benefits might cover mortgage or credit card payments. The coverage is generally overpriced and provisions are restrictive.

Investable Assets

This is only the portion of your assets that is not earmarked for some other goal, such as your retirement. It should also be reduced by the living expenses you will have to pay out of your own pocket during the waiting period.

Spouse's Income

You can add this in only if it isn't already being used for living expenses or other planning goals.

After examining each of these potential sources of income, you can include the ones you feel comfortable relying on, taking note of the waiting and benefit periods in each case. If you map out all of the income sources on a time line drawn on a sheet of paper, you'll be able to get a ballpark estimate of how much disability income coverage you need. However, the amount that you actually buy may be determined by the carrier's issue and participation limits and what you can afford.

SHOPPING FOR DISABILITY INCOME INSURANCE

Here are some suggestions for finding a reasonably priced product:

- Keep in mind that policy provisions are more important than price. A policy that doesn't pay benefits when you need them is no bargain at any price.

- Get a specimen copy of the contract and riders and read every word. It's your choice: You can read the contract *before* you make the purchase or *after* you've become disabled and are not receiving the benefits you thought you were entitled to.

- Look at the trade-offs between benefits and cost. Unless you have a lot of money to spend on disability income insurance, decide which types of benefits are of most value to you. To construct proposals for comparison, start with an adequate amount of total disability coverage, and then add additional benefits as your budget allows. Figure 9.3 gives you one possible format.

- Ask about flexibility. Can you adjust the waiting period, benefit period, and other options as your needs change?

- Look at both low-load and agent-sold products. If you decide to use an agent, look for someone with experience in selling disability income insurance. You'll pay the same commissions and get more expertise.

Figure 9.4. Constructing Proposals for Comparison

	Annual Cost
Total disability	_____
(monthly benefit:)	
(benefit period:)	
(waiting period:)	
Higher monthly benefit ( )	_____
Longer benefit period ( )	_____
Shorter waiting period ( )	_____
Future increase options	_____
Residual disability benefits	_____
Own-occupation definition of disability	_____
Social Security substitute	_____
Cost-of-living adjustments	_____
Other: _____	
Other: _____	
Other: _____	
Total	_____

- Try to determine the company's record of fair payment of claims. Sources of information include agents, financial planners, and consumer complaint logs maintained by the company and by your state insurance department. In interpreting the responses, don't forget that companies have a legitimate right to investigate suspicious claims to protect themselves against fraud.

- Choose a participating (i.e., dividend-paying) policy if you're willing to accept some of the risk of higher morbidity rates, in exchange for the possibility of a lower long-term cost if experience improves. Choose a nonparticipating policy if you want to lock in today's premium rates for the life of the policy.

- If a contractual provision is ambiguous, ask for written clarification from an officer of the company. This is a common practice for disability income insurance, so you needn't feel that you're making an unusual request.

10

CHOOSING A COMPANY

There are more than two thousand life insurance companies in the United States, but six hundred of them account for over 99 percent of the life insurance and annuities sold to individuals—and some of those are probably not licensed in your state. New York residents, for example, have fewer than two hundred companies to choose from.

IMPORTANT CONSIDERATIONS

In evaluating an insurance company, prospective policyholders should focus on two questions in particular: Is the company organizationally and financially stable? Will the company treat you fairly after you buy the product?

Stability

Stability is clearly a key consideration in deciding whether to do business with an insurer. If the company gets into financial trouble, you can experience delays in receiving benefits or, worse, suffer a loss. If a company changes hands, the new owners often conduct a thorough review of the product portfolio, with an eye toward realizing the "hidden values" that led them to buy the company. That's probably not good news for existing policyholders.

Of course, none of this would matter if you could quickly move from one company to another at the first sign of trouble, as you can with banks. However, many insurance products have stiff surrender penalties that last for years; some products, such as immediate annuities, do not allow surrenders at all. You may also be locked in if your health deteriorates and you are no longer insurable at standard rates.

Some insurance buyers assume that state *guaranty associations*, also called *guaranty funds*, will protect them in the event of company insolvency, but there are several reasons not to be so complacent:

1. A few states do not have a guaranty association.

2. Liability is typically limited to $100,000 for cash values and $300,000 for death benefits, although some states are more generous. Excessively high product guarantees may not be honored; in these cases, your benefits can be reduced below the amounts that were "guaranteed" by the insolvent insurer. Some investment-oriented products may not be covered. Also, you may not be covered if you buy a policy from a company that is not licensed in your state.

3. You may experience delays in receiving payments. Unlike the Federal Deposit Insurance Corporation, state guaranty funds have no funds; instead, they operate on an assessment basis. When an insolvency occurs, each member company pays a small percentage of its in-state premiums into the fund, subject to an annual maximum. In some cases, it could take years to recover losses.

4. The guaranty fund may not be triggered at all, since state regulators exercise discretion in how they handle impaired insurers. This can involve such arcane legal issues as the difference between an interim and a final order of liquidation.

Although the guaranty association system has been strengthened in recent years, it is still a safety net with holes. For more information about your state's association, contact your state insurance department or the National Organization of Life and Health Insurance Guaranty Associations (NOLHGA, 13873 Park Center Road, Suite 329, Herndon, VA 22071).

Fairness

As mentioned in Chapter 1, it's hard to know if an insurance company has consistently been fair to its existing policyholders. In fact, it's not always clear what "fair" means. Is it fair to use high profit margins on old business to subsidize new business? Is it fair to charge expenses for AIDS claims against policyholders in all states, regardless of each state's incidence of AIDS? Is it fair to change from a portfolio average to a new-money method of allocating investment income in order to remain competitive when interest rates rise? All of these questions are debatable.

The best way to judge fairness is to have an independent actuarial consulting firm conduct a comprehensive review of a company's pricing practices, to determine if they fall within reasonable bounds. For the time being, this is impractical. Instead, you'll have to settle for published dividend and interest rate histories, the "Past repricing actions" section of our product profiles, the limited commentary in *Best's Insurance Reports*, and each company's own declarations of how wonderfully it has treated its customers. Some questions worth asking:

- In what ways are existing policyholders treated differently from new policyholders? (You can't judge whether the differences are justified until you know what they are.)

- How do actual benefits relate to what was illustrated at the time of issue?

- When benefits are added to new contracts, are they offered to existing policyholders as well?

- When tax law changes render an insurance program obsolete, how does the company assist its customers?

- Does the company keep its commitment to provide adequate service as long as a contract is in force?

Companies that treat their policyholders fairly will be able to point to specific actions taken in the past that address all of these questions.

INDUSTRY OUTLOOK

Because of the well-publicized failure of so many savings and loan institutions, more questions are being raised about the financial health of the life insurance industry. Are we heading toward another national crisis? The majority view among analysts is that:

- Many life insurance companies are not as strong as they used to be because of smaller profit margins, increased investment and underwriting risks, and reduced agent loyalty. Competition has created good values for consumers—perhaps too good—and companies now have to figure out how to design competitive products that are also profitable.

- On the whole, the life insurance industry will muddle through whatever problems it faces. Comparisons with the S&L industry are inappropriate because there is no evidence of widespread fraud; most companies are reasonably well-run; state regulators are getting tougher because they want to preserve their autonomy, and they know that Congress is watching them; actuaries pride themselves on being able to quantify risks, and they don't want their reputations trashed; the industry knows that it sells promises and that without public confidence it will have nothing to sell.

- As a result of mergers, acquisitions, and insolvencies, fewer life insurance companies will exist in the United States. Soothsayers disagree on how much consolidation will take place, however. One regulator predicts that 20 percent of all companies will disappear—mostly through mergers and acquisitions—within the next ten years; a prominent actuary says 50 percent. An insurance company president believes that only three hundred companies will still be around in fifteen years. Since this is just a guessing game, you might want to enter your own prediction.

Of course, the majority view is not shared by everyone. Some observers believe that the idea of rating the claims-paying ability of large, established companies is silly. The claims will be paid, period, so don't worry about it.

At the other extreme, a Florida research firm warns that "the coming insurance industry crisis could destroy your financial future" and leave your heirs impoverished. Fortunately, you can prevent this from happening if you just send them $49 for a Personal Insurance Safety Report. You'll get their proprietary Safety Index—claimed to be "generally reliable" even though it has no track record—and some other safety measures derived from publicly available financial statements.

A PREPARATORY EXERCISE

Before you begin shopping for a safe company, do this: Scan the newspaper for a week and take note of every instance in which someone is reported to be amazed, astonished, surprised, shocked, or stunned. If it's a typical week, you'll have a long list, and you'll be in the right frame of mind to listen to the predictions of the experts. (You might even find yourself making up headlines just for fun, like "Insurer Placed Under State Supervision; Analysts Stunned.")

No one can predict with 100 percent accuracy which companies will be in business ten years from now and which ones won't. In fact, it's possible that future insolvencies will arise from causes that are unmentioned today. Ten years ago the greatest threat to solvency was disintermediation, as policy-holders surrendered their contracts or took out loans, thereby forcing companies to sell investments at a loss or use new premium dollars to finance the outflow. If all policyholders had demanded their cash values, most of the largest U.S. insurers would have been unable to pay. Today, the most publicized threats to solvency are asset defaults from junk bonds and real estate, AIDS, low profit margins, and inadequate capitalization. Who knows what the topics of discussion will be ten years from now?

EVALUATING FINANCIAL STRENGTH

You can judge the usefulness of any approach to evaluating financial strength by keeping these questions in mind:

- Does it identify companies that will get into trouble? Ideally, you want to avoid all of the unsound companies.

- Does it identify companies that will *not* get into trouble? You don't want to have your choices restricted unnecessarily. For example, the simple rule that you should avoid all insurance companies will keep you away from all of the troubled ones, but it also mislabels the sound companies.

- How much warning does it give? For deferred annuities, you might only care about the next few years; for life insurance, immediate annuities, and disability income insurance, your time frame could be decades.

- Is it practical, in terms of time and money spent?

Financial Strength Ratings

For many consumers, ratings are the most familiar and useful source of information about insurance companies. There are currently four major organizations that publish ratings of financial strength or claims-paying ability.

A.M. Best. The A.M. Best Company has been evaluating the financial soundness of insurance companies since 1906. The current system of letter ratings has been in use for life/health companies since 1976. Table 10.1 shows the distribution of 1989 Best's Ratings. A *contingent* rating—indicated by a lower case "c"—is assigned when the rating is under review due to a decline in performance that does not yet warrant a downgrade. Ten *not assigned* categories are used for companies that have been in business only a few years, have experienced a significant change in ownership or direction, are very small, or have other features that make the rating system inapplicable. Complete ratings definitions are provided in Appendix F.

Table 10.1. Distribution of 1989 Best's Ratings

Rating	Number of Companies	% of Total
A+	259	18%
A	247	17
A-	28	2
B+	129	9
B	80	6
B-	6	0
C+	27	2
C	12	1
C-	1	0
Contingent		
A+c	12	1
Ac	4	0
A-c	1	0
B+c	7	0
Not Assigned	611	44
	1,424	100%

Source: A.M. Best Company. Reprinted by permission.

A.M. Best's quantitative analysis uses a series of financial tests that focus on profitability, leverage, and liquidity. A.M. Best also performs a qualitative review of the company's reinsurance, investments, policy reserves, and management. Insurance buyers often use the Best's rating as a screening device. Here are some of the possible screens (based on 1989 ratings), in order of increasing strictness:

Companies with an assigned rating:	813
Companies rated A or A+:	506
Companies rated A+:	259
Companies rated A+ for at least 10 consecutive years:	195

(The *A+ for 10 years* screen is from the September 1989 issue of *The Insurance Forum*. The list of companies may be obtained for $3 from Insurance Forum, Inc., P.O. Box 245, Ellettsville, IN 47429.)

A.M. Best's reputation has suffered in recent years as a result of some well-publicized failures. The most embarrassing was Baldwin-United, a (formerly) large issuer of single premium deferred annuities. In August 1982, A.M. Best gave several Baldwin insurance subsidiaries an A rating, noting in one case that "the company has been very ably managed in the interests of its policyholders." Eleven months later the Baldwin companies were taken over by state regulators, who ultimately found that liabilities exceeded assets by $900 million. In fairness, it should be noted that Baldwin-United fooled a lot of people, including a prominent actuarial consulting firm. A.M. Best's overall track record has been good, and academic studies have generally concluded that the Best's rating is of value in predicting future solvency. In many cases, it is also the only game in town; no other organization comes close to monitoring the number of companies that A.M. Best does, although Standard & Poor's has announced a major expansion of its rating service, scheduled for spring 1990.

Other rating organizations. In recent years, three well-known credit-rating firms—Standard & Poor's, Moody's, and Duff & Phelps—have entered the insurance rating business to satisfy demands from pension fund sponsors, corporate insurance buyers, financial advisors, agents, and consumers for a second opinion about the financial health of insurance companies. Each organization has its own rating methodology, combining both quantitative and qualitative analysis. The rating process draws on publicly available financial information as well as proprietary information obtained during meetings with each insurer's top management. In each case, financial soundness is evaluated in the context of corporate strategy, management capabilities, and the outlook for the industry as a whole. The rating agencies sometimes reach differing conclusions about a company's prospects because of their judgments about these qualitative elements and the weight that should be given to each factor that affects stability.

Each organization also has its own rating scale. Standard & Poor's uses ten major categories: AAA, AA, A, BBB, BB, B,

CCC, CC, C, and D. For categories from AA to CCC, a plus or minus sign (for example, AA+)indicates an insurer's relative standing within that category. Ratings from AAA to BB are described as *secure*, while ratings below BB are *speculative*. Within the *secure* group, a higher rating implies a longer period of expected security.

Moody's Investors Service uses nine major categories: Aaa, Aa, A, Baa, Ba, B, Caa, Ca, and C. Each category from Aa to B is divided into three subcategories, labeled 1, 2, and 3; for example, Aa1, Aa2, and Aa3. Ratings of Baa or higher are considered investment grade.

Duff & Phelps uses seven major categories: AAA, AA, A, BBB, BB, B, and CCC. For categories from AA to B, a plus or minus sign indicates relative standing within that category. Ratings of BBB or higher are considered investment grade. (Complete definitions are provided in Appendix F).

The primary impetus for alternatives to the Best's rating came from institutional investors, such as pension funds, that refused to believe that all of the insurers rated A+ could be equally strong. As Table 10.2 shows, the Standard & Poor's rating makes the finer distinctions these investors were looking for. For example, of companies rated by both agencies, almost half of those rated A+ by Best do not receive the highest rating from Standard & Poor's. It will be many years before we know if these distinctions reflect real differences in financial strength. In the meantime, you have nothing to lose by asking for a second, third, or fourth opinion.

Financial Statement Analysis

Rating agencies, regulators, securities analysts, and financial advisors routinely examine an insurer's balance sheet and income and cash flow statements for clues about its financial position. Comparisons with other companies are often made by calculating financial ratios that measure liquidity, profitability, leverage, and asset quality. For years the National Association of Insurance Commissioners (NAIC) has used a set of financial ratios to decide which insurers need to be monitored more closely. These IRIS (Insurance Regulatory Information System) ratios are:

Table 10.2. **Distribution of Standard & Poor's Ratings for Companies Rated A+ by A.M. Best**

	Best's Rating	
S&P Rating*	A+ in 1989	A+ for 10 Years
AAA	33	29
AA+	9	8
AA	8	5
AA-	4	4
A+	2	2
A	3	2
A-	1	0
Total	60	50

* As of 12/15/89

- Net change in capital and surplus
- Gross change in capital and surplus
- Net gain to total income
- Commissions and expenses to premiums and deposits
- Adequacy of investment income
- Non-admitted to admitted assets
- Real estate to capital and surplus
- Investments in affiliates to capital and surplus
- Surplus relief (a measure of reinsurance transactions)
- Change in premium
- Change in product mix
- Change in asset mix

When four or more of a company's IRIS ratios lie outside a usual range of values, a team of examiners determines if further attention is warranted.

The mixed success of the IRIS ratios in providing an early warning of insolvencies points out the limitations of financial statement analysis. According to a study conducted by the NAIC, the IRIS ratios provided at least a two-year warning of impending difficulties for only nineteen out of fifty-two companies that actually required regulatory action from 1975 to 1982. A more recent study, covering the period from 1982 to 1986, found that no single ratio identified more than two-thirds of the companies that would become insolvent three years later. Forecasting can be improved through multiple discriminant analysis (a statistical technique for identifying key variables and combining them into an overall score.) However, credit analysts generally agree that the insurance industry is one of the most difficult to evaluate using the standard techniques of financial statement analysis. If you want to do your own evaluation, at least make sure you're working with accurate statements. Companies have been known to file an amended statement in one state and forget to tell anyone else.

Cash Flow Testing

Cash flow testing is the most direct, and therefore the most promising, quantitative method of assessing the risk of insolvency. The idea is to construct a computerized model of the company's operations and then make projections of its future assets and liabilities. If projected liabilities exceed projected assets at any point in time, you can conclude that there's a potential problem.

In the 1980s, a new specialist—the *valuation actuary*—became responsible for certifying that an insurer's assets and reserves are adequate to fulfill its obligations to policyholders. As analytical tools and procedures evolve, the valuation actuary will likely be called on to comment on a company's ability to remain solvent under a wide range of adverse circumstances.

Since 1979, the Society of Actuaries has been formally studying the risks faced by insurance companies. Actuarial conferences frequently include discussions of one or more of these four contingencies:

C-1 risk: Losses from defaults and decreases in market value of assets

C-2 risk: Losses from higher-than-expected claims and expenses and from other pricing deficiencies

C-3 risk: Losses from changes in interest rates, including investment anti-selection, reinvestment risk, and changes in the present value of assets and liabilities

C-4 risk: Losses from general business risks, including mismanagement and misregulation

Actuaries have also created new concepts of *surplus* to help them determine how much capital is needed to support a company's various product lines. In addition to financial statement surplus, there's target surplus, cash flow surplus, solvency surplus, solidity surplus, and vitality surplus.

A company's financial condition is not just "very good" or "so-so." Instead, valuation actuaries talk about the *probability of ruin*; that is, what the chances are that the company will have insufficient assets at some point during the measurement period. A one percent probability of ruin seems to be accepted as a reasonable benchmark for a well-managed company. A few countries require insurance companies to submit a valuation actuary's report as part of the solvency monitoring process. In the United States, some states now require cash flow testing for certain product lines but not for the company as a whole. The projections are generally made for five to ten years; apparently, regulators and actuaries do not feel they can make longer-range forecasts with any degree of confidence.

Like financial statement analysis, cash flow testing has its limitations. Because the results depend on a whole series of assumptions, there are bound to be surprises. The October 1987 stock market crash forced many analysts to re-examine their assumptions about the probability distribution of stock returns. The corporate takeovers of 1988 provided new information about the risks of high-grade corporate bonds. Perhaps the next recession will help actuaries refine their modeling assumptions for junk bonds. Despite shortcomings, cash flow testing will probably become an important analytical tool for regulators, company management, and rating agencies. If you're visiting a company's home office and happen to see a valuation actuary's report lying around, be sure to sneak a peek.

Management Quality

Writing in the May 1989 issue of *The Actuary*, Richard K. Kischuk, a principal of Crown Point Management Consultants, Inc., noted:

> A company's management systems, rather than external forces, tend to be the key determinants of risk. This was the leading cause of insurance company failure in the Great Depression, and it still is today. In traditional approaches, this risk has been swept into a catchall category called C-4 and is ignored by most companies. But it is the main reason why some companies can operate safely with relatively little surplus, while no amount of surplus is enough for other companies.

Management quality is important, but it is also difficult to assess. Securities analysts, rating agencies, and company insiders are probably best positioned to render a judgment. Patricia L. Guinn, a consulting actuary at Tillinghast/Towers Perrin, divides insurance company cultures into five categories: superior performers, risk takers, strategic loss makers, stupid fools, and cheats. You want to avoid the stupid fools and cheats.

Preconceptions, Speculations, Beliefs, and Prejudices

Every advisor has pet ideas about what to look for in an insurance company. It's hard to know what to think about this. What does it mean, for example, when a financial planner professes to look at the S&P rating *and* the five-year trend in capital and surplus. Is he saying that Standard & Poor's forgot to look at capital and surplus when they assigned the rating or that they didn't give it the weight it deserves? Is there really some value added by his extra scrutiny or is he just trying to impress the listener? It's tempting to latch on to one piece of information—for example, a large amount of junk bonds in company A's portfolio—and conclude that company A is taking more risks than company B. However, what matters is the entire collection of risks, not just the most salient one. Some risks are additive, some are multiplicative, and some are offsetting. Unless you're prepared to examine them all together, you're probably just wasting your time.

On the other hand, should you set aside your beliefs just because you can't prove them? You might sympathize with the Colorado financial planner who, when asked what empirical evidence he had to support his methodology, snapped, "If we had to wait around for empirical evidence, we'd never get anything done." Personal beliefs are an inevitable part of the evaluation process.

Here's a compilation of the warnings that you might run across: Beware of rapid growth, stagnation, junk bonds, corporate bonds with "event risk," affiliated securities, long-term bonds, mortgages in depressed real estate markets, common stocks, policy loans, aggressive underwriting, companies not licensed in New York, companies paying more in policyholder dividends than they are earning, very small companies, companies that specialize in just one or two products, high lapse rates, high operating expenses, fancy surplus-generating transactions, and hot-shot entrepreneurs.

One final warning: Beware of heeding all these warnings; because if you do, there won't be any insurance companies that you can do business with.

Suggestions for Choosing a Company

Here are a few suggestions for finding an appropriate insurer:

- At minimum, look for companies with a consistent A or A+ rating from A.M. Best. If you can get a second opinion from Standard & Poor's, Moody's, or Duff & Phelps, so much the better. You can narrow the list down further by taking into account other features, such as size or investment strategy.

- For maximum risk avoidance, bordering on paranoia, choose one of the industry's leviathans that meet these four tests: (1) an A+ Best's rating for at least ten years, (2) a top rating (AAA or Aaa) by at least one other agency, (3) no rating below a top rating by any of the major agencies, and (4) in business for at least one hundred years (a period that includes financial panics, epidemics, and many business cycles). The top ten companies that meet these criteria, ranked by 1988 assets, are: Prudential, Metropolitan, Aetna, New York Life, Connecticut General, John Hancock, Northwestern Mutual, Massachusetts Mutual, Principal Mutual, and Manufacturers Life. Some of these companies got where they are today by gouging consumers in the nineteenth century, but that was then and this is now. You may have to settle for an agent-sold policy if you follow this strategy.

- Remember that parent-subsidiary relationships can change, so look at the ratings for the entity that will actually issue the policy. You should take a parent's rating into account only if the affiliate is so closely tied to its parent that they should be viewed as one entity.

- For more information about a company, check any or all of the following: the profiles in this book, the unabridged reports in *Best's Insurance Reports* (available in many libraries or you can get an abridged version from the company), the analytical reports prepared by other rating agencies, the statutory annual statement filed with state insurance departments, and, for stock companies, the annual and quarterly reports required by the SEC.

- Ignore any intercompany comparisons prepared by insurance companies. Through a clever selection of measuring rods, every major insurer can produce a report that shows why it is #1.

- In working with agents and other advisors, remember that it's easy to create an impressive checklist (see sidebar), but the burden of proof is on the advisor to demonstrate that it actually accomplishes something. One way to deal with an overstuffed closet is to pull everything out and then decide—one object at a time—what you want to put back in. Financial advisors' due diligence procedures are in need of a similar housecleaning.

- If you're making a large purchase, consider using more than one company. This may increase your costs, because of duplicate policy fees and other pricing features, but the greater peace of mind might be worth it.

On Due Diligence Checklists

Due diligence has become an important issue for agents and financial planners as they try to establish a more professional image. There are many opinions about the proper way to evaluate insurance companies and their products. Sometimes these opinions are in the form of a checklist, which the advisor fills out and keeps on file as proof that adequate research was conducted. Here's a quick lesson in the mathematics of checklist construction.

With a little coaching, anyone could come up with a list of fifty items that have some plausible connection with future solvency or product performance. Let's say you narrow the list down to ten, so that you can gain some exposure (and therefore more clients) by writing an article entitled "10 Things to Look For When Choosing an Insurance Company." If the order of the items doesn't matter, how many possible checklists would there be?

Answer: 10,272,278,170.

Now let's say there are 1 million agents, financial planners, accountants, and attorneys who give advice on insurance products. If each advisor devises a checklist, what is the probability that there will be at least 10,000 different checklists in circulation? *Answer:* 99.5 percent. So you shouldn't be surprised if you run across a lot of reasonable-sounding opinions about how to evaluate an insurance company.

(Note to interested readers: There would be a 97 percent chance of at least 25,000 different opinions, and virtually no chance of 1 million opinions. The arithmetic is essentially the same as for this classic party question: What are the odds that at least two people in a group of thirty will have the same birthday? *Answer:* 71 percent.)

11

HOW TO USE THE PRODUCT AND COMPANY PROFILES

The product and company profiles in Chapters 12 and 13 provide information about the following areas of concern to insurance buyers:
- Product design
  - How does the product work?
  - Does it have the features that you need?
- Product performance
  - How does the product stack up against similar products?
  - How might performance change in the future?
- Financial stability
  - Is the issuing company financially sound?
  - Is it likely to remain financially sound?
- Treatment of policyholders
  - Is the company equipped to deal with your problems?
  - Is the company committed to keeping its customers satisfied in the future?

The information in these profiles was obtained from each company's actuarial department; in most cases, the responses were prepared or reviewed by the company's chief actuary. To further ensure accuracy, each company reviewed the edited information before publication. Of course, no set of procedures can be foolproof, and we can only promise that any remaining errors will be corrected in the future.

Following is a brief explanation of each item in the profiles. These abbreviations are used throughout: "N/A" means the information is not available or not applicable, depending on the context. "N/D" means the information is applicable, and presumably available, but is not disclosed. "1980 CSO" means the 1980 Commissioner's Standard Ordinary Mortality Table. The many versions of this table include: male/female (M/F); nonsmoker/smoker (NS/S); age nearest birthday (ANB); and age last birthday (ALB).

TRADITIONAL WHOLE LIFE

Company: NAME

Product: NAME

Description: A brief description of the product.

Availability: States where the product is approved for sale. If approval is pending in your state, contact the company for more information.
Other restrictions: These are restrictions other than age and health. In particular, will the company accept applications signed in a state where the product is approved if the applicant is a resident of a state where the product is not approved?

Issue Ages: Minimum and maximum ages.

Maturity Date: The date or age at which the contract terminates and the owner receives the cash value.

Premium Limitations:

	First	Additional
Minimum	Premiums are generally fixed; this provides any other
Maximum	relevant information.

Face Amount Limitations:
Minimum: *Maximum:*   Minimum and maximum face amounts and
Changes: changes permitted after issue.

Valuation Basis: The interest rate, mortality table, and method used to compute reserves. This doesn't tell you much, but it might say something about future dividends. In general, a more favorable valuation basis means smaller dividends, because dividends are based on the differences between actual and valuation interest and mortality.

Dividend Determination Process: A brief description of how dividends are determined.

Illustration Practices: When you look at a policy illustration, it is important to understand what the numbers represent. The questions in this section are intended to help you make qualitative adjustments to the illustrated values for comparison purposes.

If you want to go a step further–that is, produce illustrated values using different assumptions–you will need to get assistance from the company.

Do any pricing assumptions underlying currently illustrated policy values differ from:
- *current experience?* Example: If the illustrated values are based on the assumption that mortality will continue to improve, you should keep that in mind when making comparisons with illustrated values that assume no future mortality improvements.
- *anticipated future experience?* Example: If the illustrated values are based on a current portfolio yield that is higher than current market rates, you should keep that in mind when making comparisons with illustrated values that are based on new-money rates.

Dividend Options: The ways in which dividends can be used.

Surrenders: This provides information about partial and full surrenders.

Policy Loans: Minimum and maximum amounts and other restrictions.
Interest charged and effect on dividends: This provides information about the policy loan interest rate and the effect that borrowing has on dividends.

Effective cost of borrowing: This indicates the true before-tax cost of borrowing, taking into account any changes in dividends. The after-tax cost of borrowing will depend on your tax bracket and the purpose of the loan.

Settlement Options: A list of the options available. "Standard" means the usual forms of monthly life income and fixed-period and fixed-amount installments.

Fractional Premiums:

	Modal Factor	Equivalent Annual Charge
Semi-annual	Modal factors and the annualized carrying	
Quarterly	charge for premiums paid other than annually.	
Monthly		

Riders: A list of the available riders.

Other Product Features: This is a catch-all, to take account of any product features that are not explicitly discussed elsewhere.

Treatment of Policyholders: You will be a new policyholder for a day and an existing policyholder for the rest of the time that you own the policy. This section focuses on what happens after the purchase.

Service: Who will answer your questions and handle other service needs?

During the past year, have there been any significant problems in handling requests for service? And, If so, what corrective actions have been taken? "Significant" means something that an outside observer would consider to be a problem requiring attention. It does not refer to the usual level of complaints that any company can expect when dealing with the public.

Type and frequency of communications to policyholders: What periodic statements, newsletters, etc. are sent to policyholders?

Are new contract improvements offered to existing policyholders?
This is intended to give some idea of the company's plans for
keeping its old contracts up to date. Note that because of the cost
involved, some improvements cannot reasonably be offered to
existing policyholders.

Past repricing actions: A brief description of pricing changes that
the company has made since the introduction of the product.

Comparison with "Buy Term and Invest the Difference":

Policy Year	Premium	Death Benefit	Cash Value	Before-Tax Rate of Return Average Annual	Yearly
1					
2					
3					
4					
5					
10					
15					
20					

This shows average annual rates of return and yearly
rates of return for selected holding periods for one
specific case, using moderately-low annual renewable
term rates and ignoring income taxes. These numbers
are only intended to give you an idea of how the rate
of return changes over time. You should not use them
to judge the attractiveness of the policy in your
particular situation, because the rate of return will
depend on age, face amount, premiums, and the
assumed term and tax rates.

Distributors:
Name/Address   *Compensation*
This tells you who sells the policy and how the distributors are
compensated.

UNIVERSAL LIFE

Company: NAME

Product: NAME

Description: A brief description of the product.

Availability: States where the product is approved for sale. If approval is pending in your state, contact the company for more information.

Other restrictions: These are restrictions other than age and health. In particular, will the company accept applications signed in a state where the product is approved if the applicant is a resident of a state where the product is not approved?

Issue Ages: Minimum and maximum ages.

Maturity Date: The date or age at which the contract terminates and the owner receives the cash value.

Premium Limitations:

	First	Additional
Minimum	Minimum and maximum premiums, based on contract-
Maximum	ual limitations and/or the company's current practices.

Face Amount Limitations:

Minimum:	*Maximum:*	Minimum and maximum face amounts and
Changes:		changes permitted after issue.

Contract Charges:

	Current			
	Annual			
	Yr 1	Yrs 2+	Back-end	Guaranteed
Per policy ($)	A summary of current and guaranteed			
% premium	charges, by type and policy year.			
Per $1000 face ($)				
% Account value				
Insurance				
Investment				

Current Cost of Insurance Rates:

Rate structure: A brief description, including some or all of these features:

- underwriting categories
- age-nearest-birthday versus age-last-birthday
- bands/tiers
- aggregate versus select-and-ultimate

Annual rates per $1,000 of coverage:

	Nonsmoker			Smoker		
Year	35	45	55	35	45	55
1	The current annualized cost of insurance per $1,000 of
6	net amount at risk, for selected policy years. When there
11	are several bands, the rates shown are generally for
16	amounts in the $250-500K range. Current rates are
21	shown for as many as 41 years to help you compare the
41	rate structures of different products. This can be useful
	in cases where one product has lower projected
	premiums or higher cash values in the later years, and
	you are trying to understand why.

Current Interest Rate:

Rate structure: A brief description of the interest-crediting method.
Guarantee period: Period for which the current interest rate is guaranteed not to change.
Rate-setting process: A brief description of how the company sets the current interest rate.
Investment strategy: A brief description of what the company does with your money, including types of investments, maturity, and quality. The investment strategy is important because it affects the credited interest rate.

Interest rate history:

On Amounts	Declared Rate at 1/1					
Deposited on 1/1	1985	1986	1987	1988	1989	1990

1985
1986
1987
1988
1989
1990

Changes in
new-money rate

A six-year history of credited interest rates, presented in a matrix format. Read across each row to see what rates were credited over time to policies issued at the beginning of each indicated year. Read down each column to see what rates were being paid at the beginning of any given year to policies issued in each of the last six years. The last line shows the number of times the declared interest rate on new money was changed during each year, not including any change from one year to the next.

Benchmarks: See Appendix A for benchmark rates.

Persistency Bonuses: This section describes each bonus and indicates whether or not it is guaranteed.

Illustration Practices: When you look at a policy illustration, it is important to understand what the numbers represent. The questions in this section are intended to help you make qualitative adjustments to the illustrated values for comparison purposes.

If you want to go a step further–that is, produce illustrated values using different assumptions–you will need to get assistance from the company.

Do any pricing assumptions underlying currently illustrated policy values differ from:

- *current experience?* Example: If the illustrated values are based on the assumption that mortality will continue to improve, you should keep that in mind when making comparisons with illustrated values that assume no future mortality improvements.
- *anticipated future experience?* Example: If the illustrated values are based on a current portfolio yield that is higher than current market rates, you should keep that in mind when making comparisons with illustrated values that are based on new-money rates.

Withdrawals and Surrenders: Restrictions and charges on withdrawals and surrenders.

Policy Loans: Minimum and maximum amounts and other restrictions.

Interest charged and credited: This provides information about the policy loan interest rate and the interest credited on borrowed amounts.

Effective cost of borrowing: This indicates the true before-tax cost of borrowing, taking into account any changes in credited interest. The after-tax cost of borrowing will depend on your tax bracket and the purpose of the loan.

Settlement Options: A list of the options available. "Standard" means the usual forms of monthly life income and fixed-period and fixed-amount installments.

Riders: A list of available riders.

Other Product Features: This is a catch-all, to take account of any product features that are not explicitly discussed elsewhere.

Treatment of Policyholders: You will be a new policyholder for a day and an existing policyholder for the rest of the time that you own the policy. This section focuses on what happens after the purchase.

Service: Who will answer your questions and handle other service needs?

During the past year, have there been any significant problems in handling requests for service? And, *If so, what corrective actions have been taken?* "Significant" means something that an outside observer would consider to be a problem requiring attention. It does not refer to the usual level of complaints that any company can expect when dealing with the public.

Type and frequency of communications to policyholders: What periodic statements, newsletters, etc. are sent to policyholders?

During the past year, have there been any significant delays in preparing policy statements or confirmations of transactions? And, *If so, what corrective actions have been taken?* If the insurance company does not have an adequate administrative system in place, policyholders can experience considerable delays in receiving statements.

Was the current administrative system developed in-house or purchased from an outside vendor? Can the system be upgraded as needed to meet future demands? This provides additional information about the administrative system that supports the product.

Are new contract improvements offered to existing policyholders? This is intended to give some idea of the company's plans for keeping its old contracts up to date. Note that because of the cost involved, some improvements cannot reasonably be offered to existing policyholders.

Past repricing actions: A brief description of pricing changes that the company has made since the introduction of the product.

Comparison with "Buy Term and Invest the Difference":

Policy Year	Premium	Death Benefit	Cash Value	Before-Tax Rate of Return	
				Average Annual	Yearly
1					
2					
3					
4					
5					
10					
15					
20					

This shows average annual rates of return and yearly rates of return for selected holding periods for one specific case, using moderately-low annual renewable term rates and ignoring income taxes. These numbers are only intended to give you an idea of how the rate of return changes over time. You should not use them to judge the attractiveness of the policy in your particular situation, because the rate of return will depend on age, face amount, premiums, and the assumed term and tax rates.

Distributors:

Name/Address	Compensation

This tells you who sells the policy and how the distributors are compensated.

SINGLE PREMIUM WHOLE LIFE

Company: NAME

Product: NAME

Description: A brief description of the product.

Minimum Face Amount: The minimum face amount will determine the minimum single premium, based on your age.

Other Features: When single premium whole life is being simulated by another type of product, this will refer you to the product profile for more information.

Policy Illustration:

End of Policy Year	Death Benefit	Cash Value	% Increase Cash Value
1	This shows the percentage increase in the before-tax		
2	cash surrender value from one year to the next for		
3	one specific case, based on current interest, mortality,		
4	expense, and dividend assumptions. These numbers are		
5	only intended to give you an idea of how the rate of		
10	return changes over time. You should not use them		
15	to judge the attractiveness of the policy in your 20 particular		

situation, because the percentage increases will depend on age, face amount, and the single premium.

VARIABLE LIFE

Company: NAME

Product: NAME

Description: A brief description of the product.

Availability: States where the product is approved for sale. If approval is pending in your state, contact the company for more information. *Other restrictions:* These are restrictions other than age and health. In particular, will the company accept applications signed in a state where the product is approved if the applicant is a resident of a state where the product is not approved?

Issue Ages: Minimum and maximum ages.

Maturity Date: The date or age at which the contract terminates and the owner receives the cash value.

Premium Limitations:

	First	Additional
Minimum	Minimum and maximum premiums, based on contrac-	
Maximum	tual limitations and/or the company's current practices.	

Face Amount Limitations:

Minimum:	*Maximum:*	Minimum and maximum face amounts and
Changes:		changes permitted after issue.

Contract Charges:

	Current Annual			
	Yr 1	Yrs 2+	Back-end	Guaranteed
Per policy ($) premium	A summary of current and guaranteed % charges, by type and policy year.			
Per $1000 face ($)				
% account value				
Insurance				
Investment				

Current Cost of Insurance Rates:

Rate structure: A brief description, including some or all of these features:

- underwriting categories
- age-nearest-birthday versus age-last-birthday
- bands/tiers
- aggregate versus select-and-ultimate

Annual rates per $1,000 of coverage:

	Nonsmoker			Smoker		
Year	35	45	55	35	45	55
1						
6						
11						
16						
21						
41						

The current annualized cost of insurance per $1,000 of net amount at risk, for selected policy years. When there are several bands, the rates shown are generally for amounts in the $250-500K range. Current rates are shown for as many as 41 years to help you compare the rate structures of different products. This can be useful in cases where one product has lower projected premiums or higher cash values in the later years, and you are trying to understand why.

Illustration Practices: When you look at a policy illustration, it is important to understand what the numbers represent. The questions in this section are intended to help you make qualitative adjustments to the illustrated values for comparison purposes.

If you want to go a step further–that is, produce illustrated values using different assumptions–you will need to get assistance from the company.

Do any pricing assumptions underlying currently illustrated policy values differ from:

- *current experience?* Example: If the illustrated values are based on the assumption that mortality will continue to improve, you should keep that in mind when making comparisons with illustrated values that assume no future mortality improvements.
- *anticipated future experience?* Example: If the illustrated values are based on a current portfolio yield that is higher than current market rates, you should keep that in mind when making comparisons with illustrated values that are based on new-money rates.

Investment Options:

Fund Name   Advisor

Fund name and investment advisor. This also provides a page reference where further information about each of the investment choices can be found, including: objective, decision-making process, portfolio composition, total return, expense ratio, portfolio turnover, and risk. (See page 309 for explanations.)

All performance data take account of advisory fees and other fund operating expenses, but *not* contract expenses such as the mortality and expense risk charge.This allows you to compare the insurance product funds with similar taxable mutual funds.

In comparing variable life insurance with the alternative of buying term insurance and investing in taxable mutual funds, we suggest you keep the following framework in mind:

> Policy fund performance relative to taxable funds
> - Contract expenses
> + <u>Value of tax advantages</u>
> = Performance relative to term plus taxable funds

Fixed Account: This provides additional information about the fixed-interest investment option, if any.

Settlement Options: For variable options, the minimum and/or current assumed interest rate may be given.

Portfolio Allocation Provisions:
Allocation of premiums: Restrictions on allocation of pre-
Transfers between accounts: miums and transfers between
                                       investment portfolios.

Withdrawals and Surrenders: Restrictions and charges on withdrawals and surrenders.

Policy Loans: Minimum and maximum amounts and other restrictions. *Interest charged and credited:* This provides information about the policy loan interest rate and the interest credited on borrowed amounts.
Effective cost of borrowing: This indicates the true before-tax cost of borrowing, taking into account any changes in investment return. The after-tax cost of borrowing will depend on your tax bracket and the purpose of the loan.

Death Benefit Guarantee: A brief description of the guaranteed death benefit provision, if any.

Riders: A list of available riders.

Other Product Features: This is a catch-all, to take account of any product features that are not explicitly discussed elsewhere.

Treatment of Policyholders: You will be a new policyholder for a day and an existing policyholder for the rest of the time that you own the policy. This section focuses on what happens after the purchase.

Service: Who will answer your questions and handle other service needs?

During the past year, have there been any significant problems in handling requests for service? And, If so, what corrective actions have been taken? "Significant" means something that an outside observer would consider to be a problem requiring attention. It does not refer to the usual level of complaints that any company can expect when dealing with the public.

Type and frequency of communications to policyholders: What periodic statements, newsletters, etc. are sent to policyholders?

During the past year, have there been any significant delays in preparing policy statements or confirmations of transactions? And, If so, what corrective actions have been taken? If the insurance company does not have an adequate administrative system in place, policyholders can experience considerable delays in receiving statements.

Was the current administrative system developed in-house or purchased from an outside vendor? Can the system be upgraded as needed to meet future demands? This provides additional information about the administrative system that supports the product.

Are new contract improvements offered to existing policyholders? This is intended to give some idea of the company's plans for keeping its old contracts up to date. Note that because of the cost involved, some improvements cannot reasonably be offered to existing policyholders.

Past repricing actions: A brief description of pricing changes that the company has made since the introduction of the product.

Comparison with "Buy Term and Invest the Difference":

Policy Year	Premium	Death Benefit	Cash Value	Before-Tax Rate of Return	
				Average Annual	Yearly
1					
2					
3					
4					
5					
10					
15					
20					

This shows average annual rates of return and yearly rates of return for selected holding periods for one specific case, using moderately-low annual renewable term rates and ignoring income taxes. These numbers are only intended to give you an idea of how the rate of return changes over time. You should not use them to judge the attractiveness of the policy in your particular situation, because the rate of return will depend on age, face amount, premiums, and the assumed term and tax rates.

Distributors:

Name/Address	Compensation

This tells you who sells the policy and how the distributors are compensated.

SURVIVORSHIP

Survivorship policies come in various forms, including traditional whole life, universal life, and variable life. The profile format will generally follow the format for the appropriate product type, with these changes:

Face Amount Limitations: *Can the policy be split apart into single-life policies?* This tells you if the survivorship policy can be separated into two single life policies. This may be important if the unlimited marital deduction is repealed or in cases of divorce.

Current Cost of Insurance Rates: When applicable, the table shows the current annual cost of insurance rates per $1,000 of coverage for five pairs of insureds of the same issue age.

TERM

Company:	NAME
Product:	NAME

Description: A brief description of the product.

Availability: States where the product is approved for sale. If approval is pending in your state, contact the company for more information. *Other restrictions:* These are restrictions other than age and health. In particular, will the company accept applications signed in a state where the product is approved if the applicant is a resident of a state where the product is not approved?

Issue Ages: Minimum and maximum ages.

Underwriting Classes: A list of the risk classes that determine what premiums you will be charged; for example, male/female, non-smoker/smoker, preferred/standard.

Face Amount Limitations:
Minimum: Maximum: Minimum and maximum face amounts and
Changes: changes permitted after issue.

Rate Structure: A brief description of the important features, including bands, policy fee, guarantee period, renewability, re-entry provision, discount for prepayment of premiums, and modal factors and annualized carrying charge for fractional premiums.

	Modal Factor	Equivalent Annual Charge
Semi-annual		
Quarterly		Modal factors for fractional premiums.
Monthly		

Other comments:

Convertibility: Important features of the convertibility provision, if any.

Settlement Options: A list of the options available. "Standard" means the usual forms of monthly life income and fixed-period and fixed-amount installments.

Riders: A list of available riders.

Other Product Features: This is a catch-all, to take account of any product features that are not explicitly discussed elsewhere.

Policy Illustration: This shows the present value of premiums for selected holding periods for one specific case. We have chosen to use the present value of premiums rather than the more common "interest-adjusted cost index" for two reasons:

1. The present value of premiums gives you a better idea whether or not it is worth your time to continue shopping for a cheaper policy.
2. Present value is a concept that will serve you well in other investment areas, whereas the interest-adjusted cost index is a parochial measure that was concocted only to compare insurance products. We assume that most people would prefer not to spend time understanding something of limited use, when there is an equivalent comparative measure that has wider application. However, if you insist, you can easily convert the present value of premiums into a standard cost index by dividing the present value by the following numbers:

1 year	1.000 (same)
5 years	4.546
10 years	8.108
20 years	13.085

Treatment of Policyholders: You will be a new policyholder for a day and an existing policyholder for the rest of the time that you own the policy. This section focuses on what happens after the purchase.

Service: Who will answer your questions and handle other service needs?

Past repricing actions: A brief description of pricing changes that the company has made since the introduction of the product.

Distributors:

Name/Address   *Compensation*

This tells you who sells the policy and how the distributors are compensated.

DEFERRED ANNUITIES

Company: NAME

Product: NAME

Description: A brief description of the product.

Availability: States where the product is approved for sale. If approval is pending in your state, contact the company for more information.

Other restrictions: These are restrictions other than age and health. In particular, will the company accept applications signed in a state where the product is approved if the applicant is a resident of a state where the product is not approved?

Issue Ages: Minimum and maximum ages.

Premium Limitations:

	First	Additional
Minimum	Minimum and maximum premiums, based on contrac-
Maximum	tual limitations and/or the company's current practices.

Contract Charges:

	Current			
	Annual			
	Yr 1	Yrs 2+	Back-End	Guaranteed
Per policy ($)	A summary of current and guaranteed			
% premium	charges, by type and contract year.			
% account value				

Current Interest Rate:
Rate structure: A brief description of the interest-crediting method.
Guarantee period: Period for which the current interest rate is guaranteed not to change.
Rate-setting process: A brief description of how the company sets the current interest rate.
Investment strategy: A brief description of what the company does with your money, including types of investments, maturity, and quality. The investment strategy is important because it affects the credited interest rate.

Interest rate history:

On Amounts	Declared Rate at 1/1					
Deposited on 1/1	1985	1986	1987	1988	1989	1990
1985						
1986						
1987						
1988						
1989						
1990						
Changes in new-money rate						

A six-year history of credited interest rates, presented in a matrix format. Read across each row to see what rates were credited over time to contracts issued at the beginning of each indicated year. Read down each column to see what rates were being paid at the beginning of any given year to contracts issued in each of the last six years. The last line shows the number of times the declared interest rate on new money was changed during each year, not including any change from one year to the next.

Benchmarks: See Appendix A for benchmark rates.

Withdrawals and Surrenders: Restrictions and charges on withdrawals and surrenders.

Bailout Provision: Important features of the bailout provision, if any.

Settlement Options: A list of the options available. "Standard" means the usual forms of monthly life income and fixed-period and fixed-amount installments.

Other Product Features: This is a catch-all, to take account of any product features that are not explicitly discussed elsewhere.

Treatment of Policyholders: You will be a new policyholder for a day and an existing policyholder for the rest of the time that you own the policy. This section focuses on what happens after the purchase.

Service: Who will answer your questions and handle other service needs?

During the past year, have there been any significant problems in handling requests for service? And, If so, what corrective actions have been taken? If the insurance company does not have an adequate administrative system in place, policyholders can experience considerable delays in receiving statements. "Significant" means something that an outside observer would consider to be a problem requiring attention. It does not refer to the usual level of complaints that any company can expect when dealing with the public.

Are new contract improvements offered to existing policyholders? This is intended to give some idea of the company's plans for keeping its old contracts up to date. Note that some improvements cannot reasonably be offered to existing policyholders, because of the cost involved.

Distributors:

Name/Address   *Compensation*

This tells you who sells the policy and how the distributors are compensated.

VARIABLE ANNUITIES

Company: NAME

Product: NAME

Description: A brief description of the product.

Availability: States where the product is approved for sale. If approval is pending in your state, contact the company for more information.
Other restrictions: These are restrictions other than age and health. In particular, will the company accept applications signed in a state where the product is approved if the applicant is a resident of a state where the product is not approved?

Issue Ages: Minimum and maximum ages.

Premium Limitations:

	First	Additional
Minimum	Minimum and maximum premiums, based on contract-	
Maximum	ual limitations and/or the company's current practices.	

Contract Charges:

	Current			
	Annual			
	Yr 1	Yrs 2+	Back-End	Guaranteed
Per policy ($)	A summary of current and guaranteed			
% premium	charges, by type and contract year.			
% account value				
Investment				

Investment Options:

Fund Name   Advisor

Fund name and investment advisor. This also provides a page reference where further information about each of the investment choices can be found, including: objective, decision-making process, portfolio composition, total return, expense ratio, portfolio turnover, and risk. (See page 309 for explanations).

All performance data take account of advisory fees and other fund operating expenses, but *not* contract expenses such as the mortality and expense risk charge.This allows you to compare the insurance product funds with similar taxable mutual funds.

In comparing the alternative of investing in taxable mutual funds, we suggest you keep the following framework in mind:

>   Contract fund performance relative to taxable funds
> - Contract expenses
> + Value of tax deferral
> = Performance relative to taxable funds

Fixed Account: This provides additional information about the fixed-interest investment option, if any.

Portfolio Allocation Provisions:
Allocation of premiums: Restrictions on allocation of pre-
Transfers between accounts: miums and transfers between
                                   investment portfolios.

Withdrawals and Surrenders: Restrictions and charges on withdrawals and surrenders.

Annuity Options: A list of the options available. "Standard" means the usual forms of monthly life income and fixed-period and fixed-amount installments. For variable options, the minimum and/or current assumed interest rate may be given.

Death Benefit: A brief description of the death benefit provision.

Other Product Features: This is a catch-all, to take account of any product features that are not explicitly discussed elsewhere.

Treatment of Policyholders: You will be a new policyholder for a day and an existing policyholder for the rest of the time that you own the policy. This section focuses on what happens after the purchase.

Service: Who will answer your questions and handle other service needs?

During the past year, have there been any significant problems in handling requests for service? And, If so, what corrective actions have been taken? "Significant" means something that an outside observer would consider to be a problem requiring attention. It does not refer to the usual level of complaints that any company can expect when dealing with the public.

Type and frequency of communications to policyholders: What periodic statements, newsletters, etc. are sent to policyholders?

During the past year, have there been any significant delays in preparing policy statements or confirmations of transactions? And, If so, what corrective actions have been taken? If the insurance company does not have an adequate administrative system in place, policyholders can experience considerable delays in receiving statements.

Was the current administrative system developed in-house or purchased from an outside vendor? Can the system be upgraded as needed to meet future demands? This provides additional information about the administrative system that supports the product.

Are new contract improvements offered to existing policyholders? This is intended to give some idea of the company's plans for keeping its old contracts up to date. Note that because of the cost involved, some improvements cannot reasonably be offered to existing policyholders.

Past repricing actions: A brief description of pricing changes that the company has made since the introduction of the product.

Distributors:

Name/Address   *Compensation*
This tells you who sells the policy and how the distributors are compensated.

IMMEDIATE ANNUITIES

Company: NAME

Product: NAME

Description: A brief description of the product.

Availability: States where the product is approved for sale. If approval is pending in your state, contact the company for more information.
Other restrictions: These are restrictions other than age and health. In particular, will the company accept applications signed in a state where the product is approved if the applicant is a resident of a state where the product is not approved?

Issue Ages: Minimum and maximum ages.

Premium Limitations:
Minimum: *Maximum:* Minimum and maximum premiums allowed.

Contract Charges: A summary of charges, including policy fee and state premium tax.

Payment Options: A list of the options available. "Standard" means the usual forms of monthly life income and fixed-period and fixed-amount installments.

Participation in Company Experience: Are payments fixed for life, or can they vary with the company's interest and mortality experience?

Rate-Setting Process: A brief description of how the annuity rates are determined.

Other Features: This is a catch-all, to take account of any product features that are not explicitly discussed elsewhere.

Monthly Income per $1,000 Single Premium at 1/1:

Nonqualified rates:

Selected Statistics: <u>1985</u> <u>1986</u> <u>1987</u> <u>1988</u> <u>1989</u> <u>1990</u>

Life income
<u>Age 65</u>
–Male   Rates for selected cases.
–Female   Excludes contract charges.

Benchmark: See Appendix A for benchmark rates.

Policyholder Service: Who will answer your questions and handle other service needs?

Distributors:
Name/Address   *Compensation*
  This tells you who sells the polcy and how the distributors are compensated.

FIDELITY VARIABLE PRODUCT FUNDS

Advisor: NAME

Product: NAME

___

Funding Vehicle for: A list of the low-load products that offer the fund as an investment option.

Objective: The fund's stated investment objective.

Investment Decision-Making Process: A brief description of how the advisor makes purchase/sale decisions.

Portfolio (date):   A breakdown of the investments by major category.   Other information may also be provided when appropriate.

Selected Statistics:

	1984	1985	1986	1987	1988	1989

Total return (%)　　　　Total return for each calendar year, including
Expense ratio (%)　　　 advisory fees and operating expenses and
Portfolio turnover (%)　*excluding* other contract expenses, such as
Net assets (mill.$)　　　the mortality and expense risk charge. Expense ratio and portfolio turnover for each fiscal year. Net assets at each calendar year-end.

Benchmark:　　　　　　The suggested benchmark(s) can be found in Appendix A.

Risk (variablity of total returns):

Risk can be defined in many ways. Here, risk is shown graphically as the distribution of monthly returns since inception. For portfolios with a sufficient history, there may also be a graph of the distribution of annualized returns for all rolling one-year and/or three-year periods. (Example: For a fund with a 36-month performance record, there would be 25 rolling one-year periods; i.e., months 1-12, 2-13, 3-14, and so on.) In a sense, these graphs show you all of the possible experiences of investors who entered the fund at the beginning of a month and left one month, one year, or three years later.

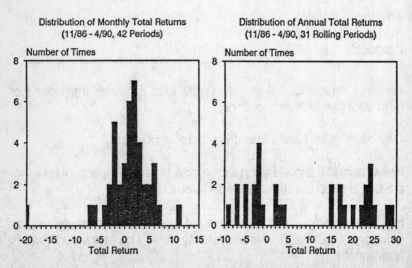

Distribution of Monthly Total Returns
(11/86 - 4/90, 42 Periods)

Distribution of Annual Total Returns
(11/86 - 4/90, 31 Rolling Periods)

DISABILITY INCOME

Company: NAME

Product: NAME

Description: A brief description of the product.

Availability: States where the product is approved for sale. If approval is pending in your state, contact the company for more information.

Other restrictions: These are restrictions other than age and health. In particular, will the company accept applications signed in a state where the product is approved if the applicant is a resident of a state where the product is not approved?

Issue Ages: Minimum and maximum ages.

Monthly Benefit Limitations:

> <u>Minimum</u>   <u>Maximum</u>
> Minimum and maximum monthly benefits and limitations on changes.

Definition of Disability: When do you qualify for benefits?

Definition of Recurrent Disability: When is a second period of disability considered to be a continuation of the first?

Waiting Period: How long do you have to be disabled before you can receive benefits?

Benefit Period: What is the maximum period during which you can receive benefits?

Other Features: This section contains information about partial disability, integration with Social Security benefits, cost of living adjustments, future increases in coverage, and other product features.

Fractional Premiums:

	Modal Factor	Equivalent Annual Charge
Semi-annual	Modal factors and annualized carrying charge	
Quarterly	for premiums paid other than annually.	
Monthly		

Illustrative Annual Premium:

Waiting Period	Annual Premium
Sample rates for one specific case.	

Policyholder Service: Who will answer your questions and handle other service needs?

Distributors:

Name/Address	Compensation
This tells you who sells the policy and how the distributors are compensated.	

HOW TO USE THE COMPANY PROFILES

The company profiles complement the product profiles and should be used together. We have also provided abridged reports on several insurers whose low-load products are not profiled.

COMPANY NAME   Telephone Number
Address
City, State Zip

Territory: This tells you where the company is licensed to do business. In some cases, you may be able to buy insurance from companies that are not licensed in your state. However, this is generally not recommended, because you might not be covered by your state's guaranty fund in the event of insolvency. There may be other legal problems, so consult with an attorney before-hand.

Ratings: Ratings of financial strength for the last ten years from the major rating organizations. Few companies are rated by all four agencies, and most companies are only rated by A.M. Best. (See Appendix F for a description of the rating categories.)

Methods of Assuring Future Solvency: This provides additional information about how management addresses the risks that every company faces. Companies were asked to consider these two related questions:

1. What makes you think that your company will still be in business in ten years?
2. Why should an insurance buyer believe that your company will still be in business in ten years?

Selected Statistics — 1989: This gives you some idea of the absolute and relative size of the company, for several financial measures. Size rankings are based on an annual survey prepared by The National Underwriter Company (1988 is the latest year available). There are over 2,000 life and health insurance companies in the United States, but the top 600 account for almost all of the policies sold directly to individuals.

Individual life and annuity premiums are "direct" only, and do not include amounts received under reinsurance arrangements. Also, amounts shown for individual annuity premiums may or may not include contracts sold through brokerage firms, due to inconsistencies in reporting.

Selected Statistics — 1985-1989: This graph shows the five-year trend for four financial measures: premiums, capital & surplus, assets, and life insurance in force. The graph uses a logarithmic scale to make it easier to compare growth rates. A straight line means the rate of change (increase or decrease) is constant. An increasing slope means an increasing growth rate. You can also compare the growth rates for different measures by simply looking at the slopes of the corresponding lines.

Distribution of First-Year Premium Income by Line of Business: This shows the relative importance of the company's low-load individual life and annuity business for the last five years. First-year premium income includes direct first-year and single premium business; it does not include reinsurance transactions. (When premium income from reinsurance is significant, this will be indicated in a footnote.)

History: A brief chronology, with emphasis on changes of ownership and sales of blocks of business during the last five years. A slash (/) separating the names of owners indicates a parent-subsidiary relationship; a backslash (\) indicates a subsidiary-parent relationship.

Treatment of Policyholders: This is arguably one of the most important elements of a company profile. We had originally intended to provide a list of specific actions that companies had taken to benefit existing policyholders. However, it became apparent that some actions could be interpreted in various ways, or companies could selectively choose what to present, so we decided to omit this and wait until we can present a more comprehensive picture.

In the meantime, this section lists the number and major categories of complaints related to individual life and annuity products. Large companies are likely to have more complaints because of their size, so you should look at these numbers in relation to the number of policies issued and oustanding.

Segmentation of General Account: For internal management purposes, many insurance companies divide their general account into several portfolios, or *segments*, in accordance with the characteristics of each product line. This section provides a brief description of the company's investment allocation practices.

Reinsurance: Consumers are usually unaware of the transactions that take place between the primary carrier and its reinsurers, but stable reinsurance relationships can help a company provide competitive products. You can assume that a reinsurance company will be involved whenever a policy's net amount at risk exceeds the primary carrier's retention level.

Balance Sheet: This provides additional information about the company's investments and their relationship to total capital and surplus. It should be used for raising questions to be explored further with an advisor or the company, rather than for arriving at any conclusions.

All amounts are based on the company's statutory annual statement. Under statutory accounting, bonds (including junk bonds) in good standing are carried at *amortized value*; that is, original cost with adjustments for discounts or premiums. Bonds in default are generally carried at market value. Mortgages are carried at principal outstanding; in the event of default, the principal balance is transferred to real estate. Preferred stocks with stable dividends are carried at cost; others are carried at market value, as are all common stocks. Real estate is carried at cost less depreciation. Most furniture and equipment is *non-admitted*; that is, it is not included as a statutory asset.

Note that "non-investment grade bonds" includes certain unrated private placements; it is not just publicly-traded junk bonds. Also, the breakdown of bonds by quality and maturity may not add up to 100 percent, because this information comes from two annual statement exhibits that do not tie together. Amounts excluded represent bonds of all quality categories that are due to mature in one year or less.

The *Mandatory Securities Valuation Reserve* (MSVR) is a liability that insurance companies are required to establish to provide a cushion against potential losses on bonds and preferred and common stocks. As such, it is often treated as an additional element of capital and surplus. To be conservative, however, we have chosen to ignore it in computing percentages.

You can get an idea of the company's relative investment mix and capitalization (with or without the MSVR) by looking at the balance sheet of the life insurance industry as a whole, in Appendix A. The aggregate data is for 1988, the latest year available.

Additional Information: For more information about the company, see *Best's Insurance Reports*, available in many libraries. When a company is rated by other organizations, an analytical report may also be available from the company or rating agency. (See Appendix F.)

12

PRODUCT PROFILES

TRADITIONAL WHOLE LIFE

Company: MASSACHUSETTS SAVINGS BANK
LIFE INSURANCE

Product: ECONOLIFE

Description: Economatic-type whole life. Yearly renewable term during first year; then 60% straight life and 40% term rider. Fixed premiums payable for life. Pays dividends. Unisex rates.

Availability: MA
Other restrictions: Must live or work in Massachusetts at time of issue.

Issue Ages: 18-70   **Maturity Date:** Age 100

Premium Limitations:

	First	Additional
Minimum	Fixed	Fixed
Maximum	Fixed	Fixed

Face Amount Limitations:
Minimum: $50,000   *Maximum:* $250,000
Changes: Not available, except by partial surrender.

Valuation Basis: 1980 CSO-C 5%, net level method.

Dividend Determination Process: Traditional three-factor formula (interest, mortality, expenses). Dividend interest rate is currently 8.5%, determined on a portfolio basis. In 1989, 30 issuing banks paid higher rates on pre-1979 policies. Mortality experience of all issuing banks is pooled to reduce fluctuations.

Illustration Practices: *Do any pricing assumptions underlying currently illustrated policy values differ from:*
• *current experience?* No
• *anticipated future experience?* No

Dividend Options: Cash, reduce premium, accumulate at interest, paid-up additions.

Surrenders: Cash value is equal to full net level terminal reserve at end of second policy year. Face amount can be reduced by partial surrenders.

Policy Loans:
Interest charged: Variable rate, based on Moody's Corporate Bond Yield Average or 6%, whichever is higher. Payable in advance.
Effect on dividends: None
Effective cost of borrowing: Same as interest charged.

Settlement Options: Currently available, but not guaranteed.

Fractional Premiums:

	Modal Factor	Equivalent Annual Charge
Semi-annual	0.51	8.3%
Quarterly	0.26	11.2
Monthly	N/A	–

Riders:
- Yearly Renewable Term
- Waiver of Premium
- Child
- Decreasing Term

Other Product Features: Unisex rates only. AIDS/ARC exclusion (waived with submission of satisfactory blood test).

Treatment of Policyholders:
Service: Provided by issuing and agency banks, backed up by central office in Woburn. No 800 number.

During the past year, have there been any significant problems in handling requests for service? No

Type and frequency of communications to policyholders:
- Annual premium/dividend notice

Are new contract improvements offered to existing policyholders?
There is no particular tradition. Very low overhead does not allow exotic updates, etc.

Past repricing actions: Dividend scales are changed periodically.

Comparison with "Buy Term and Invest the Difference":
Unisex nonsmoker, age 45, assuming dividends buy additional insurance.

Policy Year	Premium	Death Benefit	Cash Value	Before-Tax Rate of Return* Average Annual	Yearly
1	$2,990	$250,000	$2,570	(0.3)%	(0.3)%
2	2,990	250,000	5,417	3.9	6.1
3	2,990	250,000	8,469	5.5	7.1
4	2,990	250,000	11,733	6.3	7.6
5	2,990	250,000	15,227	6.8	7.9
10	2,990	250,000	36,763	7.7	8.1
15	2,990	250,000	67,001	7.9	8.1
20	2,990	270,624	110,475	8.0	8.5

*Based on unisex term rates; ignores income tax upon surrender. Rate of return will depend on age, face amount, premiums, and term and tax rates.

Distributors:

Name/Address	*Compensation*
SBLI issuing and agency banks	Sold by salaried representatives.

Company: NEW YORK SAVINGS BANK LIFE INSURANCE

Product: WHOLE LIFE

Description: Whole life with fixed premiums payable for life (straight life) or for 20 years (20 payment life). Pays dividends.

Availability: NY
Other restrictions: Must live or work in New York at time of issue.

Issue Ages: 0-70   **Maturity Date:** Age 100

Premium Limitations:

	First	Additional
Minimum	Fixed & level. Fractional premiums: at least $40.	
Maximum	Based on face amount limitations.	

Face Amount Limitations:
Minimum: $2,000 *Maximum:* $50,000 ($350,000 term conversion)
Changes: None

Valuation Basis: 1980 CSO 4.75%, Modified Preliminary Term.

Dividend Determination Process: SBLI Fund establishes premium rates and recommends a dividend scale, using a traditional three-factor formula (interest, mortality, expenses). Dividends are the same for all SBLI issuing banks for the first seven years; after that, dividends may vary, based on each bank's accumulated surplus, expenses, and investment experience. Mortality experience of all issuing banks is pooled to reduce fluctuations. Investment experience is determined on a portfolio-average basis.

Illustration Practices: *Do any pricing assumptions underlying currently illustrated policy values differ from:*
• *current experience?* No
• *anticipated future experience?* No

Dividend Options: Cash, reduce premium, accumulate at interest, paid-up additions, one-year term insurance.

Surrenders: Partial surrenders are subject to company approval.

Policy Loans:
Interest charged: Variable rate, based on Moody's Corporate Bond Yield Average or 5.75%, whichever is higher. Payable in advance.
As of 3/90: 9.65%
Effect on dividends: None
Effective cost of borrowing: Same as interest charged.

Settlement Options: Standard

Fractional Premiums:

	Modal Factor	Equivalent Annual Charge
Semi-annual	0.52	17.4%
Quarterly	0.265	17.1
Monthly	0.10	51.2

Riders:
- Accidental Death Benefit
- Spouse Insurance (10-year renewable term)
- Waiver of Premium
- Children's Rider (term to age 21)

Other Product Features: N/A

Treatment of Policyholders:
Service: Provided by issuing banks, backed up by SBLI Fund, by mail or over-the-counter.

During the past year, have there been any significant problems in handling requests for service? Problems can arise in preparation of IRS 1099 forms; company does not maintain premium or dividend histories.

If so, what corrective actions have been taken? Policyholders should avoid transactions that generate taxable income; i.e., should use dividends to buy paid-up additions and access cash values via policy loans, rather than surrender.

Type and frequency of communications to policyholders:
• Annual premium/dividend notice   • Annual newsletter

Are new contract improvements offered to existing policyholders?
Hard to generalize. When rating by sex was introduced, no change was made to existing policies. Special offers are sometimes made to recent issues when lower rates are introduced.

Past repricing actions: No change to dividend scale since 1985. Some changes–nearly all increases–by individual banks for old policies.

Comparison with "Buy Term and Invest the Difference":
Male nonsmoker, age 45, assuming dividends buy paid-up additions.

Policy Year	Premium	Death Benefit	Cash Value	Before-Tax Rate of Return* Average Annual	Yearly
1	$980	$50,000	$122	(86.4)%	(86.4)%
2	980	50,403	287	(74.3)	(71.5)
3	980	50,905	1,487	(26.7)	26.5
4	980	51,570	2,766	(9.3)	18.9
5	980	52,477	4,193	(1.3)	16.1
10	980	60,219	13,615	8.4	11.8
15	980	74,081	26,938	9.2	10.3
20	980	94,835	46,862	9.4	9.3

*Based on moderately-low term rates; ignores income tax upon surrender. Rate of return will depend on age, face amount, premiums, and term and tax rates.

Distributors:

Name/Address	*Compensation*
SBLI issuing banks	Sold by salaried representatives.

Company: USAA LIFE INSURANCE COMPANY

Product: WHOLE LIFE

Description: Fixed premium whole life. Pays dividends.

Availability: All states
Pending: MN, NV, NY, PA, WV
Other restrictions: Will only accept applications from state of residence.

Issue Ages: 0-80   **Maturity Date:** Age 100

Premium Limitations:

	First	Additional
Minimum	Fixed	Fixed
Maximum	Fixed	Fixed

Face Amount Limitations:
Minimum: $25,000   *Maximum:* None
Changes: No post-issue adjustments allowed.

Valuation Basis: 1980 CSO (NS/S) 4.5% net level method

Dividend Determination Process: Dividends are determined using the Contribution Method, with a three-factor formula. The interest contribution is based on interest earned on the reserve at the end of the prior policy year plus the net premium. The interest rate is the dividend rate–currently 9.25%–less the 4.5% valuation rate. The mortality contribution is based on the difference between the 1980 CSO valuation mortality rate and the expected mortality rate, which is 65% of 1986 Bragg Mortality. This difference is applied to the net amount at risk to produce the mortality component of the dividend. The expense contribution is the difference between actual expenses and the expected expenses that are priced into the gross premium; this component is generally negative.

Illustration Practices: *Do any pricing assumptions underlying currently illustrated policy values differ from:*
• *current experience?* No
• *anticipated future experience?* No

Dividend Options: Standard

Surrenders: No partial surrenders are allowed.

Policy Loans:
Interest charged: **7.4%** fixed rate, in advance (8%, in arrears).
Effect on dividends: Direct Recognition anticipated in one year.
Effective cost of borrowing: 8% plus reduction in dividends.

Fractional Premiums:

	Modal Factor	Equivalent Annual Charge
Semi-annual	0.51	8.3%
Quarterly	0.26	11.2
Monthly	0.085	4.4

Settlement Options: Standard

Riders:
• Waiver of Premium   • Accidental Death Benefit
• Child

Other Product Features: Vanishing premium option.

Treatment of Policyholders:
Service: By mail or 800 number.

During the past year, have there been any significant problems in handling requests for service? No

Type and frequency of communications to policyholders:
• Annual statement   • Corporate publications
                                       (6-8 times per year)

Are new contract improvements offered to existing policyholders?
Yes

Past repricing actions: None

Comparison with "Buy Term and Invest the Difference":
Male nonsmoker, age 45, assuming dividends buy paid-up additions.

Policy Year	Premium	Beg.-Yr. Death Benefit	End-Yr. Cash Value	Before-Tax Rate of Return* Average Annual	Yearly
1	$3,750	$200,140	$813	(76.2)%	(76.2)%
2	3,750	201,899	2,433	(51.6)	(41.8)
3	3,750	204,189	7,034	(17.0)	22.2
4	3,750	207,013	12,111	(3.9)	17.5
5	3,750	210,384	17,502	1.8	14.2
10	3,750	236,163	50,813	8.1	10.1
15	3,750	280,322	96,469	8.6	9.2
20	3,750	348,384	164,616	8.8	9.5

*Based on moderately-low term rates; ignores income tax upon surrender. Rate of return will depend on age, face amount, premiums, and term and tax rates.

Distributors:

Name/Address
USAA Financial Services
USAA Building
San Antonio, TX 78288
800/531-8000
512/498-8000

Compensation
Sold by salaried
representatives.

UNIVERSAL LIFE

Company: AMERITAS LIFE INSURANCE CORPORATION

Product: LOW-LOAD UNISON

Description: Flexible-premium universal life. Unisex.

Availability: All states except DC, ME, NY
Pending: NJ
Other restrictions: Product must be approved in state of residence.

Issue Ages: 20-70   **Maturity Date:** Age 95

Premium Limitations:

	First	Additional
Minimum	Sum of first-year charges.	
Maximum	As allowed by current tax law.	

Face Amount Limitations:
Minimum: $50,000   *Maximum:* $5,000,000 (without prior approval)
Changes: One per year. Increases allowed after first year with evidence of insurability. Decreases cannot reduce face amount below $50,000.

Contract Charges:

	Current			
	Annual			
	Yr 1	Yrs 2+	Back-end	Guaranteed
Per policy ($)	48	48		75
% premium	2.5	2.5		2.5
Per $1000 face ($)				
% account value				
Insurance	See COI rates			1980 CSO Unisex
Investment	Declared interest rate is net of asset charges			

Current Cost of Insurance Rates:

Rate structure: 10-year select and ultimate. No bands. Unisex. Non-smoker/smoker. Age nearest birthday.

Annual rates per $1,000 of coverage:

	Unisex Nonsmoker			Unisex Smoker		
Year	35	45	55	35	45	55
1	1.13	2.03	4.19	1.98	3.46	7.72
6	1.56	3.31	6.93	2.47	5.65	12.35
11	2.01	4.96	13.34	3.85	10.01	24.14
16	3.17	8.22	21.70	6.29	16.02	35.35
21	4.96	13.34	34.67	10.01	24.14	51.61
31	13.34	34.67	83.61	24.14	51.61	100.16
41	34.67	83.61	–	51.61	100.16	–

Current Interest Rate:

Rate structure: Hybrid new money/portfolio average approach. New premiums receive rates that reflect current market conditions. Values that have been with the company over 12 months receive pooled rates based on earnings of assets supporting interest-sensitive products. Guaranteed minimum rate: 4.5%.

Guarantee period: Interest rates on all new premiums: 12 months. Renewal rates: One month.

Rate-setting process: New money and renewal rates are approved monthly by company management and ratified by Board of Directors. Trends in investment markets, anticipated premium flows, earnings on existing assets, and competition are considered. Targeted spread between earned and credited rates is 1.35% for Years 1-8 and 0.75% thereafter, reflecting the recovery of acquisition costs.

Investment strategy: Intermediate-term bonds and mortgage loans with a maturity of 3-7 years. Investment policy is to invest in bonds of investment grade (Baa) or better.

Interest rate history:

On Amounts Deposited on 1/1	Declared Rate at 1/1					
	1985	1986	1987	1988	1989	1990
1985						
1986						
1987						
1988						
1989						8.90	8.90
1990						8.40
Changes in new-money rate					0	2

Benchmarks: Tillinghast Universal Life Analytic Study; CDs.

Persistency Bonuses: None

Illustration Practices: *Do any pricing assumptions underlying currently illustrated policy values differ from:*
• *current experience?* No
• *anticipated future experience?* No, however, company intends to re-price product to reflect any improvements in experience as they occur, and it does not anticipate any deterioration in experience.

Withdrawals and Surrenders: *Withdrawals:* After three months; one per policy year. $500 minimum. Remaining surrender value cannot be less than $1,000. *Charge:* $25 current, $50 guaranteed. No charge on full surrenders.

Policy Loans:
Interest charged: 7%, in arrears (4.5% under Reduced Rate Rider)
Interest credited: 4.5%
Effective cost of borrowing: 7% plus difference between current credited rate and 4.5% (4.5% plus lost interest for amounts borrowed under Reduced Rate Rider)

Settlement Options: Standard

Riders:
- Reduced Rate: Free and automatic; at age 65 or year 10, whichever is later, reduces loan interest rate to 4.5% for amounts up to rider limit.

- Cost Recovery: Free and automatic for issue ages 0-65; gives option to withdraw sum of all premiums or $100,000, whichever is less, without reducing the specified face amount.

- Waiver Cost of Insurance: Waives COI charges if insured is disabled for six months.

- Child Protection: $10,000 on each eligible child through age 25; convertible to $50,000 universal life at age 25.

Other Product Features: 10-day free look. Eligible to receive dividends, but none expected (current interest, expense, and COI charges are used to pass experience on to policyholders).

Treatment of Policyholders:
Service: 800 number for questions. All servicing done through mail or fee-for-service planner.

During the past year, have there been any significant problems in handling requests for service? No

Type and frequency of communications to policyholders:
- Annual report
- Confirmation of changes to contract
- Planned premium billing notice
- Semi-annual policyowner newsletter (pending)

During the past year, have there been any significant delays in preparing policy statements or confirmations of transactions? No

Was the current administrative system developed in-house or purchased from an outside vendor? Outside vendor.

Can the system be upgraded as needed to meet future demands? Yes. In-house or outside.

Are new contract improvements offered to existing policyholders?
Yes. Pricing factors are updated regularly to reflect current
experience trends. When practical, new riders are added to all
policies.

Past repricing actions: None

Comparison with "Buy Term and Invest the Difference":
Unisex nonsmoker, age 45, based on 8.65% interest and current
charges.

Policy Year	Premium	Death Benefit	Cash Value	Before-Tax Rate of Return * Average Annual	Yearly
1	$3,750	$250,000	$3,401	1.9%	1.9%
2	3,750	250,000	7,050	4.1	5.2
3	3,750	250,000	10,971	5.3	6.5
4	3,750	250,000	15,179	6.0	7.1
5	3,750	250,000	19,695	6.4	7.5
10	3,750	250,000	47,876	7.4	8.0
15	3,750	250,000	91,489	8.1	8.8
20	3,750	250,000	158,344	8.4	9.1

*Based on unisex term rates; ignores income tax upon surrender. Rate of return will
depend on age, face amount, premiums, and term and tax rates.

Distributors:

Name/Address	*Compensation*
Ameritas Marketing Corp. 800/255-9678 Field distributors: • Fee-only planners • Direct-writing representatives	• Fee for services • Field marketing allowance paid by company.

Company: AMERITAS LIFE INSURANCE CORPORATION

Product: LOW-LOAD UNIVERSAL LIFE

Description: Flexible premium universal life.

Availability: All states except DC, MA, ME, MT, NY
Pending: NJ
Other restrictions: Product must be approved in state of residence.

Issue Ages: 0-80   **Maturity Date:** Age 95

Premium Limitations:

	First	Additional
Minimum	Varies by age and sex.	
Maximum	As allowed by current tax law.	

Face Amount Limitations:
Minimum: $100,000   *Maximum:* $10,000,000
Changes: Increases allowed after first year with evidence of insurability. Decreases cannot reduce face amount below $100,000 in years 1-3 and $75,000 thereafter. Limit is one change per year.

Contract Charges:

	Current		Back-end	Guaranteed
	Annual			
	Yr 1	Yrs 2+		
Per policy ($)	48	48		75
% premium	0	0*		2.5
Per $1000 face ($)				
% account value				
Insurance	See COI rates			1980 CSO M/F NS/S
Investment	Declared interest rate is net of asset charges			

*There is a percent-of-premium administrative charge for face amount increases; percentage varies by policy year.

Current Cost of Insurance Rates:

Rate structure: Male/female; nonsmoker/smoker. Age nearest birthday. No bands. 8-year select and ultimate.

Annual rates per $1,000 of coverage:

	Male Nonsmoker				Female Nonsmoker		
Year	35	45	55		35	45	55
1	0.77	1.46	2.33		0.77	1.33	1.91
6	2.27	4.59	9.53		1.87	3.35	6.29
11	1.55	4.28	11.31		1.20	2.81	7.65
16	2.56	7.19	18.22		1.82	4.66	11.89
21	4.28	11.31	30.09		2.81	7.65	19.10
31	11.31	30.09	82.26		7.65	19.10	54.32
41	30.09	82.26	-		19.10	54.32	-

	Male Smoker				Female Smoker		
Year	35	45	55		35	45	55
1	1.31	2.49	3.90		0.80	1.40	1.97
6	3.07	6.30	14.13		2.40	4.20	8.19
11	3.93	8.99	20.74		2.62	5.83	12.73
16	6.11	13.53	30.40		3.82	8.76	19.71
21	8.99	20.74	43.65		5.83	12.73	28.01
31	20.74	43.65	90.35		12.73	28.01	64.04
41	43.65	90.35	-		28.01	64.04	-

Current Interest Rate:

Rate structure: Hybrid new money/portfolio average approach. New premiums receive rates that reflect current market conditions. Values that have been with the company over 12 months receive pooled rates based on earnings of assets supporting interest-sensitive products. Guaranteed minimum rate: 4.5%.

Guarantee period: Interest rates on all new premiums: 12 months. Renewal rates: One month.

Rate-setting process: New money and renewal rates are approved monthly by company management and ratified by Board of Directors. Trends in investment markets, anticipated premium flows, earnings on existing assets, and competition are considered. Targeted spread between earned and credited rates is 1.5% for years 1-8 and 0.75% thereafter, reflecting the recovery of acquisition costs.

Investment strategy: Intermediate-term bonds and mortgage loans with a maturity of 3-7 years. Investment policy is to invest in bonds of investment grade (Baa) or better.

Interest rate history:

On Amounts Deposited on 1/1	Declared Rate at 1/1					
	1985	1986	1987	1988	1989	1990
1985						
1986						
1987			8.45	9.75	9.00	8.75
1988				8.75	9.00	8.75
1989					8.75	8.75
1990						8.25
Changes in new-money rate		2	3	2	2	

Benchmarks: Tillinghast Universal Life Analytic Study; CDs.

Persistency Bonuses: None

Illustration Practices: *Do any pricing assumptions underlying currently illustrated policy values differ from:*
• *current experience?* No
• *anticipated future experience?* No, however, company intends to re-price product to reflect any improvements in experience as they occur, and it does not anticipate any deterioration in experience.

Withdrawals and Surrenders: *Withdrawals:* After three months; one per policy year. $500 minimum. Remaining surrender value cannot be less than $1,000. *Charge:* $25 current, $50 guaranteed. No charge on full surrenders.

Policy Loans:
Interest charged: 7%, in arrears (4.5% under Reduced Rate Rider)
Interest credited: 4.5%
Effective cost of borrowing: 7% plus difference between current credited rate and 4.5% (4.5% plus lost interest for amounts borrowed under Reduced Rate Rider)

Settlement Options: Standard

Riders:
• Reduced Rate: Free and automatic; at age 65 or year 10, whichever is later, reduces loan interest rate to 4.5% for amounts up to rider limit.

• Cost Recovery: Free and automatic for issue ages 0-65; gives option to withdraw sum of all premiums or $100,000, whichever is less, without reducing the specified face amount.

• Payor Waiver Cost of Insurance: For issue ages 0-14, waives COI charges if adult premium payer is disabled for six months.

• Waiver Cost of Insurance: Waives COI charge if insured is disabled for six months.

• Covered Insured: Term insurance on insured or another person.

• Guaranteed Insurability: For issue ages 0-34, guarantees right to increase coverage by up to $50,000 on two option dates.

• Child Protection: $10,000 on each eligible child through age 25; convertible to $50,000 universal life at age 25.

Other Product Features: 10-day free look. Eligible to receive dividends, but none expected (current interest, expense, and COI charges are used to pass experience on to policyholders).

Treatment of Policyholders:
Service: 800 number for questions. All servicing done through mail or fee-for-service planners.

During the past year, have there been any significant problems in handling requests for service? No

Type and frequency of communications to policyholders:
• Annual report
• Confirmation of contract changes
• Planned premium billing notice
• Semi-annual policyowner newsletter (pending)

During the past year, have there been any significant delays in preparing policy statements or confirmations of transactions? No

Was the current administrative system developed in-house or purchased from an outside vendor? Outside vendor.

Can the system be upgraded as needed to meet future demands? Yes. In-house or outside.

Are new contract improvements offered to existing policyholders? Yes. Pricing factors are updated regularly to reflect current experience trends. When practical, new riders are added to all policies.

Past repricing action–1987: COI rates and interest rate margins adjusted for all policies, producing higher future cash values in almost all cases. Cost Recovery rider added to all policies.

Comparison with "Buy Term and Invest the Difference":
Male nonsmoker, age 45, based on 8.5% interest and current charges.

Policy Year	Premium	Death Benefit	Cash Value	Before-Tax Rate of Return* Average Annual	Yearly
1	$3,750	$250,000	$3,644	9.5%	9.5%
2	3,750	250,000	7,442	8.2	7.5
3	3,750	250,000	11,387	7.5	6.7
4	3,750	250,000	15,501	7.1	6.5
5	3,750	250,000	19,818	6.9	6.5
10	3,750	250,000	48,540	7.9	9.5
15	3,750	250,000	94,050	8.5	9.2
20	3,750	250,000	164,196	8.8	9.3

*Based on moderately-low term rates; ignores income tax upon surrender. Rate of return will depend on age, face amount, premiums, and term and tax rates.

Distributors:

Name/Address	_Compensation_
Ameritas Marketing Corp. 800/255-9678 Field distributors: • Fee-only planners • Direct-writing representatives	• Fee for services • Field marketing allowance paid by company.

Company: JOHN ALDEN LIFE INSURANCE COMPANY

Product: PIONEER UNIVERSAL LIFE

Description: Flexible premium universal life.

Availability: All states, except MA, NY
Pending: NJ, PA
Other restrictions: Application accepted in state where insured works if it does not violate state law.

Issue Ages: 18-75   **Maturity Date:** Age 95

Premium Limitations:

	First	Additional
Minimum	First-year COI.	$25 bank draft, $50 other modes.
Maximum	As allowed by current tax law; unscheduled payments are subject to company approval.	

Face Amount Limitations:
Minimum: $100,000   *Maximum:* None
Changes: Change in option and/or face amount allowed after first year; increase or decrease must be at least $5,000.

Contract Charges:

	Current			
	Annual			
	Yr 1	Yrs 2+	Back-end	Guaranteed
Per policy ($)				
% premium				
Per $1000 face ($)			Note 1	Note 1
% account value				
Insurance	See COI rates			1980 CSO M/F NS/S
Investment	Declared interest rate is net of asset charges			

Note 1: Surrender charge is a declining amount per $1,000 initial face amount, as follows: Months 1-11, $2.50; months 12-23, $1.88; months 24-35, $1.25; months 36-47, $0.63; $0 thereafter.

Current Cost of Insurance Rates:

Rate structure: Male/female, nonsmoker/smoker. Age last birthday.
Bands: $100-249K, 250-499K, 500-999K, 1000+. Reverse select.
Each face amount increase is treated as a separate component,
with COI rates based on applicable band.

Annual rates per $1,000 of coverage (for $250-499K band):

Year	Male Nonsmoker 35	45	55	Female Nonsmoker 35	45	55
1	1.48	2.95	6.31	1.29	2.55	4.80
6	2.03	4.51	9.41	1.85	3.54	6.05
11	2.17	4.40	9.74	1.94	3.65	6.76
16	3.15	6.42	16.65	2.69	4.60	9.14
21	4.40	9.74	28.00	3.65	6.76	17.45
31	9.74	28.00	75.54	6.76	17.45	63.03
41	28.00	75.54	-	17.45	63.03	-

Year	Male Smoker 35	45	55	Female Smoker 35	45	55
1	2.58	5.61	10.62	1.91	3.99	7.14
6	3.93	7.52	14.92	3.00	5.28	6.52
11	4.72	8.94	18.10	2.94	5.26	9.35
16	6.34	12.57	23.38	3.89	6.52	12.10
21	8.94	18.10	35.84	5.26	9.35	20.79
31	18.10	35.84	81.24	9.35	20.79	70.00
41	35.84	81.24	-	20.79	70.00	-

Current Interest Rate:

Rate structure: Hybrid new money/portfolio average approach.
New money pools are established periodically. As credited rates
converge, money pools can be combined under a portfolio average
approach. Guaranteed rate: 5.5%.

Guarantee period: None

Rate-setting process: By committee; meets at irregular intervals.

Investment strategy: Segregated portfolio: Bonds 65%; mortgages 30%; short-term investments for liquidity 5%. Bonds and mortgages are intermediate-term (8-year average).

Interest rate history:

On Amounts	Declared Rate at 1/1[*]					
Deposited on 1/1	1985	1986	1987	1988	1989	1990
1985						
1986						
1987			10.00	10.00	9.00	9.00
1988				9.50	9.50	9.50
1989					9.00	9.00
1990						9.00
Changes in new-money rate					0	

[*]Low-load product not available before 1/89; earlier rates are for load product with similar spread requirements.

Benchmarks: Tillinghast Universal Life Analytic Study; CDs.

Persistency Bonuses: None

Illustration Practices: Do any pricing assumptions underlying currently illustrated policy values differ from:
• *current experience?* No
• *anticipated future experience?* No

Withdrawals and Surrenders: *Partial surrender:* Must leave at least $500 or enough to cover monthly deductions to next anniversary. $25 charge. *Full surrender:* Subject to declining charge (see Contract charges).

Policy Loans: No restrictions.
Interest charged: Currently 7.4%, in arrears. Guaranteed rate: Higher of Moody's Corporate Bond Yield Average or current gross interest rate plus 1%.
Interest credited: Currently 7.25%. Guaranteed rate: 5.5%.
Effective cost of borrowing: Currently 7.4% plus difference between credited rate on unborrowed amounts and 7.25%.

Settlement Options: Standard

Riders:
- Disability Waiver of
  Monthly Deduction
- Other Insured
- Cost of Living
- Child

Other Product Features: 20-day free look.

Treatment of Policyholders:
Service: By mail or 800 number.

During the past year, have there been any significant problems in handling requests for service? No

Type and frequency of communications to policyholders:
- Annual statement

During the past year, have there been any significant delays in preparing policy statements or confirmations of transactions? No
Was the current administrative system developed in-house or purchased from an outside vendor? Purchased from Cybertek.

Can the system be upgraded as needed to meet future demands? Yes. By Cybertek or in-house.

Are new contract improvements offered to existing policyholders? Yes. Under the same policy form.

Past repricing actions: None

Comparison with "Buy Term and Invest the Difference":

Male nonsmoker, age 45, based on 9.0% interest and current charges.

Policy Year	Premium	Death Benefit	Cash Value	Before-Tax Rate of Return* Average Annual	Yearly
1	$3,750	$250,000	$2,967	(10.8)%	(10.8)%
2	3,750	250,000	6,845	2.4	9.6
3	3,750	250,000	11,029	5.8	9.5
4	3,750	250,000	15,551	7.2	9.5
5	3,750	250,000	20,281	7.7	8.7
10	3,750	250,000	50,854	8.7	9.1
15	3,750	250,000	98,713	9.0	9.4
20	3,750	250,000	172,798	9.2	9.3

*Based on moderately-low term rates; ignores income tax upon surrender. Rate of return will depend on age, face amount, premiums, and term and tax rates.

Distributors–exclusive:

Name/Address
Fee For Service
Airport Executive Center
2203 North Lois Avenue, Suite 814
Tampa, FL 33607
813/874-5662

Compensation
Marketing costs paid
by company; fees paid
by buyer.

Company: LINCOLN BENEFIT LIFE COMPANY

Product: ACHIEVER VI

Description: Flexible premium universal life.

Availability: All states except CA, CT, FL, IA, MA, NH, NJ, NY, OR, TX
Other restrictions: Application must be signed in a state where product is approved.

Issue Ages: 0-80　　　　　　　　　　　**Maturity Date:** Age 95

Premium Limitations:

	First	Additional
Minimum	First year charges.	$10
Maximum	As allowed by current tax law.	

Face Amount Limitations:
Minimum: $10,000 (Ages 0-14); $100,000 (Ages 15-80)
Maximum: $10,000,000
Changes: One per month. Option changes allowed; face amount cannot be reduced below $25,000 for issue ages 15-80.

Contract Charges:

	Current			
	Annual			
	Yr 1	Yrs 2+	Back-end	Guaranteed
Per policy ($)	24	24		24
% premium	3.5	3.5		3.5
Per $1000 face ($)			Note 1	Note 1
% account value				
Insurance	See COI rates			1980 CSO M/F NS/S ALB
Investment	Declared interest rate is net of asset charges			

Note 1: Surrender charge is $5 per $1,000 face amount in the first year, declining by by $0.50 per year to $0 in year 11.

Current Cost of Insurance Rates:
Rate structure: Aggregate (attained-age). Age last birthday. No bands.

Annual rates per $1,000 of coverage:

	Male Nonsmoker			Female Nonsmoker		
Year	35	45	55	35	45	55
1	0.84	1.68	3.84	0.72	1.44	2.88
6	1.08	2.40	6.36	0.96	1.92	4.20
11	1.68	3.84	10.80	1.44	2.88	6.72
16	2.40	6.36	17.52	1.92	4.20	10.44
21	3.84	10.80	33.12	2.88	6.72	20.64
31	10.80	33.12	100.44	6.72	20.64	77.40
41	33.12	100.44	-	20.64	77.40	-

	Male Smoker			Female Smoker		
Year	35	45	55	35	45	55
1	1.56	3.60	8.76	1.20	2.76	5.64
6	2.28	5.52	12.96	1.92	3.96	7.56
11	3.60	8.76	19.80	2.76	5.64	11.28
16	5.52	12.96	29.52	3.96	7.56	16.44
21	8.76	19.80	49.44	5.64	11.28	27.24
31	19.80	49.44	113.76	11.28	27.24	82.80
41	49.44	113.76	-	27.24	82.80	-

Current Interest Rate:
Rate structure: Portfolio average method. Three interest rate tiers based on policy values: (1) under $5,000 earns base rate; (2) between $5,000 and $10,000 earns base rate plus 0.5%; (3) over $10,000 earns base rate plus 1.0% Guaranteed rate: 5%.

Guarantee period: None

Rate-setting process: Committee meets quarterly. Credited rates are based on yields on available and existing assets. Currently renewed quarterly.

Investment strategy: 10-year bonds, 5-year mortgages, and 7-10 year tranches of collateralized mortgage obligations (CMOs), with combined average life of about 8 years. At least 80% of investments should be in Baa (Moody's) or better quality with up to 20% in B or Ba quality. All assets are owned by Allstate, which limits assets below Baa quality to 10% overall.

Interest rate history:

On Amounts	Declared Rate at 1/1*					
Deposited on 1/1	1985	1986	1987	1988	1989	1990
1985						
1986			10.00	9.65	9.65	9.25
1987			10.00	9.65	9.65	9.25
1988				9.65	9.65	9.25
1989					9.65	9.25
1990						9.25
Changes in new-money rate		1		2	0	1

*Amounts shown are base rate. Policy values over $5,000 receive a higher rate.

Benchmarks: Tillinghast Universal Life Analytic Study; CDs.

Persistency Bonuses: None

Illustration Practices: *Do any pricing assumptions underlying currently illustrated policy values differ from:*
• *current experience?* No
• *anticipated future experience?* No

Withdrawals and Surrenders: *Withdrawals:* $25 charge; no limit on frequency. *Surrenders:* Subject to a declining charge based on the initial face amount (see contract charges).

Policy Loans:
Interest charged: Variable; currently 6% in advance (6.38%, in arrears).
Interest credited: Variable; currently 6%.

Effective cost of borrowing: Currently, 6.38% plus difference between credited rate on unborrowed amounts and 6%.

Settlement Options: Standard

Riders:
- Continuation of Premium during disability: Amount set by policy-holder, within limits
- Accidental Death
- Children's Level Term
- Additional Insureds

Other Product Features: N/A

Treatment of Policyholders:
Service: Through home office, by mail or 800 number.

During the past year, have there been any significant problems in handling requests for service? No

Type and frequency of communications to policyholders:
- Annual statement

During the past year, have there been any significant delays in preparing policy statements or confirmations of transactions? No

Was the current administrative system developed in-house or purchased from an outside vendor? Outside vendor (TCC).

Can the system be upgraded as needed to meet future demands? Yes. Planning to switch to TCC's new system (CCA) in the next five years.

Are new contract improvements offered to existing policyholders? Yes. COI and interest rate structures treat all policyholders equally regardless of purchase date.

Past repricing actions–1987: Policy loan interest rate reduced.

Comparison with "Buy Term and Invest the Difference":
Male nonsmoker, age 45, based on 9.25% interest and current charges.

Policy Year	Premium	Death Benefit	Cash Value	Before-Tax Rate of Return* Average Annual	Yearly
1	$3,750	$250,000	$2,246	(32.5)%	(32.5)%
2	3,750	250,000	6,176	4.4	11.8
3	3,750	250,000	10,460	3.1	11.3
4	3,750	250,000	15,150	6.2	11.2
5	3,750	250,000	20,259	7.7	11.0
10	3,750	250,000	54,083	9.7	10.4
15	3,750	250,000	107,037	9.9	10.1
20	3,750	250,000	193,147	10.0	10.2

*Based on moderately-low term rates; ignores income tax upon surrender. Rate of return will depend on age, face amount, premiums, and term and tax rates.

Distributors:

Name/Address
Licensed agents
(call 800-LBL-WATS for
 referral)

Compensation
Fees paid by buyer.

Company: USAA LIFE INSURANCE COMPANY

Product: UNIVERSAL LIFE

Description: Flexible premium universal life.

Availability: All states except MT
Pending: NJ
Other restrictions: Only applications from state of residence.

Issue Ages: 0-80   **Maturity Date:** Policy anniversary
after age 95.

Premium Limitations:

	First	Additional
Minimum	Enough to keep policy in force for three months.	No restrictions.
Maximum	As allowed by current tax law.	

Face Amount Limitations:
Minimum: $25,000   *Maximum:* None
Changes: After one year; $25,000 minimum increase.

Contract Charges:

	Current			
	Annual			
	Yr 1	Yrs 2+	Back-end	Guaranteed
Per policy ($)	80	30		80, 30
% premium	3.0	3.0		3.0, 3.0
Per $1000 face ($)				
% account value				
Insurance	See COI rates			1980 CSO M/F NS/S ALB
Investment	Declared interest rate is net of asset charges			

Current Cost of Insurance Rates:

Rate structure: Aggregate (attained age). Age last birthday. Three tiers: $0-100K, 100-250K, 250K+. Cost of insurance per $1,000: A blended rate depending on net amount at risk. For attained ages 0-60: $0-100K tier rates are about 125% of the $250K+ tier rates; $100-250K tier rates are about 119% of the $250K+ tier rates. For attained ages above 60: differences gradually diminish.

Annual rates per $1,000 of coverage (for $250,000+ tier):

	Male Nonsmoker			Female Nonsmoker		
Year	35	45	55	35	45	55
1	1.068	1.704	3.444	0.984	1.692	3.348
6	1.320	2.424	5.508	1.272	2.400	4.224
11	1.704	3.444	9.360	1.692	3.348	5.184
16	2.424	5.508	18.084	2.400	4.224	10.536
21	3.444	9.360	35.712	3.348	5.184	24.408
31	9.360	35.712	132.336	5.184	24.408	97.776
41	35.712	132.336	-	24.408	97.776	-

	Male Smoker			Female Smoker		
Year	35	45	55	35	45	55
1	1.740	3.024	8.304	1.560	2.856	5.484
6	2.304	4.848	11.868	2.100	3.840	7.944
11	3.024	8.304	18.780	2.856	5.484	11.400
16	4.848	11.868	31.176	3.840	7.944	17.856
21	8.304	18.780	54.528	5.484	11.400	33.048
31	18.780	54.528	132.336	11.400	33.048	97.776
41	54.528	132.336	-	33.048	97.776	-

Current Interest Rate:

Rate structure: Portfolio-average method. There are four interest rate tiers based on policy values: (1) under $25,000 earns base rate; (2) between $25,000 and $50,000 earns base rate plus 0.25%; (3) between $50,000 and $100,000 earns base rate plus 0.5%; and (4) over $100,000 earns base rate plus 0.6%. Guaranteed rate: 4.5%

Guarantee period: One month

Rate-setting process: Set monthly by Interest Rate Committee, composed of senior company officers appointed by Board of Directors. Primary considerations are current yield on segregated assets, yield on new investments, and competitors' rates.

Investment strategy: Invests primarily in utility and industrial bonds and Federally-backed mortgage pass-through securities. A small portion is invested in preferred and common stock. All bonds are Moody's Baa or better. Pass-through securities have an Aaa rating. Targeted average maturity is 5-12 years. Asset/liability matching analyses were initiated in 1989.

Interest rate history:

On Amounts	Declared Rate at 1/1[*]					
Deposited on 1/1	1985	1986	1987	1988	1989	1990
1985	11.20	10.25	9.75	9.00	8.90	8.80
1986		10.25	9.75	9.00	8.90	8.80
1987			9.75	9.00	8.90	8.80
1988				9.00	8.90	8.80
1989					8.90	8.80
1990						8.80
Changes in new-money rate	6	5	5	1	2	

[*]Amounts shown are base rate. Policy values above $25,000 receive a higher rate.

Benchmarks: Tillinghast Universal Life Analytic Study; CDs.

Persistency Bonuses: None

Illustration Practices: *Do any pricing assumptions underlying currently illustrated policy values differ from:*
- *current experience?* No
- *anticipated future experience?* No

Withdrawals and Surrenders: *Withdrawals:* $25 charge; *Full surrenders:* No charge.

Policy Loans:
Interest charged: 6.1%, in advance (6.5%, in arrears)
Interest credited: 4.5%
Effective cost of borrowing: 6.5% plus the difference between credited rate on unborrowed amounts and 4.5%.

Settlement Options: Standard

Riders:
- Waiver of Monthly Deduction
- Child
- Accidental Death Benefit

Other Product Features: 20-day free look.

Treatment of Policyholders:
Service: By mail or 800 number.

During the past year, have there been any significant problems in handling requests for service? No

Type and frequency of communications to policyholders:
- Annual statement
- Corporate publications (6-8 times per year)

During the past year, have there been any significant delays in preparing policy statements or confirmations of transactions? None.

Was the current administrative system developed in-house or purchased from an outside vendor? Outside vendor.

Can the system be upgraded as needed to meet future demands? Yes. Flexible enough to meet needs.

Are new contract improvements offered to existing policyholders? Yes

Past repricing actions:

1982: Introduced product
1983: Reduced cost of insurance rates
1984: Reduced cost of insurance rates
1985: Reduced cost of insurance rates
1987: Implemented a tiered rate structure for current cost of insurance (rate reduction for policies over $100,000) and a tiered rate structure for current interest (higher credited rates for cash values over $25,000). Introduced 1980 CSO version of product, with lower guaranteed cost of insurance, $30 policy fee, and offsetting reduction in current cost of insurance, for first $50,000.

Comparison with "Buy Term and Invest the Difference":
Male nonsmoker, age 45, based on 9.00% interest and current charges.

Policy Year	Premium	Death Benefit	Cash Value	Before-Tax Rate of Return* Average Annual	Yearly
1	$3,750	$250,000	$3,348	0.6%	0.6%
2	3,750	250,000	7,016	4.1	5.9
3	3,750	250,000	10,978	5.6	7.2
4	3,750	250,000	15,264	6.5	7.9
5	3,750	250,000	19,906	7.1	8.4
10	3,750	250,000	49,796	8.3	9.0
15	3,750	250,000	95,581	8.7	9.2
20	3,750	250,000	167,420	8.9	9.5

*Based on moderately-low term rates; ignores income tax upon surrender. Rate of return will depend on age, face amount, premiums, and term and tax rates.

Distributors:

Name/Address	*Compensation*
USAA Financial Services	Sold by salaried
USAA Building	representatives.
San Antonio, TX 78288	
800/531-8000	
512/498-8000	

SINGLE PREMIUM WHOLE LIFE

Company: AMERITAS LIFE INSURANCE CORPORATION

Product: LOW-LOAD UNISON

Description: Flexible-premium universal life, used to simulate single premium whole life. Unisex.

Minimum Face Amount: $50,000

Other Features: See universal life product profile.

Policy Illustration: Age 55, unisex nonsmoker.

Single premium: $50,000
Initial face amount: $157,434
Interest: 8.65%, current insurance and expense charges.

End of Policy Year	Death Benefit	Cash Value	% Increase Cash Value
1	$157,434	$52,450	4.9%
2	157,434	56,443	7.6
3	157,434	60,752	7.6
4	157,434	65,408	7.7
5	157,434	70,442	7.7
10	157,434	102,601	7.9
15	180,860	155,914	8.9
20	255,757	239,025	9.0

Company: AMERITAS LIFE INSURANCE CORPORATION

Product: LOW-LOAD UNIVERSAL LIFE

Description: Flexible-premium universal life, used to simulate single premium whole life.

Minimum Face Amount: $100,000

Other Features: See universal life product profile.

Policy Illustration: Age 55, male nonsmoker.

Single premium: $50,000
Initial face amount: $152,558
Interest: 8.5%, current insurance and expense charges.

End of Policy Year	Death Benefit	Cash Value	% Increase Cash Value
1	$152,558	$53,956	7.9%
2	152,558	58,087	7.7
3	152,558	62,437	7.5
4	152,558	67,047	7.4
5	152,558	71,977	7.4
10	152,558	105,477	8.6
15	187,143	161,330	8.9
20	265,278	247,924	9.0

Company: JOHN ALDEN LIFE INSURANCE COMPANY

Product: PIONEER UNIVERSAL LIFE

Description: Flexible premium universal life, used to simulate single premium whole life.

Minimum Face Amount: $100,000

Other Features: See universal life product profile.

Policy Illustration: Age 55, male nonsmoker.

Single premium: $32,304
Initial face amount: $100,000
Interest: 9.00%, current insurance and expense charges.

End of Policy Year	Death Benefit	Cash Value	% Increase Cash Value
1	$100,000	$34,586	7.1%
2	100,000	37,323	7.9
3	100,000	40,284	7.9
4	100,000	43,496	8.0
5	100,000	46,920	7.9
10	100,000	69,365	8.4
15	122,149	105,301	8.8
20	171,553	160,330	8.8

Company: LINCOLN BENEFIT LIFE COMPANY

Product: ACHIEVER VI

Description: Flexible premium universal life, used to simulate single premium whole life.

Minimum Face Amount:
Ages 0-14: $10,000
Ages 15-80: $100,000

Other Features: See universal life product profile.

Policy Illustration: Age 55, male nonsmoker.

Single premium: $50,000
Initial face amount: $152,600
Interest: 9.25%, current insurance and expense charges

End of Policy Year	Death Benefit	Cash Value	% Increase Cash Value
1	$152,600	$51,923	3.9%
2	152,600	56,860	9.5
3	152,600	62,271	9.5
4	152,600	68,214	9.5
5	152,600	74,751	9.6
10	152,600	118,966	9.9
15	221,597	191,032	9.9
20	328,504	307,013	10.0

Company: MASSACHUSETTS SAVINGS BANK LIFE INSURANCE

Product: SINGLE PREMIUM WHOLE LIFE

Description: Single premium whole life with dividends used to buy paid-up additions.

Minimum Face Amount: $2,500

Other Features: None

Policy Illustration: Age 55, unisex nonsmoker.

Single premium: $50,000
Initial face amount: $128,123

End of Policy Year	Death Benefit	Cash Value	% Increase Cash Value
1	$133,614	$51,069	2.1%
2	139,363	55,063	7.8
3	145,385	59,357	7.8
4	151,693	63,977	7.8
5	158,299	68,947	7.8
10	196,256	99,727	7.5
15	243,827	142,426	7.3
20	303,812	201,080	7.0

Company: NEW YORK SAVINGS BANK LIFE INSURANCE

Product: SINGLE PREMIUM LIFE

Description: Single premium whole life with dividends used to buy paid-up additions.

Minimum Face Amount: $1,000

Other Features: None

Policy Illustration: Age 55, male nonsmoker.

Single premium: $20,803
Initial face amount: $50,000

End of Policy Year	Death Benefit	Cash Value	% Increase Cash Value
1	$52,534	$22,384	7.6%
2	55,193	24,270	8.4
3	57,997	26,290	8.3
4	60,927	28,476	8.3
5	64,002	30,811	8.2
10	81,845	45,432	8.0
15	104,903	66,834	8.1
20	134,192	95,704	6.6

Company: USAA LIFE INSURANCE COMPANY

Product: UNIVERSAL LIFE

Description: Flexible premium universal life, used to simulate single premium whole life.

Minimum Face Amount: $25,000

Other Features: See universal life product profile.

Policy Illustration: Age 55, male nonsmoker.

Single premium: $50,000
Initial face amount: $151,236
Interest: 9.00%, current insurance and expense charges

End of Policy Year	Death Benefit	Cash Value	% Increase Cash Value
1	$151,236	$52,390	4.8%
2	151,236	56,678	8.2
3	151,236	61,354	8.3
4	151,236	66,456	8.3
5	151,236	72,029	8.4
10	151,236	108,973	8.8
15	195,012	168,114	9.1
20	278,806	260,566	9.2

VARIABLE LIFE

Company: FIDELITY/FIDELITY INVESTMENTS
LIFE INSURANCE COMPANY

Product: FIDELITY VARIABLE LIFE

Description: Variable life. Initial single premium with additional premiums allowed. Death benefit is adjusted using corridor percentage factors. Contract is a modified endowment under current law.

Availability: All states except AL, CA, DC, HI, ME, NH, NJ, NY, VT
Pending: MA, NC
Other restrictions: Policy must be deliverable to a resident of an approved state. No substandard underwriting class.

Issue Ages: 0-75
(higher with company approval)

Maturity Date: No specific age.

Premium Limitations:

	First	Additional
Minimum	$5,000	$500
Maximum	As limited by underwriting requirements; additional premiums may require evidence of insurability.	

Face Amount Limitations: Determined by premium limitations and is a function of the initial single premium and the choice of two options:
• Maximum Investment Option–minimizes face amount
• Maximum Protection Option–provides 1/3 more face amount

Contract Charges:

	Current		Back-end	Guaranteed
	Annual			
	Yr 1	Yrs 2+		
Per policy ($)				0
% premium	Note 1		Note 2	Note 2
% account value	0.85	0.85		0.85, 0.85
Insurance	See COI rates			Note 3
Investment	See fund profile			

Note 1: State premium tax in excess of 3.5%; not applicable in any states where policy is currently approved.
Note 2: Declining surrender charge, on a contract-year basis: 6, 5, 4, 3, 2, 1, 0%.
Note 3: Medical underwriting, 1980 CSO; simplified underwriting, 130%, 1980 CSO.

Current Cost of Insurance Rates:
Rate structure: Aggregate (attained-age). Age last birthday. No bands. *Underwriting classes:* Simplified, medical. Simplified class is unismoker and wider than a typical *standard* class. Unisex rates are also available.

Annual rates per $1,000 of coverage (for simplified underwriting):

Year	Male Unismoker			Female Unismoker		
	35	45	55	35	45	55
1	1.788	3.912	9.084	1.404	3.036	6.072
6	2.604	5.796	13.968	2.088	4.236	8.124
11	3.912	9.084	22.224	3.036	6.072	12.696
16	5.796	13.968	34.776	4.236	8.124	19.308
21	9.084	22.224	57.216	6.072	12.696	34.080
31	22.224	57.216	141.420	12.696	34.080	106.824
41	57.216	141.420	347.832	34.080	106.824	334.956

Illustration Practices: *Do any pricing assumptions underlying currently illustrated policy values differ from:*
• *current experience?* No. Charges other than COI are contractually guaranteed. All values use current or guaranteed COI rates.
• *anticipated future experience?* No. Current COI rates are based on best estimate of expected experience. Company does not anticipate changing these rates during the next two years. Other charges are contractually guaranteed.

Investment Options:

Fund Name*	Advisor
Asset Manager Portfolio	Fidelity Management & Research Co.
Equity-Income Portfolio	FMR
Growth Portfolio	FMR
High Income Portfolio	FMR
Money Market Portfolio	FMR
Overseas Portfolio	FMR
Short-Term Portfolio	FMR
1993 Zero Coupon Bond Portfolio	FMR
1998 Zero Coupon Bond Portfolio	FMR
2003 Zero Coupon Bond Portfolio	FMR

* For more information, see "Fidelity Variable Product Funds" starting on page 410.

Settlement Options: Fixed benefit options only. Standard; proceeds may also be left on deposit.

Portfolio Allocation Provisions:
Allocation of premiums: No less than 10% to a selected option.

Transfers between accounts: No charge. Minimum amount: $250 or fund value, if less. Allowed number of transfers is guaranteed to be at least 5 per year (currently unlimited).

Withdrawals and Surrenders: Withdrawals permitted after the first two policy years. $20 charge limit: Two per year. *Minimum amount:* $1,000; remaining contract value cannot be reduced below $5,000. Withdrawal/surrender charge: See contract charges.

Policy Loans: *Loan value:* 90% of surrender value. *Minimum loan:* $1,000, subject to state law. Collateral is held in general account.
Interest charged: 7.5%, in arrears
Interest credited: 6.0%
Effective cost of borrowing: 7.5% plus the difference between the net rate of return on the selected portfolios and 6%.

Death Benefit Guarantee: None. Death benefit will not drop below initial face amount (except due to withdrawals); however, policy will lapse if contract value is not sufficient to cover insurance charges.

Riders: None

Other Product Features: 10-day free look, with refund of premium.

Treatment of Policyholders:
Service: By phone or mail. Toll-free number to make transfers; to obtain policy value quotes, policy change forms, or other information; and to reach insurance specialists for questions about insurance plans and investment choices. Company tries to respond to all requests within 24 hours.

During the past year, have there been any significant problems in handling requests for service? No

Type and frequency of communications to policyholders:
• Confirmation of all policy transactions
• Quarterly statements of policy values and investment allocations
• Semi-annual report for separate account, with details of fund portfolios and performance

• Current prospectus sent annually

During the past year, have there been any significant delays in preparing policy statements or confirmations of transactions? No

Was the current administrative system developed in-house or purchased from an outside vendor? Policies are serviced by an independent organization that uses an administrative system developed by an outside vendor.

Can the system be upgraded as needed to meet future demands? System is maintained and enhanced by internal programming staff and vendor.

Are new contract improvements offered to existing policyholders? Yes, including any decrease in cost of insurance rates.

Past repricing actions: None

Comparison with "Buy Term and Invest the Difference":
Male unismoker, age 45, assuming 12% gross return, and 1.03% fund expense ratio.

Policy Year	Premium	Death Benefit	Cash Value	Before-Tax Rate of Return[*] Average Annual	Yearly
1	$20,000	$78,849	$20,543	3.2%	3.2%
2	0	78,849	22,647	7.0	10.8
3	0	78.849	24,929	8.2	10.7
4	0	78,849	27,408	8.8	10.5
5	0	78,849	30,104	9.1	10.4
10	0	78,849	47,130	9.5	9.6
15	0	98,931	73,829	9.5	9.7
20	0	141,392	115,895	9.6	9.8

[*]Based on moderately-low term rates that require medical underwriting; ignores income tax upon surrender. Rate of return will depend on age, face amount, premiums, and term and tax rates.

Distributors:

Name/Address
Fidelity Insurance Agency, Inc.
82 Devonshire Street
Boston, MA 02109
800/544-6666, ext. 2327

Compensation
Company pays. Up to 2% of premiums in first year; about 0.25% of contract value in renewal years, based on persistency.

Company: FIDELITY/MONARCH LIFE INSURANCE COMPANY

Product: FIDELITY FUTURE RESERVES

Description: Variable life. Initial single premium with additional premiums allowed. Death benefit is adjusted using corridor percentage factors. Contract is a modified endowment under current law.

Availability: All states

Issue Ages: 0-75

Maturity Date: Policy anniversary after age 100

Premium Limitations:

	First	Additional
Minimum	$5,000	Lesser of $1,000 or 10% of init. pr.
Maximum	None	Year 1: 100% of init. pr. Years 2-5: 25% of init. pr. Years 6+: Not allowed. May require evidence of insurability.

Face Amount Limitations: Determined by the premium and underwriting class.

Contract Charges:

	Current			Guaranteed
	Annual			
	Yr 1-10	Yrs 11+	Back-end	
Per policy ($)				0
% premium			Note 1	Note 1
% account value	1.326	1.00		1.326, 1.00
Insurance	See COI rates			1980 CSO ALB M/F
Investment	See fund profiles			

Note 1: Declining surrender charge, on a contract-year basis: 6, 5, 4, 3, 2, 1, 0%.

Current Cost of Insurance Rates:

Rate structure: Select and ultimate. Age last birthday. No bands.
Underwriting classes: Simplified nonsmoker, simplified standard,
medical nonsmoker, medical standard.

Annual rates per $1,000 of coverage (for simplified underwriting):

	Male Nonsmoker			Female Nonsmoker		
Year	35	45	55	35	45	55
1	1.30	2.81	7.04	0.88	1.92	4.40
6	1.94	4.97	12.71	1.34	3.50	7.95
11	3.92	10.37	21.60	2.30	5.20	14.72
16	6.60	15.55	40.52	3.58	9.40	22.44
21	10.37	21.60	66.88	5.20	14.72	41.64
31	21.60	66.88	162.00	14.72	41.64	118.80
41	66.88	162.00	384.91	41.64	118.80	356.91

Illustration Practices: *Do any pricing assumptions underlying
currently illustrated policy values differ from:*
• current experience? No. Charges other than COI are contractually
guaranteed. All values use current or guaranteed COI rates.

• anticipated future experience? No. Current COI rates are based
on best estimate of expected experience. Company does not
anticipate changing these rates during the next two years. Other
charges are contractually guaranteed.

Investment Options:

Fund Name*	Advisor
Asset Manager Portfolio	Fidelity Management & Research Co.
Equity-Income Portfolio	FMR
Growth Portfolio	FMR
High Income Portfolio	FMR
Overseas Portfolio	FMR
Short-Term Portfolio	FMR
Money Market Portfolio	FMR
1993 Zero Coupon Bond portfolio	FMR
1998 Zero Coupon Bond portfolio	FMR
2003 Zero Coupon Bond portfolio	FMR
Fixed Account	Monarch Life Insurance Co.

* For more information, see "Fidelity Variable Product Funds" starting on page 410.

Fixed Account: New money method; rate is guaranteed for one year. *Current rates* (as of 5/90): 8.75%. *Mimimum guaranteed rate:* 4%. Policyowner is given 30-45 days advance notice before the end of a guarantee period.

Settlement Options: Fixed benefit options only. Standard options; company's single premium annuity can be purchased at a 3% discount.

Portfolio Allocation Provisions:
Allocation of premiums: Can select up to five portfolios at one time; no minimum allocation.

Transfers between variable accounts: No charge. No minimum amount. Allowed number of transfers is guaranteed to be at least 5 per year (currently unlimited). *Transfers from fixed variable accounts:* 3% penalty during guarantee period; no charge at end of guarantee period.

Withdrawals and Surrenders: Allowed in policy years 3-12. *Limit:* One per year. *Minimum amount:* $500. *Maximum amount:* 10% of all premiums paid, with some carryover. *Withdrawals:* No charge. *Surrender charge:* See contract charges.

Policy Loans: *Loan value:* 90% of surrender value. *Minimum loan:* $1,000, subject to state law. Collateral is held in general account.
Interest charged: 7.5%, in arrears
Interest credited: 6.0%
Effective cost of borrowing: 7.5% plus the difference between the net rate of return on the selected portfolios and 6%.

Death Benefit Guarantee: Death benefit will not drop below initial face amount (except due to withdrawals). Policy will stay in force during a predetermined guarantee period, regardless of investment performance.

Riders:
- Allows partial withdrawals
- Guaranteed insurability (Allows additional payments)

Other Product Features: 10-day free look, subject to state law.

Treatment of Policyholders: See Fidelity Variable Life.

During the past year, have there been any significant problems in handling requests for service? No

Type and frequency of communications to policyholders:
- Confirmation of all policy transactions
- Quarterly statements of policy values and investment allocations
- Semi-annual report for separate account, with details of fund portfolios and performance.
- Current prospectus sent annually

During the past year, have there been any significant delays in preparing policy statements or confirmations of transactions? No

Was the current administrative system developed in-house or purchased from an outside vendor? In-house

Can the system be upgraded as needed to meet future demands? Yes. Maintained and upgraded by in-house support personnel.

Are new contract improvements offered to existing policyholders? Yes, unless there are system constraints or adverse tax consequences for the policyholder.

Past repricing actions–1989: Reduced current and guaranteed smoker COI rates.

Comparison with "Buy Term and Invest the Difference":
Male nonsmoker, age 45, assuming 12% gross return.

Policy Year	Premium	Death Benefit	Cash Value	Before-Tax Rate of Return* Average Annual	Yearly
1	$20,000	$71,810	$20,555	3.2%	3.2%
2	0	71,810	22,660	6.9	10.8
3	0	71,810	24,933	8.1	10.6
4	0	71,810	27,391	8.7	10.4
5	0	71,810	30,054	9.0	10.2
10	0	73,238	46,648	9.3	9.3
15	0	97,667	72,886	9.4	9.7
20	0	139,176	114,079	9.5	9.8

*Based on moderately-low term rates that require medical underwriting; ignores income tax upon surrender. Rate of return will depend on age, face amount, premiums, and term and tax rates.

Distributors:

Name/Address
Fidelity Insurance Agency, Inc.
82 Devonshire Street
Boston, MA 02109
800/544-6666, ext. 2327

Compensation
Paid by Monarch Life.

SURVIVORSHIP

Company: FIDELITY/MONARCH LIFE INSURANCE COMPANY

Product: FIDELITY FUTURE RESERVES
(Joint and Last Survivor)

Description: Second-to-die variable life. Initial single premium with additional premiums allowed. Death benefit is adjusted using corridor percentage factors. Contract is a modified endowment under current law.

Availability: All states except DC, HI

Issue Ages: One applicant must be over 20. None over 80.

Maturity Date: No specific age.

Premium Limitations:

	First	Additional
Minimum	$5,000	Lesser of $1,000 or 10% of init. pr.
Maximum	None	Year 1: 100% of init. pr. Years 2-5: 25% of init. pr. Years 6+: Not allowed May require evidence of insurability.

Face Amount Limitations: Determined by the premium and underwriting class.
Can the policy be split apart into single-life policies? No

Contract Charges:

	Current		Back-end	Guaranteed
	Annual			
	Yr 1-10	Yrs 11+		
Per policy ($)				
% premium			Note 1	Note 1
% account value	1.50	1.50		1.50, 1.50
Insurance	See COI rates			1980 CSO ALB
Investment	See fund profiles			

Note 1: 6% surrender charge, first 6 yrs., 0% thereafter; waived on divorce or first death.

Current Cost of Insurance Rates:
Rate structure: During the guarantee period: COI is 0.15% of account value for years 1-10 and 0.50% thereafter (see contract charges). After the guarantee period: Maximum rates are charged, based on 1980 CSO Table.

Illustration Practices: *Do any pricing assumptions underlying currently illustrated policy values differ from:*
• *current experience?* No. Charges other than COI are contractually guaranteed. All illustrated values use current or guaranteed cost of insurance rates.
• *anticipated future experience?* No. Current COI rates are based on best estimate of expected experience. Company does not anticipate changing these rates during the next two years. Other charges are contractually guaranteed.

Investment Options:

Fund Name*	Advisor
Asset Manager Portolio	Fidelity Management & Research Co.
Equity-Income Portfolio	FMR
Growth Portfolio	FMR
High Income Portfolio	FMR
Overseas Portfolio	FMR
Short-Term Portfolio	FMR
Money Market Portfolio	FMR
1993 Zero Coupon Bond Portfolio	FMR
1998 Zero Coupon Bond Portfolio	FMR
2003 Zero Coupon Bond Portfolio	FMR
Fixed Account	Monarch Life Insurance Co.

* For more information, see "Fidelity Variable Product Funds" starting on page 410.

Fixed Account: New money method; rate is guaranteed for one year. *Current rate* (as of 5/90): 8.75%. *Minimum guaranteed rate:* 4%. Policyowner is given 30-45 days advance notice before the end of a guarantee period.

Settlement Options: Fixed benefit options only. Standard.

Portfolio Allocation Provisions:
Allocation of premiums: Can select up to five portfolios at one time; no minimum allocation.

Transfers between variable accounts: No charge. No minimum amount. Allowed number of transfers is guaranteed to be at least 5 per year (currently unlimited). *Transfers from fixed to variable accounts*: 3% penalty during guarantee period; no charge at end of guarantee period.

Withdrawals and Surrenders: Allowed in some policy years, based on average of insureds' issue ages: Ages 10-59, policy years 3-12; ages 60-69, policy years 3-9; ages 70-80, policy years 3-7. *Withdrawals:* One per year; no charge. *Minimum amount:* $500. *Maximum amount:* 10% of all premiums paid, with some carryover. *Surrender charge:* 6% until year 7 (see contract charges).

Policy Loans: Loan value is 90% of surrender value. *Minimum loan:* $1,000, subject to state law. Collateral is held in general account.
Interest charged: 7.5%, in arrears
Interest credited: 6.0%
Effective cost of borrowing: 7.5% plus the difference between the net rate of return on the selected portfolios and 6%.

Death Benefit Guarantee: Death benefit will not drop below initial face amount (except due to withdrawals). Policy will stay in force during a predetermined guarantee period, regardless of investment performance.

Riders:
• Allows partial withdrawals
• Guaranteed insurability (Allows additional payments)

Other Product Features: 10-day free look, subject to state law.

Treatment of Policyholders:
Service: See Fidelity Variable Life

During the past year, have there been any significant problems in handling requests for service? No

Type and frequency of communications to policyholders:
- Confirmation of all policy transactions
- Quarterly statements of policy values and investment allocations
- Semi-annual report for separate account, with details of fund portfolios and performance.
- Current prospectus sent annually

During the past year, have there been any significant delays in preparing policy statements or confirmations of transactions? No

Was the current administrative system developed in-house or purchased from an outside vendor? In-house.

Can the system be upgraded as needed to meet future demands? Can be maintained and upgraded by in-house support personnel.

Are new contract improvements offered to existing policyholders? Yes, unless there are system constraints or adverse tax consequences for the policyholder.

Past repricing actions–1989: Reduced current and guaranteed smoker cost of insurance rates.

Distributors:

Name/Address	*Compensation*
Fidelity Insurance Agency, Inc.	Paid by Monarch Life.
82 Devonshire Street	
Boston, MA 02109	
800/544-6666, ext. 2327	

Company: JOHN ALDEN LIFE INSURANCE COMPANY

Product: PIONEER SURVIVORSHIP LIFE

Description: Second-to-die flexible premium universal life. No change in premium, cash value, or insurance charges at first death.

Availability: All states except MA, MT, NY
Pending: NJ, OR, PA, TX

Issue Ages: 20-75   **Maturity Date:** Youngest insured's age 95 (older with approval)

Premium Limitations:

	First	Additional
Minimum	No limitations.	
Maximum	As allowed by current tax law.	

Face Amount Limitations:
Minimum: $250,000   *Maximum:* None
Changes: Allowed after first year
Can the policy be split apart into single-life policies? Yes, without evidence of insurability.

Contract Charges:

	Current			
	Annual			
	Yr 1	Yrs 2+	Back-end	Guaranteed
Per policy ($)	84	84		84
% premium				
Per $1000 face ($)				
% account value				
Insurance	See COI rates			1980 CSO Joint Life
Investment	Declared interest rate is net of asset charges			

Current Cost of Insurance Rates:
Rate structure: No bands. Separate set of rates by duration for each joint equal age.

Annual rates per $1,000 of coverage (rounded to three decimal places):

Male/Female Nonsmokers, same issue age

Year	55	60	65	70	75
1	0.052	0.117	0.317	0.811	2.451
6	0.2260	0.463	0.839	2.052	4.635
11	1.080	2.115	4.246	10.201	22.896
16	3.742	8.373	16.964	39.602	75.714
21	10.699	23.777	48.511	92.324	170.238
31	48.389	85.207	146.772	-	-
41	143.464	-	-	-	-

Current Interest Rate: See Pioneer Universal Life

Persistency Bonuses: None

Illustration Practices: *Do any pricing assumptions underlying currently illustrated policy values differ from:*
• *current experience?* No
• *anticipated future experience?* No

Withdrawals and Surrenders: *Withdrawals:* $25 charge. Must leave at least $500 or enough to cover deductions until end of contract year. *Surrenders:* No charge.

Policy Loans:
Interest charged: Variable; currently 8%
Interest credited: 0.75% less than rate charged
Effective cost of borrowing: Currently, 8% plus difference between credited rate on borrowed amounts and 7.25%.

Settlement Options: Standard

Riders:
• Survivorship Waiver of Monthly Deductions: Waives mortality charges upon death of covered insured.
• Cost of Living Adjustment: Increases face amount each year per Consumer Price Index; $3 million cap.

Other Product Features: N/A

Treatment of Policyholders:
Service: By mail or 800 number

Type and frequency of communications to policyholders:
• Annual statement

Was the current administrative system developed in-house or purchased from an outside vendor? Purchased from Cybertek.
Can the system be upgraded as needed to meet future demands? Will be upgraded in-house.

Are new contract improvements offered to existing policyholders? Will consider.

Past repricing actions: None; new product.

Distributors–exclusive:

Name/Address	*Compensation*
Fee For Service	Marketing costs
Airport Executive Center	paid by company;
2203 North Lois Avenue, Suite 814	fees paid by
Tampa, FL 33607	buyer.
813/874-5662	

TERM

Company: AMERITAS LIFE INSURANCE CORPORATION

Product: LOW-LOAD 5 YEAR RENEWABLE TERM

Description: 5-year level term. Renewable to age 80 and convertible for five years.

Availability: All states pending except DC, NY, ME
Other restrictions: Product must be approved in state of residence.

Issue Ages: 20-65

Underwriting Classes: Preferred nonsmoker, nonsmoker, smoker. About 50% of nonsmokers are expected to qualify for the preferred nonsmoker class. *Underwriting considerations:* Tobacco use, family history, blood profile, urinalysis, personal history.

Face Amount Limitations:
Minimum: $100,000   *Maximum:* $5,000,000
Changes: None allowed. New policy required.

Rate Structure: 5-year level term. Current and guaranteed rates. Current rates are issue-age-specific for 15 years and attained age thereafter (i.e., select and ultimate).

Bands: $100-250K; 250K-1M; 1M+
Policy fee: $35
Guarantee period: 3 years. Company intends to keep premiums level for each 5-year period, but reserves the right to make adjustments as actual experience requires.
Renewability: To age 80
Re-entry: None
Discount for prepayment: None

Fractional premiums:

	Modal Factor	Equivalent Annual Charge
Semi-annual	0.505	4.1%
Quarterly	0.260	11.2
Monthly	0.085	4.4

Other comments: N/A

Convertibility: For five years to any level-death-benefit cash value policy.

Settlement Options: Standard

Riders:
- Waiver of Premium
- Child Protection

Other Product Features: N/A

Policy Illustration:
$250,000 face amount, male nonsmoker, age 35.

		Present Value of Premiums at 5%
One year:		$280
Five years:	Current w/reversion	N/A
	Current w/o reversion	1,273
	Guaranteed	1,678
Ten years:	Current w/reversion	N/A
	Current w/o reversion	2,502
	Guaranteed	4,251
Twenty years:	Current w/reversion	N/A
	Current w/o reversion	5,777
	Guaranteed	10,612

Benchmark: Tillinghast TERMinology.

Treatment of Policyholders:
Service: 800 number for questions. All servicing through mail or fee-for-service planners.

Past repricing actions: None. New product.

Distributors:

Name/Address	Compensation
Ameritas Marketing Corp. 800/255-9678 Field Distributors:	
• Fee-only planners	• Fee for services.
• Direct-writing representatives	• Field marketing allowance paid by company.

Company: LINCOLN BENEFIT LIFE COMPANY

Product: ENTREPRENEUR II

Description: Annual renewable term. Two premium schedules: current and guaranteed. Renewable for 10 years.

Availability: All states except CA, CT, FL, IA, NH, NJ, NY, OR
Other restrictions: Application must be signed in a state where product is approved.

Issue Ages: 18-70

Underwriting Classes: Standard (smoker); preferred (nonsmoker).

Face Amount Limitations:
Minimum: $50,000   *Maximum:* $10,000,000
Changes: Not allowed

Rate Structure: Aggregate (attained-age) rates.
Bands: $50-99K; 100-249K; 250-499K; 500K+
Policy fee: $30
Guarantee period: None
Renewability: 10 years. Must convert to cash value product or provide evidence of good health to continue for another 10 years.
Re-entry: N/A
Discount for prepayment: 9% discount for up to 10 years; prepaid premiums are refundable but not guaranteed. Implicit rate of return: 9.9%, one year; 4.8%, two years.

Fractional premiums:

	Modal Factor	Equivalent Annual Charge
Semi-annual	0.52	17.4%
Quarterly	0.27	23.3
Monthly	0.089	15.7

Other comments:
- Five-year setback for female rates
- Low-load rates are discounted about 25% from commissionable version of product.

Convertibility: To universal life or decreasing term during 10-year renewability period.

Settlement Options: Standard

Riders:
- Waiver of Premium
- Accidental Death Benefit
- Child

Other Product Features: N/A

Policy Illustration:
$250,000 face amount, male nonsmoker, age 35.

		Present Value of Premiums at 5%
One year:		$215
Five years:	Current w/reversion	N/A
	Current w/o reversion	1,030
	Guaranteed	2,909
Ten years:	Current w/reversion	N/A
	Current w/o reversion	2,188
	Guaranteed	6,544
Twenty years:	Current w/reversion	5,565
	Current w/o reversion	N/A
	Guaranteed	14,963

Benchmark: Tillinghast TERMinology.

Treatment of Policyholders:
Service: Through home office, by mail or 800 number.

Past repricing actions: None

Distributors:

Name/Address	*Compensation*
Licensed agents	Fees paid by buyer.
(call 800-LBL-WATS	
for referral)	

Company: MASSACHUSETTS SAVINGS BANK LIFE INSURANCE

Product: YEARLY RENEWABLE TERM

Description: One-year renewable and convertible term to age 70. Scheduled and maximum premiums. Pays dividends beginning at age 39.

Availability: MA
Other restrictions: Must live or work in Massachusetts at time of issue.

Issue Ages: 5-64

Underwriting Classes: Unisex nonsmoker–no cigarette usage for one year. Unisex standard.

Face Amount Limitations:
Minimum: $10,000   *Maximum:* $250,000 ($50,000 for ages 5-15)
Changes: Not allowed.

Rate Structure: Attained age rates.
Bands: $10-100K; 100-250K; 250K+
Policy fee: $35
Guarantee period: One year
Renewability: To age 70
Re-entry: Not provided
Discount for prepayment: None

Fractional premiums:

	Modal Factor	Equivalent Annual Charge
Semi-annual	0.51	8.3%
Quarterly	0.26	11.2
Monthly	N/A	-

Other comments: AIDS/ARC exclusion (waived with submission of satisfactory blood test). "$99 special" for $100,000 policy for nonsmokers ages 18-30 (level premium through age 30).

Convertibility: To age 65

Settlement Options: Currently available, but not guaranteed.

Riders:
- Waiver of Premium (Allows conversion to whole life at age 65)
- Child

Other Product Features: None

Policy Illustration:
$250,000 face amount, unisex nonsmoker, age 35. Includes dividends.

		Present Value of Premiums at 5%
One year:		$225
Five years:	Current w/reversion	N/A
	Current w/o reversion	1,106
	Guaranteed	1,791
Ten years:	Current w/reversion	N/A
	Current w/o reversion	2,226
	Guaranteed	4,313
Twenty years:	Current w/reversion	N/A
	Current w/o reversion	5,526
	Guaranteed	10,657

Benchmark: Tillinghast TERMinology.

Treatment of Policyholders:
Service: By issuing and agency banks, backed up by central office in Woburn. No 800 number.

Past repricing actions: Since product introduction in 1979, actual dividends have been the same as amounts illustrated at time of issue. Premium and dividend scales were changed in 1984 and 1987.

Distributors:

Name/Address	*Compensation*
SBLI issuing and agency banks	Sold by salaried representatives.

Company: NEW YORK SAVINGS BANK LIFE INSURANCE

Product: FINANCIAL INSTITUTIONS GROUP LIFE INSURANCE (FIGLI)

Description: One-year renewable and convertible term to age 70. Individually-underwritten group policy.

Availability: NY
Other restrictions: Must live or work in New York and be a savings bank depositor at time of issue.

Issue Ages: 15-64

Underwriting Classes: Male/female; smoker/nonsmoker. Substandard available to 250%. Nonmedical underwriting in some cases.

Face Amount Limitations:
Available in these amounts only: $100,000; $150,000; $200,000; $250,000; $350,000
Changes: May re-apply for new amount on anniversary.

Rate Structure: 10-year select and ultimate.
Bands: $100-200K; 250-350K.
Policy fee: None
Guarantee period: Premiums may be increased for entire underwriting class on any anniversary.
Renewability: To age 70. (Policy can be discontinued for entire underwriting class with 31 days notice.)
Re-entry: Allowed only once. Full underwriting required.
Discount for prepayment: None

Fractional premiums:

	Modal Factor	Equivalent Annual Charge
Semi-annual	0.52	17.4%
Quarterly	0.265	17.1
Monthly	N/A	–

Other comments: None

Convertibility: To any permanent plan up to age 70.

Settlement Options: At company discretion, up to $250,000.

Riders:
- Accidental Death Benefit
- Waiver of Premium

Other Product Features: None

Policy Illustration:
$250,000 face amount, male nonsmoker, age 35.

		Present Value of Premiums at 5%*
One year:		$180
Five years:	Current w/reversion	1,040
	Current w/o reversion	1,040
	Guaranteed	N/A
Ten years:	Current w/reversion	2,502
	Current w/o reversion	2,502
	Guaranteed	N/A
Twenty years:	Current w/reversion	5,614
	Current w/o reversion	6,903
	Guaranteed	N/A

*Assumes reversion in year 11.

Treatment of Policyholders:
Service: Provided by issuing banks, backed up by SBLI Fund, by mail or over-the-counter.

Past repricing actions–1989: Rates reduced

Distributors:

Name/Address	Compensation
SBLI issuing banks	Sold by salaried representatives.

Company: USAA LIFE INSURANCE COMPANY

Product: ANNUAL RENEWABLE TERM

Description: Annual renewable term. Two premium schedules: current and guaranteed.

Availability: All states except MT
Other restrictions: Applications accepted only from state of residence.

Issue Ages: 0-65

Underwriting Classes: Nonsmoker, smoker.

Face Amount Limitations:
Minimum: $25,000   *Maximum:* None
Changes: Decrease–Policy is re-issued; no evidence of insurability is required. Increase–New policy is required; consideration is given to prior underwriting.

Rate Structure: Aggregate (attained-age) rates.
Bands: $25-100K; 100-250K; 250-500K; 500K-1M; 1M+
Policy fee: $30
Guarantee period: One year
Renewability: To age 69
Re-entry: N/A
Discount for prepayment: None

Fractional premiums:

	Modal Factor	Equivalent Annual Charge
Semi-annual	0.51	8.3%
Quarterly	0.26	11.2
Monthly	0.085	4.4

Other comments: N/A

Convertibility: To any permanent plan, to age 60.

Settlement Options: Standard

Riders:
- Waiver of Premium
- Child
- Accidental Death Benefit

Other Product Features: N/A

Policy Illustration:
$250,000 face amount, male nonsmoker, age 35.

		Present Value of Premiums at 5%
One year:		$260
Five years:	Current w/reversion	N/A
	Current w/o reversion	1,249
	Guaranteed	2,659
Ten years:	Current w/reversion	N/A
	Current w/o reversion	2,529
	Guaranteed	6,073
Twenty years:	Current w/reversion	N/A
	Current w/o reversion	6,197
	Guaranteed	14,666

Benchmark: Tillinghast TERMinology.

Treatment of Policyholders:
Service: By mail or 800 number.

Past repricing actions:
4/89: Rate reductions at some ages and amounts.
7/89: $500,000 and $1,000,000 bands added to rate structure.

Distributors:

Name/Address	*Compensation*
USAA Financial Services	Sold by salaried
USAA Building	representatives.
San Antonio, TX 78288	
800/531-8000	
512/498-8000	

Company: USAA LIFE INSURANCE COMPANY

Product: SEVEN-YEAR TERM

Description: Seven-year term. Level face amount, increasing premium. Two premium schedules: current and guaranteed. Renewable for 7 years.

Availability: Approved in all states except MT, NY
Other restrictions: Applications accepted only from state of residence.

Issue Ages: 20-65

Underwriting Classes: Nonsmoker, smoker.

Face Amount Limitations:
Minimum: Amount corresponding to $300 annualized premium.
Maximum: None
Changes: Decrease–Policy is re-issued; no evidence of insurability is required. Increase–New policy is required; consideration is given to prior underwriting.

Rate Structure: Aggregate (attained-age) rates.
Bands: $0-250K; 250-500K; 500K-1M; 1M+
Policy fee: $30
Guarantee period: One year
Renewability: 7 years. Must be re-underwritten at that time.
Re-entry: N/A
Discount for prepayment: None

Fractional premiums:

	Modal Factor	Equivalent Annual Charge
Semi-annual	0.51	8.3%
Quarterly	0.26	11.2
Monthly	0.085	4.4

Other comments: N/A

Convertibility: None

Settlement Options: Standard

Riders:
• Waiver of Premium   • Accidental Death Benefit

Other Product Features: N/A

Policy Illustration: $280,00 face amount, male nonsmoker, age 35.

		Present Value of Premiums at 5%
One year:		$302
Five years:	Current w/reversion	N/A
	Current w/o reversion	1,461
	Guaranteed	2,572
Ten years:	Current w/reversion	N/A
	Current w/o reversion	N/A
	Guaranteed	N/A
Twenty years:	Current w/reversion	N/A
	Current w/o reversion	N/A
	Guaranteed	N/A

Benchmark: Tillinghast TERMinology*.
*With adjustment for $280,000 face amount.

Treatment of Policyholders:
Service: By mail or 800 number.

Past repricing actions: None

Distributors:

Name/Address
USAA Financial Services
USAA Building
San Antonio, TX 78288
800/531-8000
512/498-8000

Compensation
Sold by salaried
representatives.

DEFERRED ANNUITIES

Company: JOHN ALDEN LIFE INSURANCE COMPANY

Product: PIONEER ANNUITY

Description: Flexible premium deferred annuity.

Availability: All states except MA, NY
Pending: NJ, OR, PA, UT
Other restrictions: Application accepted in state where insured works if it does not violate state law.

Issue Ages: 0-75. Annuitization before age 85, later upon request.

Premium Limitations:

	First	Additional
Minimum	$2,000	$25
Maximum	250,000	100,000
		(higher, with approval)

Contract Charges:

	Current			
	Annual			
	Yr 1	Yrs 2+	Back-End	Guaranteed
Per policy ($)				
% premium				
% account value			Note 1	Note 1

Note 1: Declining percent of account value: 7, 7, 7, 7, 6, 5, 4, 3, 2, 1, 0%.

Current Interest Rate:
Rate structure: New money. Guaranteed rate: 4%

Guarantee period: Calendar year; renewal rates are guaranteed not to change more often than every six months.

Rate-setting process: Committee

Investment strategy: Investment-grade, intermediate-term bonds and mortgages.

Interest rate history:

On Amounts Deposited on 1/1	Declared Rate at 1/1*					
	1985	1986	1987	1988	1989	1990
1985	10.25	10.25	10.25	9.50	9.25	9.25
1986		9.50	9.50	8.50	8.50	8.50
1987			7.50	7.50	7.50	7.50
1988				9.50	9.00	8.50
1989					9.50	9.00
1990						8.75

Changes in
new-money rate   N/A

*Product was introduced in 1989. Interest rates shown are for IRA II (1984-7), Multiflex (1988), and All Purpose (1989), load products with similar spread requirements.

Benchmarks: Tillinghast Universal life Analytic Study; CDs.

Withdrawals and Surrenders: One 10% penalty-free withdrawal during each 12-month period. 10-year declining charge on other withdrawals and surrenders (see contract charges).

Bailout Provision: None

Settlement Options: Standard

Other Product Features: During first five contract years, each contribution is increased by 4% at time of receipt; declared interest rate is earned on increased amount. This provision is contractually guaranteed.

Treatment of Policyholders:
Service: By mail or 800 number.

During the past year, have there been any significant problems in handling requests for service? No

Are new contract improvements offered to existing policyholders? Will consider on a case-by-case basis.

Distributors–exclusive:

Name/Address	Compensation
Fee For Service	Marketing costs paid
Airport Executive Center	by company; fees paid
2203 North Lois Avenue, Suite 814	by buyer.
Tampa, FL 33607	
813/874-5662	

Company: LINCOLN BENEFIT LIFE COMPANY

Product: FUTURIST II

Description: Flexible premium deferred annuity.

Availability: All states except CA, CT, FL, IA, MA, NH, NY, OR
Other restrictions: Application must be signed in a state where product is approved.

Issue Ages: 0-99. No restrictions on annuitization.

Premium Limitations:

	First	Additional
Minimum	$1,000	$25
Maximum	$1,000,000 total premium.	

Contract Charges:

	Current			
	Annual			
	Yr 1	Yrs 2+	Back-End	Guaranteed
Per policy ($)				
% premium				
% account value			Note 1	Note 1

Note 1: 5% of account value in year 1, declining by 1% per year.

Current Interest Rate:
Rate structure: Portfolio-average method. Three interest rate tiers based on accumulated values: (1) under $10,000 earns base rate; (2) between $10,000 and $25,000 earns base rate plus 0.5%; (3) over $25,000 earns base rate plus 1.0%. Guaranteed rate: 5%

Guarantee period: None

Rate-setting process: Committee meets quarterly. Credited rates are based on yields on available and existing assets. Rates are currently renewed quarterly.

Investment strategy: Similar to strategy for universal life product–bonds, mortgages, and collateralized mortgage obligations–with an average life of about 7 years, rather than 8. All assets are owned by Allstate, which limits assets of below-investment-grade quality to 10% overall.

Interest rate history:

On Amounts	Declared Rate at 1/1*					
Deposited on 1/1	1985	1986	1987	1988	1989	1990
1985		11.50	9.00	8.75	8.75	8.55
1986		11.50	9.00	8.75	8.75	8.55
1987			9.00	8.75	8.75	8.55
1988				8.75	8.75	8.55
1989					8.75	8.55
1990						8.55
Changes in new-money rate	1	2	2	0	0	

*Amounts shown are base rate. Accumulated values over $10,000 receive a higher rate.

Benchmarks: Tillinghast Universal Life Analytic Study; CDs.

Withdrawals and Surrenders: One penalty-free withdrawal of up to 10% of accumulated value each policy year; also applies to full surrenders. Withdrawal and surrender charge is declining percent of accumulated value (see contract charges).

Bailout Provision: None

Settlement Options: Standard. Others if approved by company.

Other Product Features: Pays 0.75% more than commissionable version of product, and has lower surrender charges.

Treatment of Policyholders:
Service: By home office, mail or 800 number.

During the past year, have there been any significant problems in handling requests for service? No

Are new contract improvements offered to existing policyholders? Yes

Distributors:

Name/Address	Compensation
Licensed agents	Fees paid by
(call 800-LBL-WATS for referral)	buyer.

Company: MASSACHUSETTS SAVINGS BANK LIFE INSURANCE

Product: LIFE SAVER

Description: Flexible premium deferred annuity.

Availability: MA
Other restrictions: Must live or work in Massachusetts at time of issue.

Issue Ages: 0-75. Annuitization or surrender by age 80.

Premium Limitations:

	First	Additional
Minimum	$5,000	$1,000
Maximum	No set limit.	Permission needed to put in more than in first year.

Contract Charges:

	Current			
	Annual			
	Yr 1	Yrs 2+	Back-End	Guaranteed
Per policy ($)				
% premium				
% account value			Note 1	Note 1

*Note 1: 7%, declining by 1% per year. $25 minimum charge.

Current Interest Rate:
Rate structure: New-money rate in Year 1; portfolio rate thereafter.
Guaranteed: 5% for Years 1-10; 4% thereafter.

Guarantee period: One year

Rate-setting process: Committee sets rate twice a month. Rates are keyed to yields on mortgage securities.

Investment strategy: Pooled fund; mainly Massachusetts residential mortgage loans.

Interest rate history:

On Amounts Deposited on 1/1	Declared Rate at 1/1					
	1985	1986	1987	1988	1989	1990
1985	9.00	8.50	7.00	7.50	8.25	7.75
1986		8.50	7.00	7.50	8.25	7.75
1987			7.00	7.50	8.25	7.75
1988				7.50	8.25	7.75
1989					8.25	7.75
1990						7.50
Changes in new-money rate	0	0	0	0	5	

Benchmarks: Tillinghast Universal Life Analytic Study; CDs.

Withdrawals and Surrenders: *Withdrawals:* Three each contract year; remaining balance must be at least $1,000. 7-year declining charge on withdrawals and surrenders (see contract charges).

Bailout Provision: None

Settlement Options: Standard. Guaranteed and current rates.

Other Product Features: N/A

Treatment of Policyholders:
Service: By issuing and agency banks, backed up by central office in Woburn. No 800 number.

During the past year, have there been any significant problems in handling requests for service? No

Are new contract improvements offered to existing policyholders? Yes

Distributors:
Name/Address
SBLI issuing and agency banks

Compensation
Sold by salaried representatives.

Company: USAA ANNUITY AND LIFE/USAA LIFE

Product: EXECUTIVE ANNUITY

Description: Flexible premium deferred annuity.

Availability: All states
Other restrictions: None

Issue Ages: No maximum issue or annuitization ages.

Premium Limitations:

	First	Additional
Minimum	$5,000	$100
Maximum	Subject to company approval.	

Contract Charges:

	Current			
	Annual			
	Yr 1	Yrs 2+	Back-End	Guaranteed
Per policy ($)				
% premium				
% account value			Note 1	Note 1

Note 1: Year 1, $150; Year 2, $50; thereafter, $25.

Current Interest Rate:
Rate structure: Portfolio-average approach. Guaranteed rate: 6.5% for first four years, 4% thereafter.

Guarantee period: One month

Rate-setting process: Same as for Single Premium Deferred Annuity.

Investment strategy: Same as for Single Premium Deferred Annuity.

Interest rate history:

On Amounts Deposited on 1/1	Declared Rate at 1/1					
	1985	1986	1987	1988	1989	1990
1985	9.25	8.75	8.50	8.00	8.50	8.35
1986		8.75	8.50	8.00	8.50	8.35
1987			8.50	8.00	8.50	8.35
1988				8.00	8.50	8.35
1989					8.50	8.35
1990						8.35
Changes in new-money rate	2	1	1	1	6	

Benchmarks: Tillinghast Universal Life Analytic Study; CDs.

Withdrawals and Surrenders: Charge: $150 in year 1; $50 in year 2; $25 thereafter. Charge is waived for annuitization.

Bailout Provision: None

Settlement Options: Standard

Other Product Features: Company pays state premium tax, if any.

Treatment of Policyholders:
Service: By mail or 800 number.

During the past year, have there been any significant problems in handling requests for service? No

Are new contract improvements offered to existing policyholders? Yes. A bonus interest plan is being designed to increase the interest rate for contract amounts over certain levels.

Distributors:

Name/Address	*Compensation*
USAA Financial Services	Sold by salaried
USAA Building	representatives.
San Antonio, TX 78288	
800/531-8000	
512/498-8000	

Company: USAA ANNUITY AND LIFE/USAA LIFE

Product: SINGLE PREMIUM DEFERRED ANNUITY

Description: Single premium deferred annuity.

Availability: All states
Other Restrictions: None

Issue Ages: No maximum issue or annuitization ages.

Premium Limitations:

	First	Additional
Minimum	$10,000	Not allowed.
Maximum	Subject to company approval.	

Contract Charges:

	Current			
	Annual			
	Yr 1	Yrs 2+	Back-End	Guaranteed
Per policy ($)				
% premium				
% account value			Note 1	Note 1

Note 1: 4% plus $25 for first 3 years; $25 thereafter.

Current Interest Rate:
Rate structure: New money rate for the first calendar year, then portfolio rate for all renewal years. New money rate is declared monthly; portfolio rate is declared at the beginning of each calendar year. Guaranteed rate: 4%.

Guarantee period: New money rate is guaranteed until the end of the first calendar year. Portfolio rate is guaranteed for one year.

Rate-setting process: Rates are set by Interest Rate Committee, composed of senior company officers appointed by Board of Directors. Factors taken into account include the portfolio yield, the yield on new investments, and competitors' rates.

Investment strategy: Company seeks to provide maximum security for invested funds. Assets are primarily invested in investment-quality (Moody's Baa or better) utility and industrial bonds and federally-backed mortgage pass-through securities (Moody's AAA). Because the company is licensed in New York, it is required to perform asset/liability matching tests and submit an actuarial opinion attesting to the adequacy of reserves.

Interest rate history:

On Amounts Deposited on 1/1	Declared Rate at 1/1					
	1985	1986	1987	1988	1989	1990
1985	9.00	11.00	9.25	9.10	8.80	8.70
1986		10.00	9.25	9.10	8.80	8.70
1987			8.00	9.10	8.80	8.70
1988				8.80	8.80	8.70
1989					8.80	8.70
1990						8.40
Changes in New-money rate	9	5	6	1	6	

Benchmarks: Tillinghast Universal Life Analytic Study; CDs.

Withdrawals and Surrenders: Charge: 4% plus $25 for first 3 years; $25 thereafter. Charge is waived for annuitization.

Bailout Provision: None

Settlement Options: Standard

Other Product Features: Company pays state premium tax, if any.

Treatment of Policyholders:
Service: By mail or 800 number.

During the past year, have there been any significant problems in handling requests for service? No

Are new contract improvements offered to existing policyholders? Yes. A bonus interest plan is being designed to increase the interest rate for contract amounts over certain levels.

Distributors:

Name/Address	Compensation
USAA Financial Services	Sold by salaried
USAA Building	representatives.
San Antonio, TX 78288	
800/531-8000	
512/498-8000	

VARIABLE ANNUITIES

Company: FIDELITY/FIDELITY INVESTMENTS
LIFE INSURANCE COMPANY

Product: FIDELITY RETIREMENT RESERVES

Description: Flexible premium variable annuity, with variable and fixed-rate investment and payment options.

Availability: All states except AL, CA, DE, HI, ME, NH, NY, VT (See also Fidelity Income Plus).
Other restrictions: Contract must be deliverable to a resident of an approved state.

Issue Ages: 0-80. Life annuity or lump-sum payment generally must be elected by the later of age 85 or the fifth contract year. Other options may be available.

Premium Limitations:

	First	Additional
*Minimum**	$2,500	$250 ($100 Automatic Plan)
Maximum	No specific restrictions.	

*For qualified plans, $10,000 initial; $2,500 additional.

Contract Charges:

	Current			
	Annual			
	Yr 1	Yrs 2+	Back-End	Guaranteed
Per policy ($)	Note 1			50
% premium	Note 2		Note 3	Note 3
% account value	1.00	1.00		1.00, 1.00
Investment	See fund profiles			

Note 1: $30 annual maintenance fee; currently waived if total premiums are at least $25,000.
Note 2: State premium tax, if any, is deducted when incurred, generally upon annuitization.
Note 3: Declining surrender charge, on a contract-year basis: 5, 4, 3, 2, 1, 0%. Waived upon death or annuitization. Effective 5/90, surrender charge will also be waived for 30 days following notice of: (1) decrease in Fixed Account renewal interest rate of more than 1% from expiring rate; or (2) increase in maintenance charge.

Investment Options:

Fund Name*	Advisor
Asset Manager Portfolio	Fidelity Management & Research Co.
Equity-Income Portfolio	FMR
Growth Portfolio	FMR
High Income Portfolio	FMR
Money Market Portfolio	FMR
Overseas Portfolio	FMR
Short-Term Portfolio	FMR
Fixed Account	Fidelity Investments Life Ins. Co.

* For more information, see "Fidelity Variable Product Funds" starting on page 410.

Fixed Account: New money method; rate is guaranteed through January 31 of the following year (one additional year for allocations made after October). Renewal rates may be different for each allocation; however, rates will tend to converge over time. *Current rate* (as of 1/90): 7.75%. *Minimum guaranteed rate:* 3.5%.

Portfolio Allocation Provisions:
Allocation of premiums: No less than 10% to a selected option. No more than $100,000 (including transfers) to the Fixed Account during contract year, without company approval.

Transfers: No charge.
• Between variable accounts: *Minimum amount:* $250 or account value, if less. Allowed number of transfers is guaranteed to be at least five per contract year (currently unlimited).

• From variable to fixed: *Minimum amount:* $250 or account value, if less. *Maximum:* Currently, no more than $100,000 (including premium allocations) during a contract year without company approval.

• From fixed to variable: Subject to company approval. *Current limitations:* One per contract year; amount cannot exceed greatest of (1) 25% of Fixed Account value, (2) amount transferred in previous contract year, or (3) $1,000.

Withdrawals and Surrenders: Unlimited number allowed. *Minimum amount:* $500; withdrawals may not reduce remaining value below $2,500. *Withdrawal/surrender charge:* See contract charges. No charge during any year for withdrawals up to 10% of total premiums paid (less prior withdrawals subject to penalty); noncumulative; also applicable to full surrenders.

Annuity Options: Annuity payouts may be fixed, variable, or a combination of both. Transfers between fixed and variable accounts are not allowed after annuity date; transfers between variable accounts are permitted. Standard annuity options; other options may be available upon request. Assumed interest rate for variable options is 3.5% (alternative rate may also be offered).

Death Benefit: Up to annuitant's age 70: Greater of (1) premiums less withdrawals or (2) contract value. After age 70: Contract value.

Other Product Features: 10-day free look (with return of greater of premium or cash value). Automatic Deduction Plan (pre-authorized transfers from checking account). Bail-out provision (see contract charges, Note 3). Dollar-Cost Averaging (automatic monthly transfers from money market to any other variable portfolio).

Treatment of Policyholders:
Service: By phone or mail. Toll-free number to make transfers; to obtain policy value quotes, policy change forms, or other information; and to reach insurance specialists for questions about insurance plans and investment choices. Company tries to respond to all requests within 24 hours.

During the past year, have there been any significant problems in handling requests for service? No

Type and frequency of communications to policyholders:
- Confirmation of all policy transactions
- Quarterly statements of policy values and investment allocations
- Semi-annual report for separate account, with details of fund portfolios and performance.
- Current prospectus sent annually

During the past year, have there been any significant delays in preparing policy statements or confirmations of transactions? No

Was the current administrative system developed in-house or purchased from an outside vendor? Policies are serviced by an independent organization that uses an administrative system developed by an outside vendor.

Can the system be upgraded as needed to meet future demands? Yes. System is maintained and enhanced by internal programming staff and vendor.

Are new contract improvements offered to existing policyholders? Generally, yes.

Past repricing actions–1990: Bail-out provision added.

Distributors:

Name/Address	Compensation
Fidelity Insurance Agency, Inc. 82 Devonshire Street Boston, MA 02109 800/544-6666, ext. 2327	Company pays up to 2% of premiums in first year and about 0.25% of contract value in renewal years, based on persistency.

Company: FIDELITY/PACIFIC FIDELITY LIFE
INSURANCE COMPANY

Product: FIDELITY INCOME PLUS

Description: Flexible premium variable annuity, with variable investment options and variable and fixed-rate payment options.

Availability: AL, CA, DE, ME, NH, VT (Other states: See Fidelity Retirement Reserves)
Other restrictions: Must be a resident of an approved state.

Issue Ages: 0-75. Annuitization or a lump-sum payment must be elected by age 85.

Premium Limitations:

	First	Additional
Minimum	$5,000	$500
Maximum	No specific restrictions.	

Contract Charges:

	Current		Back-End	Guaranteed
	Annual			
	Yr 1	Yrs 2+		
Per policy ($)	35	35		Note 1
% premium	Note 2			Note 2
% account value	0.80	0.80		0.80, 0.80
Investment	See fund profiles			

Note 1: Prior to annuitization, administrative charge may be increased, subject to state limitations.
Note 2: State premium tax, if any, is deducted when incurred, generally upon annuitization.

Investment Options:

Fund Name*	Advisor
Growth Portfolio	Fidelity Management & Research Co.
Equity-Income Portfolio	FMR
High Income Portfolio	FMR
Overseas Portfolio**	FMR
Short-Term Portfolio	FMR
Money Market Portfolio	FMR

* For more information, see "Fidelity Variable Product Funds" starting on page 410.

**Not available to CA residents.

Portfolio Allocation Provisions:

Allocation of premiums: Initial: At least $1,000 to each selected portfolio. Additional: At least $500 to each selected portfolio.

Transfers: Between accounts–No charge. Unlimited number. No minimum amount.

Withdrawals and Surrenders: No charge. Unlimited number. No minimum amount.

Annuity Options: Annuity payouts may be fixed or variable; only one choice is permitted. Transfers between variable accounts are allowed after annuitization. Standard annuity options; other options may be available upon request. Minimum assumed interest rate: 3.5%; offers a choice of assumed rates from 3.5%-7.5%.

Death Benefit: Contract value

Other Product Features: 10-day free look (with return of payment).

Treatment of Policyholders:
Service: By mail or 800 number to Boston Financial Data Services or Fidelity.

During the past year, have there been any significant problems in handling requests for service? No

Type and frequency of communications to policyholders:
- Confirmation of all policy transactions
- Semi-annual report for separate account, with details of fund portfolios and performance.
- Current prospectus sent annually

During the past year, have there been any significant delays in preparing policy statements or confirmations of transactions? No

Was the current administrative system developed inhouse or purchased from an outside vendor? Provided by Boston Financial Data Services (Boston, MA).

Can the system be upgraded as needed to meet future demands?

Are new contract improvements offered to existing policyholders? Yes

Past repricing actions:
1980: Product introduced; $18 annual administrative charge.
1987: Administrative charge raised to $35.

Distributors:

<u>Name/Address</u>	<u>Compensation</u>
Fidelity Insurance Agency, Inc.	Company pays; 0.55%
82 Devonshire Street	of variable account
Boston, MA 02109	assets per year.
800/544-6666, ext. 2327	

IMMEDIATE ANNUITIES

Company: LINCOLN BENEFIT LIFE COMPANY

Product: IMMEDIATE ANNUITY

Description: Single premium immediate annuity. (See "Other Features").

Availability: All states except CT, MA, NH, NY
Other restrictions: Application must be signed in a state where product is approved.

Issue Ages: 5-99

Premium Limitations:
Minimum: $5,000   *Maximum:* $2,000,000

Contract Charges:
Policy fee: 4%, negotiable

State premium tax: Varies by state

Payment Options: Standard

Participation in Company Experience: Nonparticipating; payments are fixed after issue.

Rate-Setting Process: Reviewed about once a month but are subject to change at any time. Current yields on asset mix are compared with what is needed for targeted spread.

Other Features: This is a commissionable product that allows agents to reduce or eliminate the commission, in order to increase policyholder benefits.

Monthly Income per $1,000 Single Premium at 1/1:

Nonqualified rates*:

	1985	1986	1987	1988	1989	1990
Life income						
Age 65						
–Male				10.02	9.85	9.53
–Female				9.23	9.07	8.74
Life income, 10 years certain						
Age 65						
–Male				9.49	9.34	9.03
–Female				8.97	8.81	8.50

*Excluding contract charges.

Benchmark: Best's Flitcraft Compend.

Policyholder Service: Through home office, mail or 800 number.

Distributors:

Name/Address	*Compensation*
Licensed agents	Fees paid by
(call 800-LBL-WATS	buyer.
for referral)	

Company: USAA ANNUITY AND LIFE/USAA LIFE

Product: SINGLE PREMIUM IMMEDIATE ANNUITY

Description: Single premium immediate annuity.

Availability: All states
Other Restrictions: None

Issue Ages: Any age

Premium Limitations:
Minimum: $10,000   *Maximum:* Subject to company approval

Contract Charges:
Policy fee: None

State premium tax: Paid by company

Payment Options: Standard, on a monthly, quarterly, semi-annual, or annual basis.

Participation in Company Experience: Nonparticipating; payments are fixed at issue.

Rate-Setting Process: Current interest rates are monitored weekly. Annuity rates are changed based on changes in the current earned rates. Mortality is studied periodically, and mortality tables are modified to reflect company experience.

Other Features: N/A

Monthly Income per $1,000 Single Premium at 1/1:

Nonqualified rates*:

	1985	1986	1987	1988	1989	1990
Life income						
Age 65						
–Male	11.18	11.18	8.91	9.22	9.37	9.07
–Female	10.40	10.40	8.17	8.48	8.63	8.32
Life income, 10 years certain						
Age 65						
–Male	10.48	10.48	8.53	8.83	8.98	8.68
–Female	10.00	10.00	7.99	8.29	8.43	8.14

*Excluding contract charges.

Benchmark: Best's Flitcraft Compend.

Policyholder Service: By mail or 800 number.

Distributors:

Name/Address	*Compensation*
USAA Financial Services	Sold by salaried
USAA Building	representatives.
San Antonio, TX 78288	
800/531-8000	
512/498-8000	

Company: USAA ANNUITY AND LIFE/USAA LIFE

Product: TAILORED INCOME PLAN

Description: Single premium immediate annuity with customized payout options.

Availability: All states
Other restrictions: None

Issue Ages: Any age

Premium Limitations:
Minimum: $50,000   *Maximum:* Subject to company approval

Contract Charges:
Policy fee: None

State premium tax: Paid by contract owner

Payment Options: Standard options, plus customized payout schedules for special needs.

Participation in Company Experience: Nonparticipating; payments are fixed at issue.

Rate-Setting Process: Similar to Single Premium Immediate Annuity. Rates change daily and are individually computer-generated.

Other Features: N/A

Monthly Income per $1,000 Single Premium at 1/1: N/A

Distributors:

Name/Address	*Compensation*
USAA Financial Services	Sold by salaried
USAA Building	representatives.
San Antonio, TX 78288	
800/531-8000	
512/498-8000	

FIDELITY VARIABLE PRODUCT FUNDS

Advisor: FIDELITY MANAGEMENT & RESEARCH COMPANY

Product: ASSET MANAGER PORTFOLIO

Funding Vehicle for:
- Fidelity Future Reserves
- Fidelity Income Plus
- Fidelity Retirement Reserves
- Fidelity Variable Life

Objective: Seeks high total return with reduced risk over the long term by allocating assets among stock, bonds, and money market instruments.

Investment Decision-Making Process: Involves interrelated network of in-house research analysts, portfolio managers, and investment committees. Portfolio manager works closely with research analysts and makes final investment decisions. Managers are grouped together according to broad investment objectives; within each group, investment strategies and ideas are proposed and discussed. An Investment Policy Committee is responsible for reviewing the portfolio planning and overall policies of each fund. For equity funds, an Investment Committee meets weekly to discuss the "buy, sell, hold" list, and it also directs specific research projects which support the portfolio managers.

Portfolio (12/31/89): Common stocks 28%; nonconvertible bonds 12%; U.S. Government and agency obligations 17%; repurchase agreements 43%.

Selected Statistics:

	1984	1985	1986	1987	1988	1989[*]
Total return (%)						0.8
Expense ratio (%)						2.50
Port. turnover (%)						158
Net assets (mill. $)						7.3

[*] From 9/6/89.

Advisor: FIDELITY MANAGEMENT & RESEARCH COMPANY

Product: EQUITY-INCOME PORTFOLIO

Funding Vehicle for:
- Fidelity Future Reserves
- Fidelity Income Plus
- Fidelity Retirement Reserves
- Fidelity Variable Life

Objective: Seeks reasonable income by investing primarily in income-producing equity securities, with some consideration given to the potential for capital appreciation.

Investment Decision-Making Process: See Asset Manager Portfolio.

Portfolio (12/31/89): Common stocks 74%; preferred stocks 6%; corporate bonds 11%; short-term obligations 9%.

Selected Statistics:

	1984	1985	1986	1987	1988	1989
Total return (%)				(1.1)	22.7	17.4
Expense ratio (%)				1.33	1.10	0.85
Portfolio turnover (%)				133	69	78
Net assets (mill. $)			3.8	26.4	51.8	142.6

Benchmark: S&P 500.

Risk (variablity of total returns):

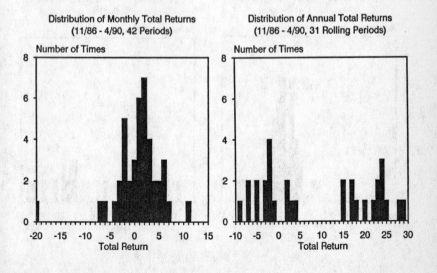

Distribution of Monthly Total Returns
(11/86 - 4/90, 42 Periods)

Distribution of Annual Total Returns
(11/86 - 4/90, 31 Rolling Periods)

Advisor: FIDELITY MANAGEMENT & RESEARCH COMPANY

Product: GROWTH PORTFOLIO

Funding Vehicle for:
- Fidelity Future Reserves
- Fidelity Income Plus
- Fidelity Retirement Reserves
- Fidelity Variable Life

Objective: Seeks to achieve capital appreciation.

Investment Decision-Making Process: See Asset Manager Portfolio.

Portfolio (12/31/89): Common stocks 88%; nonconvertible preferred stocks 1%; short-term obligations 11%.

Selected Statistics:

	1984	1985	1986	1987	1988	1989
Total return (%)				3.7	15.6	31.5
Expense ratio (%)				1.50	1.24	1.02
Portfolio turnover (%)				37	155	111
Net assets (mill. $)			2.0	18.6	28.5	77.3

Benchmark: S&P 500.

Risk (variability of total returns):

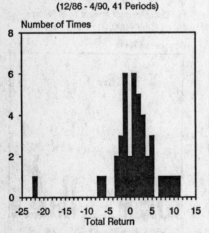

Distribution of Monthly Total Returns
(12/86 - 4/90, 41 Periods)

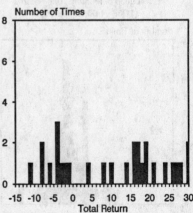

Distribution of Annual Total Returns
(12/86 - 4/90, 30 Rolling Periods)

Advisor: FIDELITY MANAGEMENT & RESEARCH COMPANY

Product: HIGH INCOME PORTFOLIO

Funding Vehicle for:
- Fidelity Future Reserves
- Fidelity Income Plus
- Fidelity Retirement Reserves
- Fidelity Variable Life

Objective: Seeks a high level of current income. Invests primarily in high-yielding, fixed-income securities. Also considers growth of capital.

Investment Decision-Making Process: See Asset Manager Portfolio.

Portfolio (12/31/89): Corporate bonds 89%; nonconvertible preferred stocks 5%; short-term obligations 6%. *Corporate bonds:* 65 companies in 13 broad sectors and 30 subsectors. *Quality distribution:* Ba2 3%; Ba3 4%; B1 16%; B2 24%; B3 28%; unrated 25%. *Largest company positions (% of total portfolio):* Kroger 49%; RJR Holdings 4.1%; Fort Howard 3.6%; Turner Broadcasting 1.9%; SCI Holdings 2.8%.

Selected Statistics:

	1984	1985	1986	1987	1988	1989
Total return (%)			17.7	1.2	11.6	(4.2)
Expense ratio (%)			1.00	1.02	0.99	0.93
Portfolio turnover (%)			78	189	139	124
Net assets (mill. $)		2.0	13.1	19.3	30.2	33.7

Benchmark: Lipper High Income Index.

Risk (variability of total returns):

Distribution of Monthly Total Returns
(10/85 - 4/90, 55 Periods)

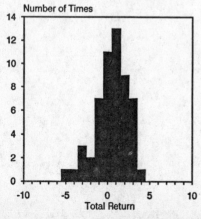

Distribution of Annual Total Returns
(10/85 - 4/90, 44 Rolling Periods)

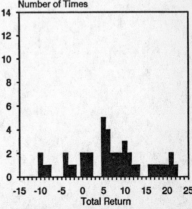

Advisor: FIDELITY MANAGEMENT & RESEARCH COMPANY

Product: MONEY MARKET PORTFOLIO

Funding Vehicle for:
- Fidelity Future Reserves
- Fidelity Income Plus
- Fidelity Retirement Reserves
- Fidelity Variable Life

Objective: Seeks to obtain as high a level of current income as is consistent with preserving capital and providing liquidity.

Investment Decision-Making Process: See Asset Manager Portfolio.

Portfolio (6/30/89): Bankers' acceptances 11%; certificates of deposit 17%; commercial paper 71%; repurchase agreements 1%.

Selected Statistics:

	1984	1985	1986	1987	1988	1989
Total return (%)	10.4	8.1	6.7	6.4	7.4	9.1
Expense ratio (%)	0.66	0.56	0.50	0.54	0.60	0.67
Net assets (mill. $)	84.0	81.9	65.2	87.8	105.6	143.0

Advisor: FIDELITY MANAGEMENT & RESEARCH COMPANY

Product: OVERSEAS PORTFOLIO

Funding Vehicle for:
- Fidelity Future Reserves
- Fidelity Income Plus
- Fidelity Retirement Reserves
- Fidelity Variable Life

Objective: Seeks long term growth of capital primarily through investments in foreign securities.

Investment Decision-Making Process: See Asset Manager Portfolio.

Portfolio (12/31/89): Common stocks 86%; preferred stocks 1%; corporate bonds 1%; short-term obligations 12%. *Common stocks:* Japan 29%; Netherlands 11%; West Germany 9%; France 9%; Italy 8%; U.K. 6%; Norway 4%; all other 10%.

Selected Statistics:

	1984	1985	1986	1987	1988	1989
Total return (%)					8.1	26.3
Expense ratio (%)					1.50	1.50
Portfolio turnover (%)					95	78
Net assets (mill. $)				6.6	9.3	25.9

Benchmark: EAFE Index.

Risk (variability of total returns):

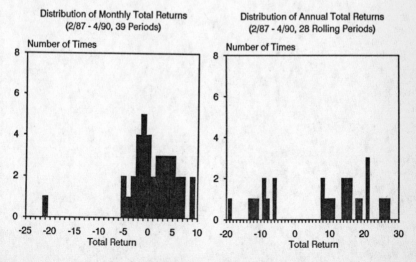

Distribution of Monthly Total Returns
(2/87 - 4/90, 39 Periods)

Distribution of Annual Total Returns
(2/87 - 4/90, 28 Rolling Periods)

Advisor: FIDELITY MANAGEMENT & RESEARCH COMPANY

Product: SHORT-TERM PORTFOLIO

Funding Vehicle for:
- Fidelity Future Reserves
- Fidelity Income Plus
- Fidelity Retirement Reserves
- Fidelity Variable Life

Objective: Seeks to obtain as high a level of current income as is consistent with preserving capital. Investments will generally be of investment grade and have an average maturity of three years or less.

Investment Decision-Making Process: See Asset Manager Portfolio.

Portfolio (12/31/89): Corporate bonds 50%; U.S. Government and agency obligations 43%; short-term obligations 7%.

Selected Statistics:

	1984	1985	1986	1987	1988	1989
Total return (%)						10.2
Expense ratio (%)						0.80
Net assets (mill. $)					2.6	6.1

Company: FIDELITY MANAGEMENT & RESEARCH COMPANY

Product: ZERO COUPON BOND PORTFOLIO

Funding Vehicle for:
- Fidelity Variable Life
- Fidelity Future Reserves

Objective: Seeks to provide a definable return over the lifetime of each portfolio. Will primarily invest in zero coupon U.S. Treasury securities with maturity dates of 1993, 1998, and 2003.

Investment Decision-Making Process: See Asset Manager Portfolio.

Portfolio (12/31/89): U.S. Treasury STRIPS 100%.

Selected Statistics:

1993 Portfolio

	1984	1985	1986	1987	1988	1989
Total return (%)						13.7
Expense ratio (%)						1.00
Net assets (mill. $)					1.0	1.6

1998 Portfolio

	1984	1985	1986	1987	1988	1989
Total return (%)						19.3
Expense ratio (%)						1.00
Net assets (mill. $)					0.7	1.4

2003 Portfolio

	1984	1985	1986	1987	1988	1989
Total return (%)						22.7
Expense ratio (%)						1.00
Net assets (mill. $)					1.1	3.3

DISABILITY INCOME

Company: USAA LIFE INSURANCE COMPANY

Product: USAA INCOME REPLACEMENT POLICY

Description: Noncancellable, level premium income replacement policy, with benefits for total and partial disability. Choice of integrated (contract benefits are reduced dollar for dollar by governmental benefits received) or non-integrated contracts. Eligible for dividends.

Availability: All states, except FL, GA, MD, MN, NJ, NY, PA, SC, VA, WI, WV
Other restrictions: Available to independent professionals, white collar workers, and business owners whose duties are performed primarily in an office environment.

Issue Ages: 18-60

Monthly Benefit Limitations:

	Minimum	Maximum
Integrated	$750	$12,000
Non-integrated	350	12,000
Changes	Increases made by rider.	

Definition of Disability:
You are disabled if: (1) You are under the care of a physician for an injury or sickness; and (2a) you have a 20% or greater loss of time at work, or (2b) you are unable to perform one or more of your substantial and material business duties, accounting for 20% or more of your earned income during the prior 12 months.

You have a Covered Income Loss, and are therefore eligible to receive monthly benefits, if you have a 20% or greater loss of earned income due to the same sickness or injury that began the waiting period.

Definition of Recurrent Disability:
For 2- or 5-year benefit period: Disability during six consecutive months of no Covered Income Loss.
For to-age-65 benefit period: Disability during 12 consecutive months of no Covered Income Loss.

Waiting Period: 30, 60, 90, 180, or 365 days.

Benefit Period: 2 or 5 years, or to age 65.

Other Features:
• Partial disability: Provided in base policy. Benefit paid is a percentage of maximum monthly benefit, equal to percentage loss of earned income. (*Example:* $4,000 monthly earned income, $2,000 maximum monthly benefit. If earned income drops 75% to $1,000, monthly benefit would be 75% of $2,000.) Earned income loss must be at least 20%. During the first six months, minimum benefit is 50%.

• Government benefit integration: Can choose between integrated and non-integrated contracts at issue. For integrated contracts, monthly benefit is reduced dollar for dollar by Government benefits received, in order to maintain same total benefit. Non-integrated contract has a higher premium.

• Cost of living adjustments: By Cost of Living Benefit Rider. Benefits adjusted annually, based on Consumer Price Index. Annual cap is 6% simple interest; lifetime cap is twice base coverage. No automatic purchase option when disability ends.

• Future benefit increases: By Additional Insurance Option Rider. $500 increment each year; earned income must be sufficient to warrant increase. Evidence of good health is not required. Options can be exercised while disabled. Premium increases are based on rate schedule in effect at date of exercise.

• Other: Own Occupation Rider. Company will calculate Covered Income Loss by considering only income from the occupation specified in the contract if: (1) at least 70% of earned income during the previous 36 months came from the specified occupation; and (2) the insured has a 100% loss of income from the specified occupation. Adequate proof must be submitted.

Fractional Premiums:

	Modal Factor	Equivalent Annual Charge
Semi-annual	0.51	8.3%
Quarterly	0.26	11.2
Monthly	0.085	4.4

Illustrative Annual Premium:
Male nonsmoker, age 35, professional,
$3,000 monthly benefit, to-age-65 benefit period.
Integrated, no riders, $30 policy fee.

Waiting Period	Annual Premium
30 days	$1,180
60	944
90	819
180	686
365	613

Policyholder Service: By USAA Life. Mail or 800 number.

Distributors:

Name/Address	Compensation
USAA Life Insurance Company	Sold by salaried
USAA Building	representatives.
San Antonio, TX 78288	
800/531-8000	
512/498-8000	

13

COMPANY PROFILES

AMERITAS LIFE INSURANCE CORPORATION   800/255-9678
5900 O Street
Lincoln, NE 68510

Territory: All states except NY

Ratings: 1990 1989 1988 1987 1986 1985 1984 1983 1982 1981

A.M. Best A+   A+   A+   A+   A+   A+   A+   A+   A+   A+

Methods of Assuring Future Solvency: Maintains a strong surplus balance as a cushion against financial risk. Maintains a balanced portfolio and a conservative investment strategy. Carefully underwrites new business to screen for AIDS; due to past geographic concentration of business, has experienced very few AIDS claims.

Selected Statistics — 1989:

	Amount	1988 Rank in U.S.
Total assets	$1,244,454,322	143
Total capital and surplus	106,369,667	-
Life insurance in force	4,650,714,000	245
Total premiums	183,664,464	213

	Premiums	Number of Policies Issued in 1989	In Force Year-End
Individual life	$51,160,029	4,690	142,098
Individual annuities	7,730,927	715	6,045

Selected Statistics — 1985-1989: (In mill. $)

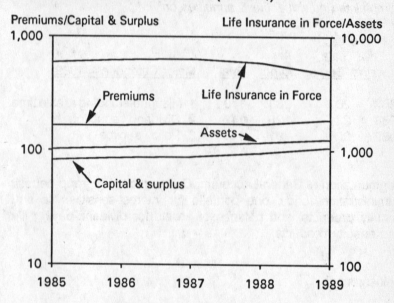

Premiums/Capital & Surplus — Life Insurance in Force/Assets

Distribution of First-Year Premium Income by Line of Business:

	Individual Life		Individual Annuities		
	Low-Load	Load	Low-Load	Load	All Other
1985	2%	41%	–	7%	50%
1986	2	39	–	5	54
1987	4	33	–	14	49
1988	6	28	–	17	49
1989	5	22	–	13	60

History:

1887: Incorporated as a stock company.
1941: Became a mutual company.
1983: Variable life subsidiary established.
1984: Group dental company established for New York.
1988: Name changed from Bankers Life Nebraska to Ameritas Life.

Treatment of Policyholders:
Complaints (individual life & annuities only):

	Filed w/ State Ins. Depts.	All Other	Total	Major Categories—1989
1987	26	85	110	1. Misunderstanding at sale time
1988	22	125	147	2. Dividend reduction
1989	22	91	113	3. Policy service

Segmentation of General Account: One portfolio for group deposit administration funds, one portfolio for interest-sensitive life and annuity products, and balance of assets for dividend-paying life and annuity products.

Reinsurance:

Retention: $400,000 to age 65   *Number of reinsurers:* 8
200,000 over age 65

Distribution by reinsurer of risks ceded and length of relationship:

	% of Risks Ceded	Reinsurer Since
Reinsurer #1	32.4%	1951
Reinsurer #2	27.2	1969
All other	40.4	N/A

Balance Sheet:

Total assets: $1,244,454,322

Asset Category	As % of Assets
Bonds	56.2%
Investment grade	55.8
Non-investment grade	
-average quality	0.3
-below average quality	0.2
-in or near default	–
1-5 years	8.1
5-10 years	15.8
10-20 years	23.3
Over 20 years	9.0
Mortgages	16.3
Performing	15.9
Non-performing	0.5
Real estate	5.1
From purchases	4.9
From foreclosures	0.2
Preferred stocks	–
Common stocks	3.2
Cash and near-cash	6.3
Policy loans	6.4
Separate account	0.6
All other	5.8
Total	100%
Affiliated investments	1.2
Nonaffiliated	98.8
Total	100%

Total liabilities: $1,138,084,656

Liability Category	As % of Assets
MSVR	2.0
All other	89.5
Total capital & surplus	$106,369,667

	As % of Assets
Total capital & surplus	8.5

FIDELITY INVESTMENTS
LIFE INSURANCE COMPANY
82 Devonshire Street, L8B
Boston, MA 02109

800/544-8888
ext. 2327

Territory: 43 states and DC

Ratings*: 1990 1989 1988 1987 1986 1985 1984 1983 1982 1981

A.M. Best N/A

*Company is not yet eligible for a Best's Rating because it does not have five consecutive years of representative operating experience. No insurance operations prior to 1984.

Methods of Assuring Future Solvency: Business consists of variable life and annuity products with limited investment risk to company. Company is a wholly-owned subsidiary of Fidelity Investments, one of the largest investment organizations in the U.S. Under current agreement with parent, company is reimbursed for approximately two-thirds of its operating expenses. Strong surplus position.

Selected Statistics — 1989:

	Amount	1988 Rank in U.S.
Total assets	$55,960,226	300+
Total capital and surplus	10,904,823	-
Life insurance in force	5,764,000	300+
Total premiums	37,506,473	300+

	Premiums	Number of Policies Issued in 1989	In Force Year-End
Individual life	$1,146,326	76	100
Individual annuities	36,360,147	1,596	1,892

Selected Statistics — 1985-1989: N/A

Distribution of First-Year Premium Income by Line of Business: All business consists of low-load variable life insurance and annuities.

History:

1981: Incorporated as a stock company, wholly owned by Provident Mutual Life Insurance Company.
1984: Began insurance operations
1986: Sold to FMR Corp. (Fidelity Investments).
1987: Changed name to Fidelity Investments Life Insurance Co.
1988: Offered variable life and annuity products.

Treatment of Policyholders:

	Filed w/ State Ins. Depts.	All Other	Total	Major Categories—1989
1989	0	7	7	1. Prospectus/contract procedures (4)
				2. Other servicing (2)
				3. Investment performance (1)

Segmentation of General Account: N/A

Reinsurance:

Retention: $100,000   *Number of reinsurers:* 2

Distribution by reinsurer of risks ceded and length of relationship:

	% of Risks Ceded	Reinsurer Since
Reinsurer #1	50.0%	1988
Reinsurer #2	50.0	1988
All other	-	-

Balance Sheet:

Total assets: $55,960,226

Asset Category	As % of Assets
Bonds	18.5%
Investment grade	18.5
Non-investment grade	-
-average quality	-
-below average quality	-
-in or near default	-
1-5 years	18.5
5-10 years	-
10-20 years	-
Over 20 years	-
Mortgages	-
Performing	-
Non-performing	-
Real estate	-
From purchases	-
From foreclosures	-
Preferred stocks	-
Common stocks	0.9
Cash and near-cash	4.2
Policy loans	
Separate account	76.0
All other	0.4
Total	100%
Affiliated investments	
Nonaffiliated	100.0
Total	100%

Total liabilities: $45,055,403

Liability Category	As % of Assets
MSVR	-
All other	80.5

Total capital & surplus:	$10,904,823

	As % of Assets
Total capital & surplus:	19.5

**JOHN ALDEN LIFE
INSURANCE COMPANY**
7300 Corporate Center Drive
Miami, FL 33126-1208

305/470-3100
Mailing address:
P.O. Box 020270
Miami, FL 33102

Territory: All states except NY

Ratings:

	1990	1989	1988	1987	1986	1985	1984	1983	1982	1981
A.M. Best	N/A*	A+c	A+c	A+	A+	A+	A+	A	A	A

*Rating not available as of 4/90.

Methods of Assuring Future Solvency: Company has a conservative investment policy; large percentage of investment-grade bonds. Company matches the duration of assets and liabilities; matching is tested by performing asset/liability matching studies with multiple scenarios. For health products, claim reserves are established based upon company experience, and a margin for adverse deviation is added.

Selected Statistics — 1989:

	Amount	1988 Rank in U.S.
Total assets	$2,328,759,876	99
Total capital and surplus	111,734,465	-
Life insurance in force	7,375,809,000	240
Total premiums	1,008,115,224	98

		Number of Policies	
	Premiums	Issued in 1989	In Force Year-End
Individual life	$19,768,838	3,546	39,838
Individual annuities	15,417,592	32,172	90,334

Selected Statistics — 1985-1989: (In mill. $)

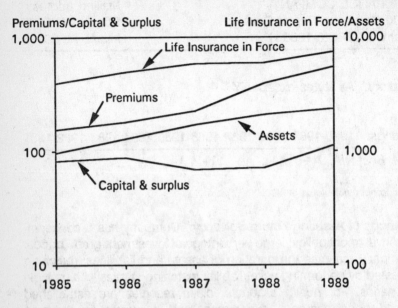

Premiums/Capital & Surplus   **Life Insurance in Force/Assets**

Distribution of First-Year Premium Income by Line of Business:

	Individual Life		Individual Annuities		
	Low-Load	Load	Low-Load	Load	All Other
1985	0%	97%	0%	3%	0%
1986	0	59	0	41	0
1987	0	48	0	52	0
1988	0	36	0	64	0
1989	3	52	1	44	0

History:

1961: Incorporated as a stock company. Owned by Aristar Capital Corporation, a wholly owned subsidiary (1983) of Great Western Savings\Great Western Financial Corporation.

1987: Acquired by John Alden Financial Corporation, which is owned by senior management, Merrill Lynch Capital Partners, GE Capital Corporation/Employers Reinsurance Corp/Kidder Peabody.

1988: Sold $455 million block of annuities (SPDA contracts issued between 1979 and 1983) to Reliance Standard Life.

Treatment of Policyholders:

Complaints (individual life & annuities only):

	Filed w/ State Ins. Depts.	All Other	Total	Major Categories—1989
1987	61	10	71	1. Marketing (15)
1988	42	9	53	2. Service (17)
1989	40	0	40	3. Underwriting/issue (7)

Segmentation of General Account: Two portfolios for interest sensitive products, one portfolio for guaranteed investment contracts, one general portfolio.

Reinsurance:

Retention: $150,000   *Number of reinsurers:* 17

Distribution by reinsurer of risks ceded and length of relationship:

	% of Risks Ceded	Reinsurer Since
Reinsurer #1	41%	1984
Reinsurer #2	40	1982
All other	19	-

Balance Sheet:

Total assets: $2,328,752,876 | *Total liabilities: $2,217,018,4*

Asset Category	As % of Assets	Liability Category	As % Assets
		MSVR	1.1
Bonds	45.7%	All other	94.1
Investment grade	42.2		
Non-investment grade		*Total capital*	
-average quality	0.3	*& surplus*	$111,734,4
-below average quality	0.3		
-in or near default	-		As % Assets
1-5 years	23.4		
5-10 years	15.0		
10-20 years	0.5	*Total capital*	
Over 20 years	3.9	*& surplus*	4.8
Mortgages	41.7		
Performing	40.9		
Non-performing	0.8		
Real estate	0.4		
From purchases	0.3		
From foreclosures	0.1		
Preferred stocks	0.3		
Common stocks	1.2		
Cash and near-cash	6.8		
Policy loans	0.9		
Separate account	-		
All other	3.0		
Total	100%		
Affiliated investments	1.5		
Nonaffiliated	98.5		
Total	100%		

LINCOLN BENEFIT LIFE COMPANY
134 South 13th Street
Lincoln, NE 68508

402/475-4061
800/525-9287
Mailing address: P. O. Box 80469
Lincoln, NE 68501

Note: Lincoln Benefit Life serves primarily as a distribution system for its parent, Allstate Life.

Territory: All states except NY

Ratings*: 1990 1989 1988 1987 1986 1985 1984 1983 1982 1981

A.M. Best	A+r	A+r	A+r	A+r	A+e	N/A	N/A	N/A	C+	C+
S&P	AAA	AAA	AAA							
Moody's	Aaa	Aaa								

*Best's rating is based on reinsurance/subsidiary relationship with Allstate; rating procedure was inapplicable during 1983-1985 due to change of ownership.

Methods of Assuring Future Solvency: All new business up to retention limit is reinsured by Allstate, which is liable for reimbursement of death benefits, cash values, and expenses. Allstate receives and invests premiums and periodically tests the adequacy of reserves, target surplus, and product pricing under stochastically-determined interest rate scenarios.

Selected Statistics — 1989
Assets:
• Lincoln Benefit Life – $65,485,000
• Allstate Life – $10,994,000,000; 1988 rank in U.S.: 27th

	Premiums	Number of Policies Issued in 1988	In Force Year-End
Individual life	N/A	11,303	54,349
Individual annuities	N/A	8,528	45,845

Selected Statistics — 1985-1989: N/A

Distribution of First-Year Premium Income by Line of Business: N/A

History:

1938: Incorporated as a stock company.
1981: Purchased by Dean Witter, which was then acquired by Sears.
1982: Ownership transferred to Sears/Allstate Insurance Company/
1984: Allstate Life. Plans formulated to use LBL to give Allstate access to individual life and annuity brokerage market.
1987: Allstate assumes all new business and almost all existing business.

Treatment of Policyholders:
Complaints (individual life & annuities only): N/A

Segmentation of General Account: N/A

Reinsurance:

All new business up to $100,000 retention limit is reinsured by Allstate. Net amounts at risk in excess of $100,000 are reinsured as follows:

Retention: $100,000   *Number of reinsurers:* 7

Distribution of premiums ceded and length of relationship:

	% of Risks Ceded	Reinsurer Since
Reinsurer #1	47%	1980
Reinsurer #2	14	1980
All other	39	-

Balance Sheet: N/A

MASSACHUSETTS SAVINGS BANK 617/938-3500
LIFE INSURANCE
P.O. Box 4046
Woburn, MA 01888-9602

Territory: MA

Ratings: 1990 1989 1988 1987 1986 1985 1984 1983 1982 1981

A.M. Best A+ A+ A+ A+ A+ A+ A+ A+ A+ A+

Methods of Assuring Future Solvency: High level of surplus in relation to liabilities. Dividends can be reduced if necessary (1989 dividends paid were 37% of year-end surplus). Term premiums on recently-issued policies can be increased if necessary. Conservative investments; no junk bonds, very limited exposure in common stocks.

Selected Statistics — 1989:

	Amount	1988 Rank in U.S.
Total assets	$709,346,176	211
Total capital and surplus	94,046,190	-
Life insurance in force	9,409,259,234	202
Total premiums	68,258,216	300+

	Premiums	Number of Policies Issued in 1989	In Force Year-End
Individual life	$58,629,120	19,726	593,331
Individual annuities	4,774,444	223	3,255

Selected Statistics — 1985-1989: (In mill. $)

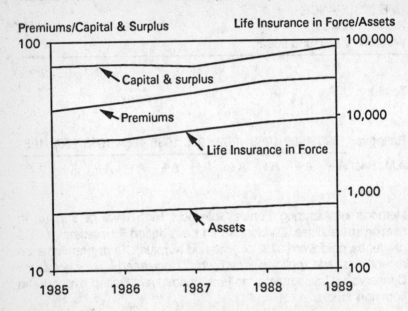

Premiums/Capital & Surplus   Life Insurance in Force/Assets

Chart showing Capital & surplus, Premiums, Life Insurance in Force, and Assets lines from 1985 to 1989.

Distribution of First-Year Premium Income by Line of Business:

| | Individual Life | | Individual Annuities | | |
	Low-Load	Load	Low-Load	Load	All Other
1988	88%		7%		5
1989	86		7		7

History:

1907: Established by Massachusetts Legislature; General Insurance Guaranty Fund created to act as guarantor of all policy obligations.

1938: Savings Bank Life Insurance Council established to provide services to issuing banks.

1977: System reorganization; SBLI Council placed under management of Guaranty Fund trustees; functional unification with Massachusetts Division of SBLI.

1987: Policy limit raised from $60,000 to $250,000.

1990: 56 issuing banks as of 4/90.

Treatment of Policyholders:
Complaints (individual life & annuities only): Total not available, but number of complaints is very low.

Segmentation of General Account: N/A

Reinsurance: None on individual policies.

Balance sheet:

Under the SBLI system, policies are backed only by the assets of the insurance department of each issuing bank, with the General Insurance Guaranty Fund as guarantor. The assets of each bank's insurance department are separate from the savings department.

Amounts shown below are for year-end 1989:

	Amount	As % of Total SBLI Assets
MSVR	$0	-%
Surplus -Guaranty Fund only	9,225,267	1.3
-Total SBLI system	94,046,190	13.3

MONARCH LIFE INSURANCE COMPANY   413/784-2000
One Monarch Place
Springfield, MA 01133

Territory: All states, Guam, Puerto Rico, and U.S. Virgin Islands

Ratings:

	1990	1989	1988	1987	1986	1985	1984	1983	1982	1981
A.M. Best	A+c	A+c	A+c	A+	A+	A+	A+	A+	A+	A+
S&P	AA-	AA-								

Methods of Assuring Future Solvency: Business consists primarily of variable life products with limited investment risk to company.

Selected Statistics — 1989:

	Amount	1988 Rank in U.S.
	$5,127,008,347	52
Total assets	138,117,060	-
Total capital and surplus	12,340,476,000	161
Life insurance in force	232,431,347	153
Total premiums		

	Premiums	Number of Policies Issued in 1989	In Force Year-End
Individual life	$56,199,589	5,694	99,909
Individual annuities	18,018,988	19	3,569

Selected Statistics — 1985-1989: N/A

Distribution: First-Year Premium Income by Line of Business, 1989:
Individual life 24%; individual annuities 8%; all other 68%.
Business is primarily commissionable.

History:

1901: Incorporated as a mutual company.
1921: Reincorporated as a stock company.
1980: Established variable life separate account.
1982: Introduced single premium variable life product.
1985: Introduced another variable life product.
1987: Introduced joint survivor variable life product; sold term, whole life, and participating annuity business to Banner Life.

Treatment of Policyholders: N/A

Segmentation of General Account: N/A

Reinsurance:

Retention: $500,000   *Number of reinsurers:* 45

Distribution by reinsurer of risks ceded and length of relationship:

	% of Risks Ceded	Reinsurer Since
Reinsurer #1	58.8%	N/A
Reinsurer #2	19.9	N/A
All other	-	-

Balance Sheet:

Total assets: $5,127,008,347

Total liabilities: $4,988,891,287

Asset Category	As % of Assets	Liability Category	As % of Assets
Bonds	9.1%	*MSVR*	0.3
Investment grade	7.4	*All other*	97.0
Non-investment grade			
-average quality	0.5	*Total capital*	
-below average quality	0.5	*& surplus:*	$138,117,060
-in or near default	-		

	As % of Assets
1-5 years	0.5
5-10 years	1.9
10-20 years	2.8
Over 20 years	3.7

	As % of Assets
Total capital	
& surplus	2.7

Asset Category	As % of Assets
Mortgages	1.3
Performing	1.3
Non-performing	-
Real estate	-
From purchases	-
From foreclosures	-
Preferred stocks	0.2
Common stocks	1.5
Cash and near-cash	1.2
Policy loans	9.3
Separate account	73.3
All other	4.1
Total	100%

Affiliated investments	1.8
Nonaffiliated	98.2
Total	100%

NEW YORK SAVINGS BANK LIFE INSURANCE   212/356-0300
460 West 34th Street
New York, NY 10001-2320

Territory: NY

Ratings:

	1990	1989	1988	1987	1986	1985	1984	1983	1982	1981
A.M. Best	A+	A+	A+	A+	A+	A+	A+	A+	A+	A+

Methods of Assuring Future Solvency: Conservatism in entering new lines of business; not on "cutting edge" in product development; no interest-sensitive or health insurance products offered. High level of surplus in relation to liabilities. Decentralized risk; each bank invests funds independently and SBLI Fund acts as guarantor for all. Regulated by New York Banking and Insurance Departments, with oversight by SBLI Fund. No agent pressure in underwriting procedures. Low lapse rates.

Selected Statistics — 1989:

	Amount	1988 Rank in U.S.
Total assets	$844,637,974	184
Total capital and surplus	90,735,880	-
Life insurance in force	16,560,729,862	128
Total premiums	113,792,025	277

	Premiums	Number of Policies Issued in 1989	Number of Policies In Force Year-End
Individual life	$82,697,928	19,809	470,604
Individual annuities	40,630	1	238

Selected Statistics — 1985-1989: (In mill. $)

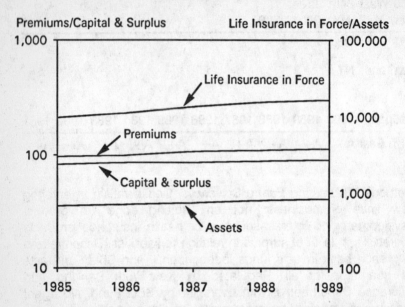

Premiums/Capital & Surplus   Life Insurance in Force/Assets

Distribution of First-Year Premium Income by Line of Business:

First-year premiums are not separated from renewal premiums. About 75% of premiums are individual life; remainder is credit and group life. All business is low-load.

History:

1939: Founded under special New York law that allowed mutual savings banks to establish an insurance department. Policies limited to $1,000 per life.

1940: Savings Bank Life Insurance Fund created to act as guarantor of all policy obligations.

1942: Policy limit raised to $3,000.

1948: Policy limit raised to $5,000.

1958: Policy limit raised to $10,000.

1967: Policy limit raised to $30,000.

1985: Policy limit raised to $50,000.

1986: Bank depositors made eligible for group insurance, in amounts up to $250,000.

1990: Group insurance limit raised to $350,000.

Treatment of Policyholders:

Policyholder complaints (individual life & annuities only):

Filed
w/ State   All
Ins. Depts.   Other   Total   Major Categories—1984-88

Complaints are not tracked   1. Servicing, 55%
by year. There were 305   2. Declined claims, 27%
complaints in total during   3. Underwriting, 18%
the 1984-88 period.

Segmentation of General Account: N/A

Reinsurance:

Reinsurance activity is negligible; used for high substandard risks only.

Balance Sheet:

Under the SBLI system, policies are backed only by the assets of the insurance department of each issuing bank, with the SBLI Fund as guarantor. The assets of each bank's insurance department must be invested in the same manner as other assets.

Amounts shown below are for year-end 1989:

	Amount	As % of Total SBLI Assets
MSVR	$4,822,142	0.4%
Surplus		
-SBLI Fund only	13,114,117	1.6
-Total SBLI system	90,735,880	10.7

PACIFIC FIDELITY LIFE
INSURANCE COMPANY
251 South Lake Avenue
Pasadena, CA 91101

319/398-8511
Mailing address:
4333 Edgewood Road, N.E.
Cedar Rapids, IA 52499

Territory: All states (except NY), Guam, and U.S. Virgin Islands

Ratings:

	1990	1989	1988	1987	1986	1985	1984	1983	1982	1981
A.M. Best	N/A*	A	A	A	A	A	A	A	A	A

* Best's rating not available as of 4/90.

Methods of Assuring Future Solvency: N/D

Selected Statistics — 1989:

	Amount	Rank in U.S.
Total assets	$956,969,045	171
Total capital and surplus	45,689,295	-
Life insurance in force	2,510,532,000	300+
Total premiums	162,675,668	178

	Premiums	Number of Policies Issued in 1989	Number of Policies In Force Year-End
Individual life	$28,612,597	1,412	24,482
Individual annuities	66,402,762	38,044	146,436

Selected Statistics — 1985-1989: N/A

Distribution: First-Year Premium Income by Line of Business, 1988: Individual life 18%; individual annuities 41%; all other 41%. Business is primarily commissionable.

History:

1956: Incorporated as a stock company.
1988: AEGON USA, Inc. formed as holding company, wholly owned by Aegon N.V., one of the ten largest European insurance companies.

Treatment of policyholders: N/A

Segmentation of General Account: N/A

Reinsurance: N/A

Balance sheet on following page

Balance Sheet:

Total assets: **$956,969,045**   *Total liabilities:* **$911,279,75⁴**

Asset Category	As % of Assets	Liability Category	As % of Assets
Bonds	62.6%	MSVR	0.1
Investment grade	60.1	All other	94.2
Non-investment grade			
-average quality	2.1	*Total capital*	
-below average quality	0.4	*& surplus*	$45,689,2⁹
-in or near default	-		
			As % of
1-5 years	4.6		Assets
5-10 years	12.1		
10-20 years	15.1		
Over 20 years	30.2		
		Total capital	
Mortgages	7.4	*& surplus*	4.8
Performing	7.3		
Non-performing	0.1		
Real estate	2.4		
From purchases	2.2		
From foreclosures	0.2		
Preferred stocks	-		
Common stocks	0.1		
Cash and near-cash	1.3		
Policy loans	7.4		
Separate account	15.5		
All other	3.3		
Total	100%		
Affiliated investments	0.1		
Nonaffiliated	99.9		
Total	100%		

USAA LIFE INSURANCE COMPANY
USAA Building
San Antonio, TX 78288

800/531-8000
512/498-8000

Territory: All states

Ratings:

	1990	1989	1988	1987	1986	1985	1984	1983	1982	1981
A.M.Best	A+	A+	A+	A+	A+	A+	A+	A+	A+	A+

Methods of Assuring Future Solvency: Since 1987, all adult applicants have been tested for AIDS, and a special reserve has been established to cover excess mortality on existing policies. Regular statutory reserves exceed state regulatory requirements. Methods of monitoring profitability are continually improved; company is beginning to price and reprice products using target surplus formulas; internal committees examine products on an ongoing basis to assure viability. Interest rate risk is controlled through investments in mortgage pass-through securities backed by Federal agencies, which are readily marketable and provide a monthly return of principal. Asset/liability matching studies are conducted on annuity products, as required by New York regulations, and a plan has been initiated to expand asset/liability management by utilizing adjustable rate mortgages, interest rate swaps, and options. Continuous contact is maintained with A.M. Best to review rating process, in order to maintain A+ rating. USAA Life is a wholly-owned subsidiary of USAA, a property/casualty insurer with strong internal surplus requirements.

Selected Statistics – 1989:

	Amount	1988 Rank in U.S.
Total assets	$1,119,750,126	164
Total capital and surplus	102,751,494	-
Life insurance in force	34,876,513,000	73
Total premiums	236,269,318	172

| | | Number of Policies | |
| | | Issued | In Force |
	Premiums	in 1989	Year-End
Individual life	$169,555,736	33,376	323,566
Individual annuities	47,434,778	643	6,312

Selected Statistics – 1985-1989: (In mill. $)

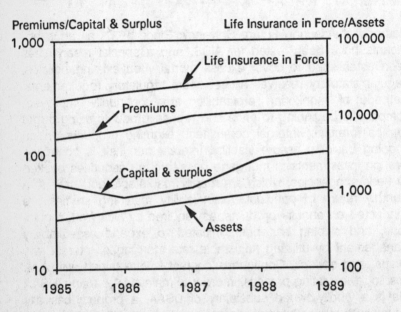

Premiums/Capital & Surplus   Life Insurance in Force/Assets

Distribution of First-Year Premium Income by Line of Business:

| | Individual Life | | Individual Annuities | | |
	Low-Load	Load	Low-Load	Load	All Other
1985	55%		44%		1
1986	65		33		2
1987	65		27		7
1988	46		45		9
1989	43		50		7

History:

1963: Incorporated as a stock company; wholly-owned by United Services Automobile Association, a property/casualty cooperative founded in 1922 by U.S. Army officers to provide low-cost automobile insurance coverage.

1979: USAA Annuity and Life Insurance Company formed as a wholly-owned subsidiary, to market and reinsure annuity contracts.

1988: Sold Multiple Employer Trust group life and long-term disability business in force.

Treatment of Policyholders:
Complaints (individual life & annuities only):

	Filed w/ State Ins. Depts.	All Other	Total	Major Categories—1989
1987	1	52	53	1. Underwriting guidelines
1988	3	39	42	2. Service
1989	6	36	42	3. Policy provisions

Segmentation of General Account: Separate portfolios are established for universal life, structured settlements, and Tailored Income Plan products; investments for these portfolios are purchased directly. All other products are backed by a general portfolio; investments are allocated to each product by reserve balance.

Reinsurance:

Retention: $400,000   *Number of reinsurers:* 11

Distribution by reinsurer of risks ceded and length of relationship:

	% of Risks Ceded	Reinsurer Since
Reinsurer #1	31%	1982
Reinsurer #2	23	1972
All other	46	-

Balance Sheet:

Total assets: $1,119,750,126

Asset Category	As % of Assets
Bonds	73.6%
Investment grade	68.8
Non-investment grade	
-average quality	2.8
-below average quality	2.0
-in or near default	-
1-5 years	5.7
5-10 years	12.4
10-20 years	9.2
Over 20 years	46.3
Mortgages	-
Performing	-
Non-performing	-
Real estate	-
From purchases	-
From foreclosures	-
Preferred stocks	7.7
Common stocks	9.5
Cash and near-cash	(0.2)
Policy loans	0.5
Separate account	-
All other	8.9
Total	100%
Affiliated investments	4.3
Nonaffiliated	95.7
Total	100%

Total liabilities: $1,016,998,63

Liability Category	As % o Assets
MSVR	2.2
All other	89.6
Total capital & surplus	$102,751,49

	As % Asset
Total capital & surplus	9.2

USAA ANNUITY AND LIFE
INSURANCE COMPANY
USAA Building
San Antonio, TX 78288

800/531-8000
512/498-8000

Territory: Licensed in 44 states and DC. Not licensed in IA, ME, NH, NJ, NY, VT

Ratings:

A.M. Best	1990	1989	1988	1987	1986	1985	1984	1983	1982	1981
A.M. Best	A	A	A	A	A	A	(Not eligible prior to 1985)			

Methods of Assuring Future Solvency: See profile of USAA Life Insurance Company. USAA Annuity and Life is a wholly-owned affiliate of USAA Life.

Selected Statistics — 1989:

	Amount	1988 Rank in U.S.
Total assets	$1,397,762,672	144
Total capital and surplus	45,727,859	-
Life insurance in force	-	-
Total premiums	215,471,168	162

	Premiums	Number of Policies Issued in 1989	In Force Year-End
Individual life	-	-	-
Individual annuities	$215,471,168	8,612	90,365

Selected Statistics — 1985-1989: (In mill. $)

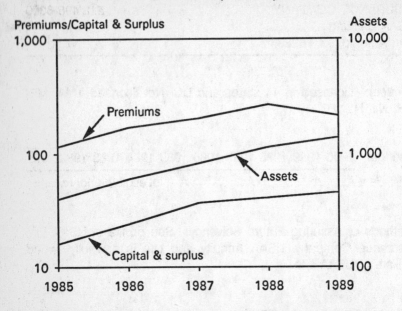

Distribution of First-Year Premium Income by Line of Business:

	Individual Life		Individual Annuities		
	Low-Load	Load	Low-Load	Load	All Other
1985			100%		
1986			100		
1987			100		
1988			100		
1989			100		

History:

1979: Incorporated as a wholly-owned subsidiary of USAA Life Insurance Company, to market and reinsure annuity contracts.

Treatment of Policyholders:
Policyholder complaints (individual life & annuities only):

	Filed w/ State Ins. Depts.	All Other	Total	Major Categories—1989
1987	0	5	5	1. Service
1988	0	9	9	2. Billing errors
1989	0	28	28	3. Policy provisions

Segmentation of General Account: Separate portfolios are established for single premium deferred annuities and guaranteed investment contracts; investments for these portfolios are purchased directly. Other annuity products are backed by a general portfolio; investments are allocated to each product by reserve balance.

Reinsurance: USAA Life Insurance Company is the only reinsurer.

Balance sheet on following page

Balance Sheet:

Total assets: $1,397,762,672

Asset Category	As % of Assets
Bonds	96.3%
Investment grade	91.0
Non-investment grade	
-average quality	2.1
-below average quality	1.0
-in or near default	-
1-5 years	12.0
5-10 years	9.1
10-20 years	5.8
Over 20 years	67.1
Mortgages	-
Performing	-
Non-performing	-
Real estate	-
From purchases	-
From foreclosures	-
Preferred stocks	0.4
Common stocks	-
Cash and near-cash	-
Policy loans	-
Separate account	-
All other	3.3
Total	100%
Affiliated investments	
Nonaffiliated	100.0
Total	100%

Total liabilities: $1,352,034,8?

Liability Category	As % of Assets
MSVR	0.8
All other	95.9

	As % of Assets
Total capital & surplus	3.3

Total capital & surplus: $45,727,859

COMPANIES WITHOUT PRODUCT PROFILES

AMERICAN LIFE INSURANCE COMPANY 212/581-1200
OF NEW YORK
810 Seventh Avenue
New York, NY 10019

Territory: All states and U.S. Virgin Islands

History: Was incorporated as a stock company in 1955. In 1987 the company was acquired by Mutual of American Life Insurance Company. It offers universal life and term insurance products through banks, agents and direct mail.

CONNECTICUT SAVINGS BANK 203/249-9391
LIFE INSURANCE
One Corporate Center
Hartford, CT 06103

Territory: CT

History: Life Insurance system was established in 1942. The company offers level premium and single premium whole life, term insurance, and flexible premium fixed annuities. All products are sold through SBLI issuing and agency banks.

TEACHERS INSURANCE AND ANNUITY 212/490-9000
ASSOCIATION OF AMERICA
730 Third Avenue
New York, NY 10017

Territory: Licensed in 33 states. Policies are issued to residents of remaining states by mail.

History: TIAA is a nonprofit stock company incorporated in 1918. It offers term, whole life, and fixed-interest annuity products; variable annuities are available from the associated College Retirement Equities Fund (CREF). All products are sold by direct mail and are only available to employees of colleges, universities, and certain other nonprofit institutions.

APPENDICES

APPENDIX A: BENCHMARKS

One-Year Certificates of Deposit

Rates as of 1/1:	1985	1986	1987	1988	1989	1990
One-year CDs	9.91	8.55	6.92	6.92	7.66	8.67

Source: Bank Rate Monitor

Other Investments

Total return with dividends reinvested as of 12/31:

	1984	1985	1986	1987	1988	1989
S&P 500*	6.10	31.57	18.55	5.32	16.66	31.53
Lipper High Income Average**	7.23	21.65	12.96	1.61	12.46	(0.88)
EAFE Index***	7.85	56.22	69.69	24.64	28.54	10.61

*Soure: Standard & Poor's Corp.

**Source: Lipper Analytical Services, Inc.

***Source: Morgan Stanley, Europe, Australia, Far East Index.

UNIVERSAL LIFE

Flexible-premium universal life new-money gross interest rates, as of 1/1:

	1985	1986	1987	1988	1989	1990
# of products	140	361	456	497	408	426
10th percentile		11.00%	9.75%	9.50%	9.50%	9.25%
25th percentile		10.75	9.40	9.20	9.00	9.00
50th percentile	11.15	10.40	9.00	9.00	9.00	8.75
75th percentile		10.00	8.75	8.75	8.60	8.50
Worst	7.86	7.00	5.84	7.00	7.25	7.25

Source: Tillinghast Universal Life Analytic Study,
            Tillinghast/Towers Perrin—by Permission.

VARIABLE LIFE

Fixed account interest rate as of 9/89:

# of products   19

10th percentile	10.00%
25th percentile	10.00
50th percentile	8.50
75th percentile	8.50
Worst	7.80

Source: Tillinghast Variable Annuity & Life User Exchange, Tillinghast/Towers Perrin—by Permission.

TERM INSURANCE

Present Value of Premiums at 5%

Male nonsmoker, age 35, $250,000 face amount. Based on current illustrations, assuming no re-entry. 511 products, as of December 1989.

	1 Year	5 Years	10 Years
10th percentile	$256	$1,364	$2,736
25th percentile	293	1,489	3,071
50th percentile	340	1,659	3,497
75th percentile	391	1,875	3,983

Source: Tillinghast TERMinology (Term Product Comparison), Tillinghast/Towers Perrin—by Permission.

DEFERRED ANNUITIES–FIXED

Single-premium deferred annuity new-money interest rates, as of 1/1:

	1988	1989	1990
# of products	223	230	308
10th percentile	9.00%	9.00%	8.65%
25th percentile	8.60	8.75	8.40
50th percentile	8.25	8.50	8.10
75th percentile	8.00	8.25	7.70
Worst	6.50	6.75	6.15

Source: Tillinghast Universal Life Analytic Study, Tillinghast/Towers Perrin—by Permission.

Flexible-premium deferred annuity new-money interest rates, as of 1/1:

	1985	1986	1987
# of products	288	260	275
10th percentile	9.25%	8.90%	8.65%
25th percentile	8.60	8.60	8.40
50th percentile	8.25	8.25	8.10
75th percentile	7.75	8.00	7.75
Worst	6.00	6.00	6.00

Source: Tillinghast Universal Life Analytic Study,
Tillinghast/Towers Perrin—by Permission.

DEFERRED ANNUITIES–VARIABLE

Fixed account interest rate as of 9/89:

# of products	29
10th percentile	9.00%
25th percentile	8.50
50th percentile	8.25
75th percentile	8.00
Worst	7.00

Source: Tillinghast Variable Annuity & Life User Exchange,
Tillinghast/Towers Perrin—by Permission.

IMMEDIATE ANNUITIES

Monthly income per $1,000 single premium, as of 2/1:

Male, age 65, monthly life income - 10 years certain. Nonqualified rates, excluding contract charges:

	1989	1990
# of products	149	136
10th percentile	$9.18	$9.09
25th percentile	8.98	8.81
50th percentile	8.72	8.62
75th percentile	8.25	8.29
Worst	6.35	7.25

Female, age 65, monthly life income - 10 years certain. Nonqualified rates, excluding contract charges:

	1989	1990
# of products	149	136
10th percentile	$8.72	$8.58
25th percentile	8.50	8.26
50th percentile	8.16	8.06
75th percentile	7.77	7.78
Worst	5.80	6.78

Source: Best's Flitcraft Compend,
         A.M. Best Company—by Permission.

INSURANCE COMPANIES

Composite Financial Information for U.S. Life Insurance Companies. Based on 1988 statutory annual statements.

Assets	% of Assets	Amount (in billions)
Bonds	48.5%	$567.5
Mortgage loans	19.6	229.1
Preferred stock	0.8	9.5
Common stock	3.8	44.3
Real estate	2.3	27.3
Policy loans	4.6	54.1
Cash & short-term investments	3.0	36.2
Other General Account assets	7.3	85.8
Separate account assets	9.9	115.7
Total	**100.0%**	**$1,169.5**

Liabilities & Capital/Surplus

	% of Assets	Amount (in billions)
MSVR	1.5%	$17.9
Other liabilities	92.0	1,075.2
Capital & surplus	6.5	76.4
Total	**100.0%**	**$1,169.5**

Premium Income

	% of Total	Amount (in billions)
Individual life	25.1%	$57.7
Individual annuities	18.3	42.2
All other [a]	56.6	130.4
Total	**100.0%**	**$230.3**

[a] Includes group life & annuities, credit life, accident & health, and industrial life (small policies sold to individuals, usually with weekly or monthly premiums).

Source: Best's Aggregates & Averages,
A.M. Best Company—by Permission.

APPENDIX B: LOW-LOAD PRODUCTS AVAILABLE FOR TAX-DEFERRED PLANS

The products listed below can be used with some types of tax-deferred retirement plans (but not IRAs):

- Ameritas Life Insurance Corp.: Pathfinder Unison
- Fidelity: Retirement Reserves
- Lincoln Benefit: Futurist II (flexible premium annuity)
- TIAA: Variable and fixed annuities
- USAA: Fixed and immediate annuities

APPPENDIX C: LOW-LOAD PRODUCTS UNDER DEVELOPMENT

The product listed below is expected to be available in 1990. Contact the company for further information.

Company	Product
Massachusetts SBLI 1 Linscott Road P.O. Box 4046 Woburn, MA 01888 617/938-3500	Graded premium life

APPENDIX D: INSURANCE PRODUCT SURVEYS

Investors may wish to consult some of these sources for more information about the products in the marketplace.

A.M. Best Company
Ambest Road
Oldwick, NJ 08858-9988
201/439-2200

Best's Flitcraft Compend — Contains summary information about several hundred whole life, universal life, and term products, including dividend and interest rate histories.

Best's Retirement Income Guide — Contains summary information about several hundred fixed annuities, variable annuities, and immediate annuities.

Best's Review (Life/Health) — Monthly magazine that contains periodic comparisons of various types of life insurance products, including historical performance.

Commerce Publishing Company
408 Olive Street
St. Louis, MO 63102
314/421-5445

Life Insurance Selling — Monthly magazine for insurance agents with periodic guides to most types of insurance products, providing summary information about contract features and commissions.
Subscription rates: $10/1 year; $22/3 years. Single issues are not available to the general public.

Consumer Reports
256 Washington Street
Mount Vernon, NY 10553
212/983-8250

Insurance Articles — Homeowners, September 1989; Medigap, June 1989; Auto, October 1988; Long-term care, May 1988; Annuities, January 1988; Life, June-August 1986.

Dow Jones & Company
200 Liberty Street
New York, NY 10281
212/416-2000

Barron's — Contains unit accumulation values for variable life and annuity funds.

Financial Planning Resources, Inc.
P.O. Box 161998
Miami, Florida 33116
305/252-4600

Variable Annuity Research & Data Service (VARDS) Report — Provides information about contract features, expenses, and fund performance for variable life and annuity products. Single-issue orders are accepted.

The National Underwriter Company
420 East 4th Street
Cincinnati, OH 45202
800/543-0874, 513/721-2140

Disability Income & Health Insurance Time Saver — Contains summary information about disability income, medicare supplement, and long-term care policies issued by over one hundred companies.

Life Rates & Data — Contains summary information about several hundred traditional whole life, interest-sensitive whole life, and universal life policies.

National Underwriter (Life/Health) — Weekly magazine that periodically contains selected annuity rates and performance data for selected variable product funds.

Quotesmith Corporation
50 North Brockway
Palatine, IL 60067
800/556-9393

Provides interactive on-line databases for term life insurance, single premium deferred annuities, and group medical and dental insurance. This service is intended for agents; however, you may be able to obtain a referral to an agent-subscriber in your area.

Securities Data Company Inc.
225 Broadway, Suite 1607
New York, NY 10007
212/765-5311

Financial Planning — Monthly magazine for financial planners with an annual survey of variable life and annuity products. Latest survey of 82 products is in the October 1989 issue.

Tillinghast/Towers Perrin
12377 Merit Drive, Suite 1200
Dallas, TX 75251-2223
214/363-2451

Note: These services are intended for insurance companies and financial advisers and are not available to the general public on a one-time-only basis.

Tillinghast Universal Life Analytic Study (TULAS) — Contains detailed comparisons and rankings of several hundred universal life policies, based on current illustrations and proprietary analyses. Also provides current interest rates for interest-sensitive whole life, single premium whole life, and deferred annuities.

TERMinology - Term Product Comparison — Provides premiums, cost rankings, and contract descriptions for several hundred term products, for male issue ages 25, 35, 45, and 55, with any specified face amount.

Variable Annuity & Life User Exchange (VALUE) — Provides information about contract features, expenses, and fund performance for variable life and annuity products.

United States Annuities
99 Hoffman Road, Suite 100
Englishtown, NJ 07726
201/521-5110

Annuity Shopper — Bimonthly publication for agents and other advisers with summary information about competitive immediate annuities, fixed deferred annuities, and guaranteed investment contracts. Single-issue orders are accepted.

APPENDIX E: FEE-FOR-SERVICE INSURANCE ADVISORS

Note: We have made no attempt to evaluate the capabilities of the organizations listed, and we caution you not to interpret inclusion on this list as a recommendation. It is your responsibility to verify that a fee-for-service advisor is qualified to offer advice in your particular situation.

Assured Enterprises, Ltd.
600 West Jackson, 8th Floor
Chicago, IL 60606
312/993-0355

Provides consulting services on a fee basis and sells low-load policies with a minimum face amount of $500,000.

Commission-based insurance agents

Some agents provide consulting services on a fee basis. Contact your state or local association of life underwriters for assistance in finding a fee-for-service agent.

Council of Life Insurance Consultants
600 West Jackson, 8th Floor
Chicago, IL 60606
312/993-0355

Provides information about low-load products and fee-for-service consultants. (Note: There may be a charge for this service.)

Fee for Service, Inc.
Airport Executive Center
2203 North Lois Avenue, Suite 814
Tampa, FL 33607
813/874-5662

Sells low-load products directly to the public and provides consulting services on a fee basis; provides support services to other fee-for-service advisors.

National Association of Personal Financial Advisors
1130 Lake Cook Road, Suite 105
Buffalo Grove, IL 60089
708/537-7722

Provides referrals and support services to fee-only financial advisors.

National Insurance Consumer Organization
121 North Payne Street
Alexandria, VA 22314
703/549-8050

Performs rate-of-return calculations for new and existing policies; publishes newsletter and acts as consumer advocate on insurance-related matters. Write to above address for information about NICO's rate-of-return service; do not send insurance policies.

Vest Insurance Marketing Corporation
1800 West Loop South, Suite 210
Houston, TX 77027-3210
800/552-3553, 713/621-1104

Sells low-load products directly to the public.

APPENDIX F: RATING ORGANIZATIONS

The organizations listed evaluate the financial stability of insurance companies and assign ratings. Analytical reports may also be available.

A.M. Best Company
Ambest Road
Oldwick, NJ 08858-9988
201/439-2200

Ratings:

A+ (Superior): Companies which have achieved superior overall performance when compared to the norms of the life/health insurance industry. Insurers generally have demonstrated the strongest ability to meet their respective policyholder and other contractual obligations.

A and A- (Excellent): Companies which have achieved excellent overall performance when compared to the norms of the life/health insurance industry. Insurers generally have demonstrated a strong ability to meet their respective policyholder and other contractual obligations.

B+ (Very Good): Companies which have achieved very good overall performance when compared to the norms of the life/health insurance industry. Insurers generally have demonstrated a very good ability to meet their policyholder and other contractual obligations.

B and B- (Good): Companies which have achieved good overall performance when compared to the norms of the life/health insurance industry. Insurers generally have demonstrated a good ability to meet their policyholder and other contractual obligations.

C+ (Fairly Good): Companies which have achieved fairly good overall performance when compared to the norms of the life/health insurance industry. Insurers generally have demonstrated a fairly good ability to meet their respective policyholder and other contractual obligations.

C and C- (Fair): Companies which have achieved fair overall performance when compared to the norms of the life/health insurance industry. Insurers generally have demonstrated a fair ability to meet their policyholder and other contractual obligations.

Rating Modifiers:

"c"– Contingent Rating: Temporarily assigned to a company when there has been a decline in the performance of its profitability, leverage and/or liquidity results, but the decline has not been significant enough to warrant an actual reduction in the company's previously assigned Rating. Evaluation may be based on the availability of more current information and/or contingent on management's successful execution of a corrective action program. Evaluation may also reflect situations involving matters of a more subjective nature.

"e" – Parent Rating: Indicates a company which meets the minimum premium size requirement, is a wholly owned subsidiary of a rated life/health insurer and maintains interim leverage and liquidity performance comparable to that of its parent, yet has not accumulated at least five consecutive years of operating experience for rating purposes. The parent company's Rating is referenced for companies which meet this criteria until the subsidiary is assigned a Rating.

"p" – Pooled Rating: Assigned to companies under common management or ownership which pool 100 percent of their net business. All premiums, expenses and losses are prorated in accordance with specified percentages that relate to the distribution of the policyholders' surplus of each member of the group. All members participating in the pooling arrangement will be assigned the same Rating and Financial Size Category, based on the group performance.

"r" – Reinsured Rating: Indicates that the Rating and Financial Size Category assigned to the company is that of an affiliated carrier which reinsures 100 percent of the company's written net business.

"w" – Watch List: Indicates the company was placed on the Rating "Watch List" during the year because it experienced a downward trend in profitability, leverage and/or liquidity performance, or other significant event affecting the operations of the subject company. The decline was not significant enough to warrant an actual reduction in the assigned Rating.

"x" – Revised Rating: Indicates the company's present Rating had been revised during the year.

"Not Assigned" Categories:

NA-1 Special Data Filing: Not applicable to Life/Health companies.

NA-2 Less than Minimum Size: Assigned to a company that complies with the requirement to file financial information via the standard NAIC Annual Statement, but does not meet the $1,500,000 minimum size requirement for annual net premium writings. Exceptions are: the company is 100 percent reinsured by a rated company; is a member of a group participating in a business pooling arrangement; was formerly assigned a Rating and is expected to meet the minimum size requirement within a reasonable period of time and in a representative manner. This classification is also assigned to a company that is virtually dormant or has no net insurance business in force.

NA-3 Insufficient Experience: Assigned to a company which meets, or is anticipated to meet, the minimum size requirement, but has not accumulated at least five consecutive years of representative operating experience. The latter includes consistency in both the types of coverages written and the relative volume of net premium writings. Additional years of experience may be required if the company exhibits substantial growth in new business or change(s) in product mix whereby the development of its business may not sufficiently mature at the end of five years to permit a satisfactory evaluation.

NA-4 Rating Procedure Inapplicable: Assigned to a company when the nature of its business and/or operations are such that normal Rating procedure for life/health insurers does not properly apply. Examples are companies writing lines of business uncommon to the life/health field; companies not soliciting business in the United States; companies which have discontinued writing new business and are in a run-off position; or companies whose sole insurance operation is the acceptance of business written directly by a parent, subsidiary or affiliated insurance company; those writing predominately property/casualty insurance under a dual charter; or companies retaining only a small portion of their premiums written.

NA-5 Significant Change: Assigned to a previously Rated company which experiences a significant change in ownership, management or book of business whereby its operating experience may be interrupted or subject to change; or any other relevant event(s) which has or may affect the general trend of a company's operations. This may include pending mergers, substantial growth in net premium writings or redirection of marketing emphasis. Depending upon the nature of the change, the Rating procedure may require a period of one to five years before a company is eligible for a Rating.

NA-6 Reinsured by Unrated Reinsurer: Assigned to a company which has a substantial portion of its book of business reinsured by unrated reinsurers and/or has reinsurance recoverables which represent a substantial portion of its policyholders' surplus due from unrated reinsurers. Exceptions are unrated foreign reinsurers that comply with reporting requirements and satisfy financial performance standards.

NA-7 Below Minimum Standards: Assigned to a company that meets the minimum size and experience requirements, but does not meet the minimum standards for a "C-" Rating.

NA-8 Incomplete Financial Information: Assigned to a company that is eligible for a Rating but fails to submit complete financial information for the current five year period under review by the established deadline. This requirement also includes all domestic life/health subsidiaries in which the company's ownership exceeds 50 percent.

NA-9 Company Request: Assigned to a company that is eligible for a Rating, but rather than incur the Rating Service Fee of $500 per company, requests that the Rating not be published. The majority of these companies, such as captives, operate in markets that do not require a Rating, but cooperate with our request for statement data in order for a report to be prepared and published on their company. This Rating can also be assigned to a company that requests that its Rating remain unpublished because it disagrees with the rating assignment and/or procedure. In this situation, the policy normally requires a minimum period of two years to elapse before the company is eligible for a Rating.

NA-10 Under State Supervision: Assigned when a company is under any form of supervision, control or restraint by state regulatory authorities including, but not limited to, conservatorship, rehabilitation or receivership.

Source: Adapted from *Best's Insurance Reports*.

Duff & Phelps Inc.
Insurance Company Claims Paying Ability Services
55 East Monroe Street, Suite 3600
Chicago, IL 60603
312/263-2610

Ratings:

AAA: Highest claims paying ability. Risk factors are negligible.

AA+, AA, AA-: Very high claims paying ability. Protection factors are strong. Risk is modest, but may vary slightly over time due to economic and/or underwriting conditions.

A+, A, A-: High claims paying ability. Protection factors are average and there is an expectation of variability in risk over time due to economic and/or underwriting conditions.

BBB+, BBB, BBB-: Below average claims paying ability. Protection factors are average. However, there is considerable variability in risk over time due to economic and/or underwriting conditions.

BB+, BB, BB-: Uncertain claims paying ability and less than investment grade quality. However, the company is deemed likely to meet these obligations when due. Protection factors will vary widely with changes in economic and/or underwriting conditions.

B+, B, B-: Possessing risk that policyholder and contractholder obligations will not be paid when due. Protection factors will vary widely with changes in economic and underwriting conditions, or company fortunes.

CCC: There is substantial risk that policyholder and contractholder obligations will not be paid when due. Company has been or is likely to be placed under state insurance department supervision.

Source: Duff & Phelps, Inc.

Moody's Investors Service
99 Church Street
New York, NY 10007
212/553-0300

Ratings:

Aaa: Insurance companies judged to be of the best quality. Their policy obligations carry the smallest degree of credit risk. While the financial strength of these companies is likely to change, such changes are most unlikely to impair their fundamentally strong position.

Aa: Insurance companies judged to be of high quality by all standards. Together with the Aaa group they comprise what are generally known as high grade companies. They are rated lower than the best companies because long term risks appear somewhat larger.

A: Insurance companies that possess many favorable attributes and are considered upper medium grade. Factors giving security to punctual payment of policyholder obligations are considered adequate, but elements may be present which suggest a susceptibility to impairment some time in the future.

Baa: Insurance companies considered as medium grade, i.e., their policyholder obligations are neither highly protected nor poorly secured. Factors giving security to punctual payment of policyholder obligations are considered adequate for the present time but certain protective elements may be lacking or may be characteristically unreliable over any great length of time. These companies' policy obligations lack outstanding investment characteristics and in fact have speculative elements as well.

Ba: Insurance companies judged to have speculative elements; their future cannot be considered as well secured. Often the ability of these companies to discharge policyholder obligations may be very moderate and thereby not well safeguarded during other good and bad times in the future. Uncertainty of position characterizes policyholder obligations of insurance companies in this class.

B: Policyholder obligations generally lack characteristics of the desirable insurance policy. Assurance of punctual payment of policyholder obligations over any long period of time is small.

Caa: Insurance companies of poor standing. They may be in default on their policyholder obligations or there may be present elements of danger with respect to punctual payment of policyholder obligations and claims.

Ca: Insurance companies which are highly speculative. Such companies are often in default on their policyholder obligations or have other marked shortcomings.

C: Insurance companies which are the lowest rated class of insurance companies and can be regarded as having extremely poor prospects of ever attaining real investment standing.

Source: Moody's Investors Service.

Standard & Poor's Corporation
Standard & Poor's Insurance Rating Services
25 Broadway
New York, NY 10004
212/208-8000

AAA: Insurers offer *superior* financial security on both an absolute and relative basis. They possess the highest safety and have an overwhelming capacity to meet policyholder obligations.

AA: Insurers offer *excellent* financial security, and their capacity to meet policyholder obligations differs only in a small degree from insurers rated "AAA."

A: Insurers offer a *strong* financial security, but their capacity to meet policyholder obligations is somewhat more susceptible to adverse changes in economic or underwriting conditions than more highly rated insurers.

BBB: Insurers offer *good* financial security, but their capacity to meet policyholder obligations is considered more vulnerable to adverse economic or underwriting conditions than that of more highly rated insurers.

BB: Insurers offer *adequate* financial security for "short-tail" or short-term policies, but their capacity to meet policyholder obligations is considered vulnerable to adverse economic or underwriting conditions and may not be adequate for "long-tail" or long-term policies.

Speculative Claims-Paying Ability

B: Insurers are currently able to meet policyholder obligations, but their vulnerability to adverse economic or underwriting conditions is considered high.

CCC: Insurers are vulnerable to adverse economic or underwriting conditions to the extent that their continued capacity to meet policyholder obligations is highly questionable unless a favorable environment prevails.

CC, C: Insurers may not be meeting all policyholder obligations, may be operating under the jurisdiction of insurance regulators, and are vulnerable to liquidation.

D: Insurers have been placed under an order of liquidation.

Source: Standard & Poor's Corporation.

APPENDIX G: STATE INSURANCE DEPARTMENTS

In addition to their primary responsibility of monitoring solvency, state insurance departments also handle consumer complaints. Here are their phone numbers:

Alabama	205/269-3550 (or 3554)
Alaska	907/465-2515
American Samoa	684/633-4116
Arizona	602/255-5400
Arkansas	501/371-1325
California	415/557-9624
Colorado	303/620-4300
Connecticut	203/566-5275
Delaware	302/736-4251
District of Columbia	202/727-5422
Florida	904/488-3440
Georgia	404/656-2056
Guam	011/671-477-1040
Hawaii	808/548-5450 (or 6522)
Idaho	208/334-2250
Illinois	217/782-4515
Indiana	317/232-2386
Iowa	515/281-5705
Kansas	913/296-7801
Kentucky	502/564-3630
Louisiana	504/342-5328

Maine	207/582-8707
Maryland	301/333-2520 (or 6300)
Massachusetts	617/727-7189
Michigan	517/373-9273
Minnesota	612/296-6848
Mississippi	601/359-3569
Missouri	314/751-2451
Montana	406/444-2040
Nebraska	402/471-2201
Nevada	702/885-4270
New Hampshire	603/271-2261
New Jersey	609/292-5363
New Mexico	505/827-4500
New York	212/602-0478 (or 0429)
North Carolina	919/733-7473
North Dakota	701/224-2440
Ohio	614/644-2658
Oklahoma	405/521-2828
Oregon	503/378-4271
Pennsylvania	717/787-5173
Puerto Rico	809/722-8686
Rhode Island	401/277-2246
South Carolina	803/737-6117
South Dakota	605/773-3563
Tennessee	615/741-2241
Texas	512/463-6464
Utah	801/530-6400
Vermont	802/828-3301
Virginia	804/786-3741
Virgin Islands	809/774-2991
Washington	206/753-7301
West Virginia	304/348-3394
Wisconsin	608/266-0102
Wyoming	307/777-7401

Source: Best's Insurance Reports, NICO Newsletter
(November/December 1988), other sources.

APPENDIX H: STANDARD MORTALITY TABLES

Mortality rates are often expressed as the number of deaths during the year per one thousand individuals alive at the beginning of the year. The 1980 Commissioners Standard Ordinary Mortality Table is used to compute required reserves for newly-issued life insurance policies. Many companies also use it to determine the guaranteed cost-of-insurance rates for universal life and similar products.

There are several versions of the 1980 CSO Table, based on sex, smoking status, age-nearest-birthday versus age-last-birthday, and aggregate versus select-and-ultimate. The annual mortality rates shown below are for six aggregate (new and existing issues combined), age-nearest-birthday versions of the table: male aggregate (nonsmoker and smoker combined), male nonsmoker, male smoker, female aggregate, female nonsmoker, and female smoker.

Note that these tables are used for conservative valuation purposes, and therefore overstate the actual chances of dying.

DEATHS PER 1,000: 1980 CSO TABLES

Male, aggregate, age nearest birthday.

Attained Age	Aggregate	Nonsmoker	Smoker
0	4.18	–	–
5	0.90	–	–
10	0.73	–	–
15	1.33	1.29	1.65
20	1.90	1.68	2.31
25	1.77	1.52	2.14
30	1.73	1.44	2.10
35	2.11	1.69	2.63
40	3.02	2.29	3.94
45	4.55	3.32	6.27
50	6.71	4.91	9.56
55	10.47	7.82	15.14
60	16.08	12.64	23.19
65	25.42	21.13	36.29
70	39.51	34.63	54.48

75	64.19	58.80	83.77
80	98.84	93.67	121.59
85	152.95	149.20	174.20
90	221.77	220.19	233.69
95	329.96	329.96	329.96
99	1000.00	1000.00	1000.00

Female, aggregate, age nearest birthday.

Attained Age	Aggregate	Nonsmoker	Smoker
0	2.89	–	–
5	0.76	–	–
10	0.68	–	–
15	0.85	0.84	0.94
20	1.05	1.01	1.16
25	1.16	1.09	1.29
30	1.35	1.24	1.55
35	1.65	1.47	1.94
40	2.42	2.08	3.00
45	3.56	2.99	4.61
50	4.96	4.19	6.54
55	7.09	6.13	9.40
60	9.47	8.51	12.51
65	14.59	13.55	19.07
70	22.11	21.20	27.95
75	38.24	37.32	46.64
80	65.99	65.12	76.26
85	116.10	115.38	126.42
90	190.75	190.39	197.01
95	317.32	317.32	317.32
99	1000.00	1000.00	1000.00

APPENDIX I: SUPPLEMENTS TO INSURANCE COMPANY ANNUAL STATEMENTS

Insurance companies are required to file a detailed annual statement with state insurance departments each year. Most of this information will be of little interest to consumers. However, two supplements to the annual statement can provide additional information about the company's products.

The supplement to Schedule M has been required since 1983 and provides dividend information. The supplement to Exhibit 8 has been required since 1987 and provides information about *nonguaranteed elements,* such as interest rates and insurance charges. Each one contains two sections of descriptive material and one set of specific questions, some of which ask about the company's ability to support its current illustrations.

These supplements are public documents; to obtain a copy, contact the company or your state insurance department (see Appendix G).

Disclosure of Dividend Practices
(Supplement to Schedule M)

Process of Dividend Determination

Description of Experience Factors (investment income, claims, expense, termination, tax)

General Interrogatories:

1. Has the contribution principle been followed in determining dividends?

2. Since this schedule was last filed, has any material change occurred with respect to the determination of policy factors?

3a. Since this schedule was last filed, have there been any changes in the scales of dividends on new or existing business authorized for illustration by the company?

3b. Since this schedule was last filed, have there been any changes in the scales of dividends apportioned for payment?

3c. For each major block of business, indicate when the dividend scale was last changed (including changes described in b. above) and indicate the extent of such change in terms of the percentage by which dividends payable under the new scale exceeded or were less than those that would have been paid in the year of change had the scale not been changed.

4. Does the dividend scale incorporate the use of projections or forecasts for any period in excess of two years beyond the effective date of the scale?

5. In the basis of determining investment income experience factors, state whether the company uses (a) a portfolio average approach, (b) an investment generation approach, or (c) a combination of the two approaches. If (b) or (c), describe the general basis used, including the issue year groupings.

6. With respect to policy loan provisions:

6a. Describe how differences in such provisions affect dividends.

6b. Does the dividend scale contain any provision for varying the amount of dividend in accordance with the extent to which an individual policy's loan provision is utilized?

7. Does the company pay termination dividends on its policies?

7a. Are they payable on death, surrender, and maturity?

7b. Are they payable or credited either upon the commencement of non-forfeiture insurance or upon termination thereof by death, surrender, or maturity?

7c. Do they reflect the incidence, size, and growth of amounts that may be attributed to the policies in question?

8. Does the undersigned believe dividends illustrated on new or existing business can be paid if current experience continues?

9. Does the undersigned believe there is a substantial probability that because of expected deterioration of experience, the dividends illustrated on new or existing business cannot be maintained for at least two years?

10. Describe any aspects of the determination of the dividend scale not covered above that involve material departures from the actuarial principles and practices of the American Academy of Actuaries applicable to the determination of dividends paid by mutual companies.

11. Describe any material changes in the basis of determination of the dividend scale that were made since this schedule was last filed and that are not covered above.

Disclosure of Nonguaranteed Element
Determination Procedures
(Supplement to Exhibit 8)

Determination Process

Description of Experience Factors (investment income, claims, expense, termination, tax)

General Interrogatories:

1. Since this statement was last filed, have there been any changes in the values of nonguaranteed elements on new or existing business authorized for illustration by the company? If yes, describe the changes that were made.

2. Since this statement was last filed, have there been any changes in the values of nonguaranteed elements actually charged or credited? If yes, describe the changes that were made.

3. Indicate to what extent any changes described in 1 or 2 vary from the policy and/or general methods and procedures last reported for the affected contracts.

4. Are the anticipated experience factors underlying any nonguaranteed elements different from current experience? If yes, describe in general terms the ways in which future experience is anticipated to differ from current experience and the nonguaranteed element factors which are affected by such anticipation.

5. State whether anticipated investment income experience factors are based on (a) a portfolio average approach, (b) an investment generation approach, or (c) other. If (b) or (c), describe the general basis used, including the investment generation groupings.

6. Describe how the company allocates anticipated experience among its various classes of business.

7. Does the undersigned believe there is a substantial probability that illustrations authorized by the company to be presented on new and existing business cannot be supported by currently anticipated experience? If yes, indicate which classes and explain.

8. Describe any aspects of the determination of nonguaranteed elements not covered above that involve material departures from the actuarial principles and practices of the American Academy of Actuaries applicable to the determination of nonguaranteed elements.

APPENDIX J: OTHER SOURCES OF INFORMATION

Essential Resources

Tax Facts 1. Comprehensive tax guide for insurance products, retirement plans, and estates and trusts, in a question-and-answer format. Published by The National Underwriter Company, 420 East 4th St., Cincinnati, OH 45202, 800/543-0874, 513/721-2140. $15.50; discount if purchased with *Tax Facts 2* (a similar tax guide for other investments).

General Information

These publications offer additional information and other perspectives on how to select and use insurance products:

American Bar Association (Real Property, Probate and Trust Law Section). *The Life Insurance Counselor: Life Insurance Products, Illustrations, and Due Diligence.* Chicago: 1989.

American Bar Association (Real Property, Probate and Trust Law Section). *The Life Insurance Counselor: Federal Income Taxation of Life Insurance.* Chicago: 1989.

American Council of Life Insurance. *Life Insurance Fact Book.* Washington, DC; revised annually (free).

Applegarth, Virginia. *How to Protect Your Family with Insurance.* Boston: Houghton Mifflin Company, 1990.

Bailard, Biehl and Kaiser, Inc. *How to Buy the Right Insurance at the Right Price.* Homewood, IL: Dow Jones-Irwin, 1989.

Baldwin, Ben G. *The Complete Book of Insurance: Protecting Your Life, Health, Property & Income.* Chicago: Probus Publishing, 1989.

Baldwin, Ben G. and William G. Droms. *The Life Insurance Investment Advisor.* Chicago: Probus Publishing, 1988.

Belth, Joseph M. *Life Insurance: A Consumer's Handbook, 2nd Ed.* Bloomington, IN: Indiana University Press, 1985.

Black, Kenneth Jr. & Harold Skipper, Jr. *Life Insurance, 11th Ed.* Englewood Cliffs, NJ: Prentice-Hall, Inc., 1987.

Brownlie, William D. *The Life Insurance Buyer's Guide.* New York: McGraw-Hill, 1989.

Dacey, Norman F. *What's Wrong with Your Life Insurance.* New York: Macmillan, 1989 (interesting anecdotes, but don't take the book too seriously).

Dorfman, Mark S. & Saul W. Adelman. *The Dow Jones-Irwin Guide to Life Insurance*. Homewood, IL: Dow Jones-Irwin, 1988.

Dorfman, Mark S. and Saul W. Adelman. *Life Insurance and Financial Planning*. Homewood, IL: Dow Jones-Irwin, 1988.

Editors of Consumer Reports with Trudy Lieberman. *Life Insurance: How to Buy the Right Policy from the Right Company at the Right Price, 2nd Ed.* New York: Consumer Reports Books, 1989.

Hunt, James H. *Taking the Bite Out of Insurance*. Alexandria, VA: National Insurance Consumer Organization, 1988.

The Insurance Forum (published by Joseph M. Belth, P.O. Box 245, Ellettsville, IN 47429), monthly investigatory newsletter on insurance topics.

Mehr, Robert I. and Sandra G. Gustavson. *Life Insurance: Theory and Practice, 4th Ed.* Homewood, IL: Richard D. Irwin, 1987.

National Insurance Consumer Organization. *Buyer's Guide to Insurance*, September 1988.

National Underwriter Company. *Field Guide to Estate Planning, Business Planning, & Employee Benefits; Comprehensive Deferred Compensation; Comprehensive Split Dollar; Tax Planning Techniques for the Closely Held Corporation.*

Tobias, Andrew. *The Invisible Bankers*. New York: Pocket Books, 1982.

Methods of Comparing Policies

There is extensive academic and professional literature on methods of comparing life insurance policies. Here's a sampling:

Auxier, Albert L. "An Examination of Selected Aspects of Price Disclosure in the Life Insurance Industry with Special Emphasis on the Interest Yield Method." Unpublished Ph.D. dissertation, University of Iowa, Iowa City, Iowa; 1974. Photocopies are available from UMI, 300 North Zeeb Road, Ann Arbor, MI 48106, (Order #7421872).

Babbel, David F. "Measuring Inflation Impact on Life Insurance Costs." *The Journal of Risk and Insurance* (September 1979).

Babbel, David F. and Kim B. Staking, "A Capital Budgeting Analysis of Life Insurance Costs in the United States: 1950-1979." *The Journal of Finance* (March 1983).

Belth, Joseph M. "The Rate of Return on the Savings Element in Cash-Value Life Insurance." *The Journal of Risk and Insurance* (December 1968).

Belth, Joseph M. "The Relationship Between Benefits and Premiums in Life Insurance." *The Journal of Risk and Insurance* (March 1969).

Belth, Joseph M. "Deceptive Sale Practices in the Life Insurance Business." *The Journal of Risk and Insurance* (June 1974).

Belth, Joseph M. "Information Disclosure to the Life Insurance Consumer." *Drake Law Review Insurance Law Annual* (December 1975), Littleton, CO: Fred B. Rothman & Co., Law Books.

Belth, Joseph M. "A Case Study in the Operation of NAIC Advisory Committees." *The Insurance Forum* (January 1985).

Belth, Joseph M. "More Pseudo Disclosure from the NAIC." *The Insurance Forum* (February 1985).

Cherin, Antony C. and Robert C. Hutchins, "The Rate of Return on Universal Life Insurance," *The Journal of Risk and Insurance* (December 1987).

Cooper, Robert W. "The NAIC and FTC Policy Summary Deadlock: A Possible Compromise." *CLU Journal* (October 1980).

D'Arcy, Stephen P. and Keun Chang Lee. "Universal/Variable Life Insurance Versus Similar Unbundled Investment Strategies." *The Journal of Risk and Insurance* (September 1987).

Formisano, Roger A. "The NAIC Model Life Insurance Solicitation Regulation: Measuring the Consumer Impact in New Jersey." *The Journal of Risk and Insurance* (March 1981).

Hutchins, Robert C. and Charles E. Quenneville. "Rate of Return Versus Interest-Adjusted Cost." *The Journal of Risk and Insurance* (March 1975).

Ingraham, Harold G., Jr. "An Analysis of Two Cost Comparison Methods—Interest Adjusted Cost vs. Linton Yield." *CLU Journal* (October 1979).

Kensicki, Peter R. "Consumer Valuation of Life Insurance—A Capital Budgeting Approach." *The Journal of Risk and Insurance* (December 1974).

Murray, Michael L. "Analyzing the Investment Value of Cash Value Life Insurance." *The Journal of Risk and Insurance* (March 1976).

National Association of Insurance Commissioners. "Interim Report of the NAIC Task Force on Life Insurance Disclosure System" (December 3, 1980, NAIC Proceedings, 1981 Vol. 1).

National Association of Insurance Commissioners. "Yield Index Advisory Committee Report" (November 25, 1985, NAIC Proceedings, 1986 Vol. 1).

Ryall, Peter L. J. "A Fast, More Meaningful Twenty-Year Net Cost Formula." *Transactions*, Vol. XXI (1969); Society of Actuaries.

Scheel, William C. "A Critique of the Interest-Adjusted Net Cost Index." *The Journal of Risk and Insurance* (June 1973).

Scheel, William C. "Company Retention—An Unreliable Indicator of the Cost of Life Insurance to the Policyholder." *The Journal of Risk and Insurance* (March 1975).

Schleef, Harold J. "Whole Life Cost Comparisons Based Upon the Year of Required Protection." *The Journal of Risk and Insurance* (March 1989).

Skipper, Harold, Jr. "An Idea Whose Time Has Passed." *Best's Review (Life/Health)* (August 1985).

Smith, Michael L. "The Life Insurance Policy as an Options Package." *The Journal of Risk and Insurance* (December 1982).

Society of Actuaries Special Committee on Cost Comparison Methods and Related Issues. "Analysis of Life Insurance Cost Comparison Index Methods" (September 1974).

Trowbridge, Charles L. "An Extension of the NAIC System for Life Insurance Cost Comparisons" and discussions. *Transactions*, Vol. XXXII (1980), Society of Actuaries.

Walden, Michael L. "The Whole Life Insurance Policy as an Options Package: An Empirical Investigation." *The Journal of Risk and Insurance* (March 1985).

Winter, Ralph A. "On the Choice of an Index for Disclosure in the Life Insurance Market: An Axiomatic Approach." *The Journal of Risk and Insurance* (December 1982).

Winter, Ralph A. "On the Rate Structure of the American Life Insurance Market." *The Journal of Finance* (March 1981).

APPENDIX K: HOW TO READ A LIFE INSURANCE POLICY ILLUSTRATION

There is no standard format for life insurance policy illustrations (also called *ledger statements*), so you will have to take a few minutes to get acquainted with each one that you receive. Each company decides what information to include and what the order and headings of the columns should be, in accordance with the sales situation.

Here are the main items to look for:

1. Insured's age. This could be age-nearest-birthday or age-last-birth-day.

2. Insured's underwriting class. This will depend on the company; the distinctions could be smoker/nonsmoker, standard/preferred, or some other classification system.

3. Initial face amount.

4. Future policy values—premium, death benefit, cash surrender value, and dividend (if any)—for each year, based on nonguaranteed interest, mortality, expense, and dividend (if any) assumptions. These amounts can be shown as of the beginning or the end of the policy year. In some cases, the column headings or footnotes will make this clear; in other cases, you'll have to figure it out for yourself or ask the company.

5. Guaranteed policy values, assuming guaranteed interest, mortality, and expenses. For dividend-paying policies, these values usually assume that no dividends are paid; however, some illustrations can be misleading, so you may need to specifically ask, "What would the premiums, death benefits, and cash surrender values be if no dividends were paid at any time?"

6. Explanations and caveats. These are usually at the end and provide additional information about the assumptions made in preparing the illustration. The comments may or may not be informative.

7. Other stuff. This includes interest-adjusted cost indexes, a summary section, and, for complicated situations, other columns of policy values. Some of these items may be required by state law.

Here's the format that one low-load company uses for a simple situation involving one insured/owner:

Policy Illustration: An Example of One Company's Format

```
                          Insurance Company Name

$250,000     Policy            Non-Smoker              Death Benefit Option A
                        Annual Initial Planned Premium $5,000.00
T. Weedledee                                               Male Age 40
```

End of Yr.	Age	Yearly Premium	Projected** Surrender Value	Projected** Death Benefit	Guaranteed## Surrender Value	Guaranteed## Death Benefit
1	41	5000	5122	250000	5122	250000
2	42	5000	10509	250000	9764	250000
3	43	5000	16241	250000	14584	250000
4	44	5000	22354	250000	19584	250000
5	45	0	23423	250000	19665	250000
6	46	0	24529	250000	19692	250000
7	47	0	25714	250000	19656	250000
8	48	0	27004	250000	19550	250000
9	49	0	28902	250000	19366	250000
10	50	0	30922	250000	19089	250000
11	51	0	33072	250000	18712	250000
12	52	0	35365	250000	18211	250000
13	53	0	37811	250000	17563	250000
14	54	0	40419	250000	16746	250000
15	55	0	43206	250000	15729	250000
16	56	0	46127	250000	14482	250000
17	57	0	49227	250000	12973	250000
18	58	0	52517	250000	11171	250000
19	59	0	56007	250000	9042	250000
20	60	0	59709	250000	6532	250000
At Age						
25	65	0	81981	250000	0	0
34	74	0	146737	250000	0	0
55	95	0	828809	837097	0	0

```
----- Summary Values (Projected)** -----|-- (5% Int. Adjusted) --
                                         |           Cost      Pmt
                                         |           Index    Index
                   Surrender     Total   |          --------------------
                     Value      Premiums |            Guaranteed
                   --------     --------  |          --------  -------
      10 Yrs         30922        20000   | 10 Yr     3.40      9.18
      20 Yrs         59709        20000   | 20 Yr     4.94      5.69
      Age 65         81981        20000   |            Projected
      Age 95        828809        20000   |          --------  -------
Life Expectancy                           | 10 Yr    -0.18      9.18
      Age 74        146737        20000   | 20 Yr    -1.19      5.69

   Presented By: T. Weedledum              11-15-89      Page 1 of 2
              THIS IS AN ILLUSTRATION, NOT A CONTRACT.         V 5.6
```

continued

Policy Illustration: An Example of One Company's Format

Insurance Company Name

$250,000   Policy   Non-Smoker   Death Benefit Option A

Annual Initial Planned Premium $5,000.00

T. Weedledee   Male Age 40

POLICY BENEFITS			PREMIUM	YEARS PAYABLE
$ 250000	Policy	Non-Smoker	$ 1105.00	54
			$ 1105.00	Initial Annual Premium

Guaranteed values assume current cost of insurance, interest rate and expenses for the entire first year.

Illustrated values will maintain coverage to age 95.

** Illustrated interest rate is 8.25%.
Actual interest rate is declared monthly with initial rate determined by date of policy issue. Minimum interest rate is 4.5%. Projected values are end of year, for illustrative purposes only and may not represent actual policy results.

Values in year nine and beyond reflect lower expense necessary after amortization of initial expense.

Interest is added to the cash value account monthly. New premiums receive interest from the date of receipt. Cost of insurance and expense charges are deducted monthly. Actual accounts values will differ from illustrated values due to rounding and will be furnished yearly in an annual report.

Cost of insurance and expense charges are based on current company experience without projections. Future changes in experience will be reflected in future charges.

This illustration is based on the assumed current interest rate for new premiums. All new premiums receive a twelve month guarantee at the rate in effect during the month the premium is received.

Since life insurance contains so many different charges and credits that are variable, the actual performance will depend on those variables. (For comparison purposes the most reliable illustrated values are the early year values).

Presented By: T. Weedledum   11-15-89   Page 2 of 2
                   THIS IS AN ILLUSTRATION, NOT A CONTRACT.   V 5.6

GLOSSARY

Accumulation unit: A variable annuity accounting measure that is used during the accumulation period to keep track of account values.

Adjustable life: (1) A more flexible version of traditional whole life that allows a policyholder to change the plan of insurance from term to whole life or whole life to term. (2) Universal life.

Aggregate: Meaning varies with context. In contrast to select and ultimate, it means that new and existing policies are combined in one pool. In contrast to nonsmoker/smoker, it means that nonsmokers and smokers are combined. May also mean that males and females are combined. See also *Select and ultimate*.

Annuitize: To convert a lump sum into a series of periodic payments.

Annuity unit: A variable annuity accounting measure that is used during the annuity period to determine payment amounts.

Antirebating law: Most states prohibit agents from rebating commissions in order to induce insurance buyers to purchase. Antirebating laws are vigorously defended by regulators and agent lobbying organizations when challenged by consumer groups. In some cases, however, agents can effectively rebate a portion of their commissions by offering clients low-commission products or riders—if the clients ask.

Antiselection (also **Adverse selection**): The natural tendency of insurance buyers to act in their own best interests when making choices. For example, a healthy insured might choose to drop a term insurance policy, whereas a terminally ill insured would "select against" the company by exercising the option to renew it. A company can also be exposed to investment antiselection, as when it allows additional amounts to be deposited at a previously guaranteed interest rate.

Asset share: The accumulated assets of a block of policies divided by the number of policies still in force. The asset share is based on the company's own internal accounting and is primarily of interest to pricing actuaries.

Asset/liability management: The process of aligning the term structure of assets and liabilities in accordance with a company's willingness to assume interest-rate, market, and default risks.

Benefit period: For disability income insurance, the maximum length of time for which benefits can be paid.

Cash value: Usually, the cash surrender value; i.e., what you get if you drop the policy. Sometimes the account value; i.e., the accumulated funds within the policy before surrender charges.

Consideration: Payments made to an insurance company in exchange for an annuity contract. See also *Premium*.

Contribution principle: The principle that dividends should be determined in accordance with the contribution made by each class of policies to the company's surplus.

Death benefit: The amount paid by the insurance company upon the death of the insured.

Direct recognition: For traditional whole life products, the practice of adjusting dividends to reflect borrowing activity.

Dividend: (1) For income tax purposes, a refund of a portion of the gross premiums. (2) A payment to policyholders based on the difference between guaranteed and actual investment, mortality, and expense experience.

Dividend history: One day an insurance agent, an engineer, and a philosopher were riding on a train through Texas. Seeing a lone black cow grazing in the distance, the insurance agent remarked, "Oh look! All of the cows in Texas are black."

"We don't know that for sure," the engineer replied. "All we can say is that at least one of the cows in Texas is black."

"We don't know that either," the philosopher scolded. "All we really know is that at least one of the cows in Texas is black on at least one of its sides."

A dividend history is a statement about one side of one cow, often used by insurance companies and agents to describe all of the cows in Texas.

Divisible surplus: The portion of surplus that is set aside each year to be distributed to policyholders through dividends.

Effective cost of borrowing: What it really costs to borrow against a life insurance policy, taking into account any reductions in dividends and interest. See also *Net cost of borrowing*.

Excess interest: For universal life policies, the interest in excess of the guaranteed rate.

Face amount: The initial death benefit of the policy, usually stated on the cover page.

Fractional premium: A premium that is paid other than annually; i.e. semiannually, quarterly, or monthly.

General account: All of an insurance company's unsegregated assets. See also *Separate account*.

Grace period: The maximum period of time during which the contract will continue in force if premiums are not paid.

Gross interest rate: For universal life, the credited interest rate.

Illustration (also **Ledger statement**): A projection that shows future premiums, death benefits, and cash values under a hypothetical (sometimes vaguely defined) set of assumptions.

Incontestability: A contractual provision that prohibits an insurance company from denying a claim after a specified period of time (typically two years) due to misstatements on the application.

Indeterminate premium: A rate structure that consists of a higher guaranteed premium and a lower actual premium that reflects anticipated experience; allows companies to offer competitive products without having to set up the large reserves that would be necessary if the lower rates were guaranteed.

Interest sensitive: Generally refers to universal life and other products with disclosed interest elements; however, even traditional whole life is interest sensitive in the sense that dividends fluctuate with interest rates. The best definition was crafted by Professor Joseph M. Belth in 1985: "Interest sensitive life insurance products are those designed to be sold with heavy emphasis on high gross interest rates at a time when consumers are sensitive to interest rates."

Investment generation method (also **Investment year method, new money method**): A method of allocating investment income among policyholders that takes account of the timing of deposits and withdrawals, producing a series of rates.

Lapse rate: The ratio of the amount of business lost during the year to the amount in force at the beginning of the year, measured in terms of face amount, premium, or number of policies. See also *Persistency*.

Ledger statement: See *Illustration*.

Life underwriter: (1) Insurance agent. (2) Home office employee responsible for assigning an applicant to an appropriate risk class.

Linton yield: The rate of return needed in order to match the cash surrender value of the whole life policy if a consumer bought term insurance and invested independently.

Minimum deposit: A method of premium payment in which the first few premiums are paid in cash and the rest are paid by borrowing against the policy.

Modified endowment contract: A life insurance contract with large premium payments during the early years that fails the so-called seven-pay test established by the Technical and Miscellaneous Revenue Act of 1988. MECs enjoy less favorable tax treatment than non-MEC life insurance contracts.

Mutual company: An insurance company that is owned by its policyholders, although it may sometimes seem as if the company is owned by no one at all. A mutual company can become a stock company by "demutualizing." See also *Stock company*.

Net amount at risk: The difference between the death benefit and the policy's internal fund (account value, cash value, or reserve, depending on the type of policy); in other words, the company's true exposure in the event of the insured's death.

Net cost of borrowing (also **Net loan cost**): The difference between what the company charges for a loan and what it credits a policyholder. This usually understates the true cost of borrowing and is therefore misleading. See also *Effective cost of borrowing*.

Net premium: (1) The guaranteed (gross) premium less dividends. (2) An actuarially determined premium that ignores expenses and is used in the computation of policy reserves, cash values, and dividends. *Net single premiums* are used in some variable life policies to link changes in the death benefit to investment performance.

New money method: See *Investment generation method*.

Nonforfeiture options: The ways in which a policyholder can terminate a premium-paying contract. The usual choices are cash value (a lump sum payment), paid-up insurance (a policy with a lower face amount, using the cash value as a single premium), and extended term insurance (a single premium term insurance policy with the same face amount and a specified duration).

Nonparticipating (also **Nonpar**): A policy that is not eligible for dividends. The distinction between participating and nonparticipating has been rendered meaningless by nontraditional products such as universal life. See also *Participating*.

Ordinary: Life insurance policies with a face amount over $1,000 that are sold to individuals; other categories are industrial life (small-denomination policies sold to individuals), group life, and credit life.

Paid-up addition: For traditional whole life policies, an additional amount of single premium, low-load whole life insurance purchased with policy dividends.

Partial surrender: (1) A proportionate reduction in the death benefit, face amount, and premium; for example, by dividing a policy in half and surrendering one of the parts. (2) A withdrawal from the cash value, with no effect on premiums. The effect on the death benefit will depend on the contract.

Participating: A policy that is eligible for dividends. See also *Nonparticipating*.

Permanent insurance: Cash value life insurance. Agents sometimes use the permanent/temporary dichotomy as a subtle marketing tool to encourage prospects to buy high-commission "permanent" cash value insurance instead of low-commission "temporary" term insurance. Consumers can defend themselves against this manipulation by remembering the words of eminent actuary Charles Trowbridge: "There is nothing more permanent than a term policy fully in force at the time of the insured's death—and nothing more temporary than a whole life policy that lapses shortly after issue."

Persistency: This refers to how long the company's policies stay in force. A block of business has good persistency if most policyholders keep their policies in force for a long time. See also *Lapse rate.*

Portfolio average method: A method of allocating investment income among policyholders by which everyone receives a pooled rate, regardless of the timing of deposits and withdrawals. See also *Investment generation method.*

Premium: The payment made by a policyholder to an insurance company. See also *Consideration.*

Pricing (also **Product development) actuary:** An actuary who is responsible for designing and repricing insurance products.

Profit test: An analysis prepared by an actuary to determine if an insurance product satisfies the issuer's profit objectives.

Refund of unearned premium: The practice of increasing the death or surrender proceeds by the unearned portion of that year's premium.

Reinsurance: A transfer of risk from one insurance company to another. The issuing, or *direct-writing,* company "cedes" a portion of its business to the reinsurer in exchange for a financial benefit. Reinsurance transactions can take place in several forms, with different impacts on each company's assets, liabilities, and surplus.

Repricing: The process of making periodic changes to policy cost factors, such as dividends and insurance charges, in accordance with the company's actual or expected experience.

Retention: (1) The maximum amount at risk a company is willing to accept on any one life. (2) A measure of policy cost that takes into account the yearly probabilities of death and lapsation. *Company retention* is the present expected value of the premiums less the present expected value of all benefits received.

Rider: A supplemental benefit that can be attached to the base policy, with or without an additional premium.

Risk classification: The sometimes-controversial process of dividing insurance applicants into groups with similar risk characteristics. It involves a mixture of science, judgment, and public policy considerations. An insurance company can either use cost-based pricing and assign applicants to different risk classes or charge everyone the same price, forcing its low-risk customers to subsidize the high-risk ones.

Segmentation: The practice of subdividing the general account for internal management purposes, in order to match assets and liabilities by product line.

Select and ultimate: Mortality rates that vary both by age and duration, with lower "select" rates during the early years to reflect the effects of medical selection. For example, the second-year rate for a 35-year-old would be higher than the first-year rate for a 36-year-old, but the "ultimate" rate at age 50 would be the same for both. See also *Aggregate*.

Separate account: A segregated portfolio of assets used for variable life, variable annuity, and pension products. See also *General account*.

Settlement (also **Payment**) **options:** The ways in which a beneficiary or policyholder can elect to receive the death or surrender proceeds, other than in a lump sum.

Single premium whole life: Generally a type of fixed-interest cash value policy, with no explicit cost of insurance charges, that is purchased with a single premium.

Solvency: A company is solvent when its statutory assets exceed its statutory liabilities.

Statutory accounting: A conservative set of accounting procedures prescribed by state regulatory agencies for the purpose of monitoring solvency. Statutory accounting differs from generally accepted accounting principles (GAAP) in the treatment of acquisition costs and the valuation of assets and liabilities.

Stock company: An insurance company that is owned by its shareholders. See also *Mutual company*.

Surplus: A company's accumulated earnings used to finance new business and to provide a cushion against unfavorable experience.

Surplus strain: The reduction in a company's capital and surplus caused by the acquisition costs and reserves needed for new business.

Survivorship life (also **Second-to-die, last-to-die, joint and last survivor**): A life insurance policy that pays off after the death of more than one person.

Target surplus (also **Benchmark surplus, dedicated surplus, required surplus**): The capital and surplus that a company allocates to a group of policies for internal management purposes, in order to maintain a favorable rating, reduce the risk of insolvency, and price its products adequately.

1035 exchange: A tax-free policy exchange under the provisions of Section 1035 of the Internal Revenue Code.

Terminal dividend: An extra dividend that is paid upon death or surrender when a policy has been in force for a certain number of years.

Three-factor formula: An actuarial formula that is often used to determine dividends, based on differences between actual and guaranteed interest, mortality, and expenses.

Tontines: A type of insurance arrangement in which benefits are forfeited by policyholders who die or drop their policies, and the released funds are used to increase the benefits of remaining policyholders. Tontines were popular in the late nineteenth century, but numerous abuses, lawsuits, and public outrage led state governments to restrict their use. Tontines are making a comeback of sorts in some of today's life insurance and annuity products.

Traditional whole life (also **Straight life, whole life**): A type of fixed-interest cash value policy with fixed premiums and undisclosed interest, mortality, and expense elements.

Underwriting: The process of assessing an applicant's risk characteristics.

Universal life: A type of fixed-interest cash value policy with separately identified interest, mortality, and expense elements. Premiums and death benefits can be either fixed or flexible.

Valuation actuary: An actuary who is responsible for certifying that a company's assets and reserves are adequate to fulfill its obligations to policyholders.

Vanishing premium: A method of premium payment in which several premiums are paid in full and the rest are paid by drawing on accumulated dividends or excess interest. An industry joke is that vanishing premium plans sometimes provide vanishing coverage, since the accumulated funds might not be sufficient to keep the policy going if interest or mortality deteriorates.

Variable life: A type of cash value policy that allows a policyholder to choose among several investment options. In general, both the death benefit and the cash value will fluctuate with investment performance.

Variable universal life: A variable life policy with flexible premiums and death benefits.

Waiting (also **Elimination**) **period:** For disability income insurance, the period between the occurrence of disability and eligibility for benefits.

Whole life: (1) Any insurance policy that provides coverage for the "whole of life," typically to age 95 or 100. (2) Traditional whole life.

INDEX

HETERICK MEMORIAL LIBRARY
368 D133i   onuu
Daily, Glenn S. / The individual investor'

3 5111 00184 1505